"There is a t[...]
Which existe[...]
Motionless a[...]
It stands alo[...]
I call it Tao and name it as Supreme . . ."

Thus the ancient Chinese philosopher-poet Lao Tzu
came to grips with the question of the origin of all
things. At the same time, halfway around the globe,
Zuni Indians searched for their answer, as had the
druids of England, the priests of Egypt, the epic poets
of India, the bards of Finland. For this was a
question that faced all humans for all time, and
from it came accounts of creation that continue to
stir us today—

SUN SONGS
Creation Myths from
Around the World

RAYMOND VAN OVER is the author and editor of over a
dozen acclaimed books, among them the Mentor editions of
I Ching and *Taoist Tales*. He is a member of the prestigious
Society for the Scientific Study of Religion and has taught
parapsychology at Hofstra University and at New York
University.

SUN SONGS
Creation Myths
from Around the World

EDITED AND WITH AN
INTRODUCTION BY
Raymond Van Over

A MERIDIAN CLASSIC

NEW AMERICAN LIBRARY

A DIVISION OF PENGUIN BOOKS USA INC., NEW YORK
PUBLISHED IN CANADA BY
PENGUIN BOOKS CANADA LIMITED, MARKHAM, ONTARIO

For Jacob Adler

*A man for all seasons,
who, in affliction, remains
surrounded by a special quality.*

Library of Congress Catalog Card Number: 79-90847

MERIDIAN TRADEMARK REG. U.S. PAT. OFF. AND FOREIGN COUNTRIES
REGISTERED TRADEMARK—MARCA REGISTRADA
HECHO EN WINNIPEG, CANADA

SIGNET, SIGNET CLASSIC, MENTOR, ONYX, PLUME, MERIDIAN and NAL BOOKS are published *in the United States* by New American Library, a division of Penguin Books USA Inc., 1633 Broadway, New York, New York 10019, and *in Canada* by Penguin Books Canada Limited, 2801 John Street, Markham, Ontario L3R 1B4

First Printing, February, 1980

First Meridian Printing, September, 1984

2 3 4 5 6 7 8 9 10

PRINTED IN CANADA

ACKNOWLEDGMENTS

This book was created under difficult circumstances, but the task was made considerably easier by Cheri Couture, and her considerate and able work on the manuscript. I am also deeply indebted to my Mentor editor, Nick Bakalar, for his patience, advice, and expertise. And, of course, nothing could have been accomplished without S.D.G.

CONTENTS

PART TWO
South America 93

PART THREE
Northern Europe and Central Asia 119

PART FOUR

Mesopotamia   167

PART FIVE

Greece   193

PART SIX

Africa   217

INTRODUCTION

The Meaning of Myths

MYTH HAS BEEN described as being basically visionary, an expansion of awareness into alternative realities. The symbols that carry the myth into completion may then be considered evocative signs leading toward a sense of wholeness, a fullness of being. If this is so, then Heraclitus was right when he wrote that "the unlike is joined together, and from the differences results the most beautiful harmony." For ancient mankind was undoubtedly puzzled by the great paradoxes, by life and death, the altering seasons, the apparent death when asleep and the peculiar sense of self-awareness when awake. Obvious questions such as how did life begin? What is death? What are stars, and the black canopy of the night sky? What lay beyond these enormous enigmas? Their myths attempted to resolve such profound and confusing questions, and therefore when reading myths we experience not so much an emotional insight as a sensation of watching something marvelous grow in the mind of early mankind.

The renowned mythologist Claude Lévi-Strauss suggests that mythical thought derives from the awareness that oppositions progress toward a natural mediation. That is, mythology provides a logical model that overcomes contradictions in a people's world view. On a personal level it reduces the anxiety one feels during conflicting or paradoxical life experiences. Thus, the myth resolves fundamental paradoxes. How, for example, can anyone accept that something is created from nothing? It seems an impossible contradiction, and yet if the logic of ancient man needed reassurance and resolution of this confusion, he could create a god who ruled the void, had the power to alter it, and thereby begin to fill it with "something."

For early man, there was no science of astronomy to explain the movement of the sun, moon, and stars. There was nothing to explain a sunrise; no science to explore the physics of an echo, or the reason for a rainbow. Without objective

1

science, early man used his imagination, his intuition, and his feelings to mold the fearsome world of nature into a meaningful and acceptable home.

But the ancient mythmaker, while untutored in a modern scientific sense, must have made astute observations regarding nature. The laws and phenomena of nature were vital for early man's survival, so it is natural that his observations would spill over into his theology and philosophy. Objective observation could have given rise to deductive insights. For example, two of the most frequent themes in creation myths are the sun and water, which are also two of the most important elements in the life of early man. It is not hard to imagine that as the sun scorched the earth and dried up crops, as it disappeared at night and was replaced by cold and dampness, as it rose in startling splendor and nourished the plants and life around them, it would become more than simply a bright, warm object illuminating the world. Its powers were obviously awesome. It had to possess characteristics larger than the common forms of nature such as trees, grass, and flowers, all of which seemed to gain life from its presence. Since the sun dominated other natural forces, it was greater than nature and therefore divine in its power.

Water possessed the same pervasive impact. It is reasonable that the Babylonian and Egyptian priest-scientists would observe the relationship between floodtides and fertile land. As plants blossomed on river-borne silt, it was logical to cultivate the nearby desert with irrigation. Water would obviously seem to be a primary and necessary ingredient for life. Perhaps from this came the idea that water was the source of all life. Like the sun, its presence meant life or death, whether crops flourished or failed. Thus both the sun and water became major powers that gave life and sustained all things. It is not surprising, therefore, that they were clothed, along with other natural powers that sustained life, in a cloak of divinity.

Myths also often tried to explain natural phenomena through personification of nature's powers. Thus, myth in a very broad sense is a symbolic narrative representing a cosmic process that carries necessary messages between the individual and the surrounding world. Creation myths, therefore, express our origins analogically and myth becomes a metaphor for our beginning.

With few exceptions, creation myths describe the origins of life—both cosmic and earthly—as emanating from a "beginningless god." Myths from a number of different cultures describe how this unborn, eternally existing god created the world. Rarely are there questions about the origin of this first divine being. It is simply accepted that "It" has existed since the beginning of time, or infinity. Regardless of the god's name, he has eternally ruled the void before creation and generally brooded over his own existence until creation commenced.

Most myths are quite specific about how things came into being. This specificity can be seen throughout the myths in this anthology. However, there are some exceptions. The Chinese mystic-philosopher Lao Tzu, for example, conceived an unnameable "Tao" that activates all life.[1] But the Tao (which means "way") is also an absolute rest, a formless quiescence before it again moves back into activity and creates form. The movement between these extremes of void and fullness, between activity and rest, between being and non-being is accomplished by what Lao Tzu called *wu wei*, or spontaneous action, which is the inexhaustible essence of all things. This complex and unique view of creation is set forth in Lao Tzu's single book, the *Tao Teh Ching*:

> There is a thing inherent and natural
> Which existed before heaven and earth,
> Motionless and fathomless,
> It stands alone and never changes;
> It pervades everything and is illimitable.
> It may be regarded as the source of the Universe.
> I do not know what it is . . .
> I call it Tao and name it as Supreme.

In some of the Hindu Vedas, there can be found a sophisticated metaphysical vision similar to that of Lao Tzu. In the *Rig Veda* we read:

> Who truly knows, and who can here declare it,
> Whence it was born and whence comes this creation?
> The gods are later than this world's beginning.
> Who knows then how it first came into being?
>
> He, the very origin of this creation,
> Whether He formed it all or did not form it,

---

[1] For a more complete description of Taoism, see Raymond Van Over, *Taoist Tales* (New York: The New American Library, 1973).

Whose gaze controls this world from highest heaven,
He knows it, or perhaps He knows not.

The greater number of myths in Hindu cosmology, however, are more specific than this almost Taoist view. Sometimes the traditional myths show glimmerings of metaphysics,
of a clear philosophical inclination within the minds of the
mythmakers.

"Mind" as the Metaphysics of Creation

Intriguing ideas thread their way through the tapestry of
creation myths. The idea that thought is equivalent, or at
least a powerful and necessary prerequisite to creation, occurs
in many myths. In the Zuni Indian myth (two versions of
which are included in this anthology; see pp. 23–26) the
creator Awonawilona was self-conceived; he created himself
from the black void surrounding him by *thinking* the world
into existence. Awonawilona created first the "thought" within
himself, which then took shape in his mind. When it moved
into space, it became full of power and began to grow, expanding and filling out its initial conception. The Persian
creator, Zurvan, also conceived a thought and gave birth to
Ahura Mazda, the god of light and goodness. This was
Zurvan's initial creation, but then, in a moment of doubt—
and Zurvan's awareness of the existence of doubt—Ahriman,
the god of darkness and malevolence, was brought into
creation.

In the Hindu Vedanta, thought and self-awareness are the
key to human enlightenment as well as creation. In the Buddhist *Dhammapada*, everything in existence is attributed to
thought, which is the source of creation. Buddha said: "All
that is, is the result of thought, it is found on thought, it is
made of thought."[2] For Buddha, clarity of right thought is the
fundamental requirement for enlightenment (which is equivalent to divinity), for salvation from the darkness and confusion that reigns on earth. For the Sufi 'Abd al-Karim Jili,
"thought is the basis of existence and the Essence which is in

[2] For a more thorough presentation of Buddhism, and the complete
translation of the *Dhammapada* and other Buddhist texts, see Raymond
Van Over, *Eastern Mysticism*, vol. 1 (New York: The New American
Library, 1977).

it, and it is a perfect manifestation of God, for Thought is the life of the spirit of the universe. It is the foundation of that life and its basis is man. Do not despise the power of thought, for by it is realized the nature of the Supreme Reality."[3] The same emphasis on thought occurs in Biblical verse and various apocryphal texts. In the apocryphal "Poem of the Gospel of St. John," there is written:

In the Beginning was Mind: and Mind was with God.
    So Mind was God. This was in the Beginning with God.
All kept coming into existence through it; and
    Apart from it came into existence not a single (thing).
What had come into existence in it was Life; and
    Life was the Light on the (true) Man.
And the Light shineth in the darkness; and the
    Darkness did not emprison it. . . .
It was the True Light, which enlighteneth every Man
    Who cometh into the world.
It was in the world; and the world kept coming into
    Existence through it.[4]

Obviously thought, or self-consciousness, and hence self-awareness, takes on a very real meaning early in mankind's history. For me, these ideas are more than just a learning experience, they create a sense of heritage, a continuum between our present hunger for understanding and our ancestors' questing minds.

Some of these myths also contain intriguing psychological ideas. In the *Brihadaranyaka Upanishad* (included in *Sun Songs* on page 000) the primal cosmic being looks around and perceives itself. This initial awareness of a "self" separate from the witness creates the ego. At the exact instant when this sense of separateness occurs, the cosmic creator experiences *fear*. But in this parable that symbolizes the Eastern evolutionary quest for total consciousness (the "pure thought" or "divine mind" just discussed), the cosmic being reasons that "as there is no one here but myself, what is there to fear."[5] As the cosmic being realizes this, the experience of

[3] For a complete reading of this and other Eastern ideas of divine "Mind," see Van Over, *Eastern Mysticism*, vol. 1.
[4] Margaret Smith, *Readings from the Mystics of Islam* (London: Luzac & Co., 1972), p. 117.
[5] See Van Over, *Eastern Mysticism*, vol. 1, for this and other Upanishads.

fear disappears. A peculiar mind-expanding myth! I read it as an expression of the provocative Indian idea that consciousness evolves toward a complete awareness of self, which involves transcending the ego, and is even able to achieve greater awareness as it moves toward enlightenment—that is, the disappearance of anxiety and confusion, because there is nothing to fear. This concept is reminiscent of a Zen koan on enlightenment where a disciple asks a master how he can free himself from bondage and achieve nirvana. The Zen master's reply is tantamount to saying there is no fear: "Who," he inquires, "has put you in bondage?"

Creation in this Upanishad, and the other myths in this anthology, involves a continual reaching out, an exuberant expanding. In fact, creation in Hinduism is defined as "what is poured forth." Hindus believe anyone understanding this becomes truly himself a creator in the continuing process of creation, a central actor in the drama of a universe in dynamic activity. Nothing in the act of creation can exist on its own; by definition, creation involves something "other." Creation myths frequently begin, therefore, with an undivided something separating into two from which creation then begins. It is this spasm of integration and disintegration that makes creation appear to be a pulsing, alive thing, a continual expansion and contraction.

Theories and Interpretations of Myths

There are many different definitions of myths:

• One interpretation of myths and their meaning argues that myths were invented by wise men to clarify and point toward a truth, but after a time they were taken literally. For example, this interpretation of myth would use the Greek god of time, Cronus, allegorically, because he devoured his children and time also devours that which it brings into existence. Such parallels can, of course, be easily made with many myths and mythic personalities.

• Some theologians believe that myths, because of their close association with ritual and religious beliefs, are only corruptions of scripture or early religious truths. This is in contrast to social myths that attempt to teach moral or ethical beliefs in accordance with the accepted religious dogma. But purely religious myths tend to embody (not necessarily ex-

plain) something of the nature of mankind's relation to nature and the transcendent or powerful. In fact, some argue
that without the visual and metaphoric power of myth, the
religious view of god becomes abstract and nonspecific; an
intangible first cause and close to being a scientific principle.
Thus, the world becomes real and the divine abstract. But
myth defines and makes manageable the awesome powers of
the universe.

• At one time a group of German scholars believed that
myths were entirely personifications of nature. Thus, many
of the mythic beings who create are associated with light, the
sun, or the moon. The Greek Apollo would therefore be a
personification of the sun, just as is the Egyptian Ra.

• In the early days of psychology, Freudians explained
myths as a mechanism of wish-fulfillment, while the Jungians
considered them expressions of unconscious dreams. But
Freud also described myths as primitive man's attempt to give
meaning to his incoherent and intense dreams. Freud and his
followers pointed to the body of myths that incorporated what
are now popularly called Freudian "symbols." The heroes of
myth often battled monsters that seemed straight from our
dreams: Marduk and Cadmus (whose stories are included
in this anthology), for example, Perseus and Jonah, and the
Eskimo's Raven (also included in *Sun Songs*) find themselves
in the bellies of a fish. Or a hero often commits incest and
other sexual transgressions. He steals fire, travels over water,
and suffers numerous trials, most of which can be interpreted
by Freudians symbolically. In short, Freud asserted that mankind's myths are expressions of the persistent dreams of the
human race and most often express the repressed desires of
primitive people. Otto Rank also contended that "myth is the
collective dream of the people." The psychologist Erich
Fromm argues that dreams and myths are similar in that they
constitute "the oldest creations of man." Fromm contends
that both dreams and myth utilize the same arcane ancient
language of symbols. Joseph Campbell goes even further, for
he considers myths have a central role in human history.
"Throughout the inhabited world, in all times and under
every circumstance, the myths of man have flourished. . . .
It would not be too much to say that myth is the secret opening through which the inexhaustible energies of the cosmos
pour into human cultural manifestation. Religions, philosophies, arts, the social forms of primitive and historic man,
prime discoveries in science and technology, the very dreams

that blister sleep, boil up from the basic, magic ring of myth."[6]

But the early psychological theories, especially of Freudians, have been harshly questioned by scholars of myth. Bronislav Malinowski, one of the most renowned students of myths, asked: "What did Freud really know about savages? He never lived with them." But by this caustic comment, Bronowski was perhaps unaware of how he characterized his own ideas by his facile use of "savages."

• Sir James Frazer, whose monumental book *The Golden Bough* dominated the study of myths for years, believed that all myths dealt with themes of death, birth, and resurrection. To a large extent, Frazer's syncretism has been replaced by the ideas of modern scholars who tend to see the myths of a single people as unique to their lives and environment. This results in the specific interpretation of one particular group's myths rather than a single general explanation for the myths of all people. Some theorists argue that such interpretations are the result of overspecialization, and therefore fail to see the "mythic" forest because of "specialist" trees.

• Another theory considers myth simply a traditional or fabulous story that concerns supernatural events or gods.[7] But myths have to be distinguished here from legends or folk-tales, which are about human events and often used to amuse or teach a lesson. "Legend," while often wrongly used as synonymous with myth, is generally defined as an unverifiable story handed down by tradition from earlier times.

• Sir Maurice Bowra defines a myth as a story which aims not at giving pleasure for its own sake, but rather at alleviating the perplexities of prescientific man because his reason was not ready to grasp them.[8] In Bowra's definition the mythic explanation of life's perplexities is more emotional than rational and works by suggesting a connection or similarity between the conflicting facts of life, and does not attempt to explain them by cause and effect. Thus, myths bring the unknown into relation with the known and break down the barriers between man and the "untractable mass of phenomena" that surrounds him.

---

[6] See Joseph Campbell, *Hero With a Thousand Faces* (New York: Meridian Books, 1970), p. 3.

[7] See H. S. Robinson and Knox Wilson, *Myths and Legends of All Nations* (New York: Bantam Books, 1961).

[8] Sir Maurice Bowra, *The Greek Experience* (New York: The New American Library, 1959), p. 115.

• Another profound student of myth is Ernst Cassirer, who has developed the theory that myths of primitive peoples contain the purest form of a unique symbolic way of perceiving the world. Cassirer argues that there is no sharp distinction in the primitive mind between the objective and subjective way of perceiving the world, and the myths it created expressed its religious (or subjective) perceptions. For this form of "mythical consciousness," there is no clear separation between the symbol and object, between fantasy and reality, between wish and fulfillment.

If Cassirer's theory is right, then it explains why our traditional standards for truth or objectivity do not work when applied to the mythical consciousness. What is most real is that which is most intense, that which evokes the deepest and most provocative feeling. Myths thus carry the force of a primary happening, an event uncompromised by logical or rational qualifiers. Judged by purely rationalistic standards the mythical perception of the world is meaningless; but confusion develops when it becomes clear that mankind rose up from this cauldron of his mythical consciousness. And if it worked for ancient man, if it allowed him to make accommodation with a hostile world, if it allowed him to identify with the powerful and often overwhelming forces of nature and thereby survive, how can it be accurately called "meaningless?" If nothing else, it was a survival mechanism in the sense that it allowed preverbal and prerational man to adapt psychologically to an alien and hostile world.

In short, it seems myths are meaningful precisely because of their continuing impact throughout mankind's history. As Gaston Bachelard pointedly asks in his *La Psychanalyse du Feu*,[9] "how could a [myth] be kept alive and perpetuated if each generation had not 'intimate reasons' for believing in it." In the early part of his career, Lévi-Strauss also felt that the significance of myths could be proven by their continued importance throughout history. Myths, after all, were "the principle way of literary expression for many peoples from prehistoric to modern times; I could not conceive that the men who told these myths were spending their time recounting absurdities."

Ultimately, defining myths or symbols is one of the most difficult and baffling undertakings. Psychology, philosophy, anthropology, linguistics, and literary criticism have all at-

9 (Paris, 1938).

tempted at one time or another to explore the elusive subject of myths. Because there are so many ingredients in myths, and they have such a broad application, it is perhaps best to view them and their influence with caution, yet with full respect for their power over the human psyche. For myths do seem to suggest an elaborate order that reflects both the internal world of mind and the external world of harsh physical realities.

Some Basic Themes of Creation Myths

While many incidental parallels can be found in the creation myths in this anthology, the surprising and perplexing fact is that the *basic* themes for myths in widely different geographical areas are strikingly similar. Some of the basic themes, and the area in which they appear, are:

(1) The idea of a primeval abyss (which is sometimes simply space, but often is an infinite watery deep) is common to India, Scandinavia, Egypt, Babylonia, Celtic Britain, and some North American Indians. (2) The originating god (or gods) is frequently awakened or eternally existing in this abyss, as in the myths of the Egyptians, Babylonians, the Hindus of India, Hebrews, and Quiché Maya. (3) Also in the myths of these cultures (including Polynesia), the originating god broods over the water. (4) Another common theme is the cosmic egg or embryo, which appears in the myths of Egypt, India, Japan, and Peru. From this ubiquitous germ emerged the Chinese P'an Ku, the Indian Brahma, the Egyptian Ra or Horus, and the Polynesian god-creator. (5) Life was also created through sound, or a sacred word spoken by the original god in the myths of the Egyptians, the Hebrews, the Celts, and the Quiché Maya. (6) A peculiar theme, but quite common, is the creation of life from the corpse or parts of the primeval god's body, as in the myths of Babylon, China, the Hindus of India, and Scandinavia. In Egypt and China, for example, the eyes of a god become the sun and moon. Mankind itself emerges from the tears of a god in Egypt, from the sweat of a god or giant in Scandinavia, from the blood and bones of a Babylonian god. In the myths of the Babylonians, the Hebrews, and some North American Indians, human beings are also created from clay mixed with various substances, such as blood. In Scandinavian and Quiché Maya myths, humanity is also created from wooden images or trees.

In China, there is the unique myth of mankind formed from worms and insects. Thus the themes of how the world and life were created are varied, and yet one can find numerous parallels. One scholar, Professor A. G. Rooth, analyzed three hundred creation myths of the North American Indians and found that most of them fit into eight types; and seven of these appear throughout the myths of people in the distant continent of Eurasia.

The obvious question arises: Why such similarity of mythic ideas and images throughout these distant cultures? Many scholars have puzzled over this phenomena, among them the renowned Claude Lévi-Strauss, who, after years of studying myths, came to the conclusion that "throughout, myths resemble one another to an extraordinary degree." Another scholar, Clyde Kluckhorn, argues that "there is an astounding similarity between myths collected in widely different regions." The scholarly argument has raged for decades and it continues to this day. No definitive answer seems yet to have developed, but theories abound.

There is, of course, no mystery when an individual culture creates a specific vision peculiar to itself and its own unique cultural and psychological requirements. What is puzzling is when one comes across the identical themes from different cultures. Some suggest that these symbols and images appear throughout myths from distant ages and cultures because there exists an affinity between them and the human mind. It is an intriguing question: Are there themes common to the inner processes of the human psyche, an ocean of experience that expresses itself in repeating images and symbols? Many contemporary analysts of myths do believe that there is a common internal psychical structure which produces these visions. But even without being able to resolve the question of a myth's origin, the great value of myths is precisely that they display important, perhaps even fundamental, visions on an historical blackboard for our study and pleasure.

My personal view after studying myths for many years is that creation myths seem to rise from the depths of the human psyche, but for what purpose no one seems to know. They clearly carry the intense human desire to shape and structure a confusing and troublesome reality, to give meaning and insight where before only shadows reigned. This seems an impulse that guided the makers of myths, and thus they become a necessary human function; for as they give shape and meaning to our lives, they also serve the needs of our age and our personal spirits. Perhaps a myth should not be analyzed as the repository of esoteric, or even exoteric, knowledge, but rather be seen as religious allegory meant to awaken consciousness, to expand awareness and insight, to offer alternative ways of viewing the world. The relationship between symbol, myth, and the religious impulse has perhaps been best caught by the monk Thomas Merton: "The true symbol does not merely point to something else. It contains in itself a structure which awakens our consciousness to a new awareness of the inner meaning of life and of reality itself."[10]

The force that underlies mythic structures is its power to evoke resonances from within, just as great art sets a reverberation resounding deep within those who come upon it. In this sense, myths continue to have a role in our lives—and in the modern age. They remain an important adjunct to our rational and scientific methods.

Myths and Modern Life

What we today consider "myths" once supported the moral order, vitalized secular and religious institutions, and stimulated the creative arts in ancient civilizations. As myths developed depth and complexity, it seems they incorporated many ancient, supportive symbols. Such myths and symbols gave life a cohesive meaning, and, as the German philosopher-poet Friedrich Nietzsche perceived, human beings need life-supporting myths. It has been conclusively shown that as these supporting systems break down, a culture can come apart at the seams. There are many examples where primitive societies disintegrated as contemporary white man's civilization intruded. Destruction begins as soon as the old beliefs are discredited. In fact, many observers of modern society are now saying that with the decline of ancient myths and other traditional beliefs there is a parallel disequilibrium in our own culture. Science has accurately "factualized" nature, but can offer no psychically satisfying symbols or myths as a replacement.[11]

10 "Symbolism: Communication or Communion?" in *New Directions* 20 (New York: New Directions, 1968), pp. 1–2.

11 See Joseph Campbell, *The Meaning of Myths* (New York: Bantam Books, 1977).

RATIONALISM AND THE POETRY OF MYTH

One of the more obvious interrelationships between myths and modern life is the transference of ritual into the scientific description of cycles and patterns. In ancient days, rituals symbolically represented recurrent acts of nature. It was reasonable that they were incorporated into social and religious rituals. A rain dance, for example, represented the need for rain (fertility) and hence, rebirth from the death of winter, drought, and barrenness. The cycles of nature thus possessed ritual and religious significance. Rituals suggesting rebirth can be found throughout the creation myths in *Sun Songs*. In applying the idea of patterns to modern life, mathematicians quantify cycles and measure them by probability theory and statistical rhythms. While more objectively structured, the idea of cycles actually performs the same service for modern as for ancient man: It allows us to identify and work within the boundaries and rhythms of the natural world.

Throughout history, knowledge has been equivalent to power; and power carries the necessity (or likelihood) of its use. Modern man uses knowledge and its power in an attempt to manipulate and control nature as did ancient man, but with different methods. Today, the ancient rituals of nature are replaced by rituals of science. Our tools are mechanical while ancient man's were poetic and symbolic. We have developed complicated and sophisticated techniques to identify the powers of nature while ancient man possessed only his imagination, his capacity for intuitive identification, and some small deductive powers. But the basic need to secure our place in what we feel is an alien world is the same, and the myths in this anthology continuously display these fundamental needs. In fact, the ability of technological man to identify the forces of nature without recourse to his technology has so atrophied that a return to mythic and intuitive awareness seems a necessary rebalancing.

At one time, ritual expressed preverbal realities—but in contemporary life we factualize and are far more prone to use language or scientific symbols to describe our relationship to nature. Whether we verbalize correctly or not is something else—but the fact remains that modern science is constantly quantifying, describing, and labeling. Often it seems our security depends upon our ability to describe, which ultimately becomes a preference even over judgment or wisdom. We have little patience for preverbal representations of the natural world. Except in the poetry of the unconscious mind—dreams and the arts—we are uncomfortable with the potent ancient symbols present in myths and legends. But precisely because we are becoming alienated from this vivid inner world, we have a need to refamiliarize ourselves with the preverbal symbols of nature. For the great distance between our inner lives and the factualized modern description of nature is diminished as we read myths and come to identify with our origins. In this sense, ancient myths are a means of finding our way home again.

Some of the more uncompromising and harsh modern rationalists argue that myths are merely false beliefs. They thrive only on ignorance, and disappear as soon as reason and science explore them. It is no secret that modern society is dominated by this type of rationalism. There is no area of our culture that is not heavily influenced by the spirit of rationalism and its impact through technology. Some ardent devotees of myths argue that modern man is incapable of preverbal awareness and is therefore doomed to live in an amythical world. Wherever the truth may lie between these conflicting claims, they all stress the incompatibility of myth and rationalism.

It is clear that science does not seem to touch human emotions; science expands our intellectual knowledge while the rest of the ingredients that compose the whole human being are displaced or ignored. It seems the true genius of mankind comes from the whole entity, from a synthesizing of mind and spirit—not a single accretion of fact as developed by analysis. The greatest scientific geniuses were those who accompanied their rational pursuits with poetic inspiration and a personal, transcending passion. And the great poetic geniuses are those who do not concern themselves with rationalism or scientific logic; rather, they labor to touch creative energies in their mythic unconscious. In this sense, myths provide a more complete picture of the human potential—for understanding of any absolute (such as creation) can only come as the result of a total commitment to synthesis, whether it be of a mythic or scientific nature.

The reason this is important is that the ineffable will always remain unnamed—if only because language is a poor tool to describe the mysterious and shrouded majesty of the universe. Scientific labels will not help. As Thomas Mann has observed, no matter how far we extend our inquiry, how far we let out our line, the ultimate foundations we seek withdraw still further into the depths. Many specialists in mythology become overly analytic and miss the point that myths contain the "ultimate mystery" that Mann talks about. For regardless of all the contemporary scholarly analysis and quantification, myths cannot be broken down into parts and retain their full significance. Mythic form dictates that each person delve into its source and discover its meaning on a personal level. This is one of the greatest values in an anthology of traditional creation myths. It is psychologically significant, for in our personal growth we often find that "under each deep another deep opens" to reveal ever-expanding, new dimensions. But this should not be a reason for despair or frustration, because to seek is a vital part of human nature; and while we may never reach the ultimate horizon we are nourished by the search itself. This is the peculiar heritage of humanity that we can identify in creation myths—a constant seeking to understand and find meaning. We must seek the delights of myth and mystery, or succumb to an ashen ennui that drains us of vitality.

No matter how hard we try to be the compleat rationalist, the fact remains that human beings are *ikonists,* imagemakers, visionaries. When we sacrifice our visions, as we have in the modern age, we close off our heritage, and we warp ourselves into floundering creatures struggling to survive in an unnatural environment. This does not mean that we must sacrifice our reason, but merely that we give more careful and respectful scrutiny to our subjective visions. Without such affectionate attention, our mythic inclinations wither, and we become disjointed and separate from our inner selves.

The human being seems an unformed, uncertain animal who often lives his time pendulum-like, swaying between certainty and confusion, arrogance and submissiveness, calm and terror. He seems to create life through vision, and so perhaps myth ultimately is the visionary screen upon which the human spirit projects its destiny.

EDITORIAL NOTES

Some may question a title like *Sun Songs* for a book on creation myths, especially since all the myths are not solar. The title is justified, however, by the enormous number of creation myths that involve the sun, and the life-giving, regenerative properties of light, throughout ancient cultures. The sun, or light, is almost universally identified with primal creative forces. Everywhere the sun plays an important, if not a central, role. Even the constantly recurring theme of the cosmic egg is associated with light, for it is like the Sanskrit *Hiranyagarbha*, the golden egg, an illumination brightening the dark cosmic chaos that exists before creation. The myths in this collection express the first yearnings of the waking human spirit, which can take the form of a bright dawning, of birth, the shape of a song, of sound that is exuberant and outreaching. They all, in every guise, convey both the image of a bright luminescence like the sun, and rhythmic pulse like a song.

I have limited the myths in this collection to a very special sort—myths that deal with the creation of the cosmos and myths that create earthly life. Many other myths, including those of death and resurrection, flood legends, and even well-known stories like the Narcissus myth can be interpreted as creation myths, for they all deal with transformation, with the dynamic process of life that is ever growing, ever moving on toward its mysterious conclusion.

And finally, no other justification for a thematic collection of creation myths is necessary beyond that it offers the reader an opportunity to see, in Joseph Campbell's words, the "cultural history of mankind as a unity," for this is what the comparative study of world mythologies compels.[12] Because I accept this principle wholeheartedly, the basic goal of this anthology is simply to introduce creation myths to the general reader and nonspecialist. Even though a great many books have been published on classical myths of the Western world, few books have dealt with the specific theme of creation, or have collected material from the more exotic corners of the world as I have tried to do with this anthology. The true value of any anthology is that it brings the reader into touch with original material that he may not otherwise have access to. This book then has the modest hope of offering a broad selection of creation myths so the reader may introduce himself to material that he may never otherwise find gathered together in his casual reading.

Some may find the lack of myths from specific countries strange. There are several reasons for this. First, no single

[12] See Joseph Campbell, op. cit., for his argument on the value of myths for modern man.

volume can be definitive when dealing with a subject as large and varied as creation myths. At best, one can offer a stimulating first reading that may urge the reader on to other books and a deeper understanding. Also, the economics of publishing dictates limitations of space. Further, in many cases a particular culture would have no extant material to draw on. It is very common for the more powerful ancient nations to strongly influence the smaller surrounding cultures. This was true, for example, with the cultures of Burma, Siam, and Indo-China generally, where the mythology was borrowed almost entirely from India and China.

For any anthologist, some things are beyond control. Opposing views of scholars regarding which translation of a particular text is best are quite common. Mythology also lends itself to secondary interpretations by scholars, who often make many inferences from partial texts and develop elaborate theories and hypotheses. Another problem peculiar to mythology is the frequent "reinterpretation" or paraphrased rendering of a myth for modern readers. If the translator is a poet, or particularly attuned to the culture whose myths he is "interpreting" for the modern reader—Sir Edwin Arnold's translations of the *Bhagavad Gita* are an example—then we are given a superior translation. But in all too many cases the "paraphraser" lacks poetic sensitivity or adequate knowledge of the original language he is rendering. I have tried to avoid this problem by choosing generally accepted translations, but without succumbing to using only scholarly "approved" renderings. This sounds easier than it is, for some of the myths are told in folktale form, while others are in traditional poetic verse. Also, each selection could be chosen for other specific reasons, sometimes having little to do with the translation. The gentle-harsh poetic verse style of the *Poetic Edda* and the Finnish *Kalevala*, for example, best represent those cultures and the themes of their myths. So I chose a verse translation over a storytelling narrative style. The simplicity and directness of the folktale style, however, seemed more appropriate to other cultures such as the North American Indian and African, so the selections were made accordingly. This technique I believe gives the reader a better opportunity to experience the culture whose myth he is reading about.

Because much early storytelling, including myths, used mnemonic devices that often included chanting and repetition, most early myths were musical in their telling. This is why many myths are in verse or song form, and why a poetic or

verse translation is closer to the original storyteller's presentation. For this reason, I have preferred verse translations to a
modern writer's retelling of an ancient tale in modern syntax.
In effect, one sacrifices ease of reading for authenticity with
this method of selection.

Mythology is on the order of poetry—and the translator of
ancient myths who retains his sensitivity to the poetic dimen-
sion is the person who renders ancient visions most accurately
for the modern reader. So what I looked for in these selections
were translations that fulfilled several different criteria, but
most importantly, the rendition chosen had to possess this
sensitive identification with the poetic spirit of myths.

PART ONE

North America

INTRODUCTION

UNLIKE MOST of the mythologies in *Sun Songs*, the North American Indian mythology lacks a systematic arrangement of mythic characters and events. In some of the tribes and groups, such as the Iroquois and the Zuni, a degree of uniformity has developed around their mythic beliefs (by using, for example, preferred characters like the Raven), but nothing to the degree where the tales lead to an epic literature as with the Aryan, Babylonian, Greek, and Norse peoples.[1]

Even though there is no great mythic architecture such as the early Aryan people had, the North American Indians possessed a diversified, rich mythic lore that varied from tribe to tribe, and sometimes even from clan to clan. Consequently, their myths must be unlaced from the tapestry of their elaborate rituals. There are five major rituals: 1. Smoke offerings to the sky and earth. 2. The purification rites, most often a sweat bath. 3. Fasting and vigil ceremonies. 4. Shamanistic and mediumistic rites invoking unseen nature powers. 5. Communal ceremonies, most often dances, that involve prayers, sacrifice, and honoring of ancestors and the dead. In all of these rituals there is the Great Spirit (often Father Sky or his manifestation, the Sun Father), Mother Earth, and her daughter the Corn Mother. Further down the hierarchy there are powers of the stars, wind, clouds, and even animals such as birds. Other animals are thought of as Guardians, or Elders, that help hunters, watch over the earth, and make sure it is replenished.

In North American Indian cosmogony the beginning is rarely creation from an absolute condition or state, such as an eternal void or abyss. A common description of creation is of a preexistent sky-world that contains the essences or images

[1] See H. B. Alexander, *The Mythology of All Races*, 13 vols. vol. X, "North American," (New York: Cooper Square Publishers, Inc., 1964).

of the "world-to-be." All that is needed is a Divine Mother that descends from heaven and initiates creation. Thereafter, heroes help to shape and make the earth habitable. They do battle with monsters and destructive forces on behalf of the newly generated creatures of the world. It is also quite common for the hero to arrive as twins, one of whom dies in the end of the tale and becomes the lord of the underworld. Throughout the creation and the subsequent travail of the heroes, there is inevitably the creation of fire, the beginning of death, and the giving of the arts and laws of life. These are themes that are universal, and appear in quite distant cultures, such as the Arctic Highlanders in the far north and the Cherokee nation in the southern United States.

All of these unseen powers weave the web of Indian myth, filling their tales with legends of mythic proportions. Consistency is not important, for the Indians' relationship to nature and its powers are so profound that literalness does not become a problem. On the more obvious level, some Indian myths are often entertainment. Others are clearly moral allegories, fables with a lesson to teach. But for the Indian, these tales are neither true nor false, neither history nor fable. If anything, they come closer to being parables, or symbolic narratives of what *is*—of reality.

ZUNI CREATION MYTHS

Zuni (New Mexico)

Cosmic Creation

In the beginning of things Awonawilona[1] was alone. There was nothing beside him in the whole space of time. Everywhere there was black darkness and void. Then Awonawilona conceived in himself the thought, and the thought took shape and got out into space and through this it stepped out into the void, into outer space, and from them came nebulae of growth and mist, full of power of growth. After the mist of nebulae came up, Awonawilona changed himself through his knowledge into another shape and became the sun, who is our father and who enlightens everything and fills everything with light, and the nebulae condensed and sank down and became water and thus the sea came into existence.

The Beginning of Newness

Before the beginning of the New-making, the All-father Father alone had being. Through ages there was nothing else except black darkness.

[1] The first Creator-Preserver, and the high God of the Zuni Indians of New Mexico. There are many myths, in many cultures, where the creator-god first conceives a thought within itself and then manifests that thought in the world. The exteriorized thought thus becomes a second being, or principle, that fills the dark void surrounding the creator. Other examples of this can be found in the Gnostic myth of Ennoia, and the Zoroastrian myth of Zurvan. Following this initial stage of creation there normally develop the opposing principles of consciousness and the unconscious, often symbolized by sun and sea, night and day, and the like. (See Raymond Van Over, *Eastern Mysticism*, vol. 1, for a description of Zurvan and an expanded analysis of this idea.) A longer, more complete telling of this same myth follows.

23

In the beginning of the New-making, the All-father Father (Awonawilona), conceived within himself and thought outward in space, and mists were created and up-lifted. Thus through his knowledge the All-container made himself the Sun, who was thus created and is the great Father. The dark spaces brightened with light. The cloud mists thickened and became water.

From his flesh, the Sun-father created the Seed-stuff of worlds, and he himself rested upon the waters. And these two, the Four-fold-containing Earth-mother and the All-covering Sky-father, the surpassing beings, with power of changing their forms even as smoke changes in the wind, were the father and mother of the soul-beings.[1]

Then as man and woman spoke these two together. "Behold!" said Earth-mother, as a great terraced bowl appeared at hand, and within it water, "This shall be the home of my tiny children. On the rim of each world-country in which they wander, terraced mountains shall stand, making in one region many mountains by which one country shall be known from another."

Then she spat on the water and struck it and stirred it with her fingers. Foam gathered about the terraced rim, mounting higher and higher. Then with her warm breath she blew across the terraces. White flecks of foam broke away and floated over the water. But the cold breath of Sky-father shattered the foam and it fell downward in fine mist and spray.

Then Earth-mother spoke:

"Even so shall white clouds float up from the great waters at the borders of the world, and clustering about the mountain terraces of the horizon, shall be broken and hardened by thy cold. Then will they shed downward, in rain-spray, the water of life, even into the hollow places of my lap. For in my lap shall nestle our children, mankind and creature-kind, for warmth in thy coldness."

So even now the trees on high mountains near the clouds and Sky-father, crouch low toward Earth-mother for warmth and protection. Warm is Earth-mother, cold our Sky-father.

[1] Another version renders this section: "The Sun-father formed the seed-stuff of twain worlds, impregnating therewith the great waters, and lo! in the heat of his light these waters of the sea grew green and scums rose upon them, waxing wide and weighty until, behold! they became the Four-fold Containing Mother-earth, and the All-covering Father-sky."

Then Sky-father said, "Even so. Yet I, too, will be helpful to our children." Then he spread his hand out with the palm downward and into all the wrinkles of his hand he set the semblance of shining yellow corn grains; in the dark of the early world-dawn they gleamed like sparks of fire.

"See," he said, pointing to the seven grains between his thumb and four fingers, "our children shall be guided by these when the Sun-father is not near and thy terraces are as darkness itself. Then shall our children be guided by lights." So Sky-father created the stars. Then he said, "And even as these grains gleam up from the water, so shall seed grain like them spring up from the earth when touched by water, to nourish our children." And thus they created the seed corn. And in many other ways they devised for their children, the soul-beings.

But the first children, in a cave of the earth, were unfinished. The cave was of sooty blackness, black as a chimney at night time, and foul. Loud became their murmurings and lamentations, until many sought to escape, growing wiser and more manlike.

But the earth was not then as we now see it. Then the Sun-father sent down two sons (sons also of the Foam-cap), the Beloved Twain, Twin Brothers of Light, yet Elder and Younger, the Right and the Left, like to question and answer in deciding and doing. To them the Sun-father imparted his own wisdom. He gave them the great cloud-bow, and for arrows the thunderbolts of the four quarters. For buckler, they had the fog-making shield, spun and woven of the floating clouds and spray. The shield supports its bearer, as clouds are supported by the wind, yet hides its bearer also. And he gave to them the fathership and control of men and of all creatures. Then the Beloved Twain, with their great cloud-bow lifted the Sky-father into the vault of the skies, that the earth might become warm and fitter for men and creatures. Then along the sun-seeking trail, they sped to the mountains westward. With magic knives they spread open the depths of the mountain and uncovered the cave in which dwelt the unfinished men and creatures. So they dwelt with men, learning to know them, and seeking to lead them out.

Now there were growing things in the depths, like grasses and vines. So the Beloved Twain breathed on the stems, growing tall toward the light as grass is wont to do, making them stronger, and twisting them upward until they formed a great ladder by which men and creatures ascended to a second cave.

Up the ladder into the second cave-world, men and the beings crowded, following closely the Two Little but Mighty Ones. Yet many fell back and were lost in the darkness. They peopled the under-world from which they escaped in after time, amid terrible earth shakings.

In this second cave it was as dark as the night of a stormy season, but larger of space and higher. Here again men and the beings increased, and their complainings grew loud. So the Twain again increased the growth of the ladder, and again led men upward, not all at once, but in six bands, to become the fathers of the six kinds of men, the yellow, the tawny gray, the red, the white, the black, and the mingled. And this time also many were lost or left behind.

Now the third great cave was larger and lighter, like a valley in starlight. And again they increased in number. And again the Two led them out into a fourth cave. Here it was light like dawning, and men began to perceive and to learn variously, according to their natures, wherefore the Twain taught them first to seek the Sun-father.

Then as the last cave became filled and men learned to understand, the Two led them forth again into the great upper world, which is the World of Knowing and Seeing.

The Men of the Early Times

Eight years was but four days and four nights when the world was new. It was while such days and nights continued that men were led out, in the night-shine of the World of Seeing. For even when they saw the great star, they thought it the Sun-father himself, it so burned their eyeballs.

Men and creatures were more alike then than now. Our fathers were black, like the caves they came from; their skins were cold and scaly like those of mud creatures; their eyes were goggled like an owl's; their ears were like those of cave bats; their feet were webbed like those of walkers in wet and soft places; they had tails, long or short, as they were old or young. Men crouched when they walked, or crawled along the ground like lizards. They feared to walk straight, but crouched as before time they had in their cave worlds, that they might not stumble or fall in the uncertain light.

When the morning star arose, they blinked excessively when they beheld its brightness and cried out that now surely the

Father was coming. But it was only the elder of the Bright Ones, heralding with his shield of flame the approach of the Sun-father. And when, low down in the east, the Sun-father himself appeared, though shrouded in the mist of the world-waters, they were blinded and heated by his light and glory. They fell down wallowing and covered their eyes with their hands and arms, yet ever as they looked toward the light, they struggled toward the Sun as moths and other night creatures seek the light of a campfire. Thus they became used to the light. But when they rose and walked straight, no longer bending, and looked upon each other, they sought to clothe themselves with girdles and garments of bark and rushes. And when by walking only upon their hinder feet they were bruised by stone and sand, they plaited sandals of yucca fiber.

THE CREATION OF THE WORLD

Pima (Arizona)

In the beginning there was nothing at all except darkness. All was darkness and emptiness. For a long, long while, the darkness gathered until it became a great mass. Over this the spirit of Earth Doctor drifted to and fro like a fluffy bit of cotton in the breeze. Then Earth Doctor decided to make for himself an abiding place. So he thought within himself, "Come forth, some kind of plant," and there appeared the creosote bush. He placed this before him and set it upright. But it at once fell over. He set it upright again; again it fell. So it fell until the fourth time it remained upright. Then Earth Doctor took from his breast a little dust and flattened it into a cake. When the dust cake was still, he danced upon it, singing a magic song.

Next he created some black insects which made black gum on the creosote bush. Then he made a termite which worked with the small earth cake until it grew very large. As he sang and danced upon it, the flat world stretched out on all sides until it was as large as it is now. Then he made a round sky-cover to fit over it, round like the houses of the Pimas. But the earth shook and stretched, so that it was unsafe. So Earth Doctor made a gray spider which was to spin a web around the edges of the earth and sky, fastening them together. When this was done, the earth grew firm and solid.

Earth Doctor made water, mountains, trees, grass, and weeds—made everything as we see it now. But all was still inky blackness. Then he made a dish, poured water into it, and it became ice. He threw this round block of ice far to the north, and it fell at the place where the earth and sky were woven together. At once the ice began to gleam and shine. We call it now the sun. It rose from the ground in the north up into the sky and then fell back. Earth Doctor took it and threw it to the west where the earth and sky were sewn together. It rose into the sky and again slid back to the earth. Then he threw it to the far south, but it slid back again to the flat earth. Then at last he threw it to the east. It rose higher and higher in the sky until it reached the highest point in the round blue cover and began to slide down on the other side. And so the sun does even yet.

Then Earth Doctor poured more water into the dish and it became ice. He sang a magic song, and threw the round ball of ice to the north where the earth and sky are woven together. It gleamed and shone, but not so brightly as the sun. It became the moon, and it rose in the sky, but fell back again, just as the sun had done. So he threw the ball to the west, and then to the south, but it slid back each time to the earth. Then he threw it to the east, and it rose to the highest point in the sky-cover and began to slide down on the other side. And so it does even today, following the sun.

But Earth Doctor saw that when the sun and moon were not in the sky, all was inky darkness. So he sang a magic song, and took some water into his mouth and blew it into the sky, in a spray, to make little stars. Then he took his magic crystal and broke it into pieces and threw them into the sky, to make the larger stars. Next he took his walking stick and placed ashes on the end of it. Then he drew it across the sky to form the Milky Way. So Earth Doctor made all the stars.

THE CREATION OF MANKIND
AND THE FLOOD

Pima (Arizona)

After the world was ready, Earth Doctor made all kinds of animals and creeping things. Then he made images of clay, and told them to be people. After a while there were so many people that there was not food and water enough for all. They were never sick and none died. At last there grew to be so many they were obliged to eat each other. Then Earth Doctor, because he could not give them food and water enough, killed them all. He caught the hook of his staff into the sky and pulled it down so that it crushed all the people and all the animals, until there was nothing living on the earth. Earth Doctor made a hole through the earth with his stick, and through that he went, coming out safe, but alone, on the other side.

He called upon the sun and moon to come out of the wreck of the world and sky, and they did so. But there was no sky for them to travel through, no stars, and no Milky Way. So Earth Doctor made these all over again. Then he created another race of men and animals.

Then Coyote was born. Moon was his mother. When Coyote was large and strong he came to the land where the Pima Indians lived.

Then Elder Brother was born. Earth was his mother, and Sky his father. He was so powerful that he spoke roughly to Earth Doctor, who trembled before him. The people began to increase in numbers, just as they had done before, but Elder Brother shortened their lives, so the earth did not become so crowded. But Elder Brother did not like the people created by Earth Doctor, so he planned to destroy them again. So Elder Brother planned to create a magic baby. . . .

The screams of the baby shook the earth. They could be heard for a great distance. Then Earth Doctor called all the people together, and told them there would be a great flood. He sang a magic song and then bored a hole through the

flat earth-plain through to the other side. Some of the people
went into the hole to escape the flood that was coming, but
not very many got through. Some of the people asked Elder
Brother to help them, but he did not answer. Only Coyote
he answered. He told Coyote to find a big log and sit on it,
so that he would float on the surface of the water with the
driftwood. Elder Brother got into a big olla which he had
made, and closed it tight. So he rolled along on the ground
under the olla. He sang a magic song as he climbed into his
olla.

A young man went to the place where the baby was
screaming. Its tears were a great torrent which cut gorges in
the earth before it. The water was rising all over the earth.
He bent over the child to pick it up, and immediately both
became birds and flew above the flood. Only five birds were
saved from the flood. One was a flicker and one a vulture.
They clung by their beaks to the sky to keep themselves above
the waters, but the tail of the flicker was washed by the waves
and that is why it is stiff to this day. At last a god took pity
on them and gave them power to make "nests of down" from
their own breasts on which they floated on the water. One
of these birds was the vipisimal, and if any one injures it to
this day, the flood may come again.

Now South Doctor called his people to him and told them
that a flood was coming. He sang a magic song and he bored
a hole in the ground with a cane so that people might go
through to the other side. Others he sent to Earth Doctor, but
Earth Doctor told them they were too late. So they sent the
people to the top of a high mountain called Crooked Mountain. South Doctor sang a magic song and traced his cane
around the mountain, but that held back the waters only for
a short time. Four times he sang and traced a line around
the mountain, yet the flood rose again each time. There was
only one thing more to do.

He held his magic crystals in his left hand and sang a
song. Then he struck it with his cane. A thunder peal rang
through the mountains. He threw his staff into the water and
it cracked with a loud noise. Turning, he saw a dog near him.
He said, "How high is the tide?" The dog said, "It is very
near the top." He looked at the people as he said it. When
they heard his voice they all turned to stone. They stood just
as they were, and they are there to this day in groups: some
of the men talking, some of the women cooking, and some
crying.

But Earth Doctor escaped by enclosing himself in his reed staff, which floated upon the water. Elder Brother rolled along in his olla until he came near the mouth of the Colorado River. The olla is now called Black Mountain. After the flood he came out and visited all parts of the land.

When he met Coyote and Earth Doctor, each claimed to have been the first to appear after the flood, but at last they admitted Elder Brother was the first, so he became ruler of the world.

CREATION AND LONGEVITY

Achomawi (California)

Coyote began the creation of the earth, but Eagle completed it. Coyote scratched it up with his paws out of nothingness, but Eagle complained there were no mountains for him to perch on. So Coyote made hills, but they were not high enough. Therefore Eagle scratched up great ridges. When Eagle flew over them, his feathers dropped down, took root, and became trees. The pin feathers became bushes and plants.

Coyote and Fox together created man. They quarreled as to whether they should let men live always or not. Coyote said, "If they want to die, let them die." Fox said, "If they want to come back, let them come back." But Coyote's medicine was stronger, and nobody ever came back.

Coyote also brought fire into the world, for the Indians were freezing. He journeyed far to the west, to a place where there was fire, stole some of it, and brought it home in his ears. He kindled a fire in the mountains, and the Indians saw the smoke of it, and went up and got fire.

OLD MOLE'S CREATION

Shastika (California)

Long, long ago, before there was any earth, Old Mole burrowed underneath Somewhere, and threw up the earth which forms the world. Then Great Man created the people. But the Indians were cold.

Now in the east gleamed the white Fire Stone. Therefore Coyote journeyed eastward, and brought back the Fire Stone for the Indians. So people had fire.

In the beginning, Sun had nine brothers, all flaming hot like himself. But Coyote killed the nine brothers and so saved the world from burning up. But Moon also had nine brothers all made of ice, like himself, and the Night People almost froze to death. Therefore Coyote went away out on the eastern edge of the world with his flintstone knife. He heated stones to keep his hands warm, and as the Moons arose, he killed one after another with his flintstone knife, until he had slain nine of them. Thus the people were saved from freezing at night.

When it rains, some Indian, sick in heaven, is weeping. Long, long ago, there was a good young Indian on earth. When he died the Indians wept so that a flood came upon the earth and drowned all people except one couple.

SPIDER'S CREATION

Sia (New Mexico)

In the beginning, long, long ago, there was but one being in the lower world. This was the spider, Sussistinnako. At that time there were no other insects, no birds, animals, or any other living creature.

The spider drew a line of meal from north to south and then crossed it with another line running east and west. On each side of the first line, north of the second, he placed two small parcels. They were precious, but no one knows what was in them except Spider. Then he sat down near the parcels and began to sing. The music was low and sweet and the two parcels accompanied him, by shaking like rattles. Then two women appeared, one from each parcel.

In a short time people appeared and began walking around. Then animals, birds, and insects appeared, and the spider continued to sing until his creation was complete.

But there was no light, and as there were many people, they did not pass about much for fear of treading upon each other. The two women first created were the mothers of all. One was named Utset and she was the mother of all Indians. The other was Now-utset, and she was the mother of all other nations. While it was still dark, the spider divided the people into clans, saying to some, "You are of the Corn clan, and you are the first of all." To others he said, "You belong to the Coyote clan." So he divided them into their clans, the clans of the Bear, the Eagle, and other clans.

After Spider had nearly created the earth, Ha-arts, he thought it would be well to have rain to water it, so he created the Cloud People, the Lightning People, the Thunder People, and the Rainbow People, to work for the people of Ha-arts, the earth. He divided this creation into six parts, and each had its home in a spring in the heart of a great mountain upon whose summit was a giant tree. One was in the spruce tree on the Mountain of the North; another in the pine tree on the Mountain of the West; another in the oak tree on the Mountain of the South; and another in the aspen tree on the Mountain of the East; the fifth was on the cedar tree on the

Mountain of the Zenith; and the last in an oak on the Mountain of the Nadir.

The spider divided the world into three parts: Ha-arts, the earth; Tinia, the middle plain; and Hu-wa-ka, the upper plain. Then the spider gave to these People of the Clouds and to the rainbow, Tinia, the middle plain.

Now it was still dark, but the people of Ha-arts made houses for themselves by digging in the rocks and the earth. They could not build houses as they do now, because they could not see. In a short time Utset and Now-utset talked much to each other, saying,

"We will make light, that our people may see. We cannot tell the people now, but tomorrow will be a good day and the day after tomorrow will be a good day," meaning that their thoughts were good. So they spoke with one tongue. They said, "Now all is covered with darkness, but after a while we will have light."

Then these two mothers, being inspired by Sussistinnako, the spider, made the sun from white shell, turkis, red stone, and abalone shell. After making the sun, they carried him to the east and camped there, since there were no houses. The next morning they climbed to the top of a high mountain and dropped the sun down behind it. After a time he began to ascend. When the people saw the light they were happy.

When the sun was far off, his face was blue; as he came nearer, the face grew brighter. Yet they did not see the sun himself, but only a large mask which covered his whole body.

The people saw that the world was large and the country beautiful. When the two mothers returned to the village, they said to the people, "We are the mothers of all."

The sun lighted the world during the day, but there was no light at night. So the two mothers created the moon from a slightly black stone, many kinds of yellow stone, turkis, and a red stone, that the world might be lighted at night. But the moon traveled slowly and did not always give light. Then the two mothers created the Star People and made their eyes of sparkling white crystal that they might twinkle and brighten the world at night. When the Star People lived in the lower world they were gathered into beautiful groups; they were not scattered about as they are in the upper world.

ORIGIN OF LIGHT

Gallinomero (California)

In the earliest beginning, the darkness was thick and deep. There was no light. The animals ran here and there, always bumping into each other. The birds flew here and there, but continually knocked against each other.

Hawk and Coyote thought a long time about the darkness. Then Coyote felt his way into a swamp and found a large number of dry tule reeds. He made a ball of them. He gave the ball to Hawk, with some flints, and Hawk flew up into the sky, where he touched off the tule reeds and sent the bundle whirling around the world. But still the nights were dark, so Coyote made another bundle of tule reeds, and Hawk flew into the air with them, and touched them off with the flints. But these reeds were damp and did not burn so well. That is why the moon does not give so much light as the sun.

POKOH, THE OLD MAN[1]

Pai Ute (California)

Pokoh, Old Man, they say, created the world. Pokoh had many thoughts. He had many blankets in which he carried around gifts for men. He created every tribe out of the soil where they used to live. That is why an Indian wants to live and die in his native place. He was made of the same soil. Pokoh did not wish men to wander and travel, but to remain in their birthplace.

Long ago, Sun was a man, and was bad. Moon was good. Sun had a quiver full of arrows, and they are deadly. Sun wishes to kill all things.

Sun has two daughters (Venus and Mercury) and twenty men kill them; but after fifty days, they return to life again.

Rainbow is the sister of Pokoh, and her breast is covered with flowers.

Lightning strikes the ground and fills the flint with fire. That is the origin of fire. Some say the beaver brought fire from the east, hauling it on his broad, flat tail. That is why the beaver's tail has no hair on it, even to this day. It was burned off.

There are many worlds. Some have passed and some are still to come. In one world the Indians all creep; in another they all walk; in another they all fly. Perhaps in a world to come, Indians may walk on four legs; or they may crawl like snakes; or they may swim in the water like fish.

---

[1] These are fragments of Pai Ute Indians' ideas on creation. They comprise sayings, creation aphorisms, and fragments from songs.

THUNDER AND LIGHTNING

Maidu (California)

Great-Man created the world and all the people. At first the earth was very hot, so hot it was melted, and that is why even today there is fire in the trunk and branches of trees, and in the stones.

Lightning is Great-Man himself coming down swiftly from his world above, and tearing apart the trees with his flaming arm.

Thunder and Lightning are two great spirits who try to destroy mankind. But Rainbow is a good spirit who speaks gently to them, and persuades them to let the Indians live a little longer.

CREATION OF MAN

Miwok (California)

After Coyote had completed making the world, he began to think about creating man. He called a council of all the animals. The animals sat in a circle, just as the Indians do, with Lion at the head, in an open space in the forest. On Lion's right was Grizzly Bear; next Cinnamon Bear; and so on to Mouse, who sat at Lion's left.

Lion spoke first. Lion said he wished man to have a terrible voice, like himself, so that he could frighten all animals. He wanted man also to be well covered with hair, with fangs in his claws, and very strong teeth.

Grizzly Bear laughed. He said it was ridiculous for any one to have such a voice as Lion, because when he roared he frightened away the very prey for which he was searching. But he said man should have very great strength; that he should move silently, but very swiftly; and he should be able to seize his prey without noise.

Buck said man would look foolish without antlers. And a terrible voice was absurd, but man should have ears like a spider's web, and eyes like fire.

Mountain Sheep said the branching antlers would bother man if he got caught in a thicket. If man had horns rolled up, so that they were like a stone on each side of his head, it would give his head weight enough to butt very hard.

Then Beaver talked. Beaver said man would have to have a tail, but it should be broad and flat, so he could haul mud and sand on it. Not a furry tail, because they were troublesome on account of fleas.

Owl said man would be useless without wings.

But Mole said wings would be folly. Man would be sure to bump against the sky. Besides, if he had wings and eyes both, he would get his eyes burned out by flying too near the sun. But without eyes, he could burrow in the soft, cool earth where he could be happy.

Mouse said man needed eyes so he could see what he was eating. And nobody wanted to burrow in the damp earth. So the council broke up in a quarrel.

When it came Coyote's turn, he said the other animals were foolish because they each wanted man to be just like themselves. Coyote was sure he could make a man who would look better than Coyote himself, or any other animal. Of course he would have to have four legs, with five fingers. Man should have a strong voice, but he need not roar all the time with it. And he should have feet nearly like Grizzly Bear's, because he could then stand erect when he needed to. Grizzly Bear had no tail, and man should not have any. The eyes and ears of Buck were good, and perhaps man should have those. Then there was Fish, which had no hair, and hair was a burden much of the year. So Coyote thought man should not wear fur. And his claws should be as long as the Eagle's, so that he could hold things in them. But no animal was as cunning and crafty as Coyote, so man should have the wit of Coyote.

Then every animal set to work to make a man according to his own ideas. Each one took a lump of earth and modeled it just like himself. All but Coyote, for Coyote began to make the kind of man he had talked of in the council.

It was late when the animals stopped work and fell asleep. All but Coyote, for Coyote was the cunningest of all the animals, and he stayed awake until he had finished his model. He worked hard all night. When the other animals were fast asleep, he threw water on the lumps of earth, and so spoiled the models of the other animals. But in the morning he finished his own, and gave it life long before the others could finish theirs. Thus man was made by Coyote.

NAVAJO CREATION MYTHS

Creation

The great Navajo nation's doctrine of the dawn of the present age chronicles the adventures of the first three living beings, Coyote, who was a creator and trickster, First Man, and First Woman. Groping about their cramped first world in complete darkness, the three decided to journey to the second world, where there was a faint yellow light in the West, a glimmer of white light in the North, and a dim blue light in the South. The East, from whence they had come, was black, and there was a living being in each direction. The travelers found two people in the second world, Sun Man and Moon Man, and they observed that the three colors glowed brightly and it was day. At other times the black from the East blanketed everything and it was night. During the first day Sun Man forced his affections on First Woman, but she resisted and an argument broke out. To settle matters, all-knowing Coyote cried out, "Beings in the four directions, come here for a council so we can determine what to do; this second world is too crowded."

The beings came and everybody sat down on the ground after the proper ceremonies. Soon all present agreed with Coyote that more space was needed.

"Come," said Coyote, "let us all climb the sky ladder to the third world."

After a long, arduous climb they stepped out onto a spacious expanse of land with trees, mountains, canyons, lakes, rivers, and beauty everywhere. The People of the Mountains met Coyote and his followers.

"We are happy to welcome you," said the Mountain People, "and everything will go well here with you as long as the water monster is not disturbed."

Coyote, always thinking of tricks, considered the warning. "I'm going to search for the water monster," he mumbled as he started toward the East where the big waters were. Find-

ing the water monster's home and the water monster's two
children, Coyote liked them so well that he put his blanket
around the children and carried them away to his own home.
When the water monster Tieholtsoti returned to his home
and discovered his children were missing, he thrashed about
in a rage and went off to search all over the world for them.

"My children have been stolen," Tieholtsoti said to himself,
"so I will use my power on the waters and cover the land."

Swiftly the low places became oceans and the oceans rose
and flooded over the land and the Mountain People, after a
short council, took the mountains from the four directions
and piled them all together. All the people now climbed to
the top of the new mountain where they planted a fast-
growing hollow reed which soon grew through the sky above
the third world and into the fourth world. Up through the
reed all of the people and their animals climbed. Bringing up
the rear was Turkey, who began to climb when the flood
waters reached his tail feathers. To this day all of Turkey's
descendants have white-tipped tail feathers, proving that their
ancestor had to flee the flood.

After four days and nights of climbing, the people stepped
out onto the fourth world, which was very dim. The murky
light seemed to come from three sources, but the land and
mountains and lakes were much like those of the former
world. The broad land was divided from East to West by a
wide river. Human people lived on the North side, while the
South side was populated by animal people. The situation
seemed idyllic, but a year was as short as a day and a con-
troversy arose between men and women because time passed
too quickly.

"We are most important," said the men, "because we
build the houses and hunt for food."

"You are wrong," the women countered, "because we bear
the children, plant and harvest corn and cotton, make all of
the pottery, and even build the fires and keep them burning."

"Ah," the men replied, "but we know the proper ceremonies and dances which keep the spirits happy. We certainly
are more important than you because our ceremonies assure
good crops. You could not live without us men."

When the quarrel worsened, the men made a large canoe
and crossed the river to the South side where they built
houses, planted crops, hunted animals for their meat, and
had more food than they could eat. Meanwhile, on the North
side of the great river the women planted no corn or cotton,

and after four years they were sad. The men were sad, too, and at a council of the sexes they all decided that each needed the other and each was as important as the other. So the families were reunited after confessing the argument had been ridiculous.

They resumed the responsibilities for which each was fitted and this is how men and women learned to live together peaceably as families. Expanding their farming activities, the people spread across the land and their families grew and new families were started. Everything was fine, or should have been but for one thing. Old Coyote was living quietly in his house, and he still held the water monster's charming children captive because of his fascination for them. Unaware of the evil in their midst, the people were so happy that they were unprepared for the tragedy about to overtake them. At first the moisture in the ground was not noticed, but when the great river overflowed, the wise men said, "We must hasten and prepare for another flood!"

Once again the people struggled to move the mountains together from each of the four directions. In the middle of their cultivated land they piled the mountains together into one and climbed to the top where they planted a hollow reed as their ancestors had done so long ago. Quickly the reed grew through the sky above the fourth world.

"Badger, you must lead the way," the wise men ordered, "because you have sharp claws and can dig through the sky."

So Badger went up first through the giant hollow reed, and it was good that he did because the sky over the fourth world proved to be dirt. As Badger dug, the earth-sky became muddy, and presently all of the people emerged from the reed to discover they were in a vast sea of mud.

"What shall we do?" the people wailed. "The flood is still rising and will engulf us and we will drown."

"I can get through the mud," Locust volunteered. "I will find the way to dry land." And he scrambled through the mud, half-flying, and went up to the surface where he saw a yellow swan in the West, a blue swan in the South, a white swan in the North and a black swan in the East like the lights in the previous worlds. After listening to Locust's account of the trouble all of the people were having getting away from the flood the swans proclaimed everyone would have to pass a test in order to enter the fifth world.

"Everyone must thrust an arrow into his mouth and down through his body and pass it completely through," the swans said. "Then the arrow must be reversed and drawn up through each person's body and be brought out through the mouth," they said, as they demonstrated how easily this was done.

Locust knew he could do this bit of magic but he also knew the people could not. "I'll agree if you will do as I do," said the crafty Locust, who drove the arrow through the middle of his body—or appeared to do so—and withdrew it from his backside. Locust's magic was that his spine was very short and did not extend the length of his body, thus he was able to pass the arrow through his body below his spine.

"Now let me see you do what I have just done," Locust challenged.

"We agree that your magic is as powerful as ours," the swans replied. "Summon all your people to enter."

Up came the people in great haste, each man, woman, and child carrying his small bundle of treasured possessions. Out into the great muddy swamp they climbed, but the flood waters rose behind them and there was no dry land.

"There is the water monster," called out one of the people in a loud voice. "There is Tieholtsoti. I see his horns above the mud!"

Sure enough, the terrible water monster was there. "Come over here, all of you," Tieholtsoti commanded. "Let me see all of your belongings. Unwrap your bundles!"

The people had no other choice, and Coyote, who was among them of course, had to unwrap his blanket.

"Coyote has Tieholtsoti's children," the people murmured. "Coyote, that old trickster, is the cause of all of our troubles!"

The water monster was happy to see his beloved children and the people pushed them to Tieholtsoti without delay. The waters receded rapidly as the reunited water monster family swam away, but the people found themselves standing huddled together on a large island in the center of the swampy sea.

Now the priests ordered them to be quiet while they prayed to the black god of darkness in the East. Immediately the god cut through the mountains and the waters flowed through the canyon.

"But there is still too much mud," the people complained. "We still must stand here huddled together."

Next the priests had the people pray to the winds of the four directions, and a great wind blew for four days until the mud was dry.

"Now we can go to the land," the people rejoiced, and they did so, but because the ground was not correctly shaped the

wise men and chiefs put them to work moving great masses
of the remaining mud. On each of the four corners of the new
fifth world they made mountains which quickly hardened.
The entire world grew and the mountains grew. Instructed
by the wise men and priests, the people grabbed hold of Sun
Man and threw him into the sky. They also threw Moon Man
into the sky. Every day for four days the world grew and the
Sun rose higher into the sky until, on the fifth day, the Sun
of the fifth world was at its highest point but it stood still.

"Now it is so hot everything will be burned as quickly as it
grows," the people protested.

"We must have a sacrifice for the Sun," a wise man de-
creed and the wife of one of the high chiefs was prepared as
an offering. When the last breath and drop of blood had left
her body, the Sun began again to move in his orbit.

"This is a sign," said a wise man, "that people will die as
they grow old. Do not be afraid, for this is as it should be."
And the priest walked to the place where the people had
emerged and looked down through the great hollow reed. "I
see our chief's wife," the priest told the people. "She is happy
and healthy and is beside the great river in our old world."

The priest looked down again and listened to the woman
who had just died. Turning to the people, the priest said,
"Our chief's wife told me that everyone in this new world
will return to the old fourth world after they die and there
they will live in great happiness forever."

Sun moved across the sky from East to West every day.
During the dark of night, Moon was supreme. One day the
old priest died and Coyote—who knew everything—told the
people that this meant that a Navajo would die every day
and that during the night someone also would die. From
Coyote's interpretation of these events, the people came to
believe that anyone who looked upon a dead person would
die and this—the Navajo creation story—tells us why the
face of a dead person is covered quickly with a blanket and
the body is buried so the spirit can emerge into the other
world of eternal happiness.

Creation Myth of Begochiddy

The story starts in the Running-Pitch Place or Jahdokonth-
Hashjeshjin. The son of the Fire, whose mother is a Comet,

and Etsay-Hasteen, the first man, who is the son of Night and whose father is Nah-doklizh, which is the blue above the place where the Sun has set, were there, also Estsa-assun, the first woman, and so on. Her name has to do with the Daybreak. The earth-God is Begochiddy; he is the real creator God. He is the great God whose mother is a Ray of Sunlight and whose father is the Daylight. This earth God "built in the east a white mountain, in the south a blue mountain" and so on. First he creates below, under the earth, a sort of cosmos which is surrounded by four mountains in the four directions of the horizon. He also creates four types of ants and some bugs. In the East mountain he plants some bamboo and other things. Then, after some time, when the bamboo has grown upwards, they all climbed out on it; and "Begochiddy pulled the bamboo up into the second world and Hashjeshjin blew into the hole four times which made the hole close up and the first world burned up and is still burning."

This first world, created near the center of the earth, was only a temporary world and all its inhabitants, animals and gods, climbed up out of it and destroyed it after them. The fire world underground accounts for present-day volcanoes.

Now these first beings come into the second world: "Bego-chiddy took the earth brought from the first world and created mountains in the East, South, West and North, and plants similar to those in the first world, and he planted white cotton in the East, blue cotton in the South" and so on. Then they climb up into the third world, and there again six gods create all living things. Then they come to the fourth world; there the locust comes up through the crust which covered the third world into the fourth world which is covered with water. With the help of the locust, the people come up and settle in the fourth world.

THE MAKING OF THE WORLD

Huron

In the beginning there was nothing but water, a wide sea, which was peopled by various animals of the kind that live in and upon the water. It happened then that a woman fell down from the upper world. It is supposed that she was, by some mischance, pushed down by her husband through a rift in the sky. Though styled a woman, she was a divine personage. Two loons, which were flying over the water, happened to look up and see her falling. To save her from drowning they hastened to place themselves beneath her, joining their bodies together so as to form a cushion for her to rest on. In this way they held her up, while they cried with a loud voice to summon the other animals to their aid. The cry of the loon can be heard to a great distance, and the other creatures of the sea heard it, and assembled to learn the cause of the summons. Then came the tortoise (or "snapping turtle,") a mighty animal, which consented to relieve the loons of their burden. They placed the woman on the back of the tortoise, charging him to take care of her. The tortoise then called the other animals to a grand council, to determine what should be done to preserve the life of the woman. They decided that she must have earth to live on. The tortoise directed them all to dive to the bottom of the sea and endeavor to bring up some earth. Many attempted it—the beaver, the muskrat, the diver, and others—but without success. Some remained so long below that when they rose they were dead. The tortoise searched their mouths but could find no trace of earth. At last the toad went down, and after remaining a long time rose, exhausted and nearly dead. On searching his mouth the tortoise found in it some earth, which he gave to the woman. She took it and placed it carefully around the edge of the tortoise's shell. When thus placed, it became the beginning of dry land. The land grew and extended on every side, forming at last a great country, fit for vegetation. All was sustained by the tortoise, which still supports the earth.

Then the woman felt she was pregnant with twins. When

these came forth they evinced opposite dispositions, the one good, the other evil. Even before they were born the same characters were manifested. They struggled together, and their mother heard them disputing. The one declared his willingness to be born in the usual manner, while the other malignantly refused, and, breaking through his mother's side, killed her. She was buried, and from her body sprang the various vegetable productions which the new earth required to fit it for the habitation of man. From her head grew the pumpkin vine; from her breasts the maize; from her limbs the bean and the other useful esculents. Meanwhile the twins grew up, showing in all they did their opposing inclinations. The name of the good one was Tijuskeha, which means, something like savior, or good man. The evil brother was named Tawiskarong, meaning flinty, or flintlike, in allusion probably to his hard and cruel nature. They were not men, but supernatural beings, who were to prepare the world to be the abode of men. Finding that they could not live together, they separated, each taking his own portion of the earth. Their first act was to create animals of various kinds. The bad brother made fierce and monstrous creatures, proper to terrify and destroy mankind—serpents, panthers, wolves, bears, all of enormous size, and huge mosquitoes, "as large as turkeys." Among other things he made an immense toad, which drank up all the fresh water that was on the earth. In the meantime the good brother, in his province, was creating the innocent and useful animals. Among the rest he made the partridge. To his surprise, the bird rose in the air and flew toward the territory of Tawiskarong. Tijuskeha asked him whither he was going. The bird replied that he was going to look for water, as there was none left in that land, and he heard there was some in the dominion of Tawiskarong. Tijuskeha then began to suspect mischief. He followed the course which the partridge had taken and presently reached the land of his evil brother. Here he encountered the snakes, ferocious brutes, and enormous insects which his brother had made, and overcame them. Finally he came to the monstrous toad, which he cut open, letting the water flow forth. He did not destroy the evil animals—perhaps had not the power to do so—but he reduced them in size, so that men would be able to master them.

The spirit of his mother warned him in a dream to beware of his evil brother, who would endeavor to destroy him by treachery. Finally they encountered, and as it was evident that they could not live together on the earth, they determined to decide by a formal combat which of them should remain master of the world. It was further agreed that each should make known to the other the only weapon by which he could be overcome. This extraordinary article of their agreement was probably made necessary by the fact that without such a disclosure the contest would have lasted forever. The good brother declared that he could be destroyed only by being beaten to death with a bag full of corn, beans, or some other product of the bread kind. The evil brother rejoined that he could be killed only by the horn of a deer or of some other wild animal. They set off a fighting group, or "list," within which the combat was to take place. Tawiskarong had the first turn, or, as duellists would say, the first fire. He set upon his brother with a bag of corn or beans, chased him about the ground, and pounded him until he was nearly lifeless and lay as if dead. He revived, however (perhaps through the aid of his mother's spirit), and, recovering his strength, pursued in turn his evil brother, beating him with a deer's horn until he killed him. But the slain combatant was not utterly destroyed. He reappeared after death to his brother, and told him that he had gone to the far west, and that thenceforth all the races of men after death would go to the west, like him. "And, it is the belief of all the early Indians that after death their spirits will go to the far west, and dwell there."

(A continuation of this tale further develops the opposing character of the brothers.)

"When the brothers were preparing the land for the Indians to live in, the manner of their work was that as often as the good brother made or designed anything for the benefit of mankind, the bad brother objected, and devised something to counteract the good intention, so far as he could. Thus, when the good brother made rivers for the Indians to journey on, it was his design that each river should have a twofold current in which the streams should flow in opposite directions. Thus the Indians would be able always to float easily downstream. This convenient arrangement did not please the bad brother. He maintained that it would be too good for the people. 'Let them at least,' he said, 'have to work one way up stream.' He was not content merely to defeat his brother's design of the return current, but he created at the same time rapids and cataracts for the further delay and danger of voyagers."

CROW CREATION MYTHS

How Raven Brought the Light

Raven sat one day in the top of a tall fir, chewing a twig. He bit the end very hard because he was much troubled; and he chewed the twig because he had nothing else to do. It was so dark Raven could not see his claw when he put it up before his face. He had done that several times. Then Raven looked at his own wings, but he could not see them, even though they were pure white. Because in those days Raven was white, and so was Old Crow. Neither had a black feather on him. Now both are as black as jet and they became that way because—but that's another story.

As Raven was looking down at his claws, and chewing that twig, and thinking about the darkness, he heard a slight whirring of wings. Somebody was coming. When that somebody alighted on the fir tree, he cried, "Caw! caw! caw!"

"Well, I am glad you cried 'Caw,' Old Crow," said Raven. "In this darkness no one could see who it was."

"I am glad you spoke," said Old Crow, "because otherwise nobody would know you were here. This darkness is so thick I can feel it."

Now this happened in the Days of the Animal People, when the Earth-land was very new. Real People had not come yet, because this was even before the Days of the Grandfathers.

"Dear me!" said Old Crow, after a few minutes. "What will the Real People do when they come to the Earth-land if it is so dark?"

"They will think we haven't fixed things up very nicely," said Raven. "They'll be bumping into trees and bushes, and getting into the wrong tepees, and jostling against each other——"

"Just as we do," said Old Crow, "and the animals, too. Why, do you know, Black Bear was coming down a tree the other day, and Elk happened to be standing right underneath.

51

Black Bear couldn't see anything, of course, without any light, and he thought Elk's antlers were branches of his tree, and tried to climb out on them. Elk was terribly frightened and tried to run away, with Black Bear hanging on, and they got tangled up in the underbrush—oh, they both had an awful time. And both were so badly frightened. Black Bear said he was not used to climbing out on tree branches that ran away with him. He was quite indignant. He felt Elk had not treated him nicely, at all."

"I am tired of the dark," said Raven. "Sea Gull is my cousin, but I think he is very selfish about keeping all the light. He owns all the light there is, and the rest of us have to go without it."

"I have asked Sea Gull over and over again," said Old Crow, "to open his box of light just a little, so we can see where we are flying. But he won't. Dear me!"

Raven chewed on his twig for a long time without answering a word. Old Crow waited in silence, because he knew Raven was thinking. Raven always chewed a twig when he was thinking.

Suddenly Raven said, "I have thought of a way. "I'll *make* Sea Gull give us some light!"

"Oh!" said Old Crow in astonishment. "But how are you going to do it?"

"You wait and see. I have thought of a plan," said Raven mysteriously. And Old Crow had to wait, because Raven wouldn't tell him what he was going to do.

Now in those days everything was dark because Sea Gull owned all the light. All the light in the whole world was kept in a box in Gull's tepee. All the Animal People had talked to Gull about giving them light, especially as the Indians were coming so soon to the Earth-land, and they wanted to fix things up nicely. But Gull only said, "*No! no! no!*" and that was why things were so dark.

Sea Gull lived near the ocean, of course, and shortly after Raven and Old Crow had talked things over, Raven flew softly to his house one night. Or perhaps it was day. Raven couldn't tell, because there never had been any light on earth. Raven had once flown right into a tangle of thorn bushes near Gull's house, and had torn his feathers almost to pieces before he got out. He remembered just where those thorn bushes were, and he pulled off several branches with his beak.

Raven remembered also that there was a regular trail between Gull's tepee and the place where he always fastened his canoe. Gull always fastened it to one certain tree, and he could always find the tree without trouble, because when he went fishing he took the box of daylight with him. All he had to do to find that tree was to open the cover just a little. Raven remembered all that.

Raven put the thorn branches in the trail, and he moved very softly until the work was done, and then he rushed wildly up to Gull's tepee, shouting, "Your canoe has gone adrift! Your canoe has gone adrift!"

Sea Gull heard Raven, and he remembered the tide was going out. Without waiting to put on his moccasins, he rushed out of his house and down the trail in his bare feet. Then he cried, "*Ah-Ah-Ah*" just as sea gulls do now, because he had stepped on those thorn branches. Gull couldn't go any further, so he shouted to Raven, "Get my canoe! Save my canoe!" and went back to the house. He was much excited. Raven shouted, "All right!" but he never went near the canoe, which was safely fastened to the tree. But he waited around a while, and then went to the house. Gull spoke of those thorns in his feet.

Raven said, "Oh, I can pull them out, if you will let a little daylight out of your box." So Gull sat down on a large carved box in which he kept his dancing apron, and his dancing mask, and put the box of daylight under his wing. He opened the cover just the least little bit. Raven pulled out a thorn with an awl. Then he pulled out another. Then he said, "I could see better if you could give me more light." Gull opened the box a little more, and Raven pulled out more thorns. Soon he said, "I can't see very well. Give me more light." And Sea Gull opened the cover still more.

Raven pulled out all the thorns but one. Then he said, "This last one is hard to get at. I shall need more light." When Gull opened the box still more Raven took out the last thorn and gave his wing a sudden push. The box of daylight went rolling on the floor, and broke. Then all the daylight spilled out, and spread all over the world. Sea Gull jumped up and rushed about and tried to collect it again, but he couldn't do it. The light had spread everywhere.

Raven was so pleased to think that the light had come, that the very same day he brushed his feathers carefully, combed and oiled his hair—Raven taught the Indians how to do that after they came to the Earth-land—and painted his face red and black. Then he went to a little spring where the water was quiet, and sat there looking at himself. Raven thought he looked very well indeed, and it was the first time he had ever been able to see himself.

When Real People Were Baked

"It's high time the Real People were coming to the Earth-land," remarked Raven one day, as he sat on the topmost branch of his particular fir, talking to Old Crow. All the Animal People had been glad to see Sun again, after Raven had found him in Moon-woman's tepee, but none of them could get used to Raven's black coat. Raven had sat by the campfire and told that story over and over again—how Moon-woman piled on the green branches, which smoked instead of burned, after she had caught him in the smoke hole. And the Animal People would listen and then roll over and over on the ground, laughing. Rabbit sat up so straight on his haunches and then laughed so he wore off the end of his tail. Even to-day rabbits do not have a real tail. Porcupine would always say, "Oh, if I had only been there! I'd have shot some quills at her! Raven, you ought to have taken some of us with you!"

But Raven had known that going to Moon-woman's great tepee on that wide plain was a very dangerous piece of work.

Raven didn't like being laughed at about his black coat. He really had always wanted one, and he felt very dignified in it, but the Animal People couldn't seem to get used to it. But after a while they didn't talk so much about that, and began to discuss the Real People who were coming to the Earth-land.

"Has Great One come yet?" asked Old Crow. "I haven't seen him."

"Yes. Great One came down to the Earth-land three suns ago," said Raven. "And the Real People should soon be here. But I don't see why their coming is delayed."

No one at all knew why the coming of the Real People was delayed except Great One himself. And he wasn't telling. But this is what really happened.

Great One came down from the Sky-land to the Earth-land one beautiful summer day. First, through a hole in Sky-land he pushed down great masses of glorious white clouds, until they were piled up so high they almost touched the earth. Then he stepped through the hole, onto the cloudy heap, and took two long strides clear to the bottom. After he was fairly down, he went far south to a great wide plain, because here he was going to make the Real People. He went south, because Sun liked the south land better, and was there a great deal, and Sun was to help Great One.

Great One went to a great pile of clay which was heaped upon the plain and took a large lump of it in his fingers. He squeezed it this way and that, and rolled it, and kneaded it with his fingers until he made a man out of it. Sun had been watching him all this time. Great One covered the clay man with large leaves.

"Now, Sun," said Great One, when the man was finished, "sit up in that tree yonder and bake this man." So Sun climbed up into the top of a big maple tree and threw all the heat he had toward that clay man. Great One took a nap. When he waked up, he went at once to the clay man and took off the leaves. Why, that man was burned black!

"Oh, that will never do," said Great One, in great disgust. Then he spoke to the black man. "Go far into the south," he said. "Do not come up into this country again until I give permission." So he sent him away, and he did it so quickly that for a long, long time the Animal People never knew there was such a thing as a black man.

Great One began to make another man, while Sun wandered around for a while. When the next man was ready, Great One called to him, "Ho, Sun! Go sit on that mountain top—that one far off—and don't send so much of your heat in this direction." Then he covered the second man with large leaves so he would bake well, and took another nap.

Great One slept for a long time, and when he awakened, he rushed to the clay man and pulled all the leaves off in a great hurry. He didn't stop to think at all. And behold! The clay man was hardly baked at all. He was still white. Sun had sat too far away and had sent all his heat in another direction.

Great One was much disgusted. "Why," he said, "I don't want a white man." But there the white man was, walking about. So Great One gave him a canoe, and told him to go far off across the wide sea and not to come back until he gave permission.

Sun came up just then to see how things were going. They talked about the black man and the white man for some time. Then Great One said, "Well! I'll make another man, and this one must be right, because my magic is almost used up. Now, Sun, you sit on that tree where you did the first time, and send your heat in another direction. Then the man will bake just right."

And Sun did so. He did just as Great One had said, and Great One made a third man and covered him all up with leaves. Then he stayed awake and counted up to five hundred while Sun sat up in the tree and sent just the right amount of heat out to bake that man properly. When Great One had counted five hundred he took off the leaves, and behold! There was a red man—an Indian. He was baked just right, and he was just the kind of man Great One wanted.

Then Great One was very happy. He made a great many other men, and many women, and a few children. That is the way the Real People came to the Earth-land.

Raven heard first about the red man, and he was much pleased. Great One never told any one about the black man and the white man, and the Animal People knew nothing about them at all for a long, long time.

The Remaking of Real People[1]

"It isn't right," said Old Crow one day, as he and Raven sat on the topmost branch of a tall fir tree, "it isn't right to have a world without Real People. And since Grizzly Bear has eaten them all up, and Great One doesn't come down and make more, I think we will have to do it ourselves."

"I think so, too," said Raven, "and we must call a council. But first I think I'll have a talk with Sun and find out how he did it."

So that very noon Raven and Old Crow flew up to the top of the highest mountain—the very one where Sun rested every noon, to eat his luncheon—and had a talk with him. It was a rather gray day, else they could not have had this chat, now that Sun was so very bright.

Sun told them just how Great One had made that third man—the red one who was baked just right. But he said never a word about the black man or the white man.

"I don't believe that Great One wants me to tell that," he

said to himself, as he started off on his trail again. "I think it is better not to refer to it. They were both mistakes."

Raven called the council, and all the Animal People came, because Deer called so long and loud that every one heard about it. And they all felt, too, that it was very important to be there.

The Animal People sat in a half circle, just as they taught the Indians to do. Cougar sat at one end, in an open space in the forest; Grizzly Bear sat next to him, and Black Bear was next to him. Porcupine was there, and Owl, and Mountain Goat, and Eagle,—oh, all the Animal People were there.

Cougar spoke first. He said that Real People should have a voice like his, so that they could frighten all the Animal People. Cougar said also, "Real People should be well covered with fur, and have fangs in their claws, and very strong teeth."

Grizzly Bear laughed. "It's ridiculous," he said, "for any one to have such a voice as Cougar has." And indeed, Cougar when he shrieks has a fearful voice. Grizzly had heard him, of course, in the forest. Then Grizzly went on talking:

"The Real People should have four legs," he said firmly, "or else wings. It's absurd to make them so they can't fly— and they can't if they haven't wings—and with only two legs."

"Why, I think——" began Otter, but Grizzly interrupted him.

"I haven't finished yet," he said. "Real People should have very great strength, and move silently, but swiftly. They should be able to seize their prey without noise at all."

"Why, I think——" began Otter, but Grizzly cut him short again.

"Real People must have four legs!" he repeated. "It's all right when they fight to stand on their hind legs and fight with their forepaws—as I do—but they *must* have four legs. Or else wings."

Oh, Grizzly was very determined. You see, he had knocked over, one after another, those Real People which Great One had made, and eaten them all up—though he did it in the friendliest way—and he felt he knew just how Real People should be made.

"Oh, that's all nonsense," said Deer, speaking with great force. "Real People don't need a terrible voice, or claws with talons, but they do look foolish without antlers! Real people ought to have ears like a spider's web—soft and silky, but ears that can catch the faintest sound."

"Branching antlers would bother Real People terribly, whenever they got into thickets," said Mountain Sheep. "But if they had heavy horns, all rolled up like mine, so they were like a stone on each side of their heads, they could butt down anything."

Then Beaver talked. "Real People ought to have tails," he said, "but they should be broad and flat, like mine, so they could haul sand and mud on them when they are building their houses. A furry tail is a great bother, but they need a good, broad, serviceable tail. And they must have long, sharp front teeth so they can cut down trees."

"I agree with Grizzly on one point," said Owl. "Real People are utterly useless without wings."

"Wings are folly," exclaimed Mole. "Real People would bump against the sky if they had wings. Besides, if they had wings and eyes both, and got too near Sun, the heat and light would hurt their eyes. Real People don't need eyes to burrow in the soft cool earth where they could be happy. They surely can't be happy *on* the earth. Nobody is. The best place to live is down *in* the earth."

Then Coyote spoke. Coyote was very wise, and Raven and Old Crow listened carefully to what he said.

"It's foolish," said Coyote to the Animal People, as he looked around the council, "to talk as you have done. Real People should have a strong voice, but they don't need to shriek all the time. Of course it would be better for man to have four legs, with five fingers on each, but I'm not so sure but that two legs would be enough. Of course," he went on, "if he had feet like Grizzly's, he could stand up and walk on his hind feet whenever he wanted to fight."

"Why, I think——" said Otter, but Coyote paid no attention to him. He went right on talking.

"Fish has no fur," he remarked, "and fur is a great burden much of the time. Real People should not have fur except on their heads. And the claws on his forefeet should be long, like Eagle's, so he could hold things. And he should have keen eyes, like Eagle, which see at a great distance."

"Why, I think——" began Otter, but just then Porcupine said he wanted to say something, and everybody knew that Old Crow and Raven had good ideas, so everybody began talking at once.

Coyote tried to call the meeting to order, but nobody paid any attention to him, and they all talked at the top of their voices, until Fox said, "Everybody get a lump of clay, and make a model!"

That was just the right thing to do, and every man there wondered why he hadn't thought of that. There was a good-sized bank of reddish clay near by, so the Animal People each went there and brought back lumps of it in pieces of bark. Then each began to make a model for one of the Real People.

Supper was late that night, for all of them, because they were so interested in their clay modeling, and it was late when they got to sleep. But after a while every one was asleep except Coyote. Coyote wanted to make Real People just as he thought they should be made, so he worked hard. Now Coyote was very wise. He put his clay model far back under the lowspreading branches of a spruce tree. And that night it *rained!*

All the models were spoiled except his.

Then early in the morning, when his was still complete, Sun gave it a baking, and lo! When the Animal People waked up—they were all late because they had been so sleepy—there was Coyote's man walking around! He wore a beautiful blanket of red, with a border of blue and yellow.

Cougar shrieked when he saw him, and Grizzly stood up on his hind legs and growled. "Only two legs!" he muttered, "and no wings! What's he good for!" And Grizzly went lumbering off into the forest.

Well, nobody liked Coyote's model. Beaver looked him over and exclaimed: "No tail—and no teeth to speak of! How will he ever build a house!"

"No fur!" exclaimed Fox in contempt.

They all said things like that. Only Raven and Old Crow began to think. They went off by themselves into the topmost branch of a tall fir tree. The council had broken up in such confusion that nobody had even asked what they thought about it.

"It's a great mistake," said Old Crow indignantly, "to do important work in such a fashion as that!"

Raven chewed his twig vigorously. He was thinking. "Do you know," he said suddenly, "I'm going to send word to Great One. He ought to come down again and straighten things out. What did you do with the quill Porcupine gave you for a pen?"

"It's over at the house," said Old Crow. "I told my wife to take good care of it."

So at once they flew to Old Crow's tepee, and Raven wrote a note to Great One, telling him all about the council. He told him also that Grizzly had eaten up all the other Real People. He felt Great One should know that.

Eagle was a good friend of theirs, and Old Crow and Raven felt they could trust him. So Eagle took the note in his beak, and flew high up, almost to the hole in the sky, and laid the note on the top of the highest white cloud there. He was sure Great One would see it there. And sure enough, that evening, when Great One came to the hole in the sky to watch the sunset, he saw it there, and sent one of his men down to get it.

"Hm-m-m-m!" he said, when he had read it. "I guess I'll have to go down and straighten things out."

And he did so. When he looked over Coyote's man, he said, "That's pretty good for a beginning," but he made some changes. Then he taught him how to defend himself against Grizzly. Since then Grizzly has not been able to eat up all the Real People.

Then Raven and Old Crow felt satisfied. "Even if he doesn't have wings," added Old Crow.

Now that day Beaver worked very hard, cutting down trees with his long, sharp front teeth, and hauling mud and sand on his broad flat tail, for he was building a new dam. Beaver was indeed a very busy man. But that night, just as he put his head on his pillow in his new home, he suddenly remembered Coyote's man. "No tail!" he murmured sleepily, "and no teeth—to speak of. How *will* he ever build a house!"

CREATION MYTH OF THE GAROS

In the beginning, what is now the Earth was a vast watery plain. There was no land, and darkness was over everything.

Tatara-Rabuga determined to create the Earth, so he sent a lesser spirit, Nostu-Nopantu, in the shape of a woman, to carry out his will. There was no dry place for her to set foot on, so she took up her abode in a spider's web which was stretched over the water. Tatara-Rabuga gave her for material a handful of sand, but when she set about her task she found that she could not make the particles stick together. So she sent the big crab down under the water to fetch some clay, but it was too deep, and he was obliged to return with his errand unfulfilled. Nostu then sent Chipongnokma-Balponggitel, the small crab, to do her behest, but he was afraid, and returned without having performed his errand. Last of all, Nostu chose Chiching-Barching, a beetle, and sent him down, and he returned with a lump of clay, with the aid of which Nostu-Nopantu fashioned the Earth.

She created the Earth, which was called Mane-Pilte, and the big rocks Mojar, and the little rocks Dinjar, but all was still wet and unfit to walk upon. So Nostu prayed Tatara-Rabuga to help her, and he placed the sun in the sky, and the moon, and sent wind, and the three between them dried up and hardened the surface of the Earth.

Then Tatara gave the earth a *riking* or petticoat (the Earth is spoken of as a woman) and a *pagri* made of clouds, and caused hair to grow on her in the shape of the *prap tree* (Ficus Rumphi), the *bolong*, the *sawe* (sago palm), the *rejok* and *re* (kinds of cane), and the *ampang* (thatching grass).

Of the animals which Tatara created, the first was the hulock ape, and his mission on earth was to utter loud cries and be productive. After the hulock, the hanuman and the common brown monkey were created, and then all other beasts.

In the water, the first animal created was the frog, for he was appointed to proclaim the advent of rain to all living things by his loud croak. After the frog, the many fishes of the deep were created.

Under the Earth there was much water, but on the surface there was none. Seeing this, the creator made rivers to flow and sent Norechire-Kimrebokre, or the rain, to water the Earth, and he sent a voice (thunder) before the rain to announce its coming.

Man had not yet been created, so Tatara called around him the lesser spirits, and declared his intention of placing man on earth. He chose a goddess named Susime, and sent her down to prepare it for its new inhabitants.

The first abode of man was Amitong-Asiljong (somewhere in the east), and the first man and woman were Sani and Muni, whose children, Gancheng and Dujong, were the parents of Noro and Mande, who were the progenitors of the Garo race.

The first inhabitants of the Earth had no rice to eat, so they had to satisfy their hunger with roots and fruit which they found in the forest.

The first human beings to cultivate the soil were two dwarfs, Bonejasku and his wife Jane-Gando. They cleared the forest as is done at the present day, and Tatara-Rabuga, to whom they made an offering of pumpkins, rewarded their industry by causing rice to grow.

MAIDU CREATION MYTHS

Creation

In the beginning there was no sun, no moon, no stars. All was dark and everywhere there was only water. A raft came floating on the water. It came from the north, and in it were two persons,—Turtle (A'noshma) and Father-of-the-Secret-Society (Pehe'ipe). The stream flowed very rapidly. Then from the sky a rope of feathers, called Po'kelma, was let down, and down it came Earth-Initiate. When he reached the end of the rope, he tied it to the bow of the raft, and stepped in. His face was covered and was never seen, but his body shone like the sun. He sat down, and for a long time said nothing. At last Turtle said, "Where do you come from?" and Earth-Initiate answered, "I come from above." Then Turtle said, "Brother, can you not make for me some good dry land, so that I may sometimes come up out of the water?" Then he asked another time, "Are there going to be any people in the world?" Earth-Initiate thought a while, then said, "Yes." Turtle asked, "How long before you are going to make people?" Earth-Initiate replied, "I don't know. You want to have some dry land: well, how am I going to get any earth to make it of?" Turtle answered, "If you will tie a rock about my left arm, I'll dive for some." Earth-Initiate did as Turtle asked, and then, reaching around, took the end of a rope from somewhere, and tied it to Turtle. When Earth-Initiate came to the raft, there was no rope there: he just reached out and found one. Turtle said, "If the rope is not long enough, I'll jerk it once, and you must haul me up; if it is long enough, I'll give two jerks, and then you must pull me up quickly, as I shall have all the earth that I can carry." Just as Turtle went over the side of the boat, Father-of-the-Secret-Society began to shout loudly.

Turtle was gone a long time. He was gone six years; and when he came up, he was covered with green slime, he had been down so long. When he reached the top of the water, the only earth he had was a very little under his nails; the rest had all washed away. Earth-Initiate took with his right hand a stone knife from under his left armpit, and carefully scraped the earth out from under Turtle's nails. He put the earth in the palm of his hand, and rolled it about till it was round; it was as large as a small pebble. He laid it on the stern of the raft. By and by he went to look at it: it had not grown at all. The third time he went to look at it, it had grown so that it could be spanned by the arms. The fourth time he looked, it was as big as the world, the raft was aground, and all around were mountains as far as he could see.

When the raft had come to land, Turtle said, "I can't stay in the dark all the time. Can't you make a light, so that I can see?" Earth-Initiate replied, "Let us get out of the raft, and then we will see what we can do." So all three got out. Then, Earth-Initiate said, "Look that way, to the east! I am going to tell my sister to come up." Then it began to grow light, and day began to break; then Father-of-the-Secret-Society began to shout loudly, and the sun came up. Turtle said, "Which way is the sun going to travel?" Earth-Initiate answered, "I'll tell her to go this way, and go down there." After the sun went down, Father-of-the-Secret-Society began to cry and shout again, and it grew very dark. Earth-Initiate asked Turtle and Father-of-the-Secret-Society, "How do you like it?" and they both answered, "It is very good." Then Turtle asked, "Is that all you are going to do for us?" and Earth-Initiate answered, "No, I am going to do more yet." Then he called the stars each by its name, and they came out. When this was done, Turtle asked, "Now what shall we do?" Earth-Initiate replied, "Wait, and I'll show you." Then he made a tree grow at Ta'doiko,—the tree called Hu'kimtsa; and Earth-Initiate and Turtle and Father-of-the-Secret-Society sat in its shade for two days. The tree was very large, and had twelve different kinds of acorns growing on it.

After they had sat for two days under the tree, they all went off to see the world that Earth-Initiate had made. They started at sunrise, and were back by sunset. Earth-Initiate traveled so fast that all they could see was a ball of fire flashing about under the ground and the water. While they were gone, Coyote (Ola'li) and his dog Rattlesnake (Kaudi or So'la) came out of the ground. It is said that Coyote could see Earth-Initiate's face. When Earth-Initiate and the others came back, they found Coyote at Ta'doiko, but no one could go inside of Earth-Initiate's house. Soon after the travelers came back,

Earth-Initiate called the birds from the air, and made the trees and then the animals. He then took some mud, and of this made first a deer; and after that, he made all the other animals. Sometimes Turtle would say, "That does not look well: can't you make it some other way?"

Creating Man and Woman

Some time after this, Earth-Initiate and Coyote were at Marysville Buttes (E'stobusin Ya'mani). Earth-Initiate said, "I am going to make people." In the middle of the afternoon he began, for he had returned to Ta'doiko. He took dark red earth, mixed it with water, and made two figures,—one a man, and one a woman. He laid the man on his right side, and the woman on his left, inside his house. Then he lay down himself, flat on his back, with his arms stretched out. He lay thus and sweated all the afternoon and night. Early in the morning the woman began to tickle him in the side. He kept very still, did not laugh. By and by he got up, thrust a piece of pitch-wood into the ground and fire burst out. The two people were very white. No one today is as white as they were. Their eyes were pink, their hair was black, their teeth shone brightly, and they were very handsome. It is said that Earth-Initiate did not finish the hands of the people, as he did not know how it would be best to do it. Coyote saw the people, and suggested that they ought to have hands like his. Earth-Initiate said, "No, their hands shall be like mine." Then he finished them. When Coyote asked why their hands were to be like that, Earth-Initiate answered, "So that, if they are chased by bears, they can climb trees." This first man was called Ku'ksu; and the woman Morning-Star Woman (La'idamlulum ku'le).

When Coyote had seen the two people, he asked Earth-Initiate how he had made them. When he was told, he thought, "That is not difficult. I'll do it myself." He did just as Earth-Initiate had told him, but could not help laughing, when, early in the morning, the woman poked him in the ribs. As a result of his failing to keep still, the people were glass-eyed. Earth-Initiate said, "I told you not to laugh," but Coyote declared he had not. This was the first lie.

By and by there came to be a good many people. Earth-Initiate had wanted to have everything comfortable and easy for people, so that none of them should have to work. All fruits were easy to obtain, no one was ever to get sick and die. As the people grew numerous, Earth-Initiate did not come as often as formerly; he only came to see Ku'ksu in the night. One night he said to him, "Tomorrow morning you must go to the little lake near here. Take all the people with you. I'll make you a very old man before you get to the lake." By the time he had reached it, he was a very old man. He fell into the lake, and sank down out of sight. Pretty soon the ground began to shake, the waves overflowed the shore, and there was a great roaring under the water, like thunder. By and by Ku'ksu came up out of the water, but young again, just like a young man. Then Earth-Initiate came and spoke to the people, and said, "If you do as I tell you, everything will be well. When any of you grow old, so old that you cannot walk, come to this lake, or get someone to bring you here. You must then go down into the water as you have seen Ku'ksu do, and you will come out young again." When he had said this, he went away. He left in the night, and went up above.

DIEGUENO CREATION MYTH

(Indians of Southwest California)

In the beginning there was no earth or solid land, nothing but salt water, one vast primeval ocean. But under the sea lived two brothers, of whom the elder was named Tcaipakomat. Both of them kept their eyes shut, for if they had not done so, the salt water would have blinded them. After a while the elder brother came up to the surface and looked about him, but he could see nothing but water. The younger brother also came up, but on the way to the surface he incautiously opened his eyes, and the salt water blinded him; so when he emerged he could see nothing at all, and therefore he sank back into the depths. Left alone on the face of the deep, the elder brother now undertook the task of creating a habitable earth out of the waste of waters. First of all he made little red ants, which produced land by filling up the water solid with their tiny bodies. But still the world was dark, for as yet neither sun nor moon had been created. Tcaipakomat now caused certain black birds with flat bills to come into being; but in the darkness the birds lost their way and could not find where to roost. Next Tcaipakomat took three kinds of clay, red, yellow, and black, and thereof he made a round flat thing, which he took in his hand and threw up against the sky. It stuck there, and beginning to shed a dim light became the moon. Dissatisfied with the faint illumination of this pallid orb, Tcaipakomat took more clay, molded it into another round flat disk, and tossed it up against the other side of the sky. It stuck there and became the sun, lighting up everything with his beams. After that Tcaipakomat took a lump of light-colored clay, split it partly up, and made a man of it. Then he took a rib from the man and made a woman of it. The woman thus created out of the man's rib was called Sinyaxau or First Woman (from *siny*, "woman," and *axau*, "first"). From this first man and woman, modeled by the Creator out of clay, mankind is descended.

HOPI CREATION MYTH

(Arizona)

In the beginning there was nothing but water everywhere, and two goddesses, both named Huruing Wuhti, lived in houses in the ocean, one of them in the east, and the other in the west; and these two by their efforts caused dry land to appear in the midst of the water. Nevertheless the sun, on his daily passage across the newly created earth, noticed that there was no living being of any kind on the face of the ground, and he brought this radical defect to the notice of the two deities. Accordingly the divinities met in consultation, the eastern goddess passing over the sea on the rainbow as a bridge to visit her western colleague. Having laid their heads together they resolved to make a little bird; so the goddess of the east made a wren of clay, and together they chanted an incantation over it, so that the bird soon came to life. Then they sent out the wren to fly over the world and see whether he could discover any living being on the face of the earth; but on his return he reported that no such being existed anywhere. Afterwards the two deities created many sorts of birds and beasts in like manner, and sent them forth to inhabit the world. Last of all the two goddesses made up their mind to create man. Thereupon the eastern goddess took clay and molded out of it first a woman and afterwards a man; and the clay man and woman were brought to life just as the birds and beasts had been so before them.

MICHOACAN CREATION MYTH

(Mexico)

The great god Tucapacha first made man and woman out of clay, but when the couple went to bathe in a river they absorbed so much water that the clay of which they were composed all fell to pieces. To remedy this inconvenience the Creator applied himself again to his task and molded them afresh out of ashes, but the result was again disappointing. At last, not to be baffled, he made them of metal. His perseverance was rewarded. The man and woman were now perfectly watertight; they bathed in the river without falling in pieces, and by their union they became the progenitors of mankind.

ONGWE CREATION MYTH

In one place there were two Ongwe,[1] a man and a woman, people of high rank who lived a very religious, retired life. One day the woman went over to the place where the man lived. She had a comb, and she told him to get up as she wanted to comb his hair. He got up and she combed his hair. The same thing happened every day. But soon the woman's relative's began to whisper together because she was changed, and from day to day it became clearer that she was going to have a child. Her old mother noticed it and asked what man she had slept with, but the girl did not answer. At the same time the man fell ill and the old mother went to him and asked him if he felt ill. He answered: "Oh, Mother, I have to tell you that I am going to die." The mother said: "To die! What does that mean?" For those people who lived in Heaven did not know what dying meant; so far none of the Ongwe had ever died. The man continued: "When I die, the following things will happen: life will leave my body which will turn completely cold. O, Mother, then you must do the following: you must touch me with your hands on both my sides, and you must look fixedly at me when you see that I am dying. When you see that my breath is getting weaker and weaker you will know that I am dying, and then you must put your hands on my eyes. I will tell you something more: you must make a coffin and put my body into it as for a tomb, and then place the coffin on a high place." The woman did as she was told and everything happened as predicted. They put him in a coffin and placed that on a high place. Then the old woman asked the young woman again who was the father of her child, but again she got no answer.

The child, a girl, was born and developed quickly and was soon running about. But then she started crying, nobody knew why, and she cried for five days. The grandmother then

---

[1] "Onwge" means man-being, but also stands for archetypes of all things that later exist on earth, including images of houses, trees, animals, etc. The Ongwe were beings that the Iroquois Indians believed lived on the "other" side of heaven, which is turned away from us.

said that they should show her the coffin, and they took the child and lifted her up. When she saw her father's corpse she stopped crying, but as soon as they put her down she cried again. That happened for days, and they always had to bring her back to see the dead man. One day the child brought back a ring which the dead man had worn and they scolded her and asked her why she had taken the ring. The child said that the man had told her to take it because he was truly her father, and after that nobody said any more about it. After a time the father called to the girl from his coffin and said that now the time had come for her to marry and that she should get up very early the next morning and go to a very far away place he would show her, where she would find a chief of good repute whose name was Hoohwengdschia-woogi, which means "He who holds up the Earth," and he was the man she should marry.

So the girl got ready and left the next morning . . . but she has to cross a river where there is a dragon and the dragon is the Milky Way. She has to pass a lot of dangerous constellations as well as to withstand the attacks of the storm dragon and other dangers. Finally she arrives at this Chief's hut, beside which there is an Onodscha tree whose flowers emanate light, the light which we see on earth and which also gave light to the Ongwe. She goes into the hut, puts down her basket, and says: "You and I are going to marry." The Chief makes no reply but spreads out a carpet on which she may lie down and tells her she can stay there the whole night. The next morning he tells her to get up and work, as was usual for a woman. She is to cook maize, but while doing this she suffers great pain because he has ordered her to be naked while cooking it, and her body is burnt by the hot maize mash which spurts. But she grits her teeth and stands the pain. Each time, after she has gone through this suffering, he heals her body with oil. They are together two more nights. On the fourth day the Chief tells her she can go back home; he just sends her away again and tells her he will send her the maize as a reward for what she has done.

So the woman goes back the dangerous way she came but when she gets back to her parents she is homesick for her husband and returns to him. She makes this journey three times. The Chief is very much surprised to see her again, but he notices one day that she is pregnant. Day by day and night after night he thinks about this and cannot understand how she became pregnant, since he has never touched her physically. He is astonished. He thinks it must have happened by their breath uniting when they talked to each other. But it is quite obvious that she will give life to a child. The Chief gets upset and asks her who can have made her pregnant, but she does not understand. Then this Chief who "holds up the earth" becomes very ill and feels that he is going to die. He tells his wife that it is now quite certain that an Ongwe girl will be born and says that she should feed and nurse this girl who will grow up and must be called Gaengsdesok— "Warm Whirling Wind." The wife does not understand what he tells her, but after a time gives birth to a girl, and after ten days she takes her away. Slowly the Chief's suffering gets worse and worse. So he says that the tree Onodscha, the tree of light which stands beside his hut, must be pulled up by the roots; then the earth [which is really the cupola of the heavens] will have a hole in it, and beside that hole he is to be placed with his wife sitting near him. This is done, and as soon as the woman sits near the hole with him he says that they should look down together and that she should take Gaengsdesok on her back and wrap her up carefully in her clothes. He gives her some food and tells her to sit beside him with her legs hanging down through the hole. He tells her to look down, and while she is looking down he catches hold of her and pushes her down the hole. As soon as she starts to fall through the hole the Chief gets up and feels much better. He says that now he is again the Old One, that he feels all right again, and that the tree Onodscha should be erected again. He was jealous of the Northern Lights and the Fire Dragon with his white body—one of the dragons she had walked past; that was why he had become ill, for he had thought that perhaps one of them was the father of the child, and because of his jealousy he had pushed her through the hole.

The woman who had been pushed through the hole in heaven sinks down through the deep darkness. Everything around her is a dark blue color; she can see nothing and does not know what will happen to her as she sinks further and further down. Sometimes she sees something but does not know what it is. It is the surface of a great water with a lot of water birds swimming about on it. One of the birds suddenly calls out and says that a human being, a woman, is coming up out of the water—he is looking into the water and sees the mirage—but another bird says that she is not coming up out of the water but falling down from heaven.

The birds consult together as to what they can do to save the woman. They all fly up together, and when they reach the woman they take her on their backs and slowly come down with her. Meanwhile a big tortoise comes up to the surface of the water, and the birds deposit her on its big back.

Then a number of birds try to dive for earth, and in the end one of them succeeds in bringing some up. They spread it on the back of the tortoise, and when they do this the earth remains there and spreads and becomes the whole earthy surface of our world.

In the meantime the woman again becomes pregnant because during the fall the child has re-entered her womb. The birth which had already taken place in heaven becomes regressive, as it were; when the woman arrives on the back of the tortoise on earth she is again pregnant with the girl and again gives birth to Warm Whirling Wind. The mother and daughter then stay together and the girl grows up amazingly quickly. Again this girl finds an unknown man. The same theme repeats three times. In a mysterious way, she becomes pregnant. Her husband is a man who looks like an Indian; he has an arrow and later it is said that he is the spirit of the big tortoise on earth. The girl then gives birth to twins, one a positive savior type of twin who creates the world and mankind, and one a negative, devilish being who creates all the destructive things such as mosquitoes and bad animals.

ESKIMO CREATION MYTHS

Raven and the Creation of Animal Life

Eskimo (Bering Straits)

It was in the time when there were no people on the earth plain. The first man for four days lay coiled up in the pod of the beach pea. On the fifth day he stretched out his feet and burst the pod. He fell to the ground and when he stood up he was a full-grown man. Man looked all around him and then at himself. He moved his hands and arms, his neck and legs. When he looked back he saw, still hanging to the vine, the pod of the beach pea, with a hole in the lower end out of which he had dropped. When he looked about him again, he saw that he was getting farther from his starting place. The ground seemed to move up and down under his feet, and it was very soft. After a while he had a strange feeling in his stomach, so he stooped down to drink some water from a small pool at his feet. Then he felt better.

When Man looked up again he saw coming toward him, with a fluttering motion, something dark. He watched the dark thing until it stopped just in front of him. It was Raven.

As soon as Raven stopped, he raised one of his wings and pushed up his beak, as though it were a mask, to the top of his head. Thus Raven changed at once into a man. Raven stared hard at Man, moving from side to side to see him better.

Raven said, "What are you? Where did you come from? I have never seen anything like you."

Raven still stared at Man, surprised to find this new thing so much like himself. He made Man walk around a little, while he perked his head from side to side to see him better. Then Raven said again, in astonishment, "Where did you come from? I have never seen anything like you before."

Man said, "I came from the pea pod." He pointed to the plant from which he came.

"Ah, I made that vine," said Raven. "But I did not know that anything like you would come from it. Come with me to the high ground over there; it is thicker and harder. This ground I made later and it is soft and thin."

So Man and Raven walked to the higher ground which was firm and hard. Raven asked Man if he had eaten anything. Man said he had taken some of the soft stuff from one of the pools.

"Ah, you drank some water," said Raven. "Now wait for me here."

Raven drew down his beak, as though it were a mask, over his face. He at once became a bird and flew far up into the sky—far out of sight. Man waited until the fourth day. Then Raven returned bringing four berries in his claws. He pushed up his beak and so became a man again. Then he gave to Man two salmon berries and two heath berries, saying, "Here is something I made for you to eat. I wish them to be plentiful on the earth. Eat them."

Man put the berries into his mouth, one after the other, and ate them. Then he felt better. Then Raven left Man near a small creek while he went to the edge of the water. He took two pieces of clay at the water's edge, and shaped them like a pair of mountain sheep. He held them in his hand until they were dry, and then he called Man to come and see them. Man said they were pretty, so Raven told him to close his eyes. Man closed his eyes tightly. Then Raven pulled down his beak-mast, and waved his wings four times over the pieces of clay. At once they bounded away as full-grown mountain sheep. Raven told Man to look.

Man was so much pleased that Raven said, "If these animals are plentiful, perhaps people will try to kill them."

Man said, "Yes."

Then Raven said, "Well, it will be better for them to live among the steep rocks so every one cannot kill them. There only shall they be found."

Raven took two more pieces of clay and shaped them like tame reindeer. He held them in his hand until they were partly dry, then told Man to look at them. Raven again drew down his beak-mask and waved his wings four times over them. Thus they became alive, but as they were only dry in spots while Raven held them, therefore they remained brown and white, with mottled coat. Raven told Man these tame reindeer would be very few in number.

Again Raven took two pieces of clay and shaped them like the caribou or wild reindeer. But he held them in his hands only a little while so that only the bellies of the reindeer became dry and white. Then Raven drew down his beak-mask, and waved his wings over them, and they bounded away. But because only their bellies were dry and white while Raven held them, therefore the wild reindeer is brown except its white belly.

Raven said to Man, "These animals will be very common. People will kill many of them."

Thus Raven began to create the animals.

Raven said one day to Man, "You are lonely by yourself. I will make you a companion." He went to some white clay at a spot distant from the clay of which he had made animals, and made of the clay a figure almost like Man. Raven kept looking at Man while he shaped the figure. Then he took fine water grass from the creek and fastened it on the back of the head for hair. When the clay was shaped, Raven drew down his beak-mask and waved his wings over it. The clay became a beautiful girl. The girl was white and fair because Raven let the clay dry entirely before he waved his wings over it.

Raven took the girl to Man. "There is a companion for you," he said.

Now in the days of the first people on the earth plain, there were no mountains far or near. No rain ever fell and there were no winds. The sun shone always very brightly.

Then Raven showed the first people on the earth plain how to sleep warmly in the dry moss when they were tired. Raven himself drew down his beak-mask and went to sleep like a bird.

When Raven awakened, he went back to the creek. Here he made two sticklebacks, two graylings, and two blackfish. When these were swimming about in the water, he called Man to see them. Man raised his hand in surprise and the sticklebacks darted away. Raven told him the graylings would be found in clear mountain streams, while the sticklebacks would live along the coast, and that both would be good for food.

Raven next made the shrewmouse. He said, "The shrewmouse will not be good for food. It will prevent the earth plain from looking bare and cheerless."

In this way Raven was busy several days, making birds and fishes and animals. He showed each of them to Man and explained what they were good for. Then Raven flew into the sky, far, far away, and was gone four days. When he came back he brought a salmon to Man.

But Raven noticed that the ponds and lakes were silent and lonely, so he made water bugs to flit upon the surface of the water. He also made the beaver and the muskrat to live around the borders of the ponds. Raven told Man that the beavers would live along the streams and build strong houses, so Man must build a strong house also. Raven said the beavers would be very cunning and only good hunters could catch them. He also told Man how to catch the muskrat and how to use its skin for clothing.

Raven also made flies and mosquitoes and other insects to make the earth plain more cheerful. At first mosquitoes were like flies; they did not bite. One day Man killed a deer. After he had cut it up and placed the fat on a bush, he fell asleep. When he awoke he found the mosquitoes had eaten all of it. Then Man was very angry and scolded the mosquitoes. He said, "Never eat meat again. Eat men." Before that mosquitoes never bit people.

When the first baby came on the earth plain, Raven rubbed it all over with white clay. He told Man it would grow into a man like himself. The next morning the baby was a big boy. He ran around pulling up grass and flowers that Raven had planted. By the third day the baby was a full-grown man.

Then another baby was born on the earth plain. She was rubbed over with the white clay. The next day the baby was a big girl, walking around. On the third day she was a full-grown woman.

Now Raven began to be afraid that men would kill all the creatures he had made. He was afraid they would kill them for food and clothing. Therefore Raven went to a creek nearby. He took white clay and shaped it like a bear. Then he waved his wings over it, and the clay became a bear. But Raven jumped very quickly to one side when the bear became alive because it looked fiercely around and growled. Then Raven showed the bear to Man and told him to be careful. He said the bear was very fierce and would tear him to pieces if he disturbed it.

Then Raven made the seals, and taught Man how to catch them. He also taught Man how to make strong lines from sealskin, and snares for the deer.

Then Raven went away to the place of the pea vine.

When he reached the pea vine he found three other men

had just fallen from the same pod that Man had fallen from.
These men were looking about them in wonder. Raven led
them away from the pea vine, but in a different direction
from the first man. He brought them close to the sea. Raven
stayed with these three men a long time. He taught them how
to take wood from the bushes and small trees he planted in
hollows and sheltered places, and to make a fire drill, and
also a bow. He made many more plants and birds which like
the seacoast, but he did not make so many as in the land
where Man lived. He taught these men how to make bows and
arrows, spears and nets, and how to use them; and also how
to capture the seals, which were now plentiful in the sea.
Then he taught them how to make kayaks, and how to build
houses of drift logs and of bushes, covered with earth. Then
he made wives for these men, and went back to Man.

When Raven reached the land where Man lived, he thought
the earth plain still looked bare. So, while the others slept,
Raven planted birch and spruce and cottonwood trees to
grow in the low places. Then he woke up the people, who
were pleased with the trees.

Then Raven taught Man how to make fire with the fire
drill, and to place the spark of tinder in a bunch of dry grass
and to wave it about until it blazed, and then to put dry wood
upon it. He showed them how to roast fish on a stick, and
how to make fish traps of splints and willow bark, and how
to dry salmon for winter use.

Where Man lived there was now a large village because the
people did everything as Raven told them, and therefore all
the babies grew up in three days. One day Raven came back
and sat down by Man by the creek and they talked of many
things. Man asked Raven about the skyland. Man wanted to
see the skyland which Raven had made. Therefore Raven
took Man to the land in the sky.

Man found that the skyland was a very beautiful country,
and that it had a much better climate than his land. But the
people who lived there were very small. Their heads did not
reach to Man's hips. The people wore fur clothing, with beautiful patterns, such as people on earth now wear, because
Man showed his people how to make them. In the lakes were
strange animals which would have killed Man if he had tried
to drink of the water. In a dry lake bed, thickly covered with
tall grass, Man saw a wonderful animal resting upon the tips
of the grasses. It had a long head and six legs. It had fine,
thick hair, and on the back of the head were two thick, short

horns which bent forward and then curved back at the tips. Raven told Man it took many people to kill this animal.

Then they came to a round hole in the sky and around the edge of the hole was short grass, glowing like fire. Raven said, "This is the star called the moon-dog." Some of the grass had been pulled up. Raven said he had taken some to start the first fire on earth.

Then Raven said to Man, "Shut your eyes. I will take you to another country." Man climbed upon Raven's back and they dropped down through the star hole. They floated a long, long time through the air, then they floated through something else. When they stopped Raven saw he was at the bottom of the sea. Man could breathe there, but it seemed foggy. Raven said that was the appearance of the water. Then Raven said, "I want to make some new animals here; but you must not walk about. You lie down and if you get tired, turn over on the other side."

Man went to sleep lying on one side, and slept a long while. When he waked up, he wanted to turn over, but he could not. Then Man thought, "I wish I could turn over," and at once he turned. As he turned, he was surprised to see that his body was covered with long, white hairs; and his fingers were long claws. Then he went to sleep again. This he did three times more. Then when he woke up, Raven stood by him. Raven said, "I have changed you into a white bear. How do you like it?" Man could not make a sound until Raven waved his wings over him. Then he said he did not like it; if he was a bear he would have to live on the sea, while his son lived on land; so Man should feel badly. Then Raven struck the white skin with his wings and it fell off. So Man became himself again. But Raven took the empty bearskin, and placed one of his own tail feathers inside it for a spine. Then he waved his wing over it, and a white bear arose. Ever since then white bears have been found on the frozen sea.

Raven said, "How many times did you turn over?"

Man said, "Four."

Raven said, "You slept just four years."

Then Raven made other animals. He made the a-mi-kuk, a large, slimy animal, with thick skin, and with four long, wide-spreading arms. This is a fierce animal and lives in the sea. It wraps its four long arms around a man or a kayak and drags it under the water. A man cannot escape it. If he climbs out of his kayak on the ice, the a-mi-kuk will dart underneath and break the ice. If Man runs away on shore, the a-mi-kuk pursues him by burrowing through the earth. No man can escape from it when once it pursues him.

Then Raven showed Man the walrus, and the dog walrus, with head and teeth like a dog. It always swam with large herds of walrus and with a stroke of its tail could kill a man. He showed him whales and the grampus. Raven told Man that only good hunters could kill a whale, but when one was killed an entire village could feast on it. He showed him also the sea fox, which is so fierce it kills men; and the sea otter, which is like the land otter but has finer fur, tipped with white, and other fishes and animals as they rose to the surface of the water.

Then Raven said, "Close your eyes. Hold fast to me."

Then Man found himself on the shore near his home. The village was very large. His wife was very old and his son was an old man. The people gave him place of honor in the kashim, and made him their headsman. So Man taught the young men many things.

Now Man wanted again to see the skyland, so Raven and Man went up among the dwarf people and lived there a long time. But on earth the village grew very large; the men killed many animals.

Now in those days, the sun shone always very brightly. No rain ever fell and no winds blew.

Man and Raven were angry because the people killed many animals. They took a long line and a grass basket, one night, and caught ten reindeer which they put into the basket. Now in those days reindeer had sharp teeth, like dogs. The next night Raven took the reindeer and let them down on the earth close to Man's village. Raven said, "Break down the first house you see and kill the people. Men are becoming too many." The reindeer did as Raven commanded. They stamped on the house and broke it down. They ate up the people with their sharp, wolflike teeth. The next night, Raven let the reindeer down; again they broke down a house and ate up the people with their sharp teeth.

The village people were much frightened. The third night they covered the third house with a mixture of deer fat and berries. On the third night when the reindeer began to tear down the third house, their mouths were filled with the fat and sour berries. Then the reindeer ran away, shaking their heads so violently that all their long, sharp teeth fell out. Ever since then reindeer have had small teeth and cannot harm people.

After the reindeer ran away, Raven and Man returned to the skyland. Man said, "If the people do not stop killing so many animals, they will kill everything you have made. It would be better to take the sun away from them. Then it will be dark and people will die."

Raven said, "That is right. You stay here. I will go and take away the sun."

So Raven went away and took the sun out of the sky. He put it in a skin bag and carried it far away, to a distant part of the skyland. Then it became dark on earth.

The people on earth were frightened when the sun vanished. They offered Raven presents of food and furs if he would bring back the sun. Raven said, "No." After a while Raven felt sorry for them, so he let them have a little light. He held up the sun in one hand for two days so people could hunt and secure food. Then he put the sun in the skin bag again and the earth was dark. Then, after a long time, when the people made him many gifts, he would let them have a little light again.

Now Raven had a brother living in the village. He was sorry for the earth people. So Raven's brother thought a long time. Then he died. The people put him in a grave box and had a burial feast. Then they left the grave box. At once Raven's brother slipped out of the box and went away from the village. He hid his raven mask and coat in a tree. Soon Raven's wife came for water. When she took up a dipperful to drink, Raven's brother, by magic, became a small leaf. He fell into the water and Raven's wife swallowed him. . . .

When Raven-Boy was born he grew very rapidly. He was running about when he was only a few days old. He cried for the sun which was in the skin bag, hanging on the rafters. Raven was fond of the boy so he let him play with the sun; yet he was afraid Raven-Boy would lose the sun, so he watched him. When Raven-Boy began to play out of doors, he cried and begged for the sun. Raven said, "No." Then Raven-Boy cried more than ever. At last Raven gave him the sun in the house. Raven-Boy played with it a long while. When no one was looking, he ran quickly out of the house. He ran to the tree, put on his raven mask and coat, and flew far away with the sun in the skin bag. When Raven-Boy was far up in the sky, he heard Raven call, "Do not hide the sun. Let it out of the bag. Do not keep it always dark." Raven thought the boy had stolen it for himself.

Raven-Boy flew to the place where the sun belonged. He tore off the skin covering and put the sun in its place. Then he saw a broad path leading far away. He followed it to the side of a hole fringed with short, bright grass. He remembered that Raven had said, "Do not keep it always dark," therefore he made the sky turn, with all the stars and the sun. Thus it is now sometimes dark and sometimes light.

Raven-Boy picked some of the short, bright grass by the edge of the sky hole and stuck it into the sky. This is the morning star.

Raven-Boy went down to the earth. The people were glad to see him. They said, "What has become of Man, who went into the skyland with Raven?" Now this was the first time that Raven-Boy had heard of Man. He started to fly up into the sky, but he could get only a small distance above the earth. When he found he could not get back to the sky, Raven-Boy wandered to the second village, where lived the men who had come from the pod of the beach pea. Raven-Boy there married a wife and he had many children. But the children could not fly to the sky. They had lost the magic power. Therefore the ravens now flutter over the tundras like other birds.

How the Rivers Were Formed

Tlingit (Wrangell)

Petrel was the first person created by Raven-at-the-head-of-Nass. He was keeper of the fresh water. No one else might touch it. Now the spring he owned was on a rocky island called Dekino, Fort-far-out, where the well may still be seen. Raven stole a great mouthful of water, but as he flew over the country drops spilled out of his beak. These drops made the rivers: the Nass, Skeena, Stikine, and Chilkat. Raven said, "The water that I drop down upon the earth, here and there, will whirl all the time. There will be plenty of water, but it will not flood the world."

Now before this time, Raven was pure white. But when he stole the water from Petrel he tried to fly out of the smoke hole. Petrel cried, "Spirits of the smoke hole, hold him fast." So the smoke-hole spirits held Raven until the smoke blackened his white coat.

The Origin of Fire

Tlingit

Long ago, in the days of the animal people, Raven saw a fire far out at sea. He tied a piece of pitch to Chicken Hawk's bill. He said, "Go out to the fire, touch it with the pitchwood, and bring it back." Chicken Hawk did so. The fire stuck to the pitchwood and he brought it back to Raven. Then Raven put the fire into the rock and into the red cedar. Then he said, "Thus shall you get your fire—from this rock and from this red cedar." The tribes did as he told them.

The Bringing of the Light by Raven

Eskimo (Lower Yukon)

In the first days, the sun and moon were in the sky. Then the sun and moon were taken away and people had only the light of the stars. Even the magic of the shamans failed to bring back the light.

Now there was an orphan boy in the village who sat with the humble people over the entrance way of the kashim. He was despised by every one. When the magic of the shamans failed to bring back the sun and moon into the sky the boy mocked them. He said, "What fine shamans you must be. You cannot bring back the light, but I can." Then the shamans were angry and beat the boy and drove him out of the kashim. Now this boy was like any other boy until he put on a raven coat he had. Then he became Raven.

Now the boy went to his aunt's house. He told her the shamans had failed to bring back the light, and they had beaten him when he mocked them. The boy said, "Where are the sun and moon?"

The aunt said, "I do not know."

The boy said, "I am sure you know. Look what a finely sewed coat you wear. You could not sew it that way if you did not know where the light is."

Thus they argued.

Then the aunt said, "If you wish to find the light, go far

to the south. Go on snowshoes. You will know the place when you get there."

The boy put on his snowshoes and set off toward the south. Many days he traveled and the darkness was always the same. When he had gone a very long way he saw far in front of him a ray of light. Then the boy hurried on. As he went farther the light showed again, plainer than before. Then it vanished for a time. Thus it kept appearing and vanishing.

At last the boy came to a large hill. One side was brightly lighted; the other side was black as night. Close to the hill was a hut. A man was shoveling snow from in front of it. The man tossed the snow high in the air; then the light could not be seen until the snow fell. Then the man tossed the snow again. So the light kept appearing and disappearing. Close to the house was a large ball of fire.

The boy stopped and began to plan how to steal the ball of light.

Then the boy walked up to the man. He said, "Why do you throw up the snow? It hides the light from our village."

The man said, "I am not hiding the light. I am cleaning away the snow. Who are you? Where did you come from?"

The boy said, "It is so dark at our village I do not want to stay there. I came here to live with you."

"All the time?" asked the man.

"Yes," said the boy.

The man said, "All right. Come into the house with me." Then he dropped his shovel on the ground. He stooped down to lead the way through the underground passage into the house. He let the curtain fall in front of the door as he passed, because he thought the boy was close beside him.

Then the boy caught up the ball of light. He put it in the turned-up flap of his fur coat. Then he picked up the shovel and ran away toward the north. He ran until his feet were tired. Then he put on his raven coat and flew away. He flew rapidly to the north. Raven could hear the man shriek behind him. The man was pursuing him. But Raven flew faster. Then the man cried, "Keep the light; but give me my shovel."

Raven said, "No, you cannot have your shovel. You made our village dark." So Raven flew faster.

Now as Raven flew, he broke off a little piece of the light. This made day. Then he went on a long time in darkness, until he broke off another piece of light. Thus it was day again. So as Raven flew to the village he broke off the pieces

of light. When Raven reached the kashim of his own village
he threw away the last piece. He went into the kashim and
said to the shamans, "I have brought back the light. It will
be light and then dark, so as to make day and night."

After this Raven went out upon the ice because his home
was on the seacoast. Then a great wind arose, and the ice
drifted with him across the sea to the land on the other side.

Thus Raven brought back the light. It is night and day, as
he said it would be. But sometimes the nights are very long
because Raven traveled a long way without throwing away
a piece of the light.

The Origin of the Winds

Tlingit

Now Raven went off to a certain place and created West
Wind. Raven said to it, "You shall be my son's daughter. No
matter how hard you blow, you shall hurt nobody."

Raven also made South Wind. When South Wind climbs
on top of a rock it never ceases to blow.

Raven made North Wind and on top of a mountain he
made a house for it with ice hanging down the sides. Then
he went in and said to North Wind, "Your back is white."
That is why mountains are white with snow.

Origin of Land and People

Eskimo (Lower Yukon)

In the beginning there was water over all the earth. There
were no people. It was very cold. The water was covered with
ice, and the ice pieces ground together, making long ridges
and hummocks.

Then a man came from the other side of the great water
and stopped on the ice hills. He took for his wife a wolf.
Then their children grew up. Each pair spoke a different
language from that of their parents, or from that of their
brothers and sisters. So each pair went out in a different
direction and built houses on the ice hills. Then the snow

melted and ran down the hillsides. It scooped out ravines and river beds and made the earth. Thus the earth was made and the people. That is why so many different languages are spoken.

Creation of the World

Athapascan (Upper Yukon)

A long time ago, water flowed all over the world. There was one family and they made a big raft. Then they put animals on the raft.

Now there was no land but all water, so the people wanted to make a world. The man tied a cord around a beaver and sent him down to find the bottom of the water. But the beaver got only halfway and drowned. Then the man tied a string around a muskrat and sent him down. Muskrat drowned, but he reached the bottom and got a little mud on his hands. Then the man took the mud out of the muskrat's hands into his palm. He let it dry and then crumbled it to dust. Then he blew the dust out of his palm all over the waters. This made the world.

Origin of Mankind

Eskimo (Bering Straits)

Long, long ago, a man and a woman came down from the sky and landed on one of the Diomede Islands. They lived there a long while, but they had no children. At last one day the man took some walrus ivory, and from this he carved five dolls, just like people. Then he took some wood and made from it five more dolls. Then, one night, when all were finished, he set them off to one side, all ten in a row. The next morning the dolls had become people. The ivory dolls became men, therefore they are brave and hardy; but the wooden dolls became women, therefore they are soft and timid. From these ten dolls came all the people of the Diomede Islands.

The First Woman

Eskimo (Bering Straits)

Long, long ago there were many men living in the north-land, but there was no woman among them. Far away in the southland lived one woman. At last one of the young men in the northland traveled south to the home of the woman and married her. He thought, "I have a wife, while the son of the headsman has none."

Now the son of the headsman had also started to travel to the home of the woman in the southland. He stood in the passage to the house and heard the husband talking to himself. So he waited until all the people were asleep. Then the son of the headsman crept into the house and began to drag the woman away. He caught her by her shoulders.

Then the husband was awakened. He ran to the passage and caught the woman by her feet. So the men pulled until they pulled the woman in two. The son of the headsman carried the upper part of her body to the north. Then they began to carve wood to make each woman complete. Thus there were now two women.

The woman in the south was a good dancer; but she could not do fine needlework in sewing the furs, because her hands were wooden. The woman in the north was a poor dancer, because her feet were wooden, but she could sew with fine stitches in the furs. So all the women of the north are skillful with their hands, and all the women of the south are good dancers, even to this day. Thus you may know that the tale is true.

Origin of the Wind

Athapascan (Upper Yukon)

A long time ago, when all were men, there was no wind. Now Bear used to go about with a bag on his back. The animal people wanted to know what was in the bag. Many times they asked Bear but he would not tell them. One day Bear fell asleep with the bag on his back. Then a man saw him asleep. The man cut the bag and found the wind in it. Therefore the wind escaped and has never since been caught.

Creation As Awakening and Creation by Accident

Eskimo

People do not like to think. They do not like to work with the things which are difficult to grasp and that is perhaps the reason why we know so little about Heaven and Earth and the origin of men and animals. Perhaps, and perhaps not. It is very difficult to understand how we came into existence and where we go when we die. Darkness lies over the beginning and over the end. How could one know more about the most numinous which surrounds us and which keeps us alive, about that which we call air and Heaven and sea, and what we call the human and all his dwelling places and the animals and the fishes and the seas and the lakes. Nobody can know anything for sure about the beginning of life. But whoever opens his eyes and his ears and tries to remember what the old people said, might fill the emptiness of his thought by this or that knowledge.

That is why we like to listen to those people who bring us information from the experience of dead generations, because all the old myths which our forefathers tell are what the dead people tell us. We can still talk to all the many people who were wise a long time ago but we know so few like to listen. My grandmother knew a lot of surprising things about old facts and from her I know what I am going to tell you now.

Heaven came into existence before the Earth, but it was not older because when it came into existence the Earth was also already forming. It had already a firm crust before there was any land and before there was also the first living being about whom we know anything. This being we called Tulun-gersaq, or Father Raven, because he created all life on earth and in human beings and is the origin of everything. He was not an ordinary bird but a holy life-power which was in everything which existed in this world in which we now live. But he, too, began in the shape of a human being (so don't think of Father Raven as a raven, he only became a raven) and was groping in the dark and all his deeds were completely casual until it became manifest to him who he was and what he should do.

He sat crouching in the darkness when he suddenly awoke to consciousness and discovered himself. He did not know where he was or how he had come into being, but he breathed and had life, he lived. Everything around him was in darkness and he could not see anything. With his hands he groped around, touching objects, and his fingers touched clay wherever he expanded them. The earth was clay and everything around him was dead clay. He let his fingers pass over the clay and then he found his face and he felt that he had a nose and eyes and a mouth and also that he had arms and legs, as we have. He was a human being, a man. Above his forehead he felt a hard little knot but did not know why it was there, he had no idea that he would once become a raven and that this little knot would grow and become his beak. He sank into meditation. Now he suddenly understood that he was a free being, something independent which was not connected with all his surroundings. He crept over the clay, slowly and carefully. He wanted to find out where he was. Suddenly his hands met an empty space ahead of him and he knew he should not go further. Then he broke off a bit of the clay and threw it into the depths. He listened because he wanted to hear when it reached the bottom, but he heard nothing so he moved away from the abyss and found a hard object which he buried in the clay. He did not know why he did this, but he did it, and then again sat in meditation and wondered what could be in all this deep darkness which surrounded him. Then he heard a whirring in the air and a very small, light creature alighted on his hand. With the other hand he touched it and felt that it had a beak and wings, and warm, soft feathers on its body and tiny naked feet. It was a little sparrow and he realized that this sparrow had been there before he had and had come toward him in the darkness and had hopped around him and that he had not noticed it before he touched it.

As this man liked social contact he became bolder and crept more courageously over the earth and approached a place where he had buried something before and it had made roots and had become alive: a bush had grown and the earth was no longer sterile for the naked clay was now covered with bushes; it also had grass. But the man still felt lonely, and so he formed from clay a figure which resembled his own and then he again sat crouching and waiting. As soon

as the new human being became alive it started to dig the
earth with its hands. It had no peace, but restlessly, constantly dug in the earth around, and he discovered that this
other human being had a different psychological make-up
from himself, and that it had a hot, quick temper and a violent attitude. He did not like it and therefore took it and
dragged it to the abyss and threw it in. This being, it is said,
later became Tornaq, the evil spirit, from whom all the evil
spirits on earth stem. Then the man crept back to the tree
which he had planted, and behold there were other trees
there, tree after tree. It had become a forest with rich soil,
and plants had grown there. He touched them all with his
hands and felt their form and smelled them, but he could not
see them. So he felt impelled to know more about the earth
which he had himself found and he crept around with the
little sparrow which always flew over his head. He could not
see it, but always heard its wings and sometimes it alighted
on his head or on his hand. But the man crept about because
he did not dare to walk upright in the dark, and everywhere
he found water and so discovered that he was on an island.
Now he wanted to know what was below in the abyss and he
asked the little sparrow to go down and find out. At this the
sparrow flew away and stayed away for a long time, and when
it came back it said that far below in the abyss there was
land, new land which had just started to crust over. The man
decided to go down and asked the sparrow to sit on his knees.
Then he found out how it was made, and he tried to discover
how the sparrow could by its wings keep suspended in the
air. He took twigs in the forest which looked like wings and
put them on his shoulders, and the twigs were transformed
into real wings and he himself grew feathers which covered
his body, and the knot in his forehead began to grow and
form a beak. Now the man realized that he could fly like the
little sparrow and together they flew off. The man said:
"Gowk! Gowk!" and he had become a big black bird and
called himself Raven.

The land from which they came he called Heaven. It was
as far as nowadays Heaven is from the Earth, so that when
they arrived at the bottom they were completely exhausted.
Here everything was deserted and sterile, and he again planted
the land as he had done in Heaven and he flew about and
called this new land Earth. Then, in order to populate the
Earth, he created human beings. Some say he made them
out of clay in the same way as he had made the first being

in Heaven, but others say that he created man by chance, which would be even stranger than if he had created him by will power and intention.

Father Raven went about and planted herbs and flowers. He discovered some pods, and he looked at them and opened one and a human being popped out of it—beautiful and completely grown, and the Raven was so bewildered that he threw his bird mask back, and through his bewilderment he became a human being again himself. He went laughing to the newborn man and said: "Who are you and where do you come from?" The man said: "I came out of this pod" and showed the hole from which he had come. "I did not want to lie there any more so I pushed with my feet against the hole and then sprang out." Then Father Raven laughed heartily and said: "Well, well, you are an odd creature! I never saw anything like you!" Then he laughed again and added: "I, myself, planted this pod, but I did not know what would come out of it. But the earth on which we are walking is not yet finished. Do you not feel how it shakes? We should go higher where the crust is harder." And so the first man came into being and later Father Raven created all other beings.

One day an enormous black mass came out of the sea, and Father Raven helped the human beings to kill it—it was a sea monster. They cut it into bits, which they threw around, and from them came all the large islands. So, slowly, the earth grew and became a dwelling place for men and creatures.

When the earth had become what it should be the Raven assembled all the human beings and said: "I am your Father and to me you owe the land you have and your being, and you must never forget me." Then he flew away from the Earth and up to Heaven where it was still dark, but he had picked up some fire stones on the earth and with these he created the stars. What he had left he threw out in Heaven and from that there came a great fire which poured light over the Earth, and so Heaven and Earth were created. That is the way the Earth and human beings and all the animals we catch came into existence, but before them all was the Raven and even before him there was the little sparrow.

PART TWO

South America

INTRODUCTION

BECAUSE THE mythic tales of South America were translated largely by sixteenth-century Spaniards (including writers like the Spanish priest Las Casas (1474–1566), the Jesuit Acosta (1539–1600), and the historian Herrara (1559–1625), there is an early European tone to many Latin American myths, although native traditions still dominate the basic themes. However, of all South American myths the *Popol-Vuh* is one of the most complete and significant. It is the sacred book of the Quiché Maya, and details their cosmogony, religion, history, and mythology. The philosophy, language, and literary style indicate that the Quiché ("collection of the council") had reached a high degree of development.

Another major modern source for South American Indian myths was recently discovered and translated by the Villas Boas brothers, who have worked for many years with the fifteen tribes of the Xingu Indians in Central Brazil. They have collected the oral myths of this tribe whose traditions are in danger of extinction. Of their rich mythology I have selected myths that deal centrally with the creation theme. In this fullsome, bizarre mythology the reader can find many of the thematic elements that are part of the South American Indian mythic consciousness.

Like the myths of North America, the South American Indian mythic beliefs are characterized by animated gods immersed in nature, a world where spirits and deities dramatically interact with nature and human beings. The myths in Part Two cover the South American continent.

POPOL-VUH, CREATION MYTHS
OF THE QUICHÉ MAYA

Creation of the Cosmos

This is the account of how all was in suspense, all calm, in silence; all motionless, still, and the expanse of the sky was empty.

This is the first account, the first narrative. There was neither man, nor animal, birds, fishes, crabs, trees, stones, caves, ravines, grasses, nor forests; there was only the sky.

The surface of the earth had not appeared. There was only the calm sea and the great expanse of the sky.

There was nothing brought together, nothing which could make a noise, nor anything which might move, or tremble, or could make noise in the sky.

There was nothing standing; only the calm water, the placid sea, alone and tranquil. Nothing existed.

There was only immobility and silence in the darkness, in the night. Only the Creator, the Maker, Tepeu, Gucumatz, [and] the Forefathers, were in the water surrounded with light. They were hidden under green and blue feathers, and were therefore called Gucumatz.[1] By nature they were great sages and great thinkers. In this manner the sky existed and also the Heart of Heaven, which is the name of God and thus He is called.

Then came the word. Tepeu and Gucumatz came together in darkness, in the night, and Tepeu and Gucumatz talked together. They talked then, discussing and deliberating; they agreed, they united their words and their thoughts.

Then while they meditated, it became clear to them that when dawn would break, man must appear.[2] Then they

---

[1] Gucumatz is a name the Quiché associated with water. It also was the name of a serpent with feathers that moved in water.

[2] The idea of creating man, which occurred spontaneously in the minds of the Makers, is done according to Quiché philosophy. Further, mankind was considered the ultimate, the supreme being of creation.

planned the creation, and the growth of the trees and the thickets and the birth of life and the creation of man. Thus it was arranged in the darkness and in the night by the Heart of Heaven who is called Huracán.

The first is called Caculha Huracan. The second is Chipi-Caculha. The third is Raxa-Caculha. And these three are the Heart of Heaven.

Then Tepeu and Gucumatz came together; then they conferred about life and light, what they would do so that there would be light and dawn, who it would be who would provide food and sustenance.

Thus let it be done! Let the emptiness be filled! Let the water recede and make a void, let the earth appear and become solid; let it be done. Thus they spoke. Let there be light, let there be dawn in the sky and on the earth! There shall be neither glory nor grandeur in our creation and formation until the human being is made, man is formed. So they spoke.

Then the earth was created by them. So it was, in truth, that they created the earth. Earth! they said, and instantly it was made.

Like the mist, like a cloud, and like a cloud of dust was the creation, when the mountains appeared from the water; and instantly the mountains grew.

Only by a miracle, only by magic art were the mountains and valleys formed; and instantly the groves of cypresses and pines put forth shoots together on the surface of the earth.[8]

And thus Gucumatz was filled with joy, and exclaimed: "Your coming has been fruitful, Heart of Heaven; and you, Huracan, and you, Chipi-Caculha, Raxa-Caculha!"

"Our work, our creation shall be finished," they answered.

First the earth was formed, the mountains and the valleys; the currents of water were divided, the rivulets were running freely between the hills, and the water was separated when the high mountains appeared.

Thus was the earth created, when it was formed by the Heart of Heaven, the Heart of Earth, as they are called who first made it fruitful, when the sky was in suspense, and the earth was submerged in the water.

---

[8] The translator notes that the word *puz naual* is used to indicate the magic power to create or transform one thing into another. Another term, *puz naual haleb*, was the sorcery used by the Indians to transform themselves into balls of fire, eagles, and animals.

So it was that they made perfect the work, when they did it after thinking and meditating upon it.

Then they made the small wild animals, the guardians of the woods, the spirits of the mountains,[4] the deer, the birds, pumas, jaguars, serpents, snakes, vipers, guardians of the thickets.

And the Forefathers asked: "Shall there be only silence and calm under the trees, under the vines? It is well that hereafter there be someone to guard them."

So they said when they meditated and talked. Promptly the deer and the birds were created. Immediately they gave homes to the deer and the birds. "You, deer, shall sleep in the fields by the river bank and in the ravines. Here you shall be amongst the thicket, amongst the pasture; in the woods you shall multiply, you shall walk on four feet and they will support you. Thus be it done!" So it was they spoke.

Then they also assigned homes to the birds big and small. "You shall live in the trees and in the vines. There you shall make your nests; and there you shall multiply; there you shall increase in the branches of the trees and in the vines." Thus the deer and the birds were told; they did their duty at once, and all sought their homes and their nests.

And the creation of all the four-footed animals and the birds being finished, they were told by the Creator and the Maker and the Forefathers: "Speak, cry, warble, call, speak each one according to your variety, each, according to your kind." So was it said to the deer, the birds, pumas, jaguars, and serpents.

"Speak, then, our names, praise us, your mother, your father. Invoke then, Huracan, Chipi-Caculha, Raxa-Caculha, the Heart of Heaven, the Heart of Earth, the Creator, the Maker, the Forefathers; speak, invoke us, adore us," they were told.

But they could not make them speak like men; they only hissed and screamed and cackled; they were unable to make words, and each screamed in a different way.

---

[4] Literally, the "little man of the forest." In ancient times the Indians believed that the forests were occupied with these little beings, guardians, spirits of the forests. Another translator describes them as "the hob-goblin which walks in the mountains." The ancient Cakchiquel are supposed to have spoken with these little men who were also the spirits of the volcano of Fuego.

When the Creator and the Maker saw that it was impossible for them to talk to each other, they said: "It is impossible for them to say our names, the names of us, their Creators and Makers." "This is not well," said the Forefathers to each other.

Then they said to them: "Because it has not been possible for you to talk, you shall be changed. We have changed our minds: Your food, your pasture, your homes, and your nests you shall have; they shall be the ravines and the woods, because it has not been possible for you to adore us or invoke us. There shall be those who adore us, we shall make other [beings] who shall be obedient. Accept your destiny: your flesh shall be torn to pieces. So shall it be. This shall be your lot." So they said, when they made known their will to the large and small animals which are on the face of the earth.

They wished to give them another trial; they wished to make another attempt; they wished to make [all living things] adore them.

But they could not understand each other's speech; they could succeed in nothing, and could do nothing. For this reason they were sacrificed, and the animals which were on earth were condemned to be killed and eaten.

For this reason another attempt had to be made to create and make men by the Creator, the Maker, and the Forefathers.

"Let us try again! Already dawn draws near: Let us make him who shall nourish and sustain us! What shall we do to be invoked, in order to be remembered on earth? We have already tried with our first creations, our first creatures; but we could not make them praise and venerate us. So, then, let us try to make obedient, respectful beings who will nourish and sustain us." Thus they spoke.

Then was the creation and the formation. Of earth, of mud, they made [man's] flesh. But they saw that it was not good. It melted away, it was soft, did not move, had no strength, it fell down, it was limp, it could not move its head, its face fell to one side, its sight was blurred, it could not look behind. At first it spoke, but had no mind. Quickly it soaked in the water and could not stand.

And the Creator and the Maker said: "Let us try again because our creatures will not be able to walk nor multiply. Let us consider this," they said.

Then they broke up and destroyed their work and their

creation. And they said: "What shall we do to perfect it, in order that our worshipers, our invokers, will be successful?"

Thus they spoke when they conferred again: "Let us say again to Xpiyacoc, Xmucane, Hunahpu-Vuch, Hunahpu-Utiu: 'Cast your lot again. Try to create again.' " In this manner the Creator and the Maker spoke to Xpiyacoc and Xmucane.

Then they spoke to those soothsayers, the Grandmother of the day, the Grandmother of the Dawn, as they were called by the Creator and the Maker, and whose names were Xpiyacoc and Xmucane.

And said Huracan, Tepeu, and Gucumatz when they spoke to the soothsayer, to the Maker, who are the diviners: "You must work together and find the means so that man, whom we shall make, man, whom we are going to make, will nourish and sustain us, invoke and remember us."

"Enter, then, into council, grandmother, grandfather, our grandmother, our grandfather, Xpiyacoc, Xmucane, make light, make dawn, have us invoked, have us adored, have us remembered by created man, by made man, by mortal man. Thus be it done.

"Let your nature be known, Hunahpu-Vuch, Hunahpu-Utiu, twice mother, twice father, Nim-Ac, Nima-Tziis,[5] the master of emeralds, the worker in jewels, the sculptor, the carver, the maker of beautiful plates, the maker of green gourds, the master of resin, the master Toltecat,[6] grandmother of the sun, grandmother of dawn, as you will be called by our works and our creatures.

"Cast the lot with your grains of corn and the *tzite*.[7] Do it thus, and we shall know if we are to make, or carve his mouth and eyes out of wood." Thus the diviners were told.

They went down at once to make their divination, and cast

[5] Nim-Ac is the "two times father," and carries the image of a large wild boar. Nima-Tziis is the mother and symbolized by the image of a large tapir. The tapir was the sacred animal of the Tzetla Indians of Chiapas and, according to legend, Votan took a tapir with him and it multiplied in the waters of the Soconusco River. The Nim-Ac and Nima-Tziis male and female designation give sexual definition to the two members of the Creator-couple.

[6] The Tolteca were skilled silversmiths who, according to legend, were taught the art by Quetzalcoatl himself.

[7] The *tzite* fruit is a pod which contains red grains resembling beans. The Indians used the grains, together with corn, in their fortunetelling and witchcraft.

their lots with the corn and the *tzite*. "Fate! Creature!"[8] said an old woman and an old man. And this old man was the one who cast the lots with Tzite, the one called Xpiyacoc.[9] And the old woman was the diviner, the maker, called Chiracan Xmucane.

Beginning the divination, they said: "Get together, grasp each other! Speak, that we may hear." They said, "Say if it is well that the wood be got together and that it be carved by the Creator and the Maker, and if this [man of wood] is he who must nourish and sustain us when there is light when it is day!

"Thou, corn; thou, *tzite;* thou, fate; thou, creature; get together, take each other," they said to the corn, to the *tzite*, to fate, to the creature. "Come to sacrifice here, Heart of Heaven; do not punish Tepeu and Gucumatz!"[10]

Then they talked and spoke the truth: "Your figures of wood shall come out well; they shall speak and talk on earth."

"So may it be," they answered when they spoke.

And instantly the figures were made of wood. They looked like men, talked like men, and populated the surface of the earth.

They existed and multiplied; they had daughters, they had sons, these wooden figures; but they did not have souls, nor minds, they did not remember their Creator, their Maker; they walked on all fours, aimlessly.

They no longer remembered the Heart of Heaven and therefore they fell out of favor. It was merely a trial, an attempt at man. At first they spoke, but their face was without expression; their feet and hands had no strength; they had no blood, nor substance, nor moisture, nor flesh; their cheeks were dry, their feet and hands were dry, and their flesh was yellow.

Therefore, they no longer thought of their Creator nor their Maker, nor of those who made them and cared for them.

These were the first men who existed in great numbers on the face of the earth.

---

8 The translator notes that the first word here is "sun," but that it also means "fate."

9 Xpiyacoc is the "sorcerer" who here tells fortune by the grains of the *tzite*.

10 The passage is an invitation to the Heart of Heaven to take part in the casting of lots and to not let the diviners fail.

Creation of Man

Here, then, is the beginning of when it was decided to make man, and when what must enter into the flesh of man was sought.

And the Forefathers, the Creators and Makers, who were called Tepeu and Gucumatz, said: "The time of dawn has come, let the work be finished, and let those who are to nourish and sustain us appear, the noble sons, the civilized vassals; let man appear, humanity, on the face of the earth." Thus they spoke.

They assembled, came together and held council in the darkness and in the night; then they sought and discussed, and here they reflected and thought. In this way their decisions came clearly to light and they found and discovered what must enter into the flesh of man.

It was just before the sun, the moon, and the stars appeared over the Creators and Makers.

From Paxil, from Cayala,[1] as they were called, came the yellow ears of corn and the white ears of corn.

These are the names of the animals which brought the food: *yac* (the mountain cat), *utiu* (the coyote), *quel* (a small parrot), and *hoh* (the crow). These four animals gave tidings of the yellow ears of corn and the white ears of corn, they told them that they should go to Paxil and they showed them the road to Paxil.[2]

---

[1] Paxil means "separation," the spreading of waters, or inundation. Cayala is derived from *cay*, meaning "rotten," or putrid matter in water. Both words seem to describe mythological locations that suffered the same kind of flooding phenomenon found around the Nile. But neither place has ever been actually located. The same flooding that brought disaster and sediment also brought fertile land, and hence these places are considered the spots where corn and other staples of economic life developed.

[2] The translator notes that when the Creator and the Maker made man, they had nothing with which to feed him until they found corn in Paxil. Even then they had to fight two animals, the coyote and the crow, who knew where it was growing. The coyote was killed in the middle of the cornfield. From the dough of the corn, mixed with the blood of the snake, the flesh of man was fashioned. A Mexican legend tells a similar story about the discovery of corn. Azcatl, the ant, tells Quetzalcoatl that there is corn in a mountain. Quetzalcoatl immediately changes himself into a black ant and goes with Azcatl, enters the place and brings the corn back.

And thus they found the food, and this was what went into the flesh of created man, the made man; this was his blood; of this the blood of man was made. So the corn entered [into the formation of man] by the work of the Forefathers.

And in this way they were filled with joy, because they had found a beautiful land, full of pleasures, abundant in ears of yellow corn and ears of white corn, and abundant also in *pataxte* and cacao, and in innumerable *zapotes, anonas, jocotes, nantzes, matasanos,* and honey. There was an abundance of delicious food in those villages called Paxil and Cayala. There were foods of every kind, small and large foods, small plants and large plants.

The animals showed them the road. And then grinding the yellow corn and the white corn, Xmucane made nine drinks, and from this food came the strength and the flesh, and with it they created the muscles and the strength of man. This the Forefathers did, Tepeu and Gucumatz, as they were called.

After that they began to talk about the creation and the making of our first mother and father; of yellow corn and of white corn they made their flesh; of corn meal dough they made the arms and the legs of man. Only dough of corn meal went into the flesh of our first fathers, the four men, who were created.

These are the names of the first men who were created and formed: the first man was Balam-Quitze, the second, Balam-Acab, the third, Mahucutah, and the fourth was Iqui-Balam.[3]

These are the names of our first mothers and fathers.

It is said that they only were made and formed, they had no mother, they had no father. They were only called men.[4] They were not born of woman, nor were they begotten by the Creator nor by the Maker, nor by the Forefathers. Only by a miracle, by means of incantation were they created and made by the Creator, the Maker, the Forefathers, Tepeu and Gucumatz. And as they had the appearance of men, they were men; they talked, conversed, saw and heard, walked, grasped things; they were good and handsome men, and their figure was the figure of a man.

[3] These names have symbolic significance. The first means "jaguar of much laughter," or fatal laughter, like poison. The second, "jaguar of the night." The two remaining mean "not brushed," and "jaguar of moon" or, in Mayan, the black jaguar.
[4] They had no ancestors or family name, for they were the beginning of the human race.

They were endowed with intelligence; they saw and instantly they could see far, they succeeded in seeing, they succeeded in knowing all that there is in the world. When they looked, instantly they saw all around them, and they contemplated in turn the arch of heaven and the round face of the earth.

The things hidden [in the distance] they saw all, without first having to move; at once they saw the world, and so, too, from where they were, they saw it.

Great was their wisdom; their sight reached to the forests, the rocks, the lakes, the seas, the mountains, and the valleys. In truth, they were admirable men, Balam-Quitzé, Balam-Acab, Mahucutah, and Iqui-Balam.

Then the Creator and the Maker asked them: "What do you think of your condition? Do you not see? Do you not hear? Are not your speech and manner of walking good? Look, then! Contemplate the world, look [and see] if the mountains and the valleys appear! Try, then, to see!" they said to [the four first men].

And immediately they [the four first men] began to see all that was in the world. Then they gave thanks to the Creator and the Maker: "We really give you thanks, two and three times! We have been created, we have been given a mouth and a face, we speak, we hear, we think, and walk; we feel perfectly, and we know what is far and what is near. We also see the large and the small in the sky and on earth. We give you thanks, then, for having created us, oh, Creator and Maker! for having given us being, oh, our grandmother! oh, our grandfather!" they said, giving thanks for their creation and formation.

They were able to know all, and they examined the four corners, the four points of the arch of the sky and the round face of the earth.

But the Creator and the Maker did not hear this with pleasure. "It is not well what our creatures, our works say; they know all, the large and the small," they said. And so the Forefathers held counsel again. "What shall we do with them now? Let their sight reach only to that which is near; let them see only a little of the face of the earth! It is not well what they say. Perchance, are they not by nature simple creatures of our making? Must they also be gods? And if they do not reproduce and multiply when it will dawn, when the sun rises? And what if they do not multiply?" So they spoke.

"Let us check a little their desires, because it is not well what we see. Must they perchance be the equals of ourselves, their Makers, who can see afar, who know all and see all?"

Thus spoke the Heart of Heaven, Huracan, Chipi-Caculha, Raxa-Caculha, Tepeu, Gucumatz, the Forefathers, Xpiyacoc, Xmucane, the Creator and the Maker. Thus they spoke, and immediately they changed the nature of their works, of their creatures.

Then the Heart of Heaven blew mist into their eyes, which clouded their sight as when a mirror is breathed upon. Their eyes were covered and they could see only what was close, only that was clear to them.

In this way the wisdom and all the knowledge of the four men, the origin and beginning [of the Quiché race], were destroyed.

In this way were created and formed our grandfathers, our fathers, by the Heart of Heaven, the Heart of Earth.

XINGU MYTHS OF CREATION

The First Man

In the beginning there was only Mavutsinim. No one lived with him. He had no wife. He had no son, nor did he have any relatives. He was all alone.

One day he turned a shell into a woman, and he married her. When his son was born, he asked his wife, "Is it a man or a woman?"

"It is a man."

"I'll take him with me."

Then he left. The boy's mother cried and went back to her village, the lagoon, where she turned into a shell again.

"We are the grandchildren of Mavutsinim's son," say the Indians.

The First Kuarup, the Feast of the Dead

Mavutsinim wanted his dead people to come back to life. He went into the forest, cut three logs of *kuarup* wood, carried them back to the village, and painted them. After painting them, he adorned the logs with feathers, necklaces, cotton threads, and armlets of macaw feathers. Then Mavutsinim ordered poles to be fixed in the ground at the center of the village. He called for *cururu* toads and agoutis (two of each) to sing near the kuarups. On the same occasion, he brought fish and *beijus* [flat roasted bread] to the center of the village to be given out to his people. The *maraca-eps* [singers], shaking gourd rattles in their right hands, began to sing without pause to the kuarups, pleading with them to come to life. The village men kept asking Mavutsinim if the logs were actually going to turn into people or whether they would always be wood as they were. Mavutsinum answered that no, the kuarup logs were going to transform themselves into people, walk like people, and live as people do. After eating the fish, the people began to paint themselves and to shout as they did so. Everybody was shouting. The only people singing were the maracaeps. Around midday the singing ended. The people wanted to weep for the kuarups, who represented their dead, but Mavutsinim would not let them, saying that the kuarups were going to turn into people and for that reason there was nothing to weep about.

On the morning of the second day, Mavutsinim would not let his people look at the kuarups. "No one can look," he said. Mavutsinim had to keep repeating it from moment to moment. His people must wait. In the middle of the night on the second day, the logs began to move a little. The cotton thread belts and the feather armlets were trembling, the feathers moving as if shaken by the wind. The logs wanted to turn themselves into people. Mavutsinim kept telling his people not to look. They had to wait. As soon as the kuarups began to show signs of life, the singers—the cururu toads, and the agoutis—sang to make them go and wash themselves as soon as they came to life. The posts moved, trying to get out of the holes where they had been planted. At daybreak, from the waist up, the kuarups were already taking human form, with arms, breasts, and heads. The lower half was still wood. Mavutsinim kept telling his people to wait, to keep themselves from looking. "Wait . . . wait . . . wait," he said over and over. The sun began to rise. The singers never stopped singing. The kuarups' arms kept growing. One leg was already covered with flesh. But the other was still wood. Around midday, the logs were nearly real people. They were all moving around in their holes, more human than wood. Mavutsinim ordered all house entrances to be covered. Only he stayed out at the side of the kuarups. Only he could look at them, no one else. When the transformation from wood into people was nearly finished, Mavutsinim ordered the villagers to come outside and shout, make a commotion, spread joy, and laugh out loud near the kuarups. Then the people came out of their houses. Mavutsinim suggested that those who had had sexual relations with their women during the night ought to stay inside. Only one of them had had relations, and he stayed inside. But he was unable to contain his curiosity, and after a while he came out too. In that very instant, the kuarups stopped moving and turned back into wood.

Mavutsinim was furious at the young man who had failed

to follow his orders. He ranted and raved, saying, "What I wanted to do was to make the dead live again. If the man who lay with his wife had not come out, the kuarups would have turned into people, the dead would have come back to life every time a kuarup was made."

After his tirade, Mavutsinim passed sentence: "All right. From now on, it will always be this way. The dead will never come back to life again when kuarups are made. From now on, it will only be a festival."

Mavutsinim then ordered that the kuarup logs be taken out of their holes. The people wanted to take off their ornaments, but Mavutsinim would not let them. "They should remain this way," he said. And right afterward, he ordered them to be thrown into the water or into the forest. No one knows where they were thrown, but they are at the Morena today.

The Conquest of Day

In the beginning it was all dark. It was always night. There was no day. People lived around the termite hills. Everything was very confused. Nobody could see a thing. The birds defecated on top of people. There was no fire, there were no clearings, there was nothing. Only those fireflies around the termite hill existed. The brothers Kuát and Iaê, the Sun and the Moon, did not know what to do with their people: they were all dying of hunger because they could not work to get food. The brothers were hungry too and always thinking about how to make light. They wanted to create the day, but they could not think how. After much thought, they made an image of the tapir and filled it with manioc and other things that would rot and stink. After a few days, the effigy began to reek. Everything inside had spoiled and maggots were crawling all over it. The Sun wrapped the maggots up and gave the parcel to the flies, telling them to take it to the birds' village. The flies flew off and landed in the birds' village with the package of maggots. The birds surrounded the flies to find out what they had brought. The *urubutsin* [king vulture], the birds' chief, told them that the Sun intended to trick them so that he could steal the day. The urubutsin's village already had the day; they had light. The urubutsin ordered stools to be brought for the flies to sit on. Once they were seated, the chief asked, "What did you come here for?"

The flies answered him, but the urubutsin could not make out what they were saying. Nobody could understand the flies, as no one knew their language. One by one the birds questioned the flies, but none of them could understand what they said. The answer was always hum, hum, hum. They called the *xexeu* [oriole] bird to see if he could do any better.

"I doubt that I'll understand them," he said.

In fact, he too failed to understand them. So they called a relative of the xexeu, the *diarru* [congo kingbird]. The flies said something three times and he understood none of it. He told the others that he hadn't understood a thing. The other birds, his friends, had thought that he might understand the language of the flies because the xexeu speak many tongues. Then they called the *jacubim* to perform magic, but he too was unable to make anything out of the hum, hum, hum of the flies. Many other birds questioned the flies, but nothing came of it. Finally they called upon another relative of the xexeu, the *iapi-aruiap* [a lesser variety of congo kingbird]. He was able to understand them. The flies then showed the package they had brought, saying that down below, where they came from, there were lots of rotten things that were good to eat. In fact, so many things that nobody could possibly eat it all. Then they handed over the package of maggots to the birds, who consumed it all and immediately asked the flies when they could go and eat what was down there.

"You can come this very day," they answered.

The urubutsin was always carrying on about how dangerous it was down there, and before they went, they must all cut their hair. The birds shaved themselves bald and started the trip down. The urubutsin was the last to leave. The Sun and the Moon had hidden themselves inside the tapir effigy. The urubutsin went to sit at the place the Sun had prepared for him. The birds arrived and began to eat the insects. One hawk did not rush to the carcass. He perched at a distance, watching. The Sun, who was spying through holes in the effigy's head, met the hawk's glance. The hawk saw the movement from his perch and warned the birds that the tapir's eyes had moved. The birds instantly took flight, abandoning the effigy, but after a while they came back and went on eating the grubs.

Then the Moon said to the Sun, "Get ready, here he comes."

As soon as the urubutsin landed on the carcass, the Sun grabbed one of his feet and held it fast. Seeing that their chief had been captured, all the birds took off together, abandoning the tapir's carcass.

The hawk, who had been watching from a distance, said, "Didn't I tell you I saw the tapir open his eyes?"

Then the Sun told the urubutsin, "We're not going to kill you. We only want the day. That was the reason we called you."

The birds flew back to their village. Only the jacubim and the guan stayed behind. The urubutsin ordered the jacubim to go and bring back the day. The jacubim flew off and after a while came back wearing an *araviri* [armband] made of blue macaw feathers. The day began to dawn a little, and the Sun asked, "Is this the day?" The Moon told him it wasn't, it was only a blue macaw feather. As soon as the jacubim alighted, everything got dark again. Back in their village, the birds were very sad, thinking that the Sun had killed their chief. The urubutsin, trapped by the Sun, told the jacubim to go home again and this time bring back the real day. The jacubim left and returned with the crest of the *caninde* macaw, the yellow one.

As he flew back, it cleared up a little, and the Sun asked, "Is this really the day?"

"No, this is not the day. It will get dark again as soon as he touches the ground," said the Moon.

And in fact as soon as the jacubim touched the ground, it got dark again.

"What did I tell you?" the Moon said. "It still is not the real day."

The jacubim, sent away again by his captive chief, left and returned with a headdress of parrot feathers. Again it began to get light. This time, the Sun thought, it really must be the day. But the Moon said no, it would get dark again, and sure enough, as soon as the messenger landed, it got dark again.

So the Sun said to the urubutsin, "If you do not send for the real day, your people will think we have killed you here."

Hearing that, the urubutsin told the jacubim to bring the real day. The jacubim left and flew back covered with parrot feathers.

"Is this it?" asked the Sun.

"No," said the Moon, "it's the same thing as before."

The Sun said to the urubutsin in an ingratiating tone, "*Tamai* [grandfather], send for the real day so that you can leave."

The jacubim went off again. This time he flew back decked out in a headdress and armbands of red macaw feathers.

The Sun asked, "Is it right this time? Is this really it?"

"No," repeated the Moon, "it's a red macaw's feather, and this is still not the day."

At this point the urubutsin spoke in a different tone to the guan, "Now go get the real day, because I'm tired of staying here."

The guan left and came back all decked out with a headdress, earrings, armbands and leg ornaments. He glided down.

The Moon said, "This is the day. That is the true red macaw. The other one wasn't pure."

When the guan landed, everything became bright. Pleased at last, the Sun said to the urubutsin, "I did not call you, Grandfather, to kill you. It was so you could give us the day. All my people were dying of hunger in the darkness. I needed the day for planting, for hunting, and for fishing."

Then the urubutsin began to instruct the Sun and the Moon, saying, "In the morning the day is born, in the afternoon it starts to fade, and then it disappears all at once. When this happens, don't think we took it back. Don't think that. The day appears, and afterward comes the night. It will always be this way. When the night comes, don't think that it will stay dark and that we stole the day from you. Don't be afraid. It will always come back."

Then he went on, "The night is for sleeping. The day is for working: to make gardens, hunt, fish, and do all kinds of things. Sleep at night and work during the day. Always."

When the urubutsin finished speaking, the Sun began to adorn him. He shaved the top of his head with a stone, painted it with urucu, and bound a white cotton string around it. Before leaving, the urubutsin said to the Sun and the Moon, "When you kill a big animal, put it where I can see it, so that I can come and feed."

After he spoke, the urubutsin opened his wings and flew away.

PERUVIAN CREATION MYTH
OF THE INCAS

Viracocha

In other days we who are of the race of the Incas worshipped the Sun; we held that he was the greatest and most benignant of all beings, and we named ourselves the children of the Sun. We had traditions that told of the pitiable ways that we and the rest of the human race lived in before the Sun, having had compassion upon us, decided to lead us towards better ways of living. . . . Lo, now! Our Lord, the Sun, put his two children, a son and a daughter, in a boat upon Lake Titicaca. He told them they were to float upon the water until they came to where men lived. He put his golden staff into the hands of his son. He told him he was to lead men into a place where that staff, dropped upon the earth, sank deep down into it.

So the children of our Lord the Sun went upon the waters of Lake Titicaca. They came to where our fathers lived in those far days. . . . Where we live now we see villages and cities; we see streams flowing down from the mountains, and being led this way and that way to water our crops and our trees; we see flocks of llamas feeding on good grass with their lambs—countless flocks. But in those days we lived where there were thickets and barren rocks; we had no llamas; we had no crops; we knew not how to make the waters flow this way and that way; we had no villages, no cities, no temples. We lived in clefts of the rocks and holes in the ground. The covering of our bodies was of bark or of leaves, or else we went naked in the day and without covering to put over us at night. We ate roots that we pulled up out of the ground, or fought with the foxes for the dead things they were carrying away. No one bore rule amongst us, and we knew nothing of duty or kindness of one to another.

Out of their boat on Lake Titicaca came the children of our Lord to us. They brought us together; they had rule over us, and they showed us how to live as husband and wife and children, and how to know those who were leaders amongst us and how to obey those leaders. And having showed us these things they led us from the land they had found us in.

And often did he who was the son of our Lord the Sun drop the golden staff upon the ground as we went on. Sometimes the staff sank a little way into the earth, sometimes it sank to half its length in the earth. We came to a place where the golden staff, dropped by him who was the son of our Lord the Sun, sank into the earth until only its top was to be seen. And there we stayed, or, rather, there our fathers stayed, for we are many generations from the men and women who came into this place with the two who were the children of the Sun.

They showed us how to sow crops in that rich ground, and how to lead water down from the hills to water the crops and the trees. They showed us how to tame the llamas, and how to herd them and tend them as tamed beasts. They showed us how to take the wool from them and weave the wool into garments for ourselves; also, they showed us how to dye our garments so that we went brightly clad in the light of the sun. They showed us how to work in gold and silver, and how to make vessels of clay, and how to put shapes and figures upon these vessels. They showed us how to build houses, and how to build villages, and cities, and temples. And they showed us, too, how to obey the rule of those who were left to rule over us, the Incas.

Then the two who were the son and daughter of the Sun left us. Before they went from us they told us that the Sun, their father, would adopt us as his children. And so we of the Inca race became the children of the Sun. They said to us, too, "Our father, the Sun, does good to the whole world; he gives light that men may see and follow their pursuits; he makes men warm when they had been cold; he ripens their crops; he increases their flocks of llamas; he brings dew upon the ground. The Sun, our father, goes round the earth each day that he may know of man's necessities and help him to provide for them. Be like the Sun, then, far-seeing, regular in all your occupations. And bring the worship of the Sun amongst the tribes who live in darkness and ignorance."

And so these two, his son and daughter who were sent to us by the Sun, were seen no more by us. But we knew ourselves now as the children of the Sun. We subdued the tribes in his name, and brought the knowledge of his beneficence amongst them. We built a great temple to him. And the daughters of the Incas in hundreds served him as Virgins of the Sun.

Yes, but there were those amongst us who came to have other thoughts about Heaven and the ways of Heaven. "Does not the Sun go as another being directs him to go?" one of the Incas said to his councillors. "Is he not like an arrow shot onward by a man? Is he not like a llama tethered by the will of a man rather than like one who has freedom? Does he not let a little cloud obscure his splendour? Is it not plain that he may never take rest from his tasks?"

So men amongst us have said, and they who have said them have mentioned a name. Viracocha that name is. And then they would say words from rites that were known to the people of this land before the Incas came into it. They would say, "O conquering Viracocha! Thou gavest life and valour to men, saying, 'let this be a man,' and to women saying, 'let this be a woman.' Thou madest them and gavest them being! Watch over them that they may live in health and peace! Thou who art in the high heavens, and among the clouds of the tempest, grant this with long life, and accept this sacrifice, O Creator!" So those who were priests in the land before our fathers came into it prayed.

And they said that it was Viracocha who created the Sun, and created the Moon also. They said that at the beginning the Sun was not brighter than the Moon, and that in his jealousy he flung ashes upon the face of the Moon and dimmed the Moon's primal brightness. And they said that Viracocha could make great terraces of rock and clay rear themselves up with crops upon them, and that he could bring the water-courses to freshen terraces and gardens merely by striking with a hollow cane that he carried.

Now although Viracocha was so great, he obscured himself, and came back to live amongst the Gods in the guise of a beggar. None knew him for Viracocha, the Creator of all things. And he saw the Goddess Cavillaca as she sat amongst llama lambs under a lucma-tree, weaving the wool of the white llama. He saw her and he approached her. He left a ripe fruit beside her. She ate the fruit and she became with child by him.

And when her child was born her parents and her friends said to her, "You must find out who is the father of this child. Let all who live near come to this lucma-tree, and let the child crawl amongst them. The man he crawls to and touches with his hand we will know is his father."

So under the lucma-tree Cavillaca sat, and her child was with her. All who lived near came to that place, and amongst them came Viracocha, still in his beggar's dress. All came near to Cavillaca and her child. The child crawled where they stood. He came to Viracocha. He put his hand up and touched the man who was in the beggar's garb.

Then was Cavillaca made ashamed before all the Gods. She snatched up her child and held him to her. She fled away from that place. She fled towards the ocean with her child. Viracocha put on his robes of splendour and hastened after her. And as he went he cried out, "O Goddess, turn; look back at me! See how splendid I am!" But the Goddess, without turning, fled with her child from before him.

Viracocha went seeking them. As he crossed the peaks he met a condor, and the condor flew with him, and consoled him. Viracocha blessed the condor, and gave him long life and the power to traverse the wilderness and go over the highest peaks; also he gave him the right to prey upon creatures. Afterwards he met a fox; but the fox derided him, telling him that his quest was vain. He cursed the fox, saying to him that he would have to hunt at night, and that men would slay him. He met a puma, and the puma went with him and consoled him. He blessed the puma, saying that he would receive honour from men. As he went down the other side of the mountain, he came upon parrots flying from the trees of their forest. And the parrots cried out words that were of ill-omen. He cursed the parrots, saying that they would never have honour from men. But he blessed the falcon that flew with him down to the sea.

And when he came to the sea he found that Cavillaca and her child had plunged themselves into the water and had been transformed into rocks. Then Viracocha in his grief remained beside the sea.

Now beside the sea there were two virgins who were Urpihuachac's daughters. They were guarded by a serpent. Viracocha charmed the serpent with his wisdom, and the serpent permitted him to approach Urpihuachac's daughters. One flew away and became a dove. But the other lived there with Viracocha. And this Virgin of the Sea showed Viracocha where her mother kept all the fishes of the world. They were in a pond and they could not go through the waters of the world. Viracocha broke down the walls of their pond, and let them go through the streams and the lakes and the sea. And thus he let men have fishes to eat.

He lived amongst men, and he taught them many arts. He it was, as the priests of those who were here before the Incas say, showed men how to bring streams of water to their crops, and taught them how to build terraces upon the mountains where crops would grow. He set up a great cross upon the mountain Caravay. And when the bird that cries out four times at dawn cried out, and the light came upon the cross he had set up, Viracocha went from amongst men. He went down to the sea, and he walked across it towards the west. But he told those whom he had left behind that he would send messengers back who would protect them and give them renewed knowledge of all he had taught them. He left them, but men still remember the chants that those whom he left on the mountain, by the cross, cried out their longing:

Oh, hear me!
From the sky above,
In which thou mayst be,
From the sea beneath,
In which thou mayst be,
Creator of the world,
Maker of all men;
Lord of all Lords,
My eyes fail me
For longing to see thee;
For the sole desire to know thee.

LENGUA CREATION MYTH
OF PARAGUAY

The Creator, in the shape of a beetle, inhabited a hole in the earth, and he formed man and woman out of the clay which he threw up from his subterranean abode. At first the two were joined together, "like the Siamese twins," and in this very inconvenient posture they were sent out into the world, where they contended, at great disadvantage, with a race of powerful human beings whom the beetle had previously created. So the man and woman besought the beetle to separate them. He complied with their request and gave them the power to propagate their species. So they became the parents of mankind. But the beetle, having created the world, ceased to take any active part or interest in it.

PART THREE

Northern Europe and Central Asia

INTRODUCTION

DUE TO NATURAL geographic positioning, Part Three includes several different traditions: the Finno-Ugric, Celtic, Eddic, and Siberian.

Finno-Ugric Myths

The Finno-Ugric race is one of the oldest. It once possessed a common language and home, but during thousands of years it was divided into numerous small groups of people, intermingling with and influenced by many other civilizations that range as widely as the Baltic Sea, the Arctic Ocean, and Central Asia. The Finno-Ugric family branched out and formed five divisions. One of these groups, the Permian, is composed of the Votiaks in the upper Karna region and the Siryans, who settled north of there.[1] Of all the Finno-Ugric people only the Finns, the Estonians, and the Hungarians developed what may be fairly called superior civilizations. Many lived as nomads right up to modern times—for example, the Lapps, Siryans, and Voguls.

The oldest reports of the Finns' ancient religion are very brief. In fact, the earliest record of any value dates from modern times (around the sixteenth century). Serious interest in the myths and religions of the Old Finns developed with the publication of the epic *Kalevala* in 1836 and 1849. The *Kalevala* is composed mainly of folk songs and Finnish magic songs that arose in the Middle Ages. Some of the heroes' names in the *Kalevala* epic were thought to be titles of divinities. The old man Vainamoinen, for example, may be used also for a giant or divine being. Similarly, the black-

[1] For further reference see James Hastings, *Encyclopedia of Religion and Ethics*, 13 vols, vol. 6, p. 22 (New York: Charles Scribner's Sons, 1961), or *The Mythology of All Races*, 13 vols (New York: Cooper Square Publishers, Inc., 1964).

smith's name, Ilmarinen, is a form of the Ugric air god Ilmari's name.

Siberian Myths

There is very little evidence of the religious life and mythology of early Siberian settlers. Several groups seemed to have moved across that vast terrain, including some central Asiatic peoples (either "Aryan" or "Turarian"), and the Siryan group of the Finno-Ugric peoples. There are remnants of iron implements and a few Turkic-Niger inscriptions. In fact, the name "Sybir" appears as a major capital on old maps (1367) of unknown origin. The term "Neo-Siberian" has come to mean those peoples who originally came from Central Asia or Eastern Europe, but had been in Siberia for at least the last 1,000 years.

Siberian mythology is very sparse, but the Siberians seemed to possess an animistic religion with a central role played by a shaman, or medicine man. Their beliefs involved a somewhat confused supernatural power, but animistic influences were potent.[2] Even shadows on a wall have tribes and areas where they live and hunt. The rainbow and rays of the sun have "masters" who live on these bright arcs and descend to earth at will. Stones have "voices," and a stone can roll down a hill and crush a man against whom it has a grudge. With such strong animistic beliefs, it is not surprising that their myths have many major roles played by animals, which can be seen in the myths included here.

Eddic

During the early centuries of the Christian era the Teutonic people were also spread widely over central Europe, to the northern reaches of Scandinavia and even to Iceland. As with many other widespread groups of people, there was great similarity of belief in religious custom and folklore. Yet detailed myths survived in Teutonic mythology only in the *Edda*. The Eddic myths belong primarily to Iceland, Norway,

[2] For more animistic religion see James Hastings, op. cit., p. 496.

Sweden, and Denmark. In the seventeenth century a scholar-bishop discovered a work on Norse mythology called *Edda*, apparently gathered together and composed by a twelfth-century poet, Snorri Sturluson. Snorri compiled the *Edda* in order to illustrate the old myths for young poets. The *Edda* consists of thirty-four poems separated into three parts. The first part contains the myths, the cosmogony, and the final destruction of the old gods and goddesses. The second is more myths, and the third part contains rules of poetry. In the first part, Snorri uses some of the Eddic poems, including the *Voluspa*, one of the most remarkable verses of Norse mythology, that gives an account of the beginning and end of things through the mouth of a Volva, or seeress, raised from the dead by Odin. She relates how the world began, tells tales of the early heroes, dwarfs, and the first days of the gods, and closes with the prophecy of Doom. It is a beautifully severe and simple poem, and stands above all the other Eddic mythic verses.

Celtic Myths

With the recent revival of interest in Stonehenge and the "mystical" tradition of the Druid religious practices, the old Celtic religion has had many contemporary cultic, magic-oriented interpreters. But, in fact, there is little evidence that the Celts possessed or practiced any form of esoteric-wisdom religion. Much of the legend of Druidic wisdom comes from cultish enthusiasts in medieval Wales. There are no genuine ancient documents, Welsh or Irish, that indicate anything other than mythopoeic passions building on the old Druid legends. The Celts did have divinities of war, poetry, agriculture, and the otherworld, and delighted in telling stories about them, which in turn lead to a form of romantic mythmaking. But they did not turn all their goddesses into dawn maidens, or their heroes into sun gods. These mythic themes were related in beautiful stories that were embellished by the modern "mythologizers"—thus making the Druids seem a sophisticated mystery-cult, which they were not. The copious Irish and British Celtic myths must therefore be read carefully, in order to keep separate the early, older pagan myths in which the gods are immortal, and the more recent mythic interpolations by Roman civilization, Christianity, and Euro-

pean influence. In fact, one cannot even now be sure that
any one story ever existed as pagan myth and was not con-
cocted by later mythopoeic writers.[3]

According to traditional belief, Druidism was the religion
of the Celts in pre-Roman Gaul and Britain. The Druids are
now believed to have actually existed in ancient times, but
their real identity has been obscured by folklore, superstition,
and imagination. The Druids were ignored until they caught
the interest of classical scholars during the Renaissance. The
few bits of information that have come down to us from
Greek and Roman writers, and their creation of Stonehenge,
has created an image of magic, occultism, and secret ritual.
The popularity of Druidism as a "mystery religion" exists
today, and Druidic rituals are still practiced in the United
States and Europe.[4]

One of the major problems of isolating an authentic Celtic
mythic lore is the strong Roman influence on the oral mythology of the Druids. The old religion was ruthlessly disre-
garded and eventually assimilated into the Roman, and the
old Druid gods were mixed up with, and made subservient to,
the Roman gods.

The Druids had a fertile imagination and a religion containing many ideas about the universe—its creation and form
—but their teachings did not survive to modern times intact
or in detail. Some still-extant Celtic folk beliefs indicate that
primitive myths of creation did exist, in which springs and
rivers were formed from the sweat of giants or fairies. Such
creatures in those old tales apparently took the place of
divinities. In Celtic myth, the Tuatha De Danann were believed to have come from heaven and were central in both
creating Ireland and in maintaining it. Although modern
scholars cannot be sure, the Celts also probably believed in
the creation of man by descent from the gods (e.g., the Tuatha
De Danann) rather than through a spontaneous act of creation forming human life. The history of the Tuatha De
Danann is, in fact, the Celt view of the creation of man. For
example, as related by Julius Caesar, one Druidic myth taught
the descent of the Gauls from Dispater, the Celtic god of the

---

[3] See John A. MacCulloch, *The Mythology of All Races*, 13 vols.,
vol. X, *Celtic* (New York: Cooper Square Publishers, Inc., 1964), p. 19.
[4] For more information on the Druids and Celts, see C. Squire,
Mythology of the Ancient Britons (London, 1905); J. Rhys, *Celtic Folklore* (Oxford, 1901); and E. Anwyl, *Celt Religion in Pre-Christ Times*
(London, 1906).

underworld. Thus, descent from gods was attributed to early tribes or clans, families, individuals, and even plants and animals.

MYTHS OF THE TUATHA DE DANAAN

Of the four major groups of mythic peoples who migrated to ancient Ireland, the Tuatha De Danaan are the most fascinating, for they were considered to be superhuman beings by some, to be in control of powerful magic by others, and to be gods by still others—although many modern scholars believe they were an actual tribe of people living in ancient Gaul.

The Tuatha De Danaan were also considered fairies or spirits with physical form yet possessing immortality. Up to modern times, many still believed that the Tuatha De Danaan resided in *sid*, or the numerous hollow mounds scattered over Ireland. Throughout history, they have been sacrificed to in order to have good crops of corn and to prevent the cows' milk from souring. Because they possessed magical or divine powers they could also appear as animals, birds, or even as magical mist.

Some experts translate Tuatha De Danaan as "people of the goddess Danu," yet others believe *Tuatha De* means the "divine tribe," or "the men of god." From the Tuatha De Danaan comes the continuing contemporary fascination with, and belief in, Druidic magic and the supernatural powers of Ireland's pagan religion.

The Celtic myth offered in this collection is a graphic synopsis of the Tuatha De Danaan's coming to Ireland and their battles to win their place on the Emerald Island. The battles of the Tuatha De Danaan are similar to those in many other myths where the powers of light, growth, summer, and order strive to overcome the darkness, chaos, and bleakness of the destructive forces. The Babylonian Marduk battles Tiamat; the Greek Titans and Olympian gods war to establish primacy.

---

5 For more information on these complicated customs and beliefs, see James Hastings, op. cit., vol. 3, p. 277ff.

A RUMANIAN CREATION MYTH

Before the creation of the earth God and Satan were alone over the waters. When God had decided to make the earth he sent Satan to the bottom of the ocean. Satan was to bring back particles of earth in his (God's) name. Satan dived into the waters three times but did not succeed in bringing back any particles to the surface because he was attempting to take the earth in his own name. Finally, he dived a fourth time in his and in God's name. This time he at least brought some of it up, as much that is, as could remain under his fingernails (or claws). Out of this God finished a sort of cake (a clod) and sat upon it in order to rest himself. Satan thought; "God is sleeping." He thus desired to take the earth particles of the clod and throw them into the ocean. In this way he thought he would become Lord. But every time he touched the clod it grew larger, until it had become an immense earthen ball. Because of this the waters were displaced, and as God awoke he saw that there was not enough room for the waters. Since he knew no remedy, he sent the bee to the hedgehog, the wisest of all animals, which he had created in the meantime. The hedgehog did not want to give any remedy since, indeed, God was all-knowing. The bee however, hid itself and listened to the hedgehog speaking to himself. He was overheard saying; "Evidently God does not know that he must make valleys and mountains in order to make room for the waters." The bee returned to God with the news she had overheard from the wise hedgehog. The hedgehog nevertheless, cursed the bee because it had eavesdropped. Henceforth she should eat nothing but dung. God however, rewarded the bee and declared that her dung should not be dirty or despised, but should be good to eat—and this is honey.

A CENTRAL ASIATIC CREATION MYTH

When these mighty beings descended from heaven they saw a frog diving in the water. Otshirvani's companion raised it from the depths and placed it on its back on the water. "I shall sit on the stomach of the frog," said Otshirvani, "dive to the bottom and bring up what your hand finds." Chagan-Shukuty dived twice, and the second time he succeeded in bringing up some earth. Then Otshirvani told him to sprinkle it on the stomach of the frog, on which they sat. The frog itself sank out of sight and only the earth remained visible above the surface of the water. Resting there, the gods fell asleep and while they were sleeping, Shulmus, the devil, arrived and saw the two friends lying on the earth which they had just created and which was yet so small that there was scarcely room for a third on it. The devil decided to make use of his chance and drown these beings together with their earth. But when he attempted to seize hold of the edge of the earth, he no longer saw the ocean. He took the sleeping friends under his arm and began to run toward the shore with them. But while he ran the earth grew. When he saw that his attempt was vain he dropped his burden and barely succeeded in escaping when Otshirvani awoke. The latter then explained to his companion how the devil had meant to destroy them but how the earth had saved them.

A SIBERIAN-ALTAIC MYTH

In the beginning when there was nothing but water, God and the "First Man" moved about in the shape of two black geese over the waters of the primordial ocean. The devil, however, could not hide his nature, but endeavored ever to rise higher, until he finally sank down into the depths. Nearly suffocating, he was forced to call to God for help, and God raised him again into the air with the power of his word. God then spoke: "Let a stone rise from the bottom of the ocean!" When the stone appeared, Man seated himself upon it, but God asked him to dive under the water and bring land. Man brought earth in his hand and God scattered it on the surface of the water saying: "Let the world take shape!" Once more God asked Man to fetch earth. But Man then decided to take some for himself and brought a morsel in each hand. One handful he gave to God but the other he hid in his mouth, intending to create a world of his own. God threw the earth which the devil[1] had brought him beside the rest on the water, and the world at once began to expand and grow harder, but with the growing of the world the piece of earth in Man's mouth also swelled until he was about to suffocate so that he was again compelled to seek God's help. God inquired: "What was thy intention? Didst thou think thou couldst hide earth from me in thy mouth?" Man now told his secret intentions and at God's request spat the earth out of his mouth. Thus were formed the boggy places upon the earth.

---

[1] It appears that the devil and man are synonymous here. I can find no clarification for this line.

THE TUATHA DE DANAAN,
WHENCE THEY CAME

The Tuatha De Danaan,[1] or people of the Goddess Danu, were not the first "divine" inhabitants of Ireland. The first was the Race of Partholon, who came from the Other World with twenty-four males and twenty-four females, landing in Ireland on the First of May, the day sacred to Bile, the God of Death—and called Beltaine. Ireland was then one treeless, grassless plain, watered by three lakes and nine rivers, but after three hundred years' sojourn of the people of Partholon, Ireland had grown from one plain to four and there were seven new lakes. The Race itself had increased to five thousand members. This was not without struggle, for where the Gods are, there also are the great Opposers called Fomors, a race of giants, of monstrous ugliness but with a certain supernatural power. Partholon defeated their leader, Cichol the Footless, and then there was peace for three hundred years. The oldest legends say that the people of Partholon returned to the Other World whence they came; but others say that on the same fateful First of May, exactly three hundred years after their advent, there began a mysterious epidemic which lasted a week and destroyed all the Race. Knowing their end was near, they all gathered at the original first plain, so that the last survivor might more easily bury those that died.

After them came the Race of Nemed, who also landed on the Feast of Beltaine. They continued the work of the previous Race, struggled against the Fomors and defeated them in four consecutive battles. Ireland again extended to twelve new plains and four new lakes. Then Nemed died with two thousand of his people from an epidemic, and the then leaderless Race was oppressed by the Fomors, who imposed a tax that two-thirds of the children born to the Race during the year

---

[1] The Tuatha De Danaan were the gods of pagan Ireland, and were endowed with great supernatural powers.

were to be delivered up on each day of Samhain.[2] In answer to this tax, the remaining members of the Race of Nemed stormed the fortress of the Fomorian kings (there were two kings), slew one of them, but the other king fought so vigorously that out of sixteen thousand who attacked the fortress, only thirty survived and these returned whence they came or died.

From this time the land was held by a people called the Fir-Bolgs. They consisted of three tribes who divided the country between them, the most important tribe holding three provinces and the other two tribes one province each. Some authorities think they were not "divine" or "supernatural" at all, but a subject people of the Fomors. It is certain that their most important tribe was called the "Men of Domnu," while the Fomors are called the "Gods of Domnu," and also that the five provinces they held met at the Hill of Balor, and in the figure of Balor himself we find the power of the Fomors embodied. The Fir-Bolgs are supposed to have had nine supreme kings, the last of these, Eochaid, son of Erc, surnamed "the Proud," being conquered by the next "divine" Race, the Tuatha De Danaan.

The earliest tales say that these people of the Goddess Danu came from the sky, but later ones tell that they had lived on earth, and came variously from the "north" and from the "southern isles of the world." They had dwelt in four mythical cities previously to their coming to Ireland. The names of these cities were Findias, Gorias, Murias, and Falias, and in these cities they had learned poetry and magic, and had brought from each city a treasure. From Findias came the sword of Nuada, their king, from whose stroke no one ever escaped or recovered; from Gorias came the terrible lance or spear of Lugh, the great Sun God, which weapon wielded itself and thirsted so for blood, that only by steeping its head in a sleeping draught of poppy leaves could it be kept at rest; from Murias came the magic cauldron of the Dagda, and from Falias came the "stone of Fal," better known as the "stone of Destiny," which, according to legend, utters a human cry when touched by the rightful king of Erin.

This great Race lands in Ireland, like their predecessors, on the mystic "Beltaine" without the Fir-Bolgs knowing of

---

[2] Samhain was the Feast of the Autumn Equinox, and Beltaine the Feast of the Spring Equinox.

their presence. They spread druidically-formed showers and fog-sustaining shower clouds, and make the air pour down fire and blood so that the Fir-Bolgs have to shelter for three days and nights until they can use counter spells and bring back normal atmospheric conditions. War is the inevitable result, and the two armies meet at a place called "Plain of the Sea." There is a long parley first, in which the two armies admire each other's weapons and almost become friends; indeed, the envoy of the Tuatha De Danaan offers peace to the Fir-Bolgs with divisions of the land into halves, and the envoy of the Fir-Bolgs advises them to accept these conditions. Yet though the offer is made twice, the Fir-Bolg king, Eochaid the Proud, will have none of it. "Give them half and they will soon have the whole country," are his words. A truce of a hundred days is called, during which time each army has made for them weapons like those of their opponents. On Midsummer Day, the armies at last meet in battle. First thrice nine of each force fight each other and are killed. Then follows another parley, in which Nuada, king of the Tuatha De Danaan, obtains a promise that battles shall be fought with equal numbers on both sides, although the Fir-Bolg army, as a whole, numbers more than his own. Then follows a series of single combats and for four days and nights the fighting continues thus with great slaughter on both sides.

Then a Fir-Bolg champion called Sreng fights in single combat with Nuada, the king of the Gods, and shears off the latter's hand and half his shield with one blow. But the Fir-Bolg king is killed with a hundred of his men as he goes to look for water, and when finally the Fir-Bolgs have been reduced to three hundred men, the Gods offer them one-fifth part of Ireland.

KALEVALA, CREATION EPIC FROM FINLAND[1]

Birth of Vainamoinen

I AM driven by my longing,
And my understanding urges
That I should commence my singing,
And begin my recitation.
I will sing the people's legends,
And the ballads of the nation.
To my mouth the words are flowing,
And the words are gently falling,
Quickly as my tongue can shape them,
And between my teeth emerging.

    Dearest friend, and much-loved brother,
Best beloved of all companions,
Come and let us sing together,
Let us now begin our converse,
Since at length we meet together,
From two widely sundered regions.
Rarely can we meet together,
Rarely one can meet the other,
In these dismal Northern regions,
In the dreary land of Pohja.
Let us clasp our hands together,
Let us interlock our fingers;
Let us sing a cheerful measure,
Let us use our best endeavors,
While our dear ones hearken to us,
And our loved ones are instructed,

---

[1] Many consider the *Kalevala* the Finnish national epic. It is a compilation of folk verse about the heroic deeds of three giant, semi-divine brothers. They had their abode in Kaleva, a mythical land of joy and abundance. The epic involves many aspects of creation, and is rich in myth and legend. The epic has heavily influenced Finnish art. Sibelius, for example, is known to have been inspired by the *Kalevala* in composing at least half a dozen of his major works.

While the young are standing round us,
Of the rising generation,
Let them learn the words of magic,
And recall our songs and legends,
Of the belt of Vainamoinen,
Of the forge of Ilmarinen,
And of Kaukomieli's sword point,
And of Joukahainen's crossbow:
Of the utmost bounds of Pohja,
And of Kalevala's wide heathlands.

These my father sang aforetime,
As he carved his hatchet's handle,
And my mother taught me likewise,
As she turned around her spindle,
When upon the floor, an infant,
At her knees she saw me tumbling,
As a helpless child, milk-bearded,
As a babe with mouth all milky.
Tales about the Sampo failed not,
Nor the magic spells of Louhi.
Old at length became the Sampo;
Louhi vanished with her magic;
Vipunen while singing perished;
Lemminkainen in his follies.

There are many other legends;
Songs I learned of magic import;
Some beside the pathway gathered;
Others broken from the heather;
Others wrested from the bushes;
Others taken from the saplings,
Gathered from the springing verdure
Or collected from the byways,
As I passed along as herd boy,
As a child in cattle pastures,
On the hillocks, rich in honey,
On the hills, forever golden,
After Muurikki, the black one,
By the side of dappled Kimmo.

Then the Frost his songs recited,
And the rain its legends taught me;
Other songs the winds have wafted,
Or the ocean waves have drifted;
And their songs the birds have added,
And the magic spells the tree tops.

In a ball I bound them tightly;
And arranged them in a bundle;
On my little sledge I laid it,
On my sleigh I laid the bundle;
Home upon the sledge I brought it,
Then into the barn conveyed it;
In the storehouse loft I placed it,
In a little box of copper.

In the cold my song was resting,
Long remained in darkness hidden.
I must draw the songs from Coldness,
From the Frost must I withdraw them,
Bring my box into the chamber,
On the bench-end lay the casket,
Underneath this noble gable,
Underneath this roof of beauty.
Shall I ope my box of legends,
And my chest where lays are treasured?
Is the ball to be unraveled,
And the bundle's knot unfastened?
Then I'll sing so grand a ballad,
That it wondrously shall echo,
While the rye bread I am eating,
And the beer of barley drinking.
But though ale should not be brought me,
And though beer should not be offered,
I will sing, though dry my throttle,
Or will sing, with water only,
To enhance our evening's pleasure,
Celebrate the daylight's beauty,
Or the beauty of the daybreak,
When another day is dawning.

I have often heard related,
And have heard the song recited,
How the nights closed ever lonely,
And the days were shining lonely.
Only born was Vainamoinen,
And revealed the bard immortal,
Sprung from the divine Creatrix,
Born of Ilmatar, his mother.

Air's young daughter was a virgin,
Fairest daughter of Creation.
Long did she abide a virgin,
All the long days of her girlhood,

In the Air's own spacious mansions,
In those far extending regions.
    Wearily the time passed ever,
And her life became a burden,
Dwelling evermore so lonely,
Always living as a maiden,
In the Air's own spacious mansions,
In those far-extending deserts.
    After this the maid descending,
Sank upon the tossing billows,
On the open ocean's surface,
On the wide expanse of water.
    Then a storm arose in fury,
From the East a mighty tempest,
And the sea was wildly foaming,
And the waves dashed ever higher.
    Thus the tempest rocked the virgin,
And the billows drove the maiden,
O'er the ocean's azure surface,
On the crest of foaming billows,
Till the wind that blew around her,
And the sea woke life within her.
    Then she bore her heavy burden,
And the pain it brought upon her,
Seven long centuries together,
Nine times longer than a lifetime.
Yet no child was fashioned from her,
And no offspring was perfected.
    Thus she swam, the Water-Mother,
East she swam, and westward swam she,
Swam to northwest and to southwest,
And around in all directions,
In the sharpness of her torment,
In her body's fearful anguish;
Yet no child was fashioned from her,
And no offspring was perfected.
    Then she fell to weeping gently,
And in words like these expressed her:
"O how wretched is my fortune,
Wandering thus, a child unhappy!
I have wandered far already,
And I dwell beneath the heaven,
By the tempest tossed forever,
While the billows drive me onward,

O'er this wide expanse of water,
On the far-extending billows.
    "Better were it had I tarried,
Virgin in aerial regions,
Then I should not drift forever,
As the Mother of the Waters.
Here my life is cold and dreary,
Every moment now is painful,
Ever tossing on the billows,
Ever floating on the water.
    "Ukko, thou of Gods the highest,
Ruler of the whole of heaven,
Hasten here, for thou art needed;
Hasten here at my entreaty.
Free the damsel from her burden,
And release her from her tortures.
Quickly haste, and yet more quickly,
Where I long for thee so sorely."
    Short the time that passed thereafter,
Scarce a moment had passed over,
Ere a beauteous teal came flying
Lightly hovering o'er the water,
Seeking for a spot to rest in,
Searching for a home to dwell in.
    Eastward flew she, westward flew she,
Flew to northwest and to southward,
But the place she sought she found not,
Not a spot, however barren,
Where her nest she could establish,
Or a resting place could light on.
    Then she hovered, slowly moving,
And she pondered and reflected,
"If my nest in wind I 'stablish
Or should rest it on the billows,
Then the winds will overturn it,
Or the waves will drift it from me."
    Then the Mother of the Waters,
Water-Mother, maid aerial,
From the waves her knee uplifted,
Raised her shoulder from the billows,
That the teal her nest might 'stablish,
And might find a peaceful dwelling.
Then the teal, the bird so beauteous,
Hovered slow, and gazed around her,

And she saw the knee uplifted
From the blue waves of the ocean,
And she thought she saw a hillock,
Freshly green with springing verdure.
There she flew, and hovered slowly,
Gently on the knee alighting,
And her nest she there established,
And she laid her eggs all golden,
Six gold eggs she laid within it,
And a seventh she laid of iron.

O'er her eggs the teal sat brooding,
And the knee grew warm beneath her;
And she sat one day, a second,
Brooded also on the third day;
Then the Mother of the Waters,
Water-Mother, maid aerial,
Felt it hot, and felt it hotter,
And she felt her skin was heated,
Till she thought her knee was burning,
And that all her veins were melting.
Then she jerked her knee with quickness,
And her limbs convulsive shaking,
Rolled the eggs into the water,
Down amid the waves of ocean,
And to splinters they were broken,
And to fragments they were shattered.

In the ooze they were not wasted,
Nor the fragments in the water,
But a wondrous change came o'er them,
And the fragments all grew lovely.
From the cracked egg's lower fragment,
Now the solid earth was fashioned,
From the cracked egg's upper fragment,
Rose the lofty arch of heaven,
From the yolk, the upper portion,
Now became the sun's bright luster;
From the white, the upper portion,
Rose the moon that shines so brightly;
Whatso in the egg was mottled,
Now became the stars in heaven,
Whatso in the egg was blackish,
In the air as cloudlets floated.

Now the time passed quickly over,
And the years rolled quickly onward,

In the new sun's shining luster,
In the new moon's softer beaming.
Still the Water-Mother floated,
Water-Mother, maid aerial,
Ever on the peaceful waters,
On the billows' foamy surface,
With the moving waves before her,
And the heaven serene behind her.

When the ninth year had passed over,
And the summer tenth was passing,
From the sea her head she lifted,
And her forehead she uplifted,
And she then began Creation,
And she brought the world to order,
On the open ocean's surface,
On the far-extending waters.

Wheresoe'er her hand she pointed,
There she formed the jutting headlands;
Wheresoe'er her feet she rested,
There she formed the caves for fishes;
When she dived beneath the water,
There she formed the depths of ocean;
When toward the land she turned her,
There the level shores extended,
Where her feet to land extended,
Spots were formed for salmon-netting;
Where her head the land touched lightly,
There the curving bays extended.
Further from the land she floated,
And abode in open water,
And created rocks in ocean,
And the reefs that eyes behold not,
Where the ships are often shattered,
And the sailors' lives are ended.

Now the isles were formed already,
In the sea the rocks were planted;
Pillars of the sky established,
Lands and continents created;
Rocks engraved as though with figures,
And the hills were cleft with fissures.
Still unborn was Vainamoinen;
Still unborn, the bard immortal.

Vainamoinen, old and steadfast,
Rested in his mother's body

For the space of thirty summers,
And the sum of thirty winters,
Ever on the placid waters,
And upon the foaming billows.

   So he pondered and reflected
How he could continue living
In a resting place so gloomy,
In a dwelling far too narrow,
Where he could not see the moonlight,
Neither could behold the sunlight.

   Then he spake the words which follow,
And expressed his thoughts in this wise:

   "Aid me Moon, and Sun release me,
And the Great Bear lend his counsel,
Through the portal that I know not,
Through the unaccustomed passage.
From the little nest that holds me,
From a dwelling place so narrow,
To the land conduct the roamer,
To the open air conduct me,
To behold the moon in heaven,
And the splendor of the sunlight;
See the Great Bear's stars above me,
And the shining stars in heaven."

   When the moon no freedom gave him,
Neither did the sun release him,
Then he wearied of existence,
And his life became a burden.
Thereupon he moved the portal,
With his finger, fourth in number,
Opened quick the bony gateway,
With the toes upon his left foot,
With his nails beyond the threshold,
With his knees beyond the gateway.

   Headlong in the water falling,
With his hands the waves repelling,
Thus the man remained in ocean,
And the hero on the billows.

   In the sea five years he sojourned,
Waited five years, waited six years,
Seven years also, even eight years,
On the surface of the ocean,
By a nameless promontory,
Near a barren, treeless country.

On the land his knees he planted,
And upon his arms he rested,
Rose that he might view the moonbeams,
And enjoy the pleasant sunlight,
See the Great Bear's stars above him,
And the shining stars in heaven.
    Thus was ancient Vainamoinen,
He, the ever famous minstrel,
Born of the divine Creatrix,
Born of Ilmatar, his mother.

Vainamoinen's Sowing

THEN did Vainamoinen, rising,
Set his feet upon the surface
Of a sea-encircled island,
In a region bare of forest.
    There he dwelt, while years passed over,
And his dwelling he established
On the silent, voiceless island,
In a barren, treeless country.
    Then he pondered and reflected,
In his mind he turned it over,
"Who shall sow this barren country,
Thickly scattering seeds around him?"
    Pellervoinen, earth-begotten,
Sampsa, youth of smallest stature,
Came to sow the barren country,
Thickly scattering seeds around him.
    Down he stooped the seeds to scatter,
On the land and in the marshes,
Both in flat and sandy regions,
And in hard and rocky places.
On the hills he sowed the pine trees,
On the knolls he sowed the fir trees,
And in sandy places heather;
Leafy saplings in the valleys.
    In the dales he sowed the birch trees,
In the loose earth sowed the alders,
Where the ground was damp the cherries,
Likewise in the marshes, sallows.
Rowan trees in holy places,

Willows in the fenny regions,
Juniper in stony districts,
Oaks upon the banks of rivers.
    Now the trees sprang up and flourished,
And the saplings sprouted bravely.
With their bloom the firs were loaded,
And the pines their boughs extended.
In the dales the birch was sprouting,
In the loose earth rose the alders,
Where the ground was damp the cherries,
Juniper in stony districts,
Loaded with its lovely berries;
And the cherries likewise fruited.
    Vainamoinen, old and steadfast,
Came to view the work in progress,
Where the land was sown by Sampsa,
And where Pellervoinen labored.
While he saw the trees had flourished,
And the saplings sprouted bravely,
Yet had Jumala's tree, the oak tree,
Not struck down its root and sprouted.
    Therefore to its fate he left it,
Left it to enjoy its freedom,
And he waited three nights longer,
And as many days he waited.
Then he went and gazed around him,
When the week was quite completed.
Yet had Jumala's tree, the oak tree,
Not struck down its root and sprouted.
    Then he saw four lovely maidens;
Five, like brides, from water rising;
And they mowed the grassy meadow,
Down they cut the dewy herbage,
On the cloud-encompassed headland,
On the peaceful island's summit,
What they mowed, they raked together,
And in heaps the hay collected.
    From the ocean rose up Tursas,
From the waves arose the hero,
And the heaps of hay he kindled,
And the flames arose in fury.
All was soon consumed to ashes,
Till the sparks were quite extinguished.

Then among the heaps of ashes,
In the dryness of the ashes,
There a tender germ he planted,
Tender germ, of oak an acorn
Whence the beauteous plant sprang upward,
And the sapling grew and flourished,
As from earth a strawberry rises,
And it forked in both directions.
Then the branches wide extended,
And the leaves were thickly scattered,
And the summit rose to heaven,
And its leaves in air expanded.

In their course the clouds it hindered,
And the driving clouds impeded,
And it hid the shining sunlight,
And the gleaming of the moonlight.

Then the aged Vainamoinen,
Pondered deeply and reflected,
"Is there none to fell the oak tree,
And o'erthrow the tree majestic?
Sad is now the life of mortals,
And for fish to swim is dismal,
Since the air is void of sunlight,
And the gleaming of the moonlight."

But they could not find a hero,
Nowhere find a man so mighty,
Who could fell the giant oak tree,
With its hundred spreading branches.

Then the aged Vainamoinen,
Spoke the very words which follow:
"Noble mother, who hast borne me,
Luonnotar, who me hast nurtured;
Send me powers from out the ocean:
(Numerous are the powers of ocean)
So that they may fell the oak tree,
And destroy the tree so baneful,
That the sun may shine upon us,
And the pleasant moonlight glimmer."

Then a man arose from ocean,
From the waves a hero started,
Not the hugest of the hugest,
Nor the smallest of the smallest.
As a man's thumb was his stature;
Lofty as the span of woman.

Decked his head a helm of copper,
On his feet were boots of copper,
On his hands were copper gauntlets,
Gloves adorned with copper tracings;
Round his waist his belt was copper;
In his belt his ax was copper;
And the haft thereof was thumb-long,
And the blade thereof was nail-long.

Vainamoinen, old and steadfast,
Deeply pondered and reflected:
"While he seems a man in semblance,
And a hero in appearance,
Yet his height is but a thumb-length,
Scarce as lofty as an ox hoof."

Then he spoke the words which follow,
And expressed himself in this wise:
"Who are you, my little fellow,
Most contemptible of heroes,
Than a dead man scarcely stronger;
And your beauty all has vanished."

Then the puny man from ocean,
Hero of the floods, made answer:
"I'm a man as you behold me,
Small, but mighty water hero,
I have come to fell the oak tree,
And to splinter it to fragments."

Vainamoinen, old and steadfast,
Answered in the words which follow:
"You have hardly been created,
Neither made, nor so proportioned,
As to fell this mighty oak tree,
Overthrow the tree stupendous."

Scarcely had the words been spoken,
While his gaze was fixed upon him,
When the man transformed before him,
And became a mighty hero.
While his feet the earth were stamping,
To the clouds his head he lifted,
To his knees his beard was flowing,
To his spurs his locks descended.
Fathom-wide his eyes were parted,
Fathom-wide his trousers measured;
Round his knee the girth was greater,
And around his hip 'twas doubled.

Then he sharpened keen the ax blade,
Brought the polished blade to sharpness;
Six the stones on which he ground it,
Seven the stones on which he whet it.

Then the man stepped forward lightly,
Hastened on to do his mission;
Wide his trousers, and they fluttered
Round his legs as onward strode he,
And the first step taken, brought him
To the shore so soft and sandy;
With the second stride he landed
On the dun ground farther inland,
And the third step brought him quickly,
Where the oak itself was rooted.

With his ax he smote the oak tree,
With his sharpened blade he hewed it;
Once he smote it, twice he smote it,
And the third stroke wholly cleft it.
From the ax the flame was flashing,
Flame was bursting from the oak tree,
As he strove to fell the oak tree,
Overthrow the tree stupendous.
Thus the third blow was delivered,
And the oak tree fell before him,
For the mighty tree was shattered,
And the hundred boughs had fallen,
And the trunk extended eastward,
And the summit to the northwest,
And the leaves were scattered southward,
And the branches to the northward.

He who took a branch from off it,
Took prosperity unceasing,
What was broken from the summit,
Gave unending skill in magic;
He who broke a leafy branchlet,
Gathered with it love unending.
What remained of fragments scattered,
Chips of wood, and broken splinters,
On the bright expanse of ocean,
On the far-extending billows,
In the breeze were gently rocking,
On the waves were lightly drifted,
Like the boats on ocean's surface,
Like the ships amid the sea waves.

Northward drove the wind the fragments,
Where the little maid of Pohja,
Stood on beach, and washed her headdress,
And she washed her clothes and rinsed them,
On a shingle by the ocean,
On a tongue of land projecting.

On the waves she saw the fragments,
Put them in her birch-bark wallet,
In her wallet took them homeward;
In a well-closed yard she stored them.
For the arrows of the sorcerer,
For the chase to furnish weapons.

When the oak at last had fallen,
And the evil tree was leveled,
Once again the sun shone brightly,
And the pleasant moonlight glimmered,
And the clouds extended widely,
And the rainbow spanned the heavens,
O'er the cloud-encompassed headland,
And the island's misty summit.

Then the wastes were clothed with verdure,
And the woods grew up and flourished;
Leaves on trees and grass in meadows.
In the trees the birds were singing,
Loudly sang the cheery throstle;
In the tree tops called the cuckoo.

Then the earth brought forth her berries;
Shone the fields with golden blossoms;
Herbs of every species flourished;
Plants and trees of all descriptions;
But the barley would not flourish,
Nor the precious seed would ripen.

Then the aged Vainamoinen,
Walked around, and deeply pondered,
By the blue waves' sandy margin,
On the mighty ocean's border,
And six grains of corn he found there,
Seven fine seeds of corn he found there,
On the borders of the ocean,
On the yielding sandy margin.
In a marten's skin he placed them,
From the leg of summer squirrel.

Then he went to sow the fallows;
On the ground the seeds to scatter,

Near to Kaleva's own fountain,
And upon the field of Osmo.

From a tree there chirped the titmouse:
"Osmo's barley will not flourish,
Nor will Kaleva's oats prosper,
While untilled remains the country,
And uncleared remains the forest,
Nor the fire has burned it over."

Vainamoinen, old and steadfast,
Ground his axblade edge to sharpness
And began to fell the forest,
Toiling hard to clear the country.
All the lovely trees he leveled,
Sparing but a single birch tree,
That the birds might rest upon it,
And from thence might call the cuckoo.

In the sky there soared an eagle,
Of the birds of air the greatest,
And he came and gazed around him.
"Wherefore is the work unfinished,
And the birch tree still unfallen?
Wherefore spare the beauteous birch tree?"

Said the aged Vainamoinen,
"Therefore is the birch left standing,
That the birds may perch upon it:
All the birds of air may rest there."

Said the bird of air, the eagle,
"Very wisely hast thou acted,
Thus to leave the birch tree standing
And the lovely tree unfallen,
That the birds may perch upon it,
And that I myself may rest there."

Then the bird of air struck fire,
And the flames rose up in brightness,
While the north wind fanned the forest,
And the northeast wind blew fiercely.
All the trees were burned to ashes,
Till the sparks were quite extinguished.

Then the aged Vainamoinen,
Took the six seeds from his satchel,
And he took the seven small kernels,
From the marten's skin he took them,
From the leg of summer squirrel,
From the leg of summer ermine.

Then he went to sow the country,
And to scatter seeds around him,
And he spoke the words which follow:
"Now I stoop the seeds to scatter,
As from the Creator's fingers,
From the hand of Him Almighty,
That the country may be fertile,
And the corn may grow and flourish.

The Gold and Silver Bride

Afterward smith Ilmarinen
Mourned his wife throughout the evenings,
And through sleepless nights was weeping,
All the days bewailed her fasting,
And he mourned her all the mornings,
In the morning hours lamented,
Since the time his young wife perished,
Death the fair one had o'ertaken.
In his hand he swung no longer,
Copper handle of his hammer,
Nor his hammer's clang resounded,
While a month its course was running.

Said the smith, said Ilmarinen,
"Hapless youth, I know no longer,
How to pass my sad existence,
For at night I sit and sleep not,
Always in the night comes sorrow,
And my strength grows weak from trouble.

"All my evenings now are weary,
Sorrowful are all my mornings,
And the nights indeed are dismal,
Worst of all when I am waking.
Grieve I not because 'tis evening,
Sorrow not because 'tis morning,
Trouble not for other seasons;
But I sorrow for my fair one,
And I sorrow for my dear one,
Grieve for her, the dark-browed beauty.

"Sometimes in these times so dismal,
Often in my time of trouble,
Often in my dreams at midnight,

Has my hand felt out at nothing,
And my hand seized only trouble,
As it strayed about in strangeness."
    Thus the smith awhile lived wifeless,
And without his wife grew older,
Wept for two months and for three months,
But upon the fourth month after,
Gold from out the lake he gathered,
Gathered silver from the billows,
And a pile of wood collected,
Nothing short of thirty sledgeloads,
Then he burned the wood to charcoal,
Took the charcoal to the smithy.
    Of the gold he took a portion,
And he chose him out some silver,
Even like a ewe of autumn,
Even like a hare of winter,
And the gold to redness heated,
Cast the silver in the furnace,
Set his slaves to work the bellows,
And his laborers pressed the bellows.
    Toiled the slaves, and worked the bellows,
And the laborers pressed the bellows,
With their ungloved hands they pressed them,
Worked them with their naked shoulders,
While himself, smith Ilmarinen,
Carefully the fire was tending,
As he strove a bride to fashion
Out of gold and out of silver.
    Badly worked the slaves the bellows,
And the laborers did not press them,
And on this smith Ilmarinen
Went himself to work the bellows.
Once and twice he worked the bellows,
For a third time worked the bellows,
Then looked down into the furnace,
Looking closely to the bellows,
What rose up from out the furnace,
What from out the flames ascended.
    Then a ewe rose from the furnace,
And it rose from out the bellows.
One hair gold, another copper,
And the third was all of silver;

Others might therein feel pleasure,
Ilmarinen felt no pleasure.
   Said the smith, said Ilmarinen,
"Such as you a wolf may wish for,
But I want a golden consort,
One of silver half constructed."
   Thereupon smith Ilmarinen
Thrust the ewe into the furnace,
Gold unto the mass he added,
And he added silver to it,
Set his slaves to work the bellows,
And his laborers pressed the bellows.

. . . .

   Then a foal rose from the furnace,
And it rose from out the bellows,
Mane of gold, and head of silver,
And his hoofs were all of copper;
But though others it delighted,
Ilmarinen felt no pleasure.
   Said the smith, said Ilmarinen,
"Such as you a wolf may wish for,
But I want a golden consort,
One of silver half constructed."
   Thereupon smith Ilmarinen
Thrust the foal into the furnace,
Gold unto the mass he added,
And he added silver to it,
Set his slaves to work the bellows,
And his laborers pressed the bellows.

. . . .

While himself, smith Ilmarinen,
Carefully the fire was tending,
As he strove a bride to fashion,
Out of gold and out of silver.

. . . .

   Then a maid rose from the furnace,
Golden-locked, from out the bellows,
Head of silver, hair all golden,
And her figure all was lovely.
Others might have shuddered at her,
Ilmarinen was not frightened.
   Thereupon smith Ilmarinen
Set to work to shape the image,

Worked at night without cessation,
And by day he worked unresting.
Feet he fashioned for the maiden,
Fashioned feet; and hands he made her,
But the feet would not support her,
Neither would the arms embrace him.

Ears he fashioned for the maiden,
But the ears served not for hearing,
And a dainty mouth he made her,
Tender mouth and shining eyeballs,
But the mouth served not for speaking,
And the eyes served not for smiling.

Said the smith, said Ilmarinen
"She would be a pretty maiden,
If she had the art of speaking,
And had sense, and spoke discreetly."

After this he laid the maiden
On the softest of the blankets,
Smoothed for her the softest pillows,
On the silken bed he laid her.

After this smith Ilmarinen,
Quickly warmed the steaming bathroom,
Took the soap into the bathroom,
And provided twigs for bath whisks,
And of water took three tubs full,
That the little finch should wash her,
And the little goldfinch cleanse her,
Cleanse her beauty from the ashes.

When the smith had also bathed him,
Washed him to his satisfaction,
At the maiden's side he stretched him,
On the softest of the blankets,
'Neath the steel-supported hangings,
'Neath the over-arching iron.

After this smith Ilmarinen,
Even on the very first night,
Asked for coverlets in plenty,
And for blankets to protect him,
Also two and three of bearskins,
Five or six of woolen mantles,
All upon one side to lay him,
That toward the golden image.

And one side had warmth sufficient
Which was covered by the bedclothes;

That beside the youthful damsel,
Turned toward the golden image,
All that side was fully frozen,
And with frost was quite contracted,
Like the ice on lake when frozen,
Frozen into stony hardness.

Said the smith, said Ilmarinen,
"This is not so pleasant for me.
I will take the maid to Vaino,
Pass her on to Vainamoinen,
On his knee as wife to seat her,
Dovelike in his arms to nestle."

So to Vainola he took her,
And he said upon his coming,
In the very words which follow:
"O thou aged Vainamoinen,
Here I bring a damsel for you,
And a damsel fair to gaze on,
And her mouth gapes not too widely,
And her chin is not too broadened."

Vainamoinen, old and steadfast,
Looked upon the golden image,
Looked upon her head all golden,
And he spoke the words which follow:
"Wherefore have you brought her to me,
Brought to me this golden specter?"

Said the smith, said Ilmarinen,
"With the best intent I brought her,
On your knee as wife to rest her,
Dovelike in your arms to nestle."

Said the aged Vainamoinen,
"O thou smith, my dearest brother,
Thrust the damsel in the furnace,
Forge all sorts of objects from her,
Or convey her hence to Russia,
Take your image to the Saxons,
Since they wed the spoils of battle,
And they woo in fiercest combat;
But it suits not my position,
Nor to me myself is suited,
Thus to woo a bride all golden,
Or distress myself for silver."

Then dissuaded Vainamoinen,
And forbade the wave-sprung hero,

All the rising generation,
Likewise those upgrown already,
For the sake of gold to bow them,
Or debase themselves for silver,
And he spoke the words which follow,
And in words like these expressed him:
"Never, youths, however wretched,
Nor in future, upgrown heroes,
Whether you have large possessions,
Or are poor in your possessions,
In the course of all your lifetime,
While the golden moon is shining,
May you woo a golden woman,
Or distress yourselves for silver,
For the gleam of gold is freezing,
Only frost is breathed by silver."

The Theft and Re-creation of
the Sun and Moon

Vainamoinen, old and steadfast,
On his *kantele* was playing,
Long he played, and long was singing,
And was ever full of gladness.
    In the moon's house heard they playing,
Came delight to the sun's window,
And the moon came from his dwelling,
Standing on a crooked birch tree,
And the sun came from his castle,
Sitting on a fir tree's summit,
To the kantele to listen,
Filled with wonder and rejoicing.
    Louhi, Pohjola's old Mistress,
Old and gap-toothed dame of Pohja,
Set to work the sun to capture,
In her hands the moon seized likewise.
From the birch the moon she captured,
And the sun from fir tree's summit;
Straightway to her home she brought them,
To the gloomy land of Pohja.
    Then she hid the moon from shining,
In the mottled rocks she hid him,

Sang the sun to shine no longer,
Hidden in a steel-hard mountain;
And she spoke the words which follow:
"Never more again in freedom
Shall the moon arise for shining,
Nor the sun be free for shining,
If I come not to release them,
If I do not go to fetch them,
When I bring nine stallions with me,
Which a single mare has littered."

When the moon away was carried,
And the sun had been imprisoned
Deep in Pohjola's stone mountain,
In the rocks as hard as iron,
Then she stole away the brightness,
And from Vainola the fires,
And she left the house fireless,
And the rooms no flame illumined.

Therefore was the night unending,
And for long was utter darkness,
Night in Kalevala forever,
And in Vainola's fair dwellings,
Likewise in the heavens was darkness,
Darkness round the seat of Ukko.

Life without the fire was weary,
And without the light a burden,
Unto all mankind 'twas dismal,
And to Ukko's self 'twas dismal.

Ukko, then, of Gods the highest,
In the air the great Creator,
Now began to feel most strangely,
And he pondered and reflected,
What strange thing the moon had darkened,
How the sun had been obstructed,
That the moon would shine no longer,
And the sun had ceased his shining.

Then he stepped to cloudland's borders,
On the borders of the heavens,
Wearing now his pale blue stockings,
With the heels of varied color,
And he went the moon to seek for,
And he went to find the sunlight,
Yet he could not find the moonlight,
Nor the sun he could discover.

In the air a light struck Ukko,
And a flame did Ukko kindle,
From his flaming sword he struck it,
Sparks he struck from off the sword blade,
From his nails he struck the fire,
From his limbs he made it crackle,
High above aloft in heaven,
On the starry plains of heaven.
When the fire had thus been kindled,
Then he took the spark of fire,
In his golden purse he thrust it,
Placed it in his silver casket,
And he bade the maiden rock it,
Told the maid of air to rock it,
That a new moon might be fashioned,
And a new sun be constructed.
    On the long cloud's edge she sat her,
On the air-marge sat the maiden,
There it was she rocked the fire,
There she rocked the glowing brightness,
In a golden cradle rocked it,
With a silver cord she rocked it.
    Then the silver props were shaken,
Rocked about the golden cradle,
Moved the clouds and creaked the heavens,
And the props of heaven were swaying,
With the rocking of the fire,
And the rocking of the brightness.
    Thus the maid the fire was rocking,
And she rocked the fire to brightness,
With her fingers moved the fire,
With her hands the fire she tended,
And the stupid maiden dropped it,
Dropped the flame the careless maiden,
From her hands the fire dropped downward
From the fingers of its guardian.
    Then the sky was cleft asunder,
All the air was filled with windows,
Burst asunder by the fire sparks,
As the red drop quick descended,
And a gap gleamed forth in heaven,
As it through the clouds dropped downward,
Through nine heavens the drop descended,
Through six spangled vaults of heaven.

Said the aged Vainamoinen,
"Smith and brother, Ilmarinen,
Let us go and gaze around us,
And the cause perchance discover,
What the fire that just descended,
What the strange flame that has fallen
From the lofty height of heaven,
And to earth beneath descended.
Of the moon 'tis perhaps a fragment,
Of the sun perchance a segment."

Thereupon set forth the heroes,
And they wandered on, reflecting
How they might perchance discover,
How they might succeed in finding,
Where the fire had just descended,
Where the brightness had dropped downward.

And a river flowed before them,
And became a lake extensive,
And the aged Vainamoinen
Straight began a boat to fashion,
In the wood he worked upon it,
And beside him Ilmarinen
Made a rudder out of firwood,
Made it from a log of pinewood.

Thus the boat at length was ready,
Rowlocks, rudder all completed,
And they pushed it in the water,
And they rowed and steered it onward,
All along the river Nevá,
Steering round the Cape of Neva.

Ilmatar, the lovely damsel,
Eldest Daughter of Creation,
Then advanced to meet the heroes,
And in words like these addressed them:
"Who among mankind may ye be?
By what names do people call you?"

Said the aged Vainamoinen,
"You may look on us as sailors.
I am aged Vainamoinen,
Ilmarinen, smith, is with me,
But inform us of your kindred;
By what name do people call you?"

Then the matron made them answer,
"I am oldest of all women,

Of the air the oldest damsel,
And the first of all the mothers.
Five times now have I been married,
Six times as a bride attired.
Whither do you take your journey,
Whither, heroes, are you going?"
      Said the aged Vainamoinen,
And he spoke the words which follow:
"All our fires have been extinguished,
And their flames died down in darkness,
Long already were we fireless,
And in darkness were we hidden,
But at length have we determined
That the fire we ought to seek for,
Which has just dropped down from heaven,
From above the clouds has fallen."
      Then the woman gave them answer,
And she spoke the words which follow:
"Hard it is to track the fire,
And the bright flame to discover.
It has evil wrought already,
And the flame has crime committed,
For the red spark has shot downward,
And the red ball has descended
From the realms of the Creator,
Where it was by Ukko kindled,
Through the level plains of heaven,
Through the void aerial spaces,
Downward through the sooty smoke hole,
Downward through the seasoned roof tree
Of the new-built house of Tuuri,
Of a wretched roofless dwelling.
      "When the fire at length came thither,
In the new-built house of Tuuri,
Evil deeds he then accomplished,
Shocking deeds he then accomplished,
Burning up the maidens' bosoms,
Tearing at the breasts of maidens,
And the knees of boys destroying,
And the master's beard consuming.
      "And her child the mother suckled,
In a cradle of misfortune.
Thither, too, the fire rushed onward,
And its evil work accomplished,

In the cradle burned the baby,
Burning, too, the mother's bosom,
And the child went off to Mana,
And the boy went straight to Tuoni.
Thus it was the infant perished,
And was cast into destruction,
In the red flame's fiery torture,
In the anguish of its glowing.

    "Great the knowledge of the mother,
And to Manala she went not.
Means she knew to ban the fire,
And to drive away its glowing,
Through the little eye of needle,
And across the back of ax blade,
Through the sheath of glowing sword blade,
Past the ploughed land did she drive it."

    Vainamoinen, old and steadfast,
Heard her words, and then made answer:
"Whither has the fire retreated,
Whither did the pest take refuge,
Was it in the field of Tuuri,
In a lake, or in a forest?"

    Then the matron made him answer,
And she spoke the words which follow:
"When from thence the fire departed,
And the flame went wandering onward,
First it burned o'er many districts,
Many districts, many marshes,
Rushed at last into the water,
In the billows of Lake Alue,
And the fire rose up all flaming,
And the sparks arose all crackling.

    "Three times in the nights of summer,
Nine times in the nights of autumn,
Rose the lake the height of fir trees,
Roaring rose above the lake banks,
With the strength of furious fire,
With the strength of heat all flaming.

    "On the bank were thrown the fishes,
On the rocks the perch were stranded,
And the fishes looked around them,
And the perch were all reflecting
How they could continue living.
Perch were weeping for their dwellings,

Fish were weeping for their homesteads,
Perches for their rocky castles.
  "And the perch with back all crooked,
Tried to seize the streak of fire,
But the perch was not successful;
Seized upon it the blue powan.
Down he gulped the streak of fire,
And extinguished thus its brightness.
  "Then retired the Lake of Alue,
And fell back from all its margins,
Sinking to its former level
In a single night of summer.
  "When a little time passed over,
Fire pain seized on the devourer,
Anguish came upon the swallower,
Grievous suffering on the eater.
  "Up and down the fish swam turning,
Swam for one day and a second,
All along the powan's island,
Clefts in rocks where flock the salmon,
To the points of capes a thousand,
Bays among a hundred islands.
Every cape made declaration,
Every island spoke in thiswise:
  " 'Nowhere in these sluggish waters,
In the narrow Lake of Alue,
Can the wretched fish be swallowed,
Or the hapless one may perish
In the torture of the fire,
In the anguish of its glowing.'
  "But a salmon-trout o'erheard it,
And the powan blue he swallowed.
When a little time passed over,
Fire pain seized on the devourer,
Anguish came upon the swallower,
Grievous suffering on the eater.

VOLUSPO, EDDIC CREATION POEM[1]

1. Hearing I ask from the holy races,
   From Heimdall's[2] sons, both high and low;
   Thou wilt, Valfather,[3] that well I relate
   Old tales I remember of men long ago.

2. I remember yet the giants of yore,
   Who gave me bread in the days gone by;
   Nine worlds I knew, the nine in the tree
   With mighty roots beneath the mold.

3. Of old was the age when Ymir lived;
   Sea nor cool waves nor sand there were;
   Earth had not been, nor heaven above,
   But a yawning gap, and grass nowhere.

4. Then Bur's sons lifted the level land,
   Mithgarth the mighty there they made;
   The sun from the south warmed the stones of earth,
   And green was the ground with growing leeks.

5. The sun, the sister of the moon, from the south
   Her right hand cast over heaven's rim;
   No knowledge she had where her home should be,
   The moon knew not what might was his,
   The stars knew not where their stations were.

6. Then sought the gods their assembly seats,
   The holy ones, and council held;
   Names then gave they to noon and twilight,
   Morning they named, and the waning moon,
   Night and evening, the years to number.

[1] The *Voluspo*, of *The Wise-Woman's Prophecy*, is the most famous and important of all the Eddic poems of Scandinavia. In the opening Othin, the chief of gods, calls on Volva, or wise-woman, that she may advise him. She first tells him of the past, of the creation of the world, the beginning of years, the origin of the dwarfs, of the first man and woman, and of the world ash Yggdrasil (which is a tree of cosmic dimensions whose roots reach down to the depths and whose branches penetrate the sky).

[2] The Watchman of the gods.

[3] Father of the slain.

159

7. At Ithavoll met the mighty gods,
   Shrines and temples they timbered high;
   Forges they set, and they smithied ore,
   Tongs they wrought, and tools they fashioned.

8. In their dwellings at peace they played at tables,
   Of gold no lack did the gods then know,—
   Till thither came up giant-maids three,
   Huge of might, out of Jotunheim.

9. Then sought the gods their assembly seats,
   The holy ones, and council held,
   To find who should raise the race of dwarfs
   Out of Brimir's blood and the legs of Blain.

10. There was Motsognir the mightiest made
    Of all the dwarfs, and Durin next;
    Many a likeness of men they made,
    The dwarfs in the earth, as Durin said. . . .

14. The race of the dwarfs in Dvalin's throng
    Down to Lofar the list must I tell;
    The rocks they left, and through wet lands
    They sought a home in the fields of sand. . . .

17. Then from the throng did three come forth,
    From the home of the gods, the mighty and gracious;
    Two without fate on the land they found,
    Ask and Embla, empty of might.

18. Soul they had not, sense they had not,
    Heat nor motion, nor goodly hue;
    Soul gave Othin, sense gave Hönir,
    Heat gave Lothur and goodly hue.

19. An ash I know, Yggdrasil its name,
    With water white is the great tree wet;
    Thence comes the dews that fall in the dales,
    Green by Urth's well does it ever grow.

20. Thence come the maidens mighty in wisdom,
    Three from the dwelling down 'neath the tree;
    Urth is one named, Verthandi the next,
    On the wood they scored, and Skuld the third.
    Laws they made there, and life allotted
    To the sons of men, and set their fates.

21. The war I remember, the first in the world,
    When the gods with spears had smitten Gollveig,
    And in the hall of Hor had burned her,
    Three times burned, and three times born,
    Oft and again, yet ever she lives.

22. Heith they named her who sought their home,
    The wide-seeing witch, in magic wise;
    Minds she bewitched that were moved by her magic,
    To evil women a joy she was.

23. On the host his spear did Othin hurl,
    Then in the world did war first come;
    The wall that girdled the gods was broken,
    And the field by the warlike Wanes was trodden.

24. Then sought the gods their assembly seats,
    The holy ones, and council held,
    Whether the gods should tribute give,
    Or to all alike should worship belong.

25. Then sought the gods their assembly seats,
    The holy ones, and council held,
    To find who with venom the air had filled,
    Or had given Oth's bride to the giants' brood.

26. In swelling rage then rose up Thor,
    Seldom he sits when he such things hears,
    And the oaths were broken, the words and bonds,
    The mighty pledges between them made.

27. I know of the horn of Heimdall, hidden
    Under the high-reaching holy tree;
    On it there pours from Valfather's pledge
    A mighty stream: would you know yet more?

28. Alone I sat when the Old One sought me,
    The terror of gods, and gazed in mine eyes:
    "What hast thou to ask? why comest thou hither?
    Othin, I know where thine eye is hidden."

29. I know where Othin's eye is hidden,
    Deep in the wide-famed well of Mimir;
    Mead from the pledge of Othin each morn
    Does Mimir drink: would you know yet more?

30. Necklaces had I and rings from Heerfather[4]
    Wise was my speech and my magic wisdom;
    ... Widely I saw over all the worlds. ...
    By his side does Sigyn sit, nor is glad
    To see her mate: would you know yet more?

36. From the east there pours through poisoned vales
    With swords and daggers the river Slith. ...

37. Northward a hall in Nithavellir[5]
    Of gold there rose for Sindri's race;
    And in Okolnir another stood,
    Where the giant Brimir[6] his beer hall had.

38. A hall I saw, far from the sun,
    On Nastrond[7] it stands, and the doors face north;
    Venom drops through the smoke vent down,
    For around the walls do serpents wind.

39. I saw there wading through rivers wild
    Treacherous men and murderers too,
    And workers of ill with the wives of men;
    There Nithhogg[8] sucked the blood of the slain,
    And the wolf tore men; would you know yet more?

40. The giantess old in Ironwood sat,
    In the east, and bore the brood of Fenrir[9];
    Among these one in monster's guise
    Was soon to steal the sun from the sky.

41. There feeds he full on the flesh of the dead,
    And the home of the gods he reddens with gore;
    Dark grows the sun, and in summer soon
    Come mighty storms: would you know yet more?

42. On a hill there sat, and smote on his harp,
    Eggther the joyous, the giants' warder;
    Above him the cock in the bird wood crowed,
    Fair and red did Fjalar stand.

4 Father of the Host.
5 The Dark Fields.
6 Brimir is the giant (possibly Ymir) out of whose blood the dwarfs were created.
7 Land of the Dead.
8 Nithhogg is also called the "Dread Biter," because it is the dragon that lies beneath the Yggdrasil tree and gnaws its roots. The dragon thus symbolizes the destructive elements in the universe.
9 The Wolf.

43. Then to the gods crowed Gollinkambi,[10]
    He wakes the heroes in Othin's hall;
    And beneath the earth does another crow,
    The rust-red bird at the bars of Hel.

44. Now Garm howls loud before Gnipahellir,[11]
    The fetters will burst, and the wolf run free;
    Much do I know, and more can see
    Of the fate of the gods, the mighty in fight.

45. Brothers shall fight and fell each other,
    And sisters' sons shall kinship stain;
    Hard is it on earth, with mighty whoredom;
    Ax-time, sword-time, shields are sundered,
    Wind-time, wolf-time, ere the world falls;
    Nor ever shall men each other spare.

46. Fast move the sons of Mim,[12] and fate
    Is heard in the note of the Shrieking Horn;
    Loud blows Heimdall, the horn is aloft,
    In fear quake all who on Hel-roads are.

47. Yggdrasil shakes, and shiver on high
    The ancient limbs, and the giant is loose;
    To the head of Mim does Othin give heed,
    But the kinsman of Surt[13] shall slay him soon.

48. How fare the gods? how fare the elves?
    All Jotunheim[14] groans, the gods are at council;
    Loud roar the dwarfs by the doors of stone,
    The masters of the rocks: would you know yet more?

49. Now Garm howls loud before Gnipahellir,
    The fetters will burst, and the wolf run free;
    Much do I know, and more can see
    Of the fate of the gods, the mighty in fight.

10 Fjalar and Gollinkambi are two cocks. The crowing of the first wakes the giants, that of the second wakes the gods and heroes.
11 Garm is the dog who guards the gates of the Goddess Hel's kingdom, and Gnipahellir (the Cliff-Cave) is the entrance to the world of the dead.
12 The spirits of the water.
13 Surt is the giant who rules the fire world.
14 Jotunheim: the land of the giants.

50. From the east comes Hrym[15] with shield held high;
In giant-wrath does the serpent writhe;
O'er the waves he twists, and the tawny eagle
Gnaws corpses screaming; Naglfar[16] is loose.

51. O'er the sea from the north there sails a ship
With the people of Hel, at the helm stands Loki;
After the wolf do wild men follow,
And with them the brother of Byleist[17] goes.

52. Surt fares from the south with the scourge of branches,
The sun of the battle gods shone from his sword;
The crags are sundered, the giant-women sink,
The dead throng Hel-way, and heaven is cloven.

53. Now comes to Hlin[18] yet another hurt,
When Othin fares to fight with the wolf,
And Beli's fair slayer[19] seeks out Surt,
For there must fall the joy of Frigg.

54. Then comes Sigfather's mighty son,
Vithar,[20] to fight with the foaming wolf;
In the giant's son does he thrust his sword
Full to the heart: his father is avenged.

55. Hither there comes the son of Hlothyn,
The bright snake gapes to heaven above;
. . . Against the serpent goes Othin's son.

56. In anger smites the warder of earth[21]
Forth from their homes must all men flee;
Nine paces fares the son of Fjorgyn,[22]
And, slain by the serpent, fearless he sinks.

[15] The Leader of the Giants.

[16] Naglfar is the ship which was made of dead men's nails to carry the giants to battle.

[17] Or Loki.

[18] Hlin is another name for Frigg, Othin's wife.

[19] Beli's slayer is the god Freyr, who killed the giant Beli with his fist.

[20] Sigfather, which means "Father of Victory," is Othin. Othin's son, Vithar, is the silent god, famed for his great shield and his strength.

[21] Thor.

[22] The son of Fjorgyn is also Thor, who dies after becoming weakened by the serpent's venomous breath. Fjorgyn in the masculine form is a name for Othin. In the feminine it refers to Jorth, or earth goddess.

57. The sun turns black, earth sinks in the sea,
    The hot stars down from heaven are whirled;
    Fierce grows the steam and the life-feeding flame,
    Till fire leaps high about heaven itself.[23]

58. Now Garm howls loud before Gnipahellir,
    The fetters will burst, and the wolf run free;
    Much do I know, and more can see
    Of the fate of the gods, the mighty in fight.

59. Now do I see the earth anew
    Rise all green from the waves again;
    The cataracts fall, and the eagle flies,
    And fish he catches beneath the cliffs.

60. The gods in Ithavoll meet together,
    Of the terrible girdler of earth[24] they talk,
    And the mighty past they call to mind,
    And the ancient runes of the Ruler of Gods.[25]

61. In wondrous beauty once again
    Shall the golden tables stand mid the grass,
    Which the gods had owned in the days of old. . . .

62. Then fields unsowed bear ripened fruit,
    All ills grow better, and Baldr comes back;
    Baldr and Hoth dwell in Hropt's battle-hall,
    And the mighty gods: would you know yet more?[26]

63. Then Hönir wins the prophetic wand . . .
    And the sons of the brothers of Tveggi abide
    In Vindheim now: would you know yet more?[27]

[23] This stanza ends the destruction, and verse 59 begins the description of the new world which is to rise out of the wreck of the old.
[24] Mithgarthsorm lies in the sea surrounding the land.
[25] Othin.
[26] Baldr is the son of Othin and Frigg, and his death was the first great disaster to the gods. Hoth is Baldr's brother. Their story began when Frigg demanded that all created things, except the mistletoe, swear an oath that they would not harm her son Baldr. She excluded the mistletoe because she thought it too weak to trouble over. Loki, the troublemaker brought mistletoe to Baldr's blind brother Hoth and guided his hand in hurling the twig, which killed Baldr. In this verse, they return together. Their union is a symbol of the new age beginning.
[27] Tveggi is another name for Othin. Vindheim means "Home of the Wind."

64. More fair than the sun, a hall I see,
    Roofed with gold, on Gimle[28] it stands;
    There shall the righteous rulers dwell,
    And happiness ever there shall they have.

65. There comes on high, all power to hold,
    A mighty lord, all lands he rules. . . .

66. From below the dragon dark comes forth,
    Nithhogg flying from Nithafjoll;[29]
    The bodies of men on his wings he bears,
    The serpent bright: but now must I sink.[30]

---

[28] The Hall that stands on Gimle, the "abode of the blest," is the home of those who are dead and happy. As opposed to the abode of the tortured or unhappily dead.

[29] Nithhogg is the dragon at the roots of the Yggdrasil, mentioned in note 8. Nithafjoll means the "Dark Crags."

[30] Here Volva herself sinks back into the earth from whence she was called by Othin for his instruction. It is a sort of *conclusion* to her whole prophecy.

PART FOUR

Mesopotamia

INTRODUCTION

Sumero-Babylonian Mythology

SOMETIMES RICHNESS of sources causes almost as much confusion and difficulty as possessing scant material. This is the
case with the Semitic-Babylonian-Sumerian-Akkadian mythic
tradition. The Semitic mythology is a vast, complicated amal-
gam of cognate races whose spiritual histories engendered
several of the great religious movements of the world—Juda-
ism, Mohammedanism, and Christianity. As Philip Hitti writes,
"A faithful Moslem could with but few scruples subscribe to
most of the tenets of Christian belief. In fact, all three, Arabic,
Hebrew and Christian religions, were the product of one spirit
—the Semitic."[1]

Modern scholarship has confirmed that the Semitic religions,
which spread over the wide territory of Western Asia for more
than four thousand years, can be classified into two large
groups: the Sumero-Babylonian of the east and north lands
and the Arabian of the south. A third group of ancient peoples
—the Hebrews—stands by itself, and will be dealt with more
fully later. The history of the Hebrew religion is a unique element in the Semitic tradition, and developed separately from
the Sumero-Babylonian, even though the religion was deeply
influenced by Babylonian mythology.[2]

The Sumero-Babylonian cults first established themselves in
the midst of the old Canaanite, Aramaean, Phoenician, and
Moabite cults. Consequently, the legends and myths that have
come down to us from Mesopotamia are almost completely
of Sumero-Babylonian origin.

The confusion regarding this area and its early inhabitants
can be very great. For example, the Babylonians were first
called Akkadians after their capital Akkadu; the Canaanites
later became known as the Phoenicians; and even the geo-

---

[1] *History of the Arabs* (Middlesex, England: Penguin Books, 1963),
p. 9ff.
[2] See Stephen H. Langdon, *The Mythology of All Races*, 13 vols,
vol. V, Semitic (New York: Cooper Square Publishers, Inc., 1964),
pp. xvii ff.

graphical location of the ancient Near East is now called the Middle East. A short description of the early peoples of Arabia may therefore be helpful. By the middle of the 4th millennium B.C. the Babylonians, Assyrians, and later the Chaldeans occupied the Tigris-Euphrates Valley. To the west, the Amorites and Canaanites occupied Syria after 2500 B.C., and about 1800 B.C. the Aramaeans moved into Syria and the Hebrews into Palestine.

The history of the Semitic language also shows each of these groups had strong early ties. In fact, the term "Semitic" itself appears first in the Old Testament as *Shem*, (Gen. 10:1). Also, the Assyro-Babylonian, Aramaic, Hebrew, Phoenician, Ethiopic, and Arabic languages are often viewed by scholars as dialects developing out of one common tongue—the *Ursemitisch*. The clear inference is that the ancestors of the Babylonians, Assyrians, Chaldeans, Amorites, Aramaeans, Phoenicians, Hebrews, Arabians, and Abyssinians all lived at some time in the same place as one people.[3]

The *Babylonian Epic of Creation* is the principle surviving cosmological myth of Mesopotamia. It deals with creation being formed out of primeval chaos, the result of a titanic struggle between good and evil forces—the dragon of Chaos symbolized by the female serpent-dragon Tiamat, and the Sun God represented by the great Babylonian god Marduk. Thus, it is a battle between light and darkness. Tiamat means, literally, "bitter ocean," for it is from a hostile, bitter, watery chaos that life and form spring.

Ancient Canaanite and Hebrew Mythology

Practically nothing was known about the Canaanite myths until the first part of this century, when new tablet discoveries were made at Ras Shamra, the site of an ancient Syrian city called Ugarit.

The language of the tablets was found to be a cuneiform script belonging to the Semitic group, and closely related to Arabic, Aramaic, and Hebrew. This language is now known as Ugaritic, and the tablets of Ras Shamra, or Ugarit, were found to come from the fourteenth century B.C. and to contain very early Canaanite myths. Of the Ugarit, or Canaanite, myths

---

[3] See P. K. Hitti, op. cit., for more detailed information.

found on these tablets, it was impossible to discover whether their epic of creation was a connected narrative to the "Babylonian Epic of Creation." But from the texts that were deciphered and whose translation can be agreed upon, it is clear that there are traces of these early Ugarit or Canaanite myths in Hebrew mythology. For example, in the Myths of Baal, one of the few where scholars can agree on the translation and interpretation of the texts, it is apparent that the Hebrews took over much of the Baal myth, and transferred it to Yahweh when the Hebrew peoples settled in Canaan. In one form of the Baal myth, the forces of disorder and chaos are depicted as slaying the seven-headed dragon Lotan, a creature depicted in Hebrew myth as Leviathan. Further, it appears that the Akkadian myth of the slaying of the dragon Tiamat by Marduk was also influenced by this Canaanite myth.[4] The slaying of a dragon, which is central to the Babylonian myth of creation, also strongly influenced many legends and myths in the West. For example, turn to the legends of Perseus and Andromeda, Hercules and the Hydra, Siegfried and Fafnir, Beowulf and Grendel, and the Christian St. George slaying the Dragon.

There is obviously great intimacy and cross-influencing among the several Mesopotamian cultures. While the Hebrew religion remains unique in the Semitic tradition, it was influenced by the other groups in numerous and subtle ways. The Hebrew word for "the deep," or "the chaos of waters," is *tehôm*, which is a word generally recognized to be a Hebrew corruption of the Babylonian name Tiamat, or the chaos-dragon slain by Marduk. Other, more general resemblances among the different cultures exist—the Babylonian creation account, for instance, occurred over six days and the Hebrew account is averaged in a formal order over seven days. Further, the creation myths of Egypt and Babylon begin with a process of "begetting," and the Akkadia "Epic of Creation" starts out with a genealogical table, which was handed down from an earlier Sumerian form of their creation myth.[5]

With the settlement of Semitic peoples in Mesopotamia, the "ancient and crude Sumerian myths," as Professor S. H. Hooke calls them, had undergone heavy editorial revision. The crudity

---

[4] See "The Babylonian Account of the Creation" on page 175 for the telling of this myth.
[5] For further discussion see S. H. Hooke, *Middle Eastern Mythology* (Middlesex, England: Penguin Books, 1963).

of the early myths was suppressed, and a much greater degree of literary skill became evident when one compared the early Sumerian myth and the later Babylonian "Epic of Creation." Yet, there was no fundamental change of myths because the same general ideas about the universe and life were held by the Semitic settlers and their Sumerian predecessors. But when these myths were brought into the sphere of Hebrew imagination and belief, the revisions and reshaping were considerable, and essential changes took place. One of the main differences between the early myths and those of the Hebrews is that the traditional material—of which fragments can be found in Hebrew myths—has been considerably altered. God in the Hebrew design of the universe is seen as a moral, all-powerful, all-wise Being. There is an intelligent design to the universe. The design begins with creation and moves inexorably through its course with the Hebrew people, who are an instrument of that divine structure. Hebrew writers emphasized the fact that there was no witness to the divine act of creation. As Yahweh asks ironically of Job, "Where was thou when I laid the foundations of the earth?" (Job 38:4). There is throughout the creation episode of Genesis (verses 1 through 11 particularly), a continuous theme of divine purpose, and all the images and symbols of the Hebrew creation myth—the slaying of the dragon, the garden, the tree of knowledge of good and evil, the serpent—express a divine plan and intelligent purpose. Yet, these very same general elements can be found in the earlier Sumerian myths—albeit considerably altered by the later Hebrew writers. In the Sumerian version there is the same conception of a divine garden, of a time when sickness and death didn't exist and when wild animals did not prey on each other.

In a Sumerian poem called the "Epic of Emmerkar," the creation story so familiar to us from the Old Testament can still be recognized.[6]

> The land Dilmun is a pure place, the land Dilmun is a
>   clean place.
> The land Dilmun is a clean place, the land Dilmun is a
>   bright place.
> In Dilmun the raven uttered no cry,
> The kit uttered not the cry of the kit,
> The lion killed not,

---

[6] Adapted from S. H. Hooke, op. cit.

The wolf snatched not the lamb,
Unknown was the kid-killing dog,
Unknown was the grain-devouring boar . . .
The sick-eyed says not "I am sick-eyed,"
The sick-headed says not "I am sick-headed,"
Its [Dilmun's] old woman says not "I am an old woman,"
Its old man says not "I am an old man,"
Unbathed is the maid, no sparkling water is poured in the
    city,
Who crosses the river [of death?] utters no . . .
The wailing priests walk not about him,
The singer utters no wail,
By the side of the city he utters no lament.

In contrast to the problems presented in translating Sumerian texts, or in deciphering the mutilated Ugaritic tablets, ancient Hebrew literature and language offer numerous extant texts in good condition. Thus, there is a great deal of raw material from which to decipher Hebrew myths. Most of the Hebrew myths were collected by the final editors of the Old Testament into the first eleven chapters of Genesis, but while there are myths and legends scattered through the poetry and literature of the Israelites in fragmentary form, none is as complete as the Genesis creation story.

Arab Mythology

There is practically nothing to relate regarding Arabian mythology. Even monumental studies of Arab culture like Philip Hitti's 800-page *History of the Arabs*[7] doesn't mention any form of Arab mythology. He forcefully makes the point that we know comparatively little about the Arabian peninsula and the Semitic family it cradled. Yet, even though the origin of these many peoples is unknown, some scholars believe that Mesopotamia itself was the original home of the Arabs. Others believe the whole Arabian peninsula offers a more logical dwelling place for the Arabian people, as well as other Semitic tribes.

The fertile mythic imagination of the other Semitic peoples, and of the Indo-European races, did not seem to touch the

[7] Op. cit.

Arabs. They were profoundly imaginative in most other areas of life, but mythmaking somehow did not appeal to them or satisfy their needs. No satisfactory explanation has been offered to explain this lack of Arab mythology, although a number of scholars seem to accept the idea that the hardships of nomadic life in the desert was, in general, unfavorable for the development of Arabian mythological-religious feeling.[8] Perhaps, as some have suggested, the Arabs lacked the highly complex theological thinking of ancient Babylonia and Egypt. There is some scant evidence that the Arabs, at a comparatively late period, worshiped heavenly bodies, particularly the sun. But the sparse allusions to the sun, "The Rising One," or "The Burner," remain only provocative hints about early Arabian religious myths. But even these few myths have not survived down to the present age.

The small extant evidence about Arab myths comes from a few scholars and poets where they fleetingly mention customs and myths. Some little knowledge has also been gathered from allusions in the *Koran*, from which there are some selections in *Sun Songs*.

[8] For further, more technical discussion of these points, see James Hastings, *Encyclopedia of Religion and Ethics*, 13 vols, vol. 1 (New York: Charles Scribner's Sons, 1961), pp. 659ff.

THE BABYLONIAN ACCOUNT
OF THE CREATION[1]

Long since, when above the heaven had not been named, when the earth beneath still bore no name, when the ocean (apsu), the primeval, the generator of them, and the originator[2] Tiamat, who brought forth them both—their waters were mingled together; when fields were still unformed, reeds still nowhere to be seen.[3] Long since, when no one of the gods had been called into being, when no name had been named, no fates had been determined; then were created the gods, [all of them?]. Luchmu and Lachamu[4] were called into being as the first. Ages multiplied and days grew old; An-shar and Ki-shar[5] were created. Long were the days, and the years increased. Anu, Bel, and Ea were created. An-shar made Anu his first-born, and equal to himself. . . .[6]

Let the light be darkened, like night may it be. Upon hear-

---

[1] For more detailed information about the two Babylonian creation myths included here, see Donald A. Mackenzie, *Myths of Babylonia and Assyria* (London: The Gresham Publishing Co., n.d.); Lewis Spence, *Myths and Legends of Babylonia and Assyria* (London: George Harrap & Co., 1916); and Robert F. Harper, *Assyrian and Babylonian Literature* (New York: D. Appleton and Co., 1904).

[2] The translator notes that the word *mummu*, used here as "originator," also can mean "form," or "word." Mummu is the Logos of Babylonian thought, and is thus the creative principle and messenger of Apsu. See also note 6.

[3] Another translation renders "fields" as "dark chamber," noting that the word is often used to describe sacred buildings.

[4] Luchmu and Lachamu are the first male and female deities descended from Chaos. Alternative spellings for their names are Lahmu and Lahamu. These two deities continually waver between the old order of Chaos and the new order of the gods.

[5] The personification of the upper and lower worlds.

[6] There is a break here of some twenty lines in fragments of the Babylonian tablets. New fragments indicate that Apsu and Tiamat bewailed the creation of light and how their son Mummu helps them plan to change the light back again into darkness. After another break there begins the revolt of Tiamat against the upper gods, which follows from here on. In the Epic of Creation, Mummu, whose name means both form and word in Babylonian philosophy, belongs more to the monsters of Chaos and is simply a messenger of Apsu throughout this part of the epic. He is not connected with the principle of creative

ing this Apsu's face brightened up. They planned evil against the gods, their first-born. Tiamat, the mother of the gods, turned against them in hatred with all her force; she is bitterly enraged. To her turn the gods, without exception. Even those, whom Luchmu and Lachamu created, go to her aid. They are banded together, and at the side of Tiamat they advance; cursing the day (light), they follow Tiamat. Angry, plotting, restless by day and by night, ready for the fray, fuming and raging, they banded themselves together and started the revolt.

The mother of the deep (Tiamat), the creator of all, has made in addition invincible weapons, spawning monster serpents, sharp of tooth, and unsparing of fang; with poison instead of blood she filled their bodies. Monster vipers, fierce ones, she clothed with terror, decked them with awful splendor, and made them high of stature, that their aspect might inject terror and arouse horror. Their bodies are inflated, irresistible is their attack. . . .

"An-shar, your son, has sent me to you, the command of his said: Go, Gaga, my messenger, thou who rejoicest my heart, to Luchmu and Lachamu I will send thee; willingly then hear the command of my heart. Go, then, Gaga, stand before them, the word that I now tell thee, repeat unto them and say:

'An-sar, your son, has sent me to you, the command of his heart he intrusted to me, saying: "Tiamat, our mother, turned against us in hatred with all her force; she is bitterly enraged. To her turn the gods, without exception. Even those, created by you, go to her aid. They are banded together, and at the side of Tiamat they advance; cursing the day (light), they follow Tiamat. Angry, plotting, restless by day and by night, ready for the fray, fuming and raging, they banded themselves together and started the revolt. The mother of the deep, the creator of all, has made in addition invincible weapons, spawning monster-serpents, sharp of tooth, and unsparing of fang; with poison instead of blood she filled their bodies; monster-vipers, fierce ones, she clothed with terror, decked them with awful splendor and made them high of stature, that their aspect might inject terror and arouse horror. Their bodies are inflated, irresistible is their attack. The viper she created, the dragon, and the (monster) lachamu, the storm-giant, the mad hound,

---

reason, or cosmic reason, to be found in Sumerian and Babylonian philosophy under the same word—*mummu*. According to Sumerian thought water is the first creative principle, and through its indwelling creative reason (*mummu*) all things proceed.

and the scorpion-man, the raging storms, the fish-man, and the ram, provided with weapons, unmerciful, not dreading a fight; defiant of mind, invincible against all enemies.

In addition to creating thus these eleven, she exalted among the gods, her sons, that she had borne, Kingu, and made him greatest among them all, saying: 'To march before the host, let that be thy mission; Command the weapons to strike, the attack to begin.'

To be foremost in war, supreme in victory, she intrusted to him, and placed him upon a throne saying: 'By my charm and incantation I have raised thee to power among the gods. The dominion over all the gods I intrusted to thee. Lofty thou shalt be, thou my chosen spouse; Great be thy name in all the world.'

She then gave him the Tablets of Destiny, and laid them upon his breast saying: 'Thy command be never annulled, firm stand the word of thy mouth.'

Thus exalted and having obtained divine power, among the gods, her children, Kingu ruled. 'Let the opening of your mouth quench the fire; he that excels in bravery, let him rise in power.'

I sent Anu, but he dared not to face her. Nudimmud[7] was afraid and turned to flight. Then I called upon Marduk, the counsellor of gods, your son; to go against Tiamat he has set his mind. He opened his mouth and thus spoke unto me: 'When indeed I shall become your avenger, conquering Tiamat, and thus saving your lives, assemble all the gods and proclaim my control as supreme. In Ubshukenna[8] then enter ye all joyfully, and my authority instead of thine shall assume control. Let whatsoever I do remain unaltered; unchangeable and irrevocable be ever the command of my lips.'

Hasten, then, and quickly deliver your dominion to him, that he may go and meet your enemy, the mighty!"

Gaga departed and wended his way until he came to Luchmu and Lachamu, the gods, his fathers. There he prostrated himself, kissing the ground at their feet. He bowed down, rose up again, and told them his message. . . .

* * *

[7] Marduk, the hero of this epic, is the son of Ea, and the grandson of An-Shar. Ea is also later called Nudimmud, a title meaning "he who created man from clay," or "fashioner of the form of man." Under the title of Nudimmud, Ea is said to have made the sea his abode.

[8] Ubshukenna is the name of the Babylonian Chamber of Fates, the assembly room of the gods.

When Luchmu and Lachamu heard the tale, their heart became frightened, and the host of heaven's gods were wailing bitterly, saying: "What indeed has happened that they conceived hatred; we can not understand the actions of Tiamat."

Then they gathered together; the great gods, all of them, who decree fate, entered in before An-shar, and filled the chamber. They encouraged one another by gathering together, and sat down to the banquet, and partook of the meal; ate bread and mixed wine. The sweet wine confused their senses, drinking they waxed drunk, their bodies were filled with meat and drink; they became bewildered, their spirits rose, and to Marduk, their avenger, they intrusted the rule. Thereupon the gods placed Marduk on the royal throne, surpassing his fathers in power, he took his place as decider and ruler.

When Marduk had taken his seat, the gods addressed him in the following words: "Yea, thou art the honored among the great gods; thy destiny is unequaled, thy word is 'Anu'[9] indeed. O Marduk, thou art the honored among the great gods; thy destiny is unequaled, thy word is 'Anu' indeed. Henceforth thy command shall be absolute; to exalt and to abase shall be within thy power. Verily, thy word shall be supreme, thy command irresistible. None among the gods shall trespass upon thy dominion. May abundance, the desire of the shrines of the gods, while they are in want, be showered upon thy sanctuary! Marduk, as thou indeed wilt become our avenger, we gladly give thee dominion over the whole world. In the council of the gods may thy word always prevail; thy weapon be always victorious, crushing the foe and the enemy! O lord, spare thou the life of him that putteth his trust in thee; but as for the god who led the rebellion, pour out the blood of his life."

Thereupon the gods spread out in their midst a garment; to Marduk, their firstborn, they spoke: "Thy rule, O lord, shall surpass that of the gods, to vanish and to create—speak thou, and thus it shall be. Open thy mouth and command, and the garment shall disappear; Speak then again, and the garment shall reappear."

As Marduk uttered the word, the garment disappeared; and again he spoke, and, behold, the garment was there. When the gods, his fathers, beheld such power of his word, they greeted him joyfully, saying, "Marduk is king." They invested him with scepter, with throne, and with ring, and gave him a weapon,

[9] That is, equal in power to Anu.

unequaled, to kill the enemy. "Go, now," (they said), "and cut asunder the life-thread of Tiamat, let the winds carry her blood to hidden regions."[10]

Thus the gods, his fathers, fixed the destiny of Bel (Marduk), and wished him safety and success in the work upon which he entered. He made ready a bow, he girded his weapon upon him; He prepared a lance, to be used in the fight before him. A club he took also; in his right hand he grasped it. The bow and the quiver he hung at his side. He made a flash of lightning to go before him, whose midst he filled with destructive fire. He made a net wherewith to inclose the life of Tiamat. The four winds he set, so that she might not escape. The south wind and north wind, the east wind and west wind he brought near to the net, which his father Anu had given him. He created the evil wind, the storm, and the hurricane, The fourfold wind, the sevenfold wind, the whirlwind, the wind without equal; Then he let loose the winds which he had created, seven in all. To destroy the life of Tiamat, they swept along after him.

Then Bel (the lord) grasped the "storm," his mighty weapon, He mounted his chariot, an object unequaled for terror, harnessed to it the four fiery steeds, horses, ferocious, courageous, and swift; their teeth full of slaver, their bodies flecked with foam, trained in galloping, and knowing how to trample underfoot. And Marduk stood up in it, the battle-hero, looking toward right and toward left, making up his mind, armed with furor; Majestic halo surrounded his head. He made straight for her and drew nigh unto her. Where Tiamat the furious stood, he set his face.

Holding upon his lip a magic herb, he grasped it with his finger. At that hour the gods beheld him with admiration, The gods, his fathers, beheld him with admiration, indeed. Nearer drew Bel (the lord) anxious to fight Tiamat, and seeking to capture Kingu, her spouse.

When the latter saw him he became distraught, his mind deranged, his actions confused. And the gods, his helpers, who marched by his side, Beheld their leader's distress, and they looked terrified. Tiamat alone stood ground, turned not her neck, with her lip uttering taunts of defiance: "Against thee, O Bel, the gods take up the fight. Where they are gathered, there is now thy place."

But Bel brandished the "storm," his great weapon, and re-

---

10 "To be carried far away" is meant.

proached Tiamat for what she had done, saying: "Below thou
art mighty, yea! lofty above. But thy heart drove thee to stir
up destructive fight, until the gods forsook their fathers for
thee. Around thee thou hast gathered them, shown hatred to us.
Chosest Kingu to be thy husband and spouse, and bestowedst
upon him divine power. Thou hast planned strife. To the gods,
my fathers, thou didst evil. Thus, then, may thy host be tied,
thy weapons be bound. Stand! I and thou, come let us fight!"

But Tiamat, when she heard these words, acted like one
possessed, and she lost her senses. Tiamat shrieked out wild
and loud. Trembling, her whole frame shook through and
through. She uttered a spell, recited an incantation. And also
the gods of battle charm their weapons. Then they approached
one another, Tiamat and Marduk, the counselor of gods. To
the fight they rushed, advanced to the battle. Bel spread out
his net and enclosed her. The evil wind, following him, he let
loose against her; and when Tiamat opened her mouth to swallow the evil wind, Marduk quickly drove in the evil wind, ere
she could shut her lips. The terrible winds inflated her stomach;
she lost her reason; gasping, still wider she opened her mouth.
He seized his lance and plunged it down into her stomach.
Her entrails he pierced, cut through her heart. He over-
powered her and put an end to her life, threw down her carcass
and stood upon it.

Now that Tiamat, the leader, had been slain, her host
was broken up, her throng was scattered. The gods, her helpers, who marched by her side, trembled and feared, turned
backward to flight, and tried to escape, to save their lives. But
they were surrounded, so that none could escape; Bel took
them captive and broke their weapons. They were caught in
the net, they sat in the snare, and filled with their wailing the
whole wide world. Punishment they had to endure, and were
held in prison. The eleven creatures, also, which she had
created with terrors, a horde of demons, which had marched
by her side, he placed into fetters, and tied their hands; and he
trampled under his feet their resistance. Moreover, Kingu, who
had been great above all of them, he bound and did unto him
like unto the other gods,[11] tore away from him the Tablets of

---

[11] The captured, or "bound" gods include those who were cast
into the lower world and became the sons of Enmessara and the pest
demons, as well as the eleven monsters who were chained to the stars.
This is probably the origin of the legend of the Greek Titans who were
bound and chained to the stars by Marduk (or Asur in the Assyrian

Destiny, which hung on his breast; with his own seal he sealed them and laid them upon his own breast.

Now, after Marduk had conquered and defeated his foes, had brought to naught the arrogant adversary, thus fully completing An-shar's victory over his enemy, and attaining the purpose of Nudimmud, the valiant Marduk strengthened his hold on the gods that were captive; and returned to Tiamat, whom he had defeated. Bel-Marduk trampled down the body of Tiamat; with his merciless weapon he smashed open her skull, cut through the veins of her blood, and let the north wind carry it far away. His fathers beheld this, they rejoiced and were glad; presents and gifts they brought unto him. And Bel was appeased, as he gazed on Tiamat's dead body. Her corpse he divided, and wonderful feats he performed. He cut her into two halves, like a flat fish. He took one half and made the heavenly dome, pushed bars before it, and stationed watchmen. He gave them command not to let out its waters[12] (too freely); then he passed through the heavens, inspected the regions thereof, and in front of apsu he established the home of Nudimmud. Bel measured out the structure of apsu; and corresponding to it he fashioned Esharra (the earth). The great structure Esharra, which he had built as heaven, he made Anu, Bel, and Ea to inhabit as their own city. Thus, Bel-Marduk established the stations for the great gods. The stars and the constellations he fixed; he ordained the year, and marked off its sections. Twelve months he divided by three stars. And when the days of the year he had fixed according to the stars, he established the station of Nibir[13] to mark their bounds, that none of the days might deviate, nor be found lacking. The mansions of Bel and of Ea[14] he established with Nibir. He

---

version of the epic of creation). Marduk assigns each of the prisoners a constellation-prison house. Of the captured creatures of Tiamat, the Viper is the constellation Hydra; the dragon (or raging serpent) the Milky-Way; the storm-giant (or great lion) is Leo; the mad hound is Lupus; the scorpion-man is Sagittarius; the fish-man is Aquarius; and the ram (or fish-ram) is Capricorn. The captured deities assigned to the underworld are shown mercy by Marduk, who is said to have created mankind out of compassion for them. This meaning of the place of mankind in the divine order probably refers to the land of the dead to which men finally pass and become subjects to the gods of the lower world.

[12] Tiamat's blood is taken far south, and, legends say, gave name to the Red Sea.

[13] Jupiter, the planet of Marduk, is meant.

[14] That is, the north and south poles.

opened great gates on both sides of the firmament, made strong the bolts on the left and on the right. In the midst of heaven he placed the zenith. Nannar, the moon-god, he brought forth, and intrusted the night to him; placed him there, as the luminary of night, to mark off the days; month after month, he fashioned him as full moon, saying: "At the beginning of the moon, when evening begins, let thy horns shine, to mark off the heavens. . . .

When Marduk heard the words of the gods, his heart prompted him as he devised clever things. He opened his mouth speaking unto Ea, that which he conceived in his heart, giving him counsel. "Blood will I construct, bone will I cause to be.[15] Verily I will cause *Lilu* (man) to stand forth, verily his name is man. I will create Lilu, man. Verily let the cult services of the gods be imposed, and let them be pacified.[16] I will moreover skillfully contrive the ways of the gods. All together let them be honored and may they be divided into two parts."[17]

Ea replied to him, speaking to him a word; for the pacification of the gods he imparted to him a plan: "Let one of their brothers be given. He shall perish and men be fashioned. Let the great gods assemble, let this one be given and as for them may they be sure of it."

Marduk assembled the great gods, kindly he ordered them giving instruction. He opened his mouth charging the gods, the king speaking a word to the Anunnaki.[18] "Verily the former thing which we foretold to you is become true,[19] swearing true oaths by myself. Who was it that made war? That caused Tiamat to revolt and joined battle? Let him that made war be given. I will cause him to bear his transgression, but dwell ye in peace."

The Igigi, the great gods, replied, unto Lugal-dimmer-anki,[20]

[15] Marduk commanded that the bound Kingu, husband of Tiamat, be brought before Ea, Marduk's father. Kingu is slain and Ea creates man from his blood and clay. See notes 7 and 21.

[16] The idea that mankind was created primarily for the service of the gods is frequently found in early religious texts.

[17] This refers to the division of the gods of the lower and upper world into two groups.

[18] The "great gods" mean the Annunaki and Igigi, spirits that include the highest gods of the Babylonian pantheon; also called gods of earth and heaven.

[19] Marduk refers here to his oath that he would destroy Tiamat if he received the power to determine the fates from the assembly of gods.

[20] A title of Marduk, meaning, "King of the gods of heaven and earth."

counselor of the gods their lord. "It was Kingu that made war; that caused Tiamat to revolt and joined battle."

They bound him and brought him before Ea, Punishment they imposed upon him, they severed the arteries of his blood. With his blood Ea made mankind,[21] in the cult service of the gods, and he set the gods free. After Ea had created mankind and had imposed the cult service of the gods upon him, that work was past understanding, through skill of Marduk and the *wisdom* of Nudimmud. . . .[22]

Because he split asunder Tiamat without resting, let his name be Nibiru, who defeated Kirbish-Tiamat. May he direct the course of the stars of heaven, and pasture like sheep all the gods! Let him take hold of Tiamat; let him oppress and shorten her life. For future ages, forever and ever, Be this in force and do not cease, remain in force forever.

Because he created heaven and fashioned the earth, Father Bel called his name "Lord of the Universe." The names of the Igigi,[23] he received all of them. When Ea heard this, his heart rejoiced, that to his son such lofty names had been given. "Ea shall be his name, like mine. May he deliver all my binding commands, May he transmit all my commandments!"

Fifty names they gave him, according to the great gods, fifty names, and enhanced his power. The leader (king) shall harken to this and proclaim it again, the wise and the prudent likewise take it to heart. Let father relate it to son, and speak constantly thereof. May the shepherd and leader open his ears, that he may rejoice in the lord of gods, in Marduk! His land, then, may prosper; he himself remain sound; his word be constant and firm, his order obeyed; his command none shall change, not even a god.

---

21 The legend of a god being sacrificed in order to create man is extremely ancient, and occurs in many lands. There were in fact two Sumerian legends: one from Nippur in which the earthgoddess creates man from clay, and one from Eridu in which Ea instead is the creator of man from clay. In the Nippur version the mother-goddess Aruru creates man from clay only, without the use of a god's blood, or gives birth to man directly. But a Semitic legend agrees with the Babylonian version and states that Mami (Aruru) makes man from clay and blood at the order of Ea (or Enki). The blood is supplied in this Semitic tradition from a slain god. The Assyrian version of the creation of man has no connection with the Babylonian epic of creation. In the Assyrian legend all the great gods assist in making man from the blood of two "artisan gods" who are the sons of Ea.

22 Nudimmud is the title of Ea as creator of man. See notes 7 and 21.

23 The host of heaven's gods.

A SECOND BABYLONIAN ACCOUNT
OF THE CREATION

Not yet had been built the sacred house of the gods in a sacred place; no reed was planted, no tree yet grown; no brick was laid, no brick building reared; no house had been built, no city yet founded; No city had been built, no dwelling yet prepared. The Temple of Bel at Nippur was not yet erected; The Temple of Ishtar at Erech was not yet built. The ocean was not yet formed, Eridu[1] not yet built. The frame of the sacred house of the gods had not yet been erected.

The world was all one sea. At length there was a movement in the sea, and Eridu was erected, Esagila[2] was built; Esagila in the midst of the ocean, where the god Lugal-dul-azaga[3] dwells. Babylon was built, Esagila was completed. The Anunnaki, or lesser gods, he (Marduk) created at the same time, and made supreme the glorious city, the seat dear to their hearts. Marduk constructed an enclosure around the waters; he formed dust and heaped it up at the side of the enclosure, to make a dwelling for the gods, dear to their heart.

He created mankind. The goddess Aruru (the Potter), together with him, created the seed of mankind. He created the beasts of the field and the living creatures of the dry land. Tigris and Euphrates he formed, and set them in their places, and gave them good names: soil and grass, the marsh plant and the reed, and the forest he planted; the verdure of the field he produced; the lands, the marsh plant, the reed also; the wild cow and her young; the young wild ox; the ewe and her young, the lamb of the fold; meadows and forests also; the goat and mountain-goat he also brought forth.

[1] A city sacred to Ea at the mouth of the Persian Gulf. This refers to a kind of heavenly Eridu, corresponding to the earthly one.

[2] Normally the name for the great Marduk temple in Babylon, but here probably a temple in Eridu.

[3] This is another name for Ea, meaning literally "the god of the glorious abode."

Then Marduk filled in a terrace by the shore of the sea, as he had not done before. The plant he caused to sprout, and trees he raised. Bricks he fashioned in their place, brick buildings he made; houses he erected, cities he built. Cities he erected, dwellings he reared. Nippur he built, Ekur, the temple, he erected. Erech he built, Eanna, the temple, he erected.

ARABIAN CREATION MYTH

The Creation of Adam and Eve

The angels Gabriel, Michael, and Israfil were sent by God, one after another, to fetch for that purpose seven handfuls of earth from different depths, and of different colors; but the Earth being apprehensive of the consequence, and desiring them to represent her fear to God that the creature He designed to form would rebel against Him, and draw down His curse upon her, they returned without performing God's command; whereupon He sent Azrael on the same errand, who executed his commission without remorse, for which reason God appointed that angel to separate the souls from the bodies, being therefore called *the angel of death*.

The earth he had taken was carried into Arabia, to a place between Mecca and Tayef, where, being first kneaded by the angels, it was afterward fashioned by God himself into a human form, and left to dry for the space of forty days, or, as others say, as many years, the angels in the meantime often visiting it, and Eblis (then one of the angels who are nearest to God's presence, afterward the devil) among the rest; but he, not contented with looking on it, kicked it with his foot till it rang, and knowing God designed that creature to be his superior, took a secret resolution never to acknowledge him as such. After this, God animated the figure of clay and endued it with an intelligent soul, and when He had placed him in paradise, formed Eve out of his left side.

A PHOENICIAN (CANAANITE)
CREATION MYTH[1]

The beginning of all things was a dark and condensed windy air, or a breeze of thick air, and a chaos, turbid and black as Erebus[2]; and these were unbounded, and for a long series of ages destitute of form. But when this wind became enamored of its own first principles (the chaos), an intimate union took place, that connection was called Pothos; and it was the beginning of the creation of all things. And it (the chaos) knew not its own production; but from its embrace with the wind was generated Mot, which some call Ilus (Mud), but others, the putrefaction of a watery mixture. And from this sprang all the seed of the creation and the generation of the universe.

And there were certain animals without sensation, from which intelligent animals were produced, and these were called Zophasemim—that is, the overseers of the heavens—and they were formed in the shape of an egg; and from Mot shone forth the sun and the moon, the less and the greater stars.

And when the air began to send forth light, by its fiery influence on the sea and earth, winds were produced, and clouds, and very great defluxions and torrents of the heavenly waters. And when they were thus separated and carried out of their proper places by the heat of the sun, and all met again in the air, and were dashed against each other, thunder and lightnings

---

[1] The Phoenician (Canaanite) cosmogony is pantheistic and closely resembles the Babylonians', but was influenced heavily by other ancient cultures as well. The reader will find Greek and Jewish references throughout the Phoenician theology. The most important cosmogonies were collected in the book of Sanchoniathon, from which this myth was extracted by Eusebius. See the Babylonian creation myth on page 175, and compare the basic characteristics of these myths—darkness, chaos, generation of life from water, the birth of "the overseers of heaven" from an egg, the predominance of light, etc. Note also the important place fire has in this Canaanite myth and those of the Greeks and the Hebrews.

[2] Literally "darkness," but used generally to depict "a place of darkness" between the earth and Hades.

were the result; and at the sound of the thunder, the before mentioned intelligent animals were aroused, and startled by the noise, moved upon the earth and in the sea, male and female. . . .

Of the wind, Colpias, and his wife, Baau, which is interpreted Night, were begotten two mortal men, Aeon and Protogonos so called; and Aeon discovered food from trees.

The immediate descendants of these were Genus and Genea, and they dwelt in Phoenicia; and when there were great draughts they stretched forth their hands to heaven toward the sun; for him they supposed to be God, the only Lord of heaven, calling him Baalsamim, which, in the Phoenician dialect, signifies Lord of Heaven, but among the Greeks is equivalent to Zeus.

Afterward, by Genus, the son of Aeon and Protogonos, were begotten mortal children, whose names were Phos, Pur, and Phlox (Light, Fire, Flame). These found out the method of producing fire by rubbing pieces of wood against each other, and taught men the use thereof.

These begat sons of vast bulk and height, whose names were conferred upon the mountains which they occupied; thus, from them Capius, and Libanus, and Antilibanus, and Brathu, received their names.

Memrumus and Hypsuranius were the issue of these men. . . . Hypsuranius inhabited Tyre . . . and he fell into enmity with his brother Usous, who was the inventor of clothing for the body, which he made of the skins of the wild beasts which he could catch. And when there were violent storms of rain and wind, the trees about Tyre took fire. . . . And Usous, having taken a tree and broken off its boughs, was the first who dared to venture on the sea.

By these were begotten others, of whom one was named Agrus, the other Agronerus or Agrotus (Shed, the all powerful). . . . At Byblus he is called, by way of eminence, the greatest of the gods. These added to the houses, courts, porticoes, and crypts; husbandmen, and such as hunt with dogs, derive their origin from these: they are called also Aletae (Elim) and Titans (Rephaim).

From these were descended Amynus and Magus, who taught men to construct villages and tend flocks.

By these were begotten Misor (the Egyptian) and Sydyc— that is, Well-freed and Just. . . . From Misor descended Taaut, who invented the writing of the first letters. . . . But from Sydic descended the Cabiri . . . these first built a ship complete.

Then was one Eliun, called Hypsistus (the Most High), and his wife, named Beruth, and they dwelt about Byblus.

By these was begotten Epigeus, or Autochthon, whom they afterward called Ouranus (heaven). . . . But Ouranus succeeding to the kingdom of his father, contracted a marriage with his sister Ge, and had by her four sons, Ilus (El) who is called Cronus, and Betylus (Beth El), and Dagon, which signifies Siton (Bread Corn), and Atlas (Tammuz).

But by other wives Ouranus had much issue; at which Ge, being vexed and jealous of Ouranus, reproached him, so that they parted from each other. . . . He attempted, also, to kill the children whom he had by her. . . .

But when Cronus (El) arrived at man's estate, acting with the advice and by the assistance of Hermes Trismegistus (who was his scribe), he opposed himself to his father Ouranus. . . .

And to Cronus were born children, Persephone and Athena (Tanith); the former of whom died a virgin; but, by the advice of Athena and Hermes, Cronus made a scimitar and a spear of iron. Then Hermes addressed the allies of Cronus with magic words, and wrought in them a keen desire to make war against Ouranus in behalf of Ge. And Cronus, having thus overcome Ouranus in battle, drove him from his kingdom, and succeeded him in the imperial power.

In the battle was taken a well-beloved concubine of Ouranus; and Cronus bestowed her in marriage upon Dagon, and while she was with him she was delivered of the child she had conceived by Ouranus, and called his name Demarous (Baal-Tamar).

After these events, Cronus surrounded his habitation with a wall, and founded Byblos, the first city of Phoenicia. Afterward, Cronus having conceived a suspicion of his own brother Atlas (Tammuz), by the advice of Hermes threw him into a deep cavern in the earth and buried him.

At this time the descendants of the Dioscuri (Cabiri), having built some light and other more complete ships, put to sea; and being cast away over against Mount Casius, then constructed a temple. . . . And Cronus, having a son called Sadid, despatched him with his own sword . . . and in like manner he cut off the head of his own daughter. . . .

But in process of time, while Ouranus was still in banishment, he sent his daughters, Astarte (Ashtoreth), Rhea (Atargatis), and Dione (Baalath), and afterward Einarmene and Hora, to make war with Cronus; but Cronus gained the affections of these, and detained them with himself. Moreover, the god Ouranus devised Baetulia, contriving stones that moved as having life (which were supposed to fall from heaven).

And by Astarte Cronus had seven daughters, called Titanides or Artemides; by Rhea, also, he had seven sons, the youngest of whom was consecrated from his birth; also, by Dione he had daughters; and by Astarte again he had two other sons, Pothos (Chephets) and Eros.

And Dagon, after he had found out bread-corn and the plough, was called Zeus Arotrius.

To Sydyc, who was called the just, one of the Titanides bare Asclepius (Esmun), and to Cronus then were born also, in Peraea, three sons, Cronus bearing the same name with his father, and Zeus Belus (Baal) and Apollo (Baal-Samin).

Contemporary with these were Pontus, and Typhon, and Nereus, the father of Pontus; from Pontus descended Sidon, who, by the excellence of her singing, first invented the hymns or odes of praise, and Poseidon.

But to Demarous was born Melicarthus, who is also called Heracles. . . .

Ilus, who is Cronus, laid an ambuscade for his father Ouranus . . . and dismembered him over against the fountains and rivers . . . and the blood flowed into the fountains and the waters of the rivers. . . .

But Astarte, called the greatest, and Demarous, named Zeus (Baal-Tamar), and Adodus (Hadad), king of the gods, reigned over the country by the consent of Cronus: and Astarte put upon her head, as the mark of her sovereignty, a bull's head; and traveling about the habitable world, she found a star falling through the air, which she took up and consecrated in the holy island of Tyre.

Moreover Cronus visiting the different regions of the habitable world, gave to his daughter Athena the kingdom of Attica[3] "and when there happened a plague with a great mortality, Cronus offered up his only-begotten son, as a sacrifice to his father Ouranos, and circumcised himself, and compelled his allies to do the same. . . .

After these things, Cronus gave the city of Byblus to the goddess Baaltis, which is Dione, and Berytus to Poseidon and to the Cabiri. . . .

---

[3] This is clearly a Greek interpolation.

The god Taaut, having portrayed Ouranos, represented also the countenances of the gods Cronus and Dagon, and the sacred characters of the elements. He contrived also for Cronus the ensign of his royal power. . . .

And Cronus, visiting the South, gave all Egypt to the god Taaut, that it might be his kingdom.

These things the Cabiri, the seven sons of Sydyc, and their eighth brother, Asclepius (Esmun), first of all set down in their records in obedience to the commands of the god Taaut . . . and they delivered them to their successors and to foreigners: of whom one was Isiris (Osiris), the inventor of the three letters, the brother of Chna, who is called the first Phoenician.

PART FIVE

Greece

INTRODUCTION

THE GRECO-ROMAN religious and mythological tradition is, naturally, very familiar to Westerners. The Greek mythic tradition is one of the most complete in the world. Greek myths cover a wide range, and include creation myths; myths of specific terrain, as of the Peloponnesus, the northern mainland, Crete, and Attica; myths of individual heroes such as Herakles; and myths of epic adventures and events such as the voyage of the Argo and the battle of Troy. The Greeks also possessed nature myths, philosophical myths, allegorical myths, and myths of the hereafter. There are melded throughout these mythic tales the stories of the Greek gods, which are huge in number and powers. With such a vast array of material, and so much of it familiar to most readers, *Sun Songs* necessarily concentrates on a few central creation themes.[1]

As Dr. William Fox describes the Greek religion, its uniqueness and its inclination to personalize distant deities: "The intimate relation of the gods to the life interests of men gave the Greek religion its distinctive stamp; it brought the gods down to earth in the likeness and with the passions of men, so that in time of need, the worshiper had but to reach out his hand to touch his divine helper."[2] Thus the Greeks personified their gods in a number of guises: The sun itself was transmogrified into a charming, warm, creative individual god named Apollo; the god of sleep, a kin to death, was made personable and attractive as a beautiful, soft-fleshed, dreamy youth named Hypnos. The list goes on and on. See any of a number of good books on mythology by Robert Graves, J. G. Frazer, Joseph Campbell, and Jane Ellen Harrison for more on the Greeks and their inclination to humanize their gods.

[1] Because there was very little original Roman myth, Latin writers drew on the rich tradition of Greek mythology. In fact, practically all the myths of pan-Hellenic tradition became accepted Roman property.

[2] See *Mythology of All Races*, vol. 1, "Greek and Roman" (New York: Cooper Square Publishers, Inc., 1964), p. xlix.

The Greek historian Herodotus claimed that Homer and Hesiod together had determined what the Greek gods were like. Add Thales and you have the main communicators of Greek myths. The myths included in this book contain the traditional Greek creation themes—chaos, watery deeps, raging battles between contending gods, and the eventual creation of the sky, heaven, a shadowed underworld, earth, mankind, and all animal creatures. A main synopsis of all these events is contained in the long description by the eighth century B.C. Greek poet, Hesiod, in his book on the genealogy of the gods, *Theogony*, selections from which are included here.

THE FOUR RACES OF MAN

In the beginning the Olympians under Kronos created the race of the Men of Gold. In those days men lived like gods in unalloyed happiness. They did not toil with their hands, for earth brought forth her fruits without their aid. They did not know the sorrows of old age, and death to them was like passing away in a calm sleep. After they had gone hence, their spirits were appointed to dwell above the earth, guarding and helping the living.

The gods next created the Men of Silver, but they could not be compared in virtue and happiness with the men of "the elder age of golden peace." For many years they remained mere children and as soon as they came to the full strength and stature of manhood they refused to do homage to the gods and fell to slaying one another. After death they became the good spirits who live within the earth.

The Men of Bronze followed, springing from ash trees and having hearts which were hard and jealous, so that with them "lust and strife began to gnaw the world." All the works of their hands were wrought in bronze. Through their own inventions they fell from their high estate and from the light they passed away to the dark realm of King Hades unhonored and unremembered.

Zeus then placed upon earth the race of the Heroes who fought at Thebes and Troy, and when they came to the end of life the Olympian sent them to happy abodes at the very limits of the earth.

After the Heroes came the Men of Iron—the race of these wild days. Our lot is labor and vexation of spirit by day and night, nor will this cease until the race ends, which will be when the order of nature has been reversed and human affection turned to hatred.

SELECTIONS FROM HESIOD'S *THEOGONY*

Hail! daughters of Jove; and give the lovely song. And sing the sacred race of immortals ever-existing, who sprang from Earth and starry Heaven, and murky Night, whom the briny Deep nourished. Say, too, how at the first the gods and earth were born, and rivers and boundless deep, rushing with swollen stream, and shining stars, and the broad Heaven above; and the gods who were sprung from these, givers of good gifts; and say how they divided their wealth, and how they apportioned their honors, and how at the first they occupied Olympus with-its-many-ravines. Tell me these things, ye Muses, abiding in Olympian homes from the beginning, and say ye what was the first of them that rose.

In truth then foremost sprang Chaos, and next broad-bosomed Earth, ever secure seat of all the immortals, who inhabit the peaks of snow-capped Olympus, and dark dim Tartarus in a recess of Earth having-broad-ways, and Love, who is most beautiful among immortal gods. Love that relaxes the limbs, and in the breasts of all gods and all men, subdues their reason and prudent counsel. But from Chaos were born Erebus and black Night; and from Night again sprang forth Ether and Day, whom she bore after having conceived, by union with Erebus in love. And Earth, in sooth, bore first indeed like to herself (in size) starry Heaven, that he might shelter her around on all sides, that so she might be ever a secure seat for the blessed gods; and she brought forth vast mountains, lovely haunts of deities, the Nymphs who dwell along the woodland hills. She too bore also the barren Sea, rushing with swollen stream, the Deep, I mean, without delightsome love; but afterward, having bedded with Heaven, she bore deep-eddying Ocean, Caeus and Crius, Hyperion and Iapetus, Thea and Rhea, Themis, Mnemosyne, and Phoebe with golden coronet, and lovely Tethys.[1] And after these was born, youngest, wily Cronus, most savage of their children; and

---

[1] Tethys is the nursing-mother of all things, the force of nature nurturing all creation with moisture.

he hated his vigor-giving sire. Then brought she forth next
the Cyclops,[2] having an overbearing spirit, Brontes, and
Steropes, and stout-hearted Arges, who both gave to Jove his
thunder, and forged his lightnings. Now these, in sooth,
were in other respects, it is true, like to gods, but a single eye
was fixed in their mid-foreheads. And they from immortals
grew up speaking mortals, and Cyclops was their appropriate
name, because, I wot, in their foreheads one circular eye was
fixed. Strength, force, and contrivances were in their works.
But again, from Earth and Heaven sprung other three sons,
great and mighty, scarce to be mentioned, Cottus and Briareus
and Gyas, children exceeding proud. From the shoulders of
these moved actively a hundred hands, not brooking approach,
and to each above sturdy limbs there grew fifty heads from
their shoulders. Now monstrous strength is powerful, joined
with vast size. For of as many sons as were born of Earth and
Heaven, they were the fiercest, and were hated by their sire
from the very first: as soon as any of these was born, he would
hide them all, and not send them up to the light, in a cave of
the earth, and Heaven exulted over the work of mischief, while
huge Earth inly groaned, straitened as she was; and she
devised a subtle and evil scheme. For quickly having produced
a stock of white iron, she forged a large sickle, and gave the
word to her children, and said encouragingly, though troubled
in her heart: "Children of me and of a sire madly violent, if ye
would obey me, we shall avenge the baneful injury of your
father; for he was the first that devised acts of indignity." So
spake she, but fear seized on them all, I wot, nor did any of
them speak; till, having gathered courage, great and wily
Cronus bespake his dear mother thus in reply:

"Mother this deed at any rate I will undertake and accomplish, since for our sire, in sooth, of-detested-name, I care
not; for he was the first that devised acts of indignity."

Thus spake he, and huge Earth rejoiced much at heart,
and hid and planted him in ambush: in his hand she placed a
sickle with jagged teeth, and suggested to him all the stratagem.

Then came vast Heaven bringing Night with him, and, eager
for love, brooded around Earth, and lay stretched, I wot, on all
sides: but his son from out his ambush grasped at him with
his left hand, while in his right he took the huge sickle, long
and jagged-toothed, and hastily mowed off the genitals of his

---

[2] The Cyclops were also called the sons of Earth and Heaven because
they built mankind's strongholds and forged the bolts of Jove.

sire, and threw them back to be carried away behind him. In nowise vainly slipped they from his hand; for as many gory drops as ran thence, Earth received them all; and when the years rolled around, she gave birth to stern Furies, and mighty giants, gleaming in arms, with long spears in hand, and Nymphs whom men call Ashnymphs, (Meliae,) over the boundless earth. But the genitals, as after first severing them with the steel he had cast them into the heaving sea from the continent, so kept drifting along time up and down the deep, and all around kept rising a white foam from the immortal flesh; and in it a maiden was nourished; first she drew nigh divine Cythera, and thence came next to wave-washed Cyprus. Then forth stepped an awful, beauteous goddess; and beneath her delicate feet the verdure throve around: her gods and men name Aphrodite, the foam-sprung goddess, and fair-wreathed Cytherea—the first because she was nursed in foam, but Cytherea, because she touched at Cythera; and Cyprus-born, because she was born in wave-dashed Cyprus.

And her Eros accompanied and fair Desire followed, when first she was born, and came into the host of the gods. And from the beginning this honor hath she, and this part hath she obtained by lot among men and immortal gods, the amorous converse of maidens, their smiles and wiles, their sweet delights, their love, and blandishment. Now those sons, their fathers, mighty Heaven, called by surname Titans, upbraiding those whom he had himself begotten; and he was wont to say that, out-stretching their hands in infatuation, they had wrought a grave act, but that for it there should be vengeance hereafter.

Night bore also hateful Destiny, and black Fate, and Death: she bore Sleep likewise, she bore the tribe of dreams; these did the goddess, gloomy Night, bear after union with none. Next again Momus, and Care full-of-woes, and the Hesperides, whose care are the fair golden apples beyond the famous ocean, and trees yielding fruit; and she produced the Destinies, and ruthlessly punishing Fates, Clotho, Lachesis, and Atropos, who assign to men at their births to have good and evil; who also pursue transgressions both of men and gods, nor do the goddesses ever cease from dread wrath, before that, I wot, they have repaid sore vengeance to him, whosoever shall have sinned. Then bore pernicious Night Nemesis also, a woe to mortal men: and after her she brought forth Fraud, and Wanton-love, and mischievous Old Age, and stubborn-hearted

Strife. But odious Strife gave birth to grievous Trouble, and
Oblivion, and Famine, and tearful Woes.

Now these were born eldest daughters of Oceanus and
Tethys; there are, however, many others also: for thrice a
thousand are the tapering-ankled Ocean-nymphs, who truly
spreading far and near, bright children of the gods, haunt
everywhere alike earth and the depths of the lake. And again,
as many other rivers flowing with a ringing noise, sons of
Ocean, whom august Tethys bore: of all of whom 'twere difficult for mortal man to tell the names, but each individual
knows them, of as many as dwell around them. And Thia, overcome in the embrace of Hyperion,[3] brought forth the great
Sun, and bright Moon, and Morn, that shines for all that-
dwell-on-the-earth, and for immortal gods, who occupy broad
heaven. Eurybia too, a goddess among goddesses, bore to
Crius, after union in love, huge Astraeus, and Pallas, and
Perses, who was transcendent in all sciences. And to Astraeus
Morn brought forth the strong-spirited winds, Argestes,
Zephyr, swift-speeding Boreas, and Notus, when she, a goddess,
had mingled in love with a god. And after them the goddess
of morning produced the star Lucifer, and the brilliant stars
wherewith the heaven is crowned.

And Styx, daughter of Ocean, after union with Pallas, bore
within the house Zelus and beautous-ankled Victory; and she
gave birth to Strength and Force, illustrious children, whose
mansion is not apart from Jove, nor is there any seat, or any
way, where the god does not go before them; but ever sit they
beside deep-thundering Jupiter. For thus counseled Styx, imperishable Ocean-nymph, what time the Olympian Lightener
summoned all the immortal gods to broad Olympus, and said
that whoso of the gods would fight with him against the Titans,
none of them would he rob of his rewards, but each should
have the honor, to wit, that which he had aforetime among the
immortal gods. And he said that him, who was unhonored or
ungifted by Cronus, he would stablish in honor, and rewards,
according to justice. Then first I wot came imperishable Styx
to Olympus along with her children through the counsels of
her sire. And Jove honored her, and gave her exceeding gifts.
For her he ordained to be the great Oath-witness of the

[3] The Sun was worshiped by the Greeks as Hyperion. But Pindar
calls Thia the origin of light and brightness, and Catullus mentions Sol
as the son of Thia.

gods, and her children to be dwellers-with-her all their days. And even in such wise as he promised, he performed to them all forever: for he hath power and reigns mightily.

And next Phoebe came to the much-beloved couch of Coeus: then in truth having conceived, a goddess by love of a god, she bore dark-robed Latona, ever mild, gentle to mortals and immortal gods, mild from the beginning, most kindly within Olympus. And she bore renowned Asteria, whom erst Perses led to an ample palace to be called his bride. And she, becoming pregnant, brought forth Hecate, whom Jove, the son of Cronus, honored beyond all: and provided for her splendid gifts, to wit, to hold a share of earth and of barren sea. But she has obtained honor also from starry Heaven, and has been honored chiefly by immortal gods. For even now when anywhere some one of men upon-the-earth duly propitiates them by doing worthy sacrifice, he calls on Hecate: and abundant honor very speedily attends him, whose vows the goddess shall receive, that is to say, graciously, yea, and to him she presents wealth, for she has the power. For as many as were born of Earth and Heaven, and received a share of honor, of all these she has the lot, neither did the son of Cronus force any portion from her, nor did he take away as many honors as she had obtained by lot, among the elder gods, the Titans, but she hath them, as at the first the distribution was from the beginning. Nor, because she is sole-begotten, has the goddess obtained less of honor, and her prerogative on earth, and in heaven, and sea, but even still much more, seeing that Jove honors her. And to whom she wills, she is greatly present, and benefits him, and he is distinguished, whom she may will, in the form among the people; and when men arm for mortal-destroying war, then the goddess draws nigh to whom she will, kindly to proffer victory and to extend renown to them; and in judgment she sits beside august kings; and propitiously again, when men contend in the games, there the goddess stands near these also, and helps them.

And when he has conquered by strength and might, a man carries with ease a noble prize, and rejoicingly presents glory to his parents. Propitious is she also to be present with horsemen, whom she will; and to them who ply the rough silvery main; and they pray to Hecate and the loud-sounding Earthshaker. Easily too the glorious goddess presents an ample spoil, and easily is she wont to withdraw it when it is shown, that is, if she is so disposed in her mind. And (propitious along with Mercury to increase the flock in the folds) the herds of cattle, and the droves, and broad herds of goats, and flocks of fleecy sheep, if she choose in her heart, she makes great from small, and is wont to make less from being many. Thus, in truth, though being sole-begotten from her mother, she has been honored with rewards amidst all the immortals. And the son of Cronus made her the nursing-mother-of-children, who after her have beheld with their eyes the light of far-seeing Morn. Thus is she from the beginning nursing-mother, and such are her honors.

Rhea too, embraced by Cronus, bare renowned children, Vesta, Demeter, and Here of-the-golden-sandals, and mighty Hades, who inhabits halls beneath the earth, having a ruthless heart; and loud-resounding Neptune, and counseling Jupiter, father of gods as well as men, by whose thunder also the broad earth quakes. And then indeed did huge Cronus devour, namely, every one who came to the mother's knees from her holy womb, with this intent, that none other of the illustrious heaven-born might hold royal honor among the immortals. For he had heart from Earth and starry Heaven that it was fated for him, strong though he was, to be subdued by his own child, through the counsels of mighty Jove: wherefore he did not keep a careless watch, but lying in wait for them, kept devouring his own sons; while a grief not-to-be-forgotten possessed Rhea. But when at length she was about to bear Jove, the sire of gods as well as men, then it was that she essayed to supplicate her parents dear, Earth and starry Heaven, to contrive a plan how she might without observation bring forth her son, and take vengeance on the furies of their sin; against his children, whom great and wily Cronus devoured.

But they duly heard and complied with their dear daughter, and explained to her as much as it had been fated should come to pass concerning king Cronus, and his strong-hearted son. And they sent her to Lyctus, to the fertile tract of Crete, when I wot she was about to bear the youngest of her sons, mighty Jove: whom indeed vast Earth received from her to rear and nurture in broad Crete. Thereupon indeed came she, bearing him through the swift dark night, to Lyctus first, and took him in her hands and hid him in a deep cave 'neath the recesses of the divine earth, in the dense and wooded Aegean mount. But to the great prince, the son of Heaven, former sovereign of the gods, she gave a huge stone, having wrapped it in swathes: which he then took in his hands, and stowed away into his belly, wretch as he was, nor did he consider in his mind that against him for the future his own invincible and untroubled son was left instead of a stone, who was shortly about to subdue him by strength of hand, and to drive him from his honors, and himself to reign among the immortals.

Quickly then, I ween, throve the spirit and beauteous limbs of the king, and, as years came around, having been beguiled by the wise counsels of Earth, huge Cronus, wily counselor, let loose again his offspring, having been conquered by the arts and strength of his son. And first he disgorged the stone, since he swallowed it last.[4] This stone Jove fixed down upon the earth with-its-broad-ways, in divine Pytho, beneath the clefts of Parnassus, to be a monument thereafter, a marvel to mortal men. Then he loosed from destructive bonds his father's brethren, the sons of Heaven, whom his sire had bound in his folly. Who showed gratitude to him for his kindnesses, and gave him the thunder, and the smoking bolt, and lightning; but aforetime huge Earth had hidden them: trusting on these, he rules over mortals and immortals.

Iapetus, moreover, wedded the damsel Clymene, a fair-ankled Oceanid, and ascended into a common bed. And she bore him Atlas, a stout-hearted son, and brought forth exceeding-famous Menaetius, and artful Prometheus, full of various wiles, and Epimetheus of-erring-mind, who was from the first an evil to gain-seeking men: for he first, I wot, received from Jove the clay-formed woman, a virgin. But the insolent Menaetius wide-seeing Jove thrust down to Erebus, having stricken him with flaming lightning, on account of his arrogance, and overweening strength.

But Atlas upholds broad Heaven[5] by strong necessity, before the clear-voiced Hesperides, standing on earth's verge, with head and unwearied hands. For this lot counseling Jove apportioned to him. And wily-minded Prometheus he bound in indissoluble bonds, with painful chains, having thrust them through the middle of a column. And he urged against him an eagle with-wings-outspread: but it kept feeding on his immortal liver, while it would increase to a like size all-around

---

[4] Some interpret the myth of Cronus' vomiting the sons he had devoured as symbolizing a new birth, a renewal of life in a cosmic sense. From this beginning there arose new, divine laws which were later promulgated by the Delphic oracle. The stone, which Cronus is said to have thrown up, is connected with the Delphic oracle and was later honored at festivals.

[5] Atlas, according to Hesiod, is a doomed Titan bearing up the vault of heaven as punishment.

by night, to what the eagle with-wings-outspread had eaten
during the whole day before. This bird indeed, I wot, Hercules,
valiant son of fair-ankled Alemene, slew, and repelled from
the son of Iapetus the baneful pest, and released him from
his anxieties, not against the wishes of high-reigning Olympian
Jove, that so the renown of Thebes-sprung Hercules might be
yet more than aforetime over the many-feeding earth. Thus, I
ween, he honors his very famous son, through veneration for
him: and though incensed, ceased from the wrath which he
was before cherishing, because he strove in plans against the
almighty son of Cronus. For when gods and mortal men were
contending at Mecone, then did he set before him a huge ox,
having divided it with ready mind, studying to deceive the
wisdom of Jove. For here, on the one hand, he deposited the
flesh and entrails with rich fat on the hide, having covered it
with the belly of the ox; and there, on the other hand, he laid
down, having well disposed them with subtle art, the white
bones of the ox, covering them with white fat. Then it was that
the sire of gods and men addressed him, "Son of Iapetus, far-
famed among all kings, how unfairly, good friend, you have
divided the portions." Thus spake rebukingly Jupiter, skilled in
imperishable counsels. And him in his turn wily Prometheus
addressed, laughing low, but he was not forgetful of subtle
art: "Most glorious Jove, greatest of ever-living gods, choose
which of these your inclination within your breast bids you."
He spake, I ween, in subtlety: but Jove knowing imperishable
counsels was aware, in sooth, and not ignorant of his guile; and
was boding in his heart evils to mortal men, which also were
about to find accomplishment. Then with both hands lifted he
up the white fat. But he was incensed in mind, and wrath came
around him in spirit, when he saw the white bones of the ox
arranged with guileful art. And thenceforth the tribes of men
on the earth burn to the immortals white bones on fragrant
altars. Then cloud-compeling Jove addressed him, greatly dis-
pleased: "Son of Iapetus, skilled in wise plans beyond all, you
do not, good sir, I wot, yet forget subtle art." Thus spake in
his wrath Jove knowing imperishable counsels: from that time
forward in truth, ever mindful of the fraud, he did not give
the strength of untiring fire to wretched mortal men, who
dwell upon the earth.

But the good son of Iapetus cheated him, and stole the
far-seen splendor of untiring fire in a hollow fennel stalk; but
it stung high-thundering Jove to his heart's core, and incensed

his spirit, when he saw the radiance of fire conspicuous among
men. Forthwith then wrought he evil for men in requital for
the fire bestowed.

Thus it is not possible to deceive or overreach the mind of
Jove, for neither did Prometheus, guileless son of Iapetus,
escape from beneath his severe wrath; but a great chain, by
necessity, constrains him, very knowing though he is.

But when first their sire[6] become wroth in spirit against
Briareus, Cottus, and Gyes, he bound them with a strong
bond, admiring their overweening courage, and also their form
and bulk; and he made them dwell beneath the roomy earth:
then they in sooth in grief dwelling 'neath the earth, sat at
the verge, on the extremities of vast Earth, very long, afflicted,
having a great woe at heart; but them the son of Cronus, and
other immortal gods, whom fair-haired Rhea bore in the embrace of Cronus, by the counsels of Earth brought up again
to light: for she recounted to them at large everything, how
that they should along with those (Titans) gain victory and
splendid glory. Long time then they fought, incurring soul-
vexing toil, the Titan gods and as many as were born from
Cronus, in opposition to each other in stout conflicts; the one
side, the glorious Titans from lofty Othrys, and the other, I
wot, the gods, givers of good things, whom Rhea the fair-
haired had borne to Cronus, in union with him, from Olympus.
They then, I ween, in soul-distressing battle, one party with the
other, were fighting continuously more than ten years. Nor was
there any riddance or end of severe contention to either party,
and the completion of the war was extended equally to either.
But when at length Jove set before them all things agreeable,
to wit, nectar and ambrosia, on which the gods themselves
feed, a noble spirit grew in the breasts of all. And when they
had tasted the nectar and delightful ambrosia, then at length
the sire of gods and men addressed them: "Hear me, illustrious
children of Earth and Heaven, that I may speak what my
spirit within my breast prompts me to speak. For now a very
long space are we fighting, each in opposition to other, concerning victory and power, all our days, the Titan gods and as
many of us as are sprung from Cronus. Now do ye show
against the Titans in deadly fight both mighty force and hands
invincible, in gratitude for our mild loving-kindness, namely
after how many sufferings ye came back again to the light,
from afflictive bondage, through our counsels, from the murky

6 Their sire, Heaven.

gloom." Thus he spake; and him again the blameless Cottus addressed in answer: "Excellent Lord, thou dost not tell things unlearned by us: but we too are aware that thy wisdom is excellent, and excellent thine intellect, and that thou hast been to the immortals an averter of terrible destruction. And back again, from harsh bonds, have we come from the murky darkness, through thy thoughtful care, O royal son of Cronus, having experienced treatment unhoped for. Wherefore also now with steadfast purpose and prudent counsel we will protect thy might in dread conflict, fighting with the Titans in stout battles." Thus spake he: and the gods, givers of good, applauded, when they had heard his speech: and their spirit was eager for battle still more than before, and they stirred up unhappy strife all of them, female as well as male, on that day, both Titan gods, and as many as had sprung from Cronus, and they whom Jove sent up to light from Erebus, beneath the earth, terrible and strong, having overweening force. From the shoulders of these a hundred hands outsprung to all alike, and to each fifty heads grew from their shoulders over their sturdy limbs. They then were pitted against the Titans in deadly combat, holding huge rocks in their sturdy hands. But the Titans on the other side made strong their squadrons with alacrity, and both parties were showing work of hand and force at the same time, and the boundless sea re-echoed terribly, and earth resounded loudly, and broad heaven groaned, being shaken, and vast Olympus was convulsed from its base under the violence of the immortals, and a severe quaking came to murky Tartarus, namely, a hollow sound of countless chase of feet, and of strong battle-strokes: to such an extent, I ween, did they hurl groan-causing weapons. And the voice of both parties reached to starry heaven, as they cheered: for they came together with a great war cry.

Nor longer, in truth, did Jove restrain his fury, but then forthwith his heart was filled with fierceness, and he began also to exhibit all his force: then, I wot, from heaven and from Olympus together he went forth lightening continually: and the bolts close together with thunder and lightning flew duly from his sturdy hand, whirling a sacred flash, in frequent succession, while all-around life-giving Earth was crashing in conflagration, and the immense forests on all sides crackled loudly with fire. All land was boiling, and Ocean's streams, and the barren sea: warm vapor was circling the earth-born Titans, and the incessant blaze reached the divine dense-atmosphere, while flashing radiance of thunderbolt and lightning was bereaving their eyes of sight, strong heroes though they were. Fearful heat likewise possessed Chaos:[7] and it seemed, to look at, face to face, with the eye, and to hear the sound with the ear, just as if earth and broad heaven from above were threatening to meet: (for such an exceeding crash would have arisen from earth falling in ruins, and heaven dashing it down from above). Such a din there rose when the gods clashed in strife. The winds too at the same time were stirring up quaking and dust together, thunder and lightning and smoking bolt, shafts of the mighty Jove; and they were bearing shout and battle cry into the midst, one of another, then a terrible noise of dreadful strife was roused, strength of prowess was put forth, and the battle was inclined: but before that time assailing one another, they were fighting incessantly in stern conflict. Now the others, I wot, among the first ranks roused the keen fight, Cottus, Briareus, and Gyes insatiable in war, who truly were hurling from sturdy hands three hundred rocks close upon each other, and they had overshadowed the Titans with missiles, sent them 'neath the broad-wayed earth, and bound them in irksome bonds, (having conquered them with their hands, overhaughty though they were), as far beneath under earth as heaven is from the earth, for equal is the space from earth to murky Tartarus. For nine nights and days also would a brazen anvil be descending from the heaven, and come on the tenth to the earth: and nine days as well as nights again would a brazen anvil be descending from the earth, to reach on the tenth to Tartarus.[8] Around it moreover a brazen fence has been forged: and about it Night is poured in three rows around the neck; but above spring the roots of Earth and barren Sea. There, under murky darkness, the Titan gods lie hidden by the counsels of cloud-compeling Jupiter in a dark, drear place, where are the extremities of vast Earth. These may not go forth, for Neptune has placed above them brazen gates, and a wall goes around them on both sides. There dwell Gyes, and Cottus, and high-spirited Briareus, faithful guards of aegis-bearing Jove. And there are the sources and boundaries of dusky Earth, of murky Tartarus, of barren Sea, and starry Heaven, all in their order: boundaries oppressive and gloomy,

---

[7] Chaos is often used as the home of the gods infernal. It refers here to the wide void beneath the earth between it and the bottom of Tartarus.

[8] Hesiod tries to give an exact distance from heaven to earth and from earth to Tartarus. If an anvil is thrown from earth through the void beneath, it will take as many more days to reach Tartarus.

which also even gods abhor, a vast chasm, not even for a whole round of a year would one reach the pavement, after having first been within the gates: but hurricane to hurricane would bear him onward hither and thither, distressing him, and dreadful even to immortal gods is this prodigy, and there the dread abodes of gloomy Night stand shrouded in dark clouds. In front of these the son of Iapetus stands and holds broad Heaven, with his head and unwearied hands, unmovedly, where Night and Day also drawing nigh are wont to salute each other, as they cross the vast brazen threshold. The one is about to go down within, while the other comes forth abroad, nor ever doth the abode constrain both within; but constantly one at any rate being outside the dwelling, wanders over the earth, while the other again being within the abode, awaits the season of her journey, until it come; the one having a far-seeing light for men-on-the-earth, and the other, destructive Night, having Sleep, the brother of Death, in its hands, being shrouded in hazy mist.

And there the sons of obscure Night hold their habitation, Sleep and Death, dread gods: nor ever doth the bright sun look upon them with his rays, as he ascends the heaven, or descends from the heaven. Of whom indeed the one tarries on the earth and the broad surface of the sea, silently and soothingly to men; but of the other, iron is the heart, and brazen is his ruthless soul within his breast; and whomsoever of men he may have first caught, he holdeth: and he is hostile even to immortal gods. There in the front stand the resounding mansions of the infernal god, of mighty Hades, and awful Persephone besides; and a fierce dog keeps guard in front, a ruthless dog; and he has an evil trick: those who enter he fawns upon with his tail and both ears alike, yet he suffers them not to go forth back again, but lies in wait and devours whomsoever he may have caught going forth without the gates of strong Hades and dread Persephone.

PROMETHEUS AND THE
CREATION OF FIRE

In the halls of Inachos, king of Argos, Zeus beheld and loved the fair maiden Io; but when Here the queen knew it, she was very wroth and sought to slay her. Then Zeus changed the maiden into a heifer, to save her from the anger of Here; but presently Here learned that the heifer was the maiden whom she hated, and she went to Zeus and said, "Give me that which I shall desire," and Zeus answered, "Say on." Then Here said, "Give me that beautiful heifer which I see feeding in the pastures of King Inachos." So Zeus granted her prayer, for he liked not to confess what he had done to Io to save her from the wrath of Here; and Here took the heifer and bade Argos with the hundred eyes watch over it by night and by day.

For a long time Zeus sought how he might deliver the maiden from the vengeance of Here; but he strove in vain, for Argos never slept, and his hundred eyes saw everything around him, and none could approach without being seen and slain. At the last Zeus sent Hermes, the bright messenger of the gods, who stole gently toward Argos, playing soft music on his lute. Soothingly the sweet sounds fell upon his ear, and a deep sleep began to weigh down his eyelids, until Argos with the hundred eyes lay powerless before Hermes. Then Hermes drew his sharp sword, and with a single stroke he smote off his head; wherefore men called him the slayer of Argos with the hundred eyes. But the wrath of Here was fiercer than ever when she learned that her watchman was slain; and she swore that the heifer should have no rest, but wander in terror and pain from land to land. So she sent a gadfly to goad the heifer with its fiery sting over hill and valley, across sea and river, to torment her if she lay down to rest, and madden her with pain when she sought to sleep. In grief and madness she fled from the pastures of Inachos, past the city of Erechtheus into the land of Kadmos the Theban. On and on still she went, resting not by night or day, through the Dorian and Thessalian plains, until at last she came to the wild Thrakian land. Her feet bled

on the sharp stones; her body was torn by the thorns and
brambles, and tortured by the stings of the fearful gadfly. Still
she fled on and on, while the tears streamed often down her
cheeks, and her moaning showed the greatness of her agony.
"O Zeus," she said, "dost thou not see me in my misery? Thou
didst tell me once of thy love; and dost thou suffer me now to
be driven thus wildly from land to land, without hope of comfort or rest? Slay me at once, I pray thee, or suffer me to sink
into the deep sea, that so I may put off the sore burden of my
woe."

But Io knew not that, while she spake, one heard her who
had suffered even harder things from Zeus. Far above her head,
towards the desolate crags of Caucasus, the wild eagle soared
shrieking in the sky, and the vulture hovered near, as though
waiting close to some dying man till death should leave him for
its prey. Dark snow clouds brooded heavily on the mountain,
the icy wind crept lazily through the frozen air; and Io thought
that the hour of her death was come. Then, as she raised her
head, she saw far off a giant form, which seemed fastened by
nails to the naked rock; and a low groan reached her ear, as of
one in mortal pain, and she heard a voice which said, "Whence
comest thou, daughter of Inachos, into this savage wilderness?
Hath the love of Zeus driven thee thus to the icy corners of the
earth?" Then Io gazed at him in wonder and awe, and said,
"How dost thou know my name and my sorrows? and what is
thine own wrong? Tell me (if it is given to thee to know) what
awaits thee and me in the time to come; for sure I am that
thou art no mortal man. Thy giant form is as the form of gods
or heroes, who come down sometimes to mingle with the
sons of men; and great must be the wrath of Zeus, that thou
shouldst be thus tormented here." Then he said, "Maiden,
thou seest the Titan Prometheus, who brought down fire for
the children of men, and taught them how to build themselves
houses and till the earth, and how to win for themselves food
and clothing. I gave them wise thoughts and good laws and
prudent counsel, and raised them from the life of beasts to a
life which was fit for speaking men. But the son of Kronos
was afraid at my doings, lest, with the aid of men, I might hurl
him from his place and set up new gods upon his throne. So
he forgot all my good deeds in times past, how I had aided him
when the earth-born giants sought to destroy his power and
heaped rock on rock and crag on crag to smite him on his
throne; and he caught me by craft, telling me in smooth words

how that he was my friend, and that my honor should not fail in the halls of Olympos. So he took me unawares and bound me with iron chains, and bade Hephaistos take and fasten me to this mountainside, where the frost and wind and heat scorch and torment me by day and night, and the vulture gnaws my heart with its merciless beak. But my spirit is not wholly cast down; for I know that I have done good to the sons of men, and that they honor the Titan Prometheus, who has saved them from cold and hunger and sickness. And well I know, also, that the reign of Zeus shall one day come to an end, and that another shall sit at length upon his throne, even as now he sits on the throne of his father Kronos. Hither come, also, those who seek to comfort me; and thou seest before thee the daughters of Okeanos, who have but now left the green halls of their father to talk with me. Listen then to me, daughter of Inachos, and I will tell thee what shall befall thee in time to come. Hence from the ice-bound chain of Caucasus thou shalt roam into the Scythian land and the regions of the Chalybes. Thence thou shalt come to the dwelling place of the Amazons on the banks of the river Thermodon; these shall guide thee on thy way, until at length thou shalt come to a strait, which thou wilt cross, and which shall tell by its name forever where the heifer passed from Europe into Asia. But the end of thy wandering is not yet."

. . .

Long years of pain and sorrow await thee still; but my griefs shall endure for many generations. It avails not now to weep; but this comfort thou hast, that thy lot is happier than mine; and for both of us remains the surety that the right shall at last conquer, and the power of Zeus shall be brought low, even as the power of Kronos, whom he hurled from his ancient throne. Depart hence quickly, for I see Hermes the messenger drawing nigh, and perchance he comes with fresh torments for thee and me."

So Io went on her weary road, and Hermes drew nigh to Prometheus, and bade him once again yield himself to the will of the mighty Zeus. But Prometheus laughed him to scorn; and as Hermes turned to go away, the icy wind came shrieking through the air, and the dark cloud sank lower and lower down the hillside, until it covered the rock on which the body of the Titan was nailed; and the great mountain heaved with the earthquake, and the blazing thunderbolts darted fearfully through the sky. Brighter and brighter flashed the lightning, and louder pealed the thunder in the ears of Prometheus, but he quailed not for all the fiery majesty of Zeus; and still, as the storm grew fiercer and the curls of fire were wreathed around his form, his voice was heard amid the din and roar, and it spake of the day when the good shall triumph, and unjust power shall be crushed and destroyed forever.

SYMPOSIUM, PLATO'S DIALOGUES[1]

First of all I must explain the real nature of man, and the change which it has undergone—for in the beginning we were nothing like we are now. For one thing, the race was divided into three; that is to say, besides the two sexes, male and female, which we have at present, there was a third which partook of the nature of both, and for which we still have a name, though the creature itself is forgotten. For though "hermaphrodite" is only used nowadays as a term of contempt, there really was a man-woman in those days, a being which was half male and half female.

And secondly, gentlemen, each of these beings was globular in shape, with rounded back and sides, four arms and four legs, and two faces, both the same, on a cylindrical neck, and one head, with one face one side and one the other, and four ears, and two lots of privates, and all the other parts to match. They walked erect, as we do ourselves, backward or forward, whichever they pleased, but when they broke into a run they simply stuck their legs straight out and went whirling round and round like a clown turning cartwheels. And since they had eight legs, if you count their arms as well, you can imagine that they went bowling along at a pretty good speed.

The three sexes, I may say, arose as follows. The males were descended from the Sun, the females from the Earth, and the hermaphrodites from the Moon, which partakes of either sex, and they were round and they *went* round, because they took after their parents. And such, gentlemen, were their strength and energy, and such their arrogance, that they actually tried—like Ephialtes and Otus in Homer—to scale the heights of heaven and set upon the gods.

---

[1] Supposedly attributed to Aristophanes, this Greek account of the creation of man is not to be taken seriously as a creation myth. Its irreverent approach is revealing, however, of the Greeks' attitude toward the gods, creation, and humanity: The Greek gods were not the creators of the human race, for both came into existence from the bosom of the earth.

At this Zeus took counsel with the other gods as to what was to be done. They found themselves in rather an awkward position; they didn't want to blast them out of existence with thunderbolts as they did the giants, because that would be saying goodbye to all their offerings and devotions, but at the same time they couldn't let them get altogether out of hand. At last, however, after racking his brains, Zeus offered a solution.

I think I can see my way, he said, to put an end to this disturbance by weakening these people without destroying them. What I propose to do is to cut them all in half, thus killing two birds with one stone, for each one will be only half as strong, and there'll be twice as many of them, which will suit us very nicely. They can walk about, upright, on their two legs, and if, said Zeus, I have any more trouble with them, I shall split them up again, and they'll have to hop about on one.

So saying, he cut them all in half just as you or I might chop up sorb apples for pickling, or slice an egg with a hair. And as each half was ready he told Apollo to turn its face, with the half-neck that was left, toward the side that was cut away—thinking that the sight of such a gash might frighten it into keeping quiet—and then to heal the whole thing up. So Apollo turned their faces back to front, and, pulling in the skin all the way around, he stretched it over what we now call the belly—like those bags you pull together with a string—and tied up the one remaining opening so as to form what we call the navel. As for the creases that were left, he smoothed most of them away, finishing off the chest with the sort of tool a cobbler uses to smooth down the leather on the last, but he left a few puckers round about the belly and the navel, to remind us of what we suffered long ago.

Now, when the work of bisection was complete it left each half with a desperate yearning for the other, and they ran together and flung their arms around each other's necks, and asked for nothing better than to be rolled into one. So much so, that they began to die of hunger and general inertia, for neither would do anything without the other. And whenever one half was left alone by the death of its mate, it wandered about questing and clasping in the hope of finding a spare half-woman—or a whole woman, as we should call her nowadays—or half a man. And so the race was dying out.

Fortunately, however, Zeus felt so sorry for them that he devised another scheme. He moved their privates around to the front, for of course they had originally been on the out-side—which was now the back—and they had begotten and conceived not upon each other, but, like the grasshoppers, upon the earth. So now, as I say, he moved their members around to the front and made them propagate among them-selves, the male begetting upon the female—the idea being that if, in all these clippings and claspings, a man should chance upon a woman, conception would take place and the race would be continued, while if man should conjugate with a man, he might at least obtain such satisfaction as would allow him to turn his attention and his energies to the everyday affairs of life. So you see, gentlemen, how far back we can trace our innate love for one another, and how this love is always trying to reintegrate our former nature, to make two into one, and to bridge the gulf between one human being and another.

PART SIX

Africa

INTRODUCTION

As IN THE sections on North and South America, to deal with the mythology of a whole continent briefly is difficult, if not impossible. The African continent created a number of independent cultures, each with highly individualized myths. However, because there are fewer barriers to intra-group communication when dealing with a large land mass, there can be found many ideas, customs, and beliefs held in common between African groups.

As with most other ancient cultures, African myths include the idea of a Supreme Being, even though it is only a vague concept liberally sprinkled throughout the native myths.[1] The high god of African myths, however, is not always a "creator" in our sense of the word. Although the high god does often create man, African myths seem to accept that other forms of life—the inanimate world, and sometimes even all animals—are already in existence. But also, man is sometimes described as simply appearing on earth, with his origin nowhere discussed. Thus, many African myths show mankind pre-existing, as a kind of spontaneous creation from a tree, a rock, or even a hole in the ground. The Masai, for example, say that "when God came to prepare the world, he found there a Dorobo (a hunting tribe), an elephant, and a serpent." In the Baganda myth included in *Sun Songs*, Kintu, the first man who descends from heaven, is strangely isolated. His character is as unknown to the denizens of heaven as to those of earth. Kintu's survival on the earth is dependent upon his cow, until one day the sons of heaven and their sister also come down to earth. The marriage between the sister and

---

[1] Some authorities, such as A. B. Ellis, deny that the concept of a high god exists in Africa, and assert that such an idea was introduced by Europeans and missionaries. Others disagree, arguing that the names or titles of a high god exist throughout African languages. See R. S. Rattray, *Hausa Folklore, Customs, Proverbs*, etc., 2 vols. (Oxford, 1913), and Rattray's *Ashanti Proverbs* (Oxford, 1913).

Kintu, of course, leads to the successful creation of the world. The couple cultivated the land, grew crops, husbanded animal stock and, in effect, showed succeeding generations of mankind the tools of survival and civilization.

As the myths included in *Sun Songs* will show, death plays a central role in the African creation tales. Death is frequently connected in some way with the high god, and some tribes (like the Baganda) make him a son of heaven. In the more highly developed African religious myths, we again see many nature gods contending for power. Animals, both in flesh and spirit or magical form, also frequently play a central role. In fact, animals are central to a human's success or survival, as in the tale of Kintu. Interestingly, many tribes seem to be unconcerned about the creation of the earth, accepting its existence before all else was created.

CREATION

At first there was no earth. There was Okun, the ocean, stretching over all things. Above the ocean was Olorun, the sky. Okun and Olorun contained all and possessed all things that there were.

Olorun had two sons. The elder's name was Orisha. The name of the younger son was Odudua. They were living together in the sky.

Olorun called Orisha to him. He gave him a handful of earth and a hen with five claws. Olorun said to him, "Go down and make land upon Okun, the ocean."

Orisha went. On the way he found some palm wine. He drank some of it and became drunk. Then he fell asleep.

Olorun saw this. He then called Odudua and said to him, "Thy elder brother has become drunk on his way below and has fallen asleep. Go thou, take this handful of earth and the hen with five claws and make land upon Okun."

Odudua went. He took the handful of earth. He went down and laid it on the ocean. He put the hen with five claws on it. The hen began to scratch and spread the handful of earth about and forced the water aside. Much land then appeared.

The ocean grew less and less at this place and ran away through a small hole. From this small hole came holy water. This was the source of the holy river, the water of which heals and never fails.

Now Orisha was very angry because he himself had not created the earth. He and his brother fought for a long time and then both went underground and were never seen again.

WHY THE SUN SHINES BY DAY AND THE MOON BY NIGHT

In the beginning of the world the king called the people together to be given their tasks. He sent out messengers for them. He sent the dove to call the moon, and the bat to call the sun. Each messenger was given a certain time to go and return, so that they might all arrive together.

The dove went to call the moon and brought her, and the king said, "I will give you, then, the office the sun should have had, namely, that of shining by night. When you first shine people will beat their drums and blow their trumpets; they will also bring out their fetishes for you to see them, and the fetishes of twins. These are the honors I give you."

After giving the moon her office and honors, the king waited for the bat to bring the sun; but as the bat did not come the king sent the dove to look for her and bring her.

The dove went and returned with the sun. Then the king said, "Because you have stayed so long I have given to the moon the office I meant to give to you. Now I will give you the office of showing people the way to walk about."

It was on this account that the sun hated the bat, because he loitered on the way when sent to call him, and stayed longer than the time given by the king. And very soon thereafter the sun had a chance to be even with the bat.

The bat later lived at a place with only its aged mother. Shortly after their settling there, the mother suddenly fell sick unto death. The bat called for the antelope, and said to him, "Make some medicine for my mother." The antelope looked steadily at her to see what her disease was. Then he told the bat, "There is no one who has the medicine that will cure your mother except the sun." After saying this, the antelope returned home.

On another day, early in the morning, the bat arose to go to call the sun. He did not start until about seven o'clock. He met the sun on the road about eleven o'clock. And he said to the sun, "My journey was on the way to see you."

The sun replied, "If you have a word to say, speak!"

So the bat requested, "Come! make some medicine for my mother. She is sick."

But the sun replied, "I can't go to make medicine unless you meet me in my house; not here on the road. Go back; and come to me at my house tomorrow."

So the bat went back home. And the day darkened, night came, and all went to sleep.

At six o'clock the next day, the bat started out to call the sun. About nine o'clock, he met the sun on the path, and he told the sun what he had come for. But the sun said to him, "Whenever I leave my house, I do not go back, but I keep on to the end of my journey. Go back, for another day." The bat returned home again.

He made other journeys in order to see the sun at his house, five successive days; but every day he was late, and met the sun already on the way of his own journey for his own business.

Finally, on the seventh day, the bat's mother died. Then the bat, in his grief said, "It is the sun who has killed my mother! Had he made some medicine for her, she would have become well."

Very many people from afar came together that day at the mourning for the dead. The funeral was held from six o'clock in the morning until eleven o'clock of the next day. At that hour, the bat announced, "Let her be taken to the grave." He called other beasts to go into the house together with him, in order to carry out the corpse. They took up the body, and carried it on the way to the grave.

On their arrival at the grave, these beasts said to the bat, "We have a rule that, before we bury a person, we must first look upon the face to see who it is." They then opened the coffin.

When they had looked on the face, they said, "No! we can't bury this person; for, it is not our relative, it does not belong to us beasts. This person looks like us because he has teeth. And it also has a head like us. But, that it has wings, makes it look like a bird. It is a bird. Call for the birds! We shall leave." So they departed.

Then the bat called the birds to come. They came, big and little; pelicans, eagles, herons, and all the others. When they all had come together, they said to the bat, "Show us the dead body."

He said to them, "Here it is! Come! Look upon it!"

They looked at it very carefully. Then they said, "Yes! it

resembles us; for, it has wings as we have. But, about the teeth, no! We birds, none of us, have any teeth. This person does not resemble us with those teeth. It does not belong to us."

And all the birds stepped aside.

During the time that the talking had been going on, ants had come and laid hold of the body, and could not be driven away. Then one of the birds said to the bat, "I told you, you ought not to delay the burial, for many things might happen."

And all the birds and beasts went away.

The bat, left alone, said to himself, "The wicked sun alone is to blame for all of my troubles. If he had made some medicine, my mother would not be dead. So, I, the bat, and the sun shall not look on each other again. We shall have no friendship. When he appears, I shall hide myself. I won't meet him or look at him."

"And," he added, "I shall mourn for my mother always. I will make no visits. I will walk about only at night, not in the daytime, lest I meet the sun or other people."

HOW ANIMALS CAME INTO
THE WORLD

Famine in a strange land had lasted nearly three years. In that land lived a man called Kweku Tsin. As he was very hungry, Kweku Tsin looked daily in the forest to find food.

One day he happened to see three palm kernels on the ground. He picked up two stones with which to crack them. The first nut, however, slipped when he hit it, and rolled into a hole behind him. The same thing happened to the second and to the third. This annoyed Kweku very much, and he determined to go down the hole to seek his lost palm kernels.

When he reached the hole, however, he was surprised to learn that it was the entrance to a town, of which he had never before even heard. When he entered it he found deathlike silence everywhere. He cried aloud, "Is there nobody in this town?" And soon he heard a voice in reply. He went in that direction and found an old woman creeping along one of the streets. She stopped and asked why he had come there, and he quickly told her.

The old woman was very kind and sympathetic; and promised to help him, if he would do as she told him. "Go into the garden and listen attentively," said she. "You will hear the yams speak. Pass by any yam that says, 'Dig me out, dig me out!' But take the one that says, 'Do not dig me out!' Then bring it to me."

When he brought the yam, she directed him to remove the peel from it and throw the yam away. He was then to boil the rind, and while boiling, it would become a yam.

It turned out as she said, and they sat down to eat some of it. Before taking the meal the old woman requested Kweku not to look at her while she ate. He was very polite and obedient, and kept his head turned.

In the evening the old woman sent him into the garden to get one of the drums which were there. She told him, "If you come to a drum which says, 'Ding-ding,' when you touch it, take it. But be very careful not to take one which says, 'Dong-dong.' "

He carefully obeyed her orders. When he showed her the drum, she looked pleased and told him, to his great delight, that he had only to beat it if at any time he were hungry. That would bring him food in plenty. He thanked the old woman very much and went home.

As soon as Kweku Tsin reached his own home, he called his household together, and then beat the drum. All at once, food of every kind came before them, and they all ate and ate until they wanted no more.

The next day Kweku Tsin called all the people of the village together in the public square, and then beat the drum once more. In this way every family received sufficient food for its wants, and all thanked Kweku Tsin very much for thus giving them what they so much needed.

Anansi, Kweku's father, however, was jealous of his son who was able to feed the whole village. Anansi thought he, too, should have a magic drum. The people then would be grateful to him instead of to his son.

He asked the young man, therefore, where he had found the wonderful drum. His son at first refused to tell him, but Anansi gave him no peace until he had learned the whole story.

He then immediately went off toward the hole leading to the town. He carried with him an old nut which he pretended to crack; but he threw it into the hole, and jumped in after it, and hurried along to the silent village.

When he came to the first house, he cried, "Is there no one in this town?" The old woman answered as she did when the son came, and Anansi entered her home.

He was in too much haste to be polite and spoke to her very rudely, saying, "Hurry up, old woman, and get me something to eat."

The women politely asked him to go into the garden and choose the yam which should say, "Do not dig me out."

Anansi laughed at her and said, "You surely take me for a dunce. If the yam does not want me to dig it out I would be very silly to do so. I shall take the one which wants to be dug out." And so he did.

When he brought the yam to the old woman she told him, as she had told his son, to throw away the inside and boil the rind; but he refused to obey.

"Whoever heard of such a silly thing as throwing away the inside and boiling the peel," said Anansi.

[He threw away the inside] and the yam turned into stones. He then saw that it was better to do as he had been told, and boil the rind. While boiling, the rind turned into yam.

Anansi then turned in anger to the old woman and said, "You are a witch."

She took no notice of his words, but went on putting the food on the table. She placed his dinner on a small table, lower than her own, saying, "You must not look at me while I eat."

He rudely replied, "Indeed, I will look at you if I choose. And I will have my dinner at your table, not at that small one."

Again she said nothing, but she did not touch her dinner. Anansi ate his own and hers too.

When he had finished eating he said, "Now go into the garden and choose a drum. Do not take the one which sounds 'Ding-dong'; take the one which says 'Ding-ding.'"

Anansi then said, "Do you think I will take your advice, you witch? No. I will choose the drum which says 'Ding-dong.' You are just trying to play a trick on me."

He did as he wished. Having secured the drum he marched off without so much as thanking the old woman.

No sooner had he reached home, than he thought to show off his new power to the villagers. He called all to the public square, and told them to bring dishes and trays, as he was going to supply them with food. The people in great joy rushed to the spot. Anansi took his position in the midst of them, and began to beat his drum. To his surprise and horror, instead of the abundance of foodstuffs which Kweku had summoned, Anansi saw, rushing toward him, beasts and serpents of all kinds. Such things had never been seen on the earth before.

All the people except Anansi fled in every direction. He was too frightened to move and was quickly devoured by the animals. Thus he had been speedily punished for his disobedience.

Fortunately, Kweku, with his mother and sisters, had been at the outer edge of the crowd, and they easily escaped into shelter. The animals then went in all directions and ever since they have roamed wild in the forests.

SHILLUK CREATION MYTH

(White Nile)

The creator Juok molded all men out of earth, and . . . while he was engaged in the work of creation he wandered about the world. In the land of the whites he found a pure white earth or sand, and out of it he shaped white men. Then he came to the land of Egypt and out of the mud of the Nile he made red or brown men. Lastly, he came to the land of the Shilluks, and finding there black earth he created black men out of it. The way in which he modeled men was this. He took a lump of earth and said to himself, "I will make man, but he must be able to walk and run and go out into the fields, so I will give him two long legs, like the flamingo." Having done so, he thought again, "The man must be able to cultivate his millet, so I will give him two arms, one to hold the hoe, and the other to tear up the weeds." So he gave him two arms. Then he thought again, "The man must be able to see his millet, so I will give him two eyes." He did so accordingly. Next he thought to himself, "The man must be able to eat his millet, so I will give him a mouth." And a mouth he gave him accordingly. After that he thought within himself, "The man must be able to dance and speak and sing and shout, and for these purposes he must have a tongue." And a tongue he gave him accordingly. Lastly, the deity said to himself, "The man must be able to hear the noise of the dance and the speech of great men, and for that he needs two ears." So two ears he gave him, and sent him out into the world a perfect man.

PART SEVEN

Judeo-Christian

INTRODUCTION

Cosmic creation in the Judeo-Christian tradition is both simple and complex. Simple because the first three chapters of the Old Testament describe the creation for both religions. It is a book that sets the theme for the entire Bible, both Old and New Testament: that God created the universe, and that man is the pinnacle of His creation. This much is clear, but from here on everything becomes complex and the source of generations of theological arguments and schisms.

The book of Genesis is a weaving of various Hebrew writings that were, like much religious literature, edited and re-edited until they took their present shape. And while it is basically simple in structure, many commentators and critics agree with the scholar Franz Delitzsch, that "Genesis is the most difficult book of the Old Testament."[1] The basic reason for this difficulty is that the book is allegorical and symbolic. Gregory of Nyssa (c. 390 A.D.) describes the creation in Genesis as "ideas in the form of a story." The allegorical nature of the creation stories was accepted by early prominent churchmen up to the time of Augustine, and perhaps even to the middle of the fifth century. From that time on, the creation stories were increasingly believed as literal, historical records.

Another confusing aspect of the Judeo-Christian view of creation is that there are actually two clearly separate, irreconcilable creation stories in the book of Genesis. The first story (in Genesis Chapter 1, to Chapter 2, verse 3) relates how God created the cosmos, the light, the "garments" of the world, and the order of beings. The second creation story begins with Genesis, Chapter 2, Verse 4, and ends with Chapter 3, Verse 24. The second creation story gives the creator a name (Jahweh 'Elohim), creates man from the dust, and places him in a garden in Eden. Trees spring forth, rivers

---

[1] *New Commentary on Genesis*, 2 vols. (Edinburgh: T. & T. Clark, 1888), vol. 1, p. 57.

flow through the garden, and man names the animals and birds. The Creator causes man to fall asleep and Elohim creates woman from his rib. The end of the second creation tale is, of course, familiar to all Western readers as Adam and Eve transgress and are expelled from the garden.

In the first creation story, there is a description of primeval chaos, a dark, formless watery abyss out of which the world of order and light was formed. This is very similar to many creation myths in *Sun Songs*, especially the Babylonian creation that clearly influenced the Hebrew conception.[2] Creation then continues through a series of eight separate divine acts: (1) the creation of light and its separation from the primeval darkness; (2) division of the watery chaos by the firmament; (3) separation of land from the water; (4) covering of the earth with vegetation; (5) formation of the stars and other heavenly bodies; (6) creation of fishes and birds; (7) creation of land animals; (8) creation of man (and woman) in the image of God, and who have dominion over the animals.

In the second creation story, which is probably the older of the two, the earth is originally made by Jahweh and is an arid wasteland where no plant or living thing could grow. It is also mentioned that there is no "man" to till the ground. Here man is made superior to the animals by being created earlier, rather than last as in the first story. As James Hastings points out, it is probable that these conflicting creation tales are symbolic rather than literal descriptions, and that they are fragments of a fuller cosmogony that has been abridged and used as a prologue to the story of Paradise in the Garden of Eden and the Fall.[3]

By general agreement among scholars, the first creation story has been assigned to writers after the exile, when it suffered heavy editing. The second creation story is placed much earlier, and seems, according to some analysts, to be the work of a single hand. But perhaps the contrast between these two creation stories can best be seen by setting them next to each other in summary form.[4]

[2] See the introduction to Part Four, Mesopotamia, for a further discussion of the interrelationships between Hebrew myths and that of the other Semitic peoples.

[3] *Dictionary of the Bible* (New York: Charles Scribner's Sons, 1909), p. 164. For a complete analysis of this peculiar fact of Judeo-Christian creation, see James S. Forrester-Brown, *The Two Creation Stories in Genesis* (Berkeley & London: Shambhala, 1974).

[4] Adapted from S. H. Hooke, *Middle Eastern Mythology* (Middlesex, England: Penguin Books, 1963.)

Chapter 1-2:4	Chapter 2:4-25
1. Original state of universe is a watery chaos.	1. Original state of universe is waterless waste, without vegetation.
2. Work of creation is given to Elohim, and divided into six separate operations, each belonging to one day.	2. The work of creation is assigned to Yahweh Elohim, and no note of time is given.

Order of creation is:	*Order of creation is:*
1. Light.	1. Man, made out of the dust.
2. The firmament-heaven.	2. The Garden, to the east, in Eden.
3. The dry land—earth. Separation of earth from sea.	3. Trees of every kind, including the Tree of Life, and the Tree of the knowledge of Good and Evil.
4. Vegetation—three orders.	4. Animals, beasts, and birds (no mention of fish).
5. The heavenly bodies— sun, moon, and stars.	5. Woman, created out of man.
6. Birds and fishes.	
7. Animals and man, male and female together.	

There are traces of other creation myths not a part of the two in Genesis scattered throughout the Old Testament. In Job, Chapter 38, for example, there is the lovely poetic allusion to creation where Yahweh describes laying the foundations of the earth, "when the morning stars sang together, and all the sons of God shouted for joy." This paean to creation sounds very much like the rejoicing of the gods in Marduk's victory over the dragon Tiamat, rather than either of the Genesis creations. In verse 11, Yahweh also points to how he calmed the watery chaos, a theme reminiscent of the

Babylonian creation. As Yahweh says, "Hitherto shalt thou come, but no further, and here shall thy proud waves be stayed."

Finally, it is perhaps important to point out that using the category of "myth" in relation to the Gospels does not call into question their historical character. The function of myth here is to express by imagery and symbols those events that take place outside the observable causes of history. For there are many who believe that God enters into nature at moments when life and its movement through time seem beyond causes. At these moments myth becomes an extension of human perception, a delving into the dark and mysterious corners of our origins.

JUDEO-CHRISTIAN CREATION

Genesis

CHAPTER 1

In the beginning God created the heaven and the earth.

2 And the earth was without form, and void; and darkness *was* upon the face of the deep. And the Spirit of God moved upon the face of the waters.

3 And God said, Let there be light: and there was light.

4 And God saw the light, that *it was* good: and God divided the light from the darkness.

5 And God called the light Day, and the darkness he called Night. And the evening and the morning were the first day.

6 And God said, Let there be a firmament in the midst of the waters, and let it divide the waters from the waters.

7 And God made the firmament, and divided the waters which *were* under the firmament from the waters which *were* above the firmament: and it was so.

8 And God called the firmament Heaven. And the evening and the morning were the second day.

9 And God said, Let the waters under the heaven be gathered together unto one place, and let the dry *land* appear: and it was so.

10 And God called the dry *land* Earth; and the gathering together of the waters called the Seas: and God saw that *it was* good.

11 And God said, Let the earth bring forth grass, the herb yielding seed, *and* the fruit tree yielding fruit after his kind, whose seed *is* in itself, upon the earth: and it was so.

12 And the earth brought forth grass, *and* herb yielding seed after his kind, and the tree yielding fruit, whose seed *was* in itself, after his kind: and God saw that *it was* good.

13 And the evening and the morning were the third day.

14 And God said, Let there be lights in the firmament of the heaven to divide the day from the night; and let them be for signs, and for seasons, and for days, and years:

15 And let them be for lights in the firmament of the heaven to give light upon the earth: and it was so.

16 And God made two great lights; the greater light to rule the day, and the lesser light to rule the night: *he made* the stars also.

17 And God set them in the firmament of the heaven to give light upon the earth.

18 And to rule over the day and over the night, and to divide the light from the darkness: and God saw that *it was* good.

19 And the evening and the morning were the fourth day.

20 And God said, Let the waters bring forth abundantly the moving creature that hath life, and fowl *that* may fly above the earth in the open firmament of heaven.

21 And God created great whales, and every living creature that moveth, which the waters brought forth abundantly, after their kind, and every winged fowl after his kind: and God saw that *it was* good.

22 And God blessed them, saying, Be fruitful, and multiply, and fill the earth.

23 And the evening and the morning were the fifth day.

24 And God said, Let the earth bring forth the living creature after his kind, cattle, and creeping thing, and beast of the earth after his kind: and it was so.

25. And God made the beast of the earth after his kind, and cattle after their kind, and every thing that creepeth upon the earth after his kind: and God saw that *it was* good.

26 And God said, Let us make man in our image, after our likeness: and let them have dominion over the fish of the sea, and over the fowl of the air, and over the cattle, and over all the earth, and over every creeping thing that creepeth upon the earth.

27 So God created man in his *own* image, in the image of God created he him; male and female created he them.

28 And God blessed them, and God said upon them, Be fruitful, and multiply, and replenish the earth, and subdue it: and have dominion over the fish of the sea, and over the fowl of the air, and over every living thing that moveth upon the earth.

29 And God said, Behold, I have given you every herb bearing seed, which *is* upon the face of all the earth, and every tree, in the which *is* the fruit of a tree yielding seed; to you it shall be for meat.

30 And to every beast of the earth, and to every fowl of the air, and to every thing that creepeth upon the earth, wherein *there is* life, *I have given* every green herb for meat: and it was so.

31 And God saw every thing that he had made, and, behold, *it was* very good. And the evening and the morning were the sixth day.

CHAPTER 2

Thus the heavens and the earth were finished, and all the host of them.

2 And on the seventh day God ended his work which he had made; and he rested on the seventh day from all his work which he had made.

3 And God blessed the seventh day, and sanctified it: because that in it he had rested from all his work which God created and made.

The Second Creation of the Book of Genesis

CHAPTER 2

Thus the heavens and the earth were finished, and all the host of them. And on the seventh day God finished his work which he had done, and he rested on the seventh day from all his work which he had done. So God blessed the seventh day and hallowed it, because on it God rested from all his work which he had done in creation.

4 These are the generations of the heavens and the earth when they were created.

In the day that the Lord God made the earth and the heavens, when no plant of the field was yet in the earth and no herb of the field had yet sprung up—for the Lord God had not caused it to rain upon the earth, and there was no

---

[1] This "second creation" in the "Book of Genesis" is from Chapter 2, verse 4, to Chapter 3, verse 24. I have started this selection from verse 1 of Chapter 2 so there will be no loss of continuity in reading, and no confusion as to where one ends and the other begins.

man to till the ground: but a mist went up from the earth
and watered the whole face of the ground—then the Lord
God formed man of dust from the ground, and breathed into
his nostrils the breath of life; and man became a living being.
And the Lord God planted a garden in Eden, in the east; and
there he put the man whom he had formed. And out of the
ground the Lord God made to grow every tree that is pleasant
to the sight and good for food, the tree of life also in the
midst of the garden, and the tree of the knowledge of good
and evil.

10 A river flowed out of Eden to water the garden, and
there it divided and became four rivers. The name of the
first is Pishon; it is the one which flows around the whole
land of Havilah, where there is gold; and the gold of that
land is good: bdellium and onyx stone are there. The name
of the second river is Gihon; it is the one which flows around
the whole land of Cush. And the name of the third river is
Hiddekel, which flows east of Assyria. And the fourth river
is the Euphrates.

15 The Lord God took the man and put him in the garden
of Eden to till it and keep it. And the Lord God commanded
the man, saying, "You may freely eat of every tree of the
garden; but of the tree of the knowledge of good and evil
you shall not eat, for in the day that you eat of it you shall
die."

18 Then the Lord God said, "It is not good that the man
should be alone; I will make him a helper fit for him." So
out of the ground the Lord God formed every beast of the
field and every bird of the air, and brought them to the man
to see what he would call them; and whatever the man called
every living creature, that was its name. The man gave names
to all cattle, and to the birds of the air, and to every beast of
the field; but for the man there was not found a helper fit
for him. So the Lord God caused a deep sleep to fall upon
the man, and while he slept took one of his ribs and closed
up its place with flesh; and the rib which the Lord God had
taken from the man he made into a woman and brought her
to the man. Then the man said,

"This at last is bone of my bones
    and flesh of my flesh;
    she shall be called Woman,
    because she was taken out of
        Man."

Therefore a màn leaves his father and his mother and cleaves to his wife, and they become one flesh. And the man and his wife were both naked, and were not ashamed.

CHAPTER 3

Now the serpent was more subtle than any other wild creature that the Lord God had made. He said to the woman, "Did God say, 'You shall not eat of any tree of the garden'?" And the woman said to the serpent, "We may eat of the fruit of the trees of the garden; but God said, 'You shall not eat of the fruit of the tree which is in the midst of the garden, neither shall you touch it, lest you die.' " But the serpent said to the woman, "You will not die. For God knows that when you eat of it your eyes will be opened, and you will be like God, knowing good and evil." So when the woman saw that the tree was good for food, and that it was a delight to the eyes, and that the tree was to be desired to make one wise she took of its fruit and ate; and she also gave some to her husband, and he ate. Then the eyes of both were opened, and they knew that they were naked; and they sewed fig leaves together and made themselves aprons.

8 And they heard the sound of the Lord God walking in the garden in the cool of the day, and the man and his wife hid themselves from the presence of the Lord God among the trees of the garden. But the Lord God called to the man, and said to him, "Where are you?" And he said, "I heard the sound of thee in the garden, and I was afraid, because I was naked; and I hid myself." He said, "Who told you that you were naked? Have you eaten of the tree of which I commanded you not to eat?" The man said, "The woman whom thou gavest to be with me, she gave me fruit of the tree, and I ate." Then the Lord God said to the woman, "What is this that you have done?" The woman said, "The serpent beguiled me, and I ate." The Lord God said to the serpent,

"Because you have done this,
  cursed are you above all cattle,
  and above all wild animals;
upon your belly you shall go,
  and dust you shall eat
  all the days of your life.

I will put enmity between you and
    the woman,
  and between your seed and her
    seed;
he shall bruise your head,
  and you shall bruise his heel."
To the woman he said,
"I will greatly multiply your pain in
    childbearing;
  in pain you shall bring forth
    children,
yet your desire shall be for your
    husband,
  and he shall rule over you."
And to Adam he said,
"Because you have listened to the
    voice of your wife,
  and have eaten of the tree
of which I commanded you,
  'You shall not eat of it,'
cursed is the ground because of you;
  in toil you shall eat of it all the
    days of your life;
thorns and thistles it shall bring
    forth to you;
  and you shall eat the plants of
    the field.
In the sweat of your face
  you shall eat bread
till you return to the ground,
  for out of it you were taken;
you are dust,
  and to dust you shall return."

20 The man called his wife's name Eve, because she was
the mother of all living. And the Lord God made for Adam
and for his wife garments of skins, and clothed them.

22 Then the Lord God said, "Behold, the man has become
like one of us, knowing good and evil; and now, lest he put
forth his hand and take also of the tree of life, and eat, and
live for ever"—therefore the Lord God sent him forth from
the garden of Eden, to till the ground from which he was
taken. He drove out the man; and at the east of the garden

of Eden he placed the cherubim, and a flaming sword which turned every way, to guard the way to the tree of life.

The Gospel According to
Saint John 1:1-4

In the begining was the Word, and the Word was with God, and the Word was God.

2 The same was in the beginning with God.

3 All things were made by him; and without him was not any thing made that was made.

4 In him was life; and the life was the light of man.

Revelation 21:1-6

And I saw a new heaven and a new earth: for the first heaven and the first earth were passed away; and there was no more sea.

2 And I John saw the holy city, new Jerusalem, coming down from God out of heaven, prepared as a bride adorned for her husband.

3 And I heard a great voice out of heaven saying, Behold, the tabernacle of God is with men, and he will dwell with them, . . . and be their God.

4 And God shall wipe away all tears from their eyes; and there shall be no more death, neither sorrow, nor crying, neither shall there be any more pain: for the former things are passed away.

5 And he that sat upon the throne said, Behold, I make all things new. . . .

6 And he said unto me, It is done. I am Alpha and Omega, the beginning and the end. I will give upon him that is athirst of the fountain of the water of life freely."

JEWISH COSMOLOGY

From Psalm 19

To the chief Musician, A Psalm of David

The heavens declare the glory of God; and the firmament sheweth his handywork.

2 Day unto day uttereth speech, and night unto night sheweth knowledge.

3 *There* is no speech nor language, *where* their voice is not heard.

4 Their line is gone out through all the earth, and their words to the end of the world. In them hath he set a tabernacle for the sun,

5 Which *is* as a bridegroom coming out of his chamber, *and* rejoiceth as a strong man to run a race.

6 His going forth *is* from the end of the heaven, and his circuit unto the ends of it: and there is nothing hid from the heat thereof.

7 The law of the Lord *is* perfect, converting the soul: the testimony of the Lord *is* sure, making wise the simple.

From Psalm 74

12 For God *is* my King of old, working salvation in the midst of the earth.

13 Thou didst divide the sea by thy strength: thou brakest the heads of the dragons in the waters.

14 Thou brakest the heads of leviathan in pieces, *and* gavest him *to be* meat to the people inhabiting the wilderness.

15 Thou didst cleave the fountain and the flood: thou driedst up mighty rivers.

16 The day *is* thine, the night also *is* thine: thou hast prepared the light and the sun.

17 Thou hast set all the borders of the earth: thou hast made summer and winter.

From Psalm 104

Bless the Lord, O my soul, O Lord my God, thou art very great; thou art clothed with honour and majesty.

2 Who coverest *thyself* with light as *with* a garment: who stretchest out the heavens like a curtain:

3 Who layeth the beams of his chambers in the waters: who maketh the clouds his chariot: who walketh upon the wings of the wind:

4 Who maketh his angels spirits; his ministers a flaming fire:

5 *Who* laid the foundations of the earth, *that* it should not be removed for ever.

6 Thou coveredst it with the deep as *with* a garment: the waters stood above the mountains.

7 At thy rebuke they fled; at the voice of thy thunder they hasted away.

8 They go up by the mountains; they go down by the valleys unto the place which thou hast founded for them.

9 Thou hast set a bound that they may not pass over; that they turn not again to cover the earth.

10 He sendeth the springs into the valleys, *which* run among the hills.

11 They give drink to every beast of the field: the wild asses quench their thirst.

12 By them shall the fowls of the heaven have their habitation, *which* sing among the branches.

13 He watereth the hills from his chambers: the earth is satisfied with the fruit of thy works.

14 He causeth the grass to grow for the cattle, and herb for the service of man: that he may bring forth food out of the earth;

15 And wine *that* maketh glad the heart of man, *and* oil to make *his* face to shine, and bread *which* strengtheneth man's heart.

16 The trees of the Lord are full *of sap*; the cedars of Lebanon, which he hath planted;

17 Where the birds make their nests: *as for* the stork, the fir trees *are* her house.

18 The high hills *are* a refuge for the wild goats; *and* the rocks for the conies.

19 He appointed the moon for seasons: the sun knoweth his going down.

20 Thou makest darkness and it is night: wherein all the beasts of the forest do creep *forth*.

21 The young lions roar after their prey, and seek their meat from God.

22 The sun ariseth, they gather themselves together, and lay them down in their dens.

23 Man goeth forth unto his work and to his labour until the evening.

24 O Lord, how manifold are they works! In wisdom hast thou made them all: the earth is full of thy riches.

25 *So is* this great and wide sea, wherein *are* things creeping innumerable, both small and great beasts.

26 There go the ships: *there is* that leviathan, *whom* thou hast made to play therein.

27 These wait all upon thee; that thou mayest give *them* their meat in due season.

28 *That* thou givest them they gather: thou openest thine hand, they are filled with good.

29 Thou hidest thy face, they are troubled: thou takest away their breath, they die, and return to their dust.

30 Thou sendest forth thy spirit, they are created: and thou renewest the face of the earth.

31 The glory of the Lord shall endure for ever: the Lord shall rejoice in his works.

32 He looketh on the earth, and it trembleth: he toucheth the hills, and they smoke.

THE CREATION OF ADAM[1]

When the Creator wished to make man he consulted with the ministering angels beforehand, and said unto them: "We will make a man in our image."

The angels asked: "What is man that Thou shouldst remember him, and what is his purpose?"

"He will do justice," said the Lord.

And the ministering angels were divided into groups.

Some said: "Let not man be created."

But others said: "Let him be created."

Forgiveness said: "Let him be created, for he will be generous and benevolent."

Peace objected and said: "Let him not be created, for he will constantly wage wars."

Justice said: "Let him be created, for he will bring justice into the world."

Truth said: "Let him not be created, for he will be a liar."

The Creator then hurled Truth from Heaven to earth, and, in spite of the protests of the angels, man was created.

"His knowledge," said the Creator, "will excel yours, and tomorrow you will see his wisdom."

The Creator then gathered all kinds of beasts before the ministering angels, the wild and the tame beasts, as well as the birds, and the fowls of the air, and asked the ministering angels to name them, but they could not.

"Now you will see the wisdom of man," spake the Creator. "I will ask him and he will tell their names."

All the beasts and fowls of their air were then led before man, and when asked he at once replied: "This is an ox, the other an ass, yonder a horse and a camel."

"And what is your own name?"

"I" replied man, "should be called Adam because I have been created from *adama* or earth."

[1] Adapted from the *Midrash*.

THE CREATION OF EVE[2]

When the Almighty wished to create Eve He did not know from which part of Adam's body He should fashion her.

"I won't create her from his head," He said, "so that she should not be conceited.

"I won't create her from his eye, so that she should not be curious.

"I won't create her from his ear, so that she should not listen to gossip.

"I won't create her from his tongue, so that she should not be a chatterbox.

"I won't create her from his heart, so that she should not be jealous.

"I won't create her from his hand, so that she should not be grasping.

"I won't create her from his foot, so that she should not be a gadabout.

"Instead, I will fashion her from an invisible part of man, so that even when he stands naked it cannot be seen."

Then God created Eve from one of Adam's ribs, saying: "Be thou a modest and chaste woman!"

None the less, God's excellent plan miscarried. Woman is conceited, curious, a gossip, a chatterbox, is jealous, grasping and a gadabout.

[2] Adapted from the *Midrash*.

PART EIGHT

Egypt

INTRODUCTION

THE RELIGION of ancient Egypt has fascinated the Western world for generations. This is a strange fact because many more subtle and sophisticated ancient religions do not draw half as much attention. There is, for example, little that can explain away the crudity of Egyptian animal worship. These crudities have often been ignored, and the simplicities interpreted as subtleties containing hidden meaning.[1]

The first deities of ancient Egypt were in animal form. Even as the religion developed, the basic Egyptian awe of animals remained intact, with many gods portrayed as half beast, half human. Well into the historic period and the peak of early Egyptian religion, the gods were shown as animals. Usually such clear animism recedes as a religion develops, but not in Egypt. Anubis, the god of the dead and one of the most powerful deities in the Egyptian pantheon, was pictured as a jackal. In this form Anubis presided over the weighing of the heart of the deceased. Thoth, the god of learning, wisdom, and the scribe of the afterworld, was shown as either an ibis or a baboon. Khnum, a minor deity of an island in the Nile who was associated with the myths of creation, was portrayed as a ram. Khnum created each individual from clary. One of the major female gods was Hathor, who had the head of a cow on a human body (or a human head crowned with cow's horns). She is a dominant figure in many myths as the goddess of love, beauty, and childbearing. Some regarded her as a solar deity because she wore the sun disk between her horns.[2]

---

[1] For a more thorough description of this aspect of ancient Egyptian religion, see Max Muller's analysis in *The Mythology of All Races*, vol. XII, *Egyptian* (New York: Cooper Square Publishers, Inc., 1964), pp. 7 ff.

[2] For a more detailed description of the animism of Egyptian religion, see Fred G. Bratton, *Myths and Legends of the Ancient Near East* (New York: Thomas Y. Crowell Co., 1970).

However, even with its crude aspects, ancient Egyptian religion contains a dazzling array of ideas and graphic myths. Further, animism was surely not unique to the ancient Egyptians. In fact, R. R. Marett has described myths as "animatism grown picturesque." Egyptian myths seem to support this definition. One scholar, R. Pietschmann, regards its early expressions as exactly parallel to the pure animism and fetishism of Central African pagan beliefs.

The earliest clear evidence of Egyptian ideas of creation occurs in a series of writings called the Pyramid Texts. They were composed by priests of Heliopolis, a center of early Egyptian civilization, about the middle of the third millennium B.C. There was, not surprisingly, a competition between the followers of the Heliopolitan gods and those of other districts, such as Memphis. In the Heliopolitan cosmogony there is a primordial abyss of water, without form or color, called Nun. From this waste Atum, an early mysterious deity, is born and begins the work of creation. Later, Atum came to be identified with Ra, the sun god, and was known as Atum-Ra. Atum then conceived two dieties through an act of masturbation, Shu and Tefnut. (In another rendition they are created by "spitting.") From Shu and Tefnut are created Geb—a male—the earth, and Nut—a female—the sky. This designation of the earth as male and the sky as female is a striking distinction of Egyptian cosmogony—differentiating it from most other cosmogonies. From Geb and Nut are born the famous Isis and Osiris. In this way the priests of Heliopolis attempted to make their god Atum superior to all others; in fact, to have Atum give birth to all other important gods.

On the other hand the priests of Memphis countered by denying Atum, and claiming that their god Ptah was the original creator and that Atum was subservient. Ptah is described by the Memphis priests as creating the world by power of his magical word.

A remarkable feature of Egyptian creation myths is that they make little effort to create anything other than the cosmos or world. For example, they do not attempt to describe the creation of man. And while there are passing references to creation of man in various Egyptian texts, there is no emphasis on mankind's origin or purpose as in Mesopotamian and Judeo-Christian creation. Also in the creation myths of ancient Sumer more emphasis was placed on the creation of mankind and the beginning of civilization than on the origin of the cosmos, as in Egyptian myths. Egyptian myths, along with Mesopotamian and Judeo-Christian creation stories, offer us the most striking creation myths of the ancient world. But Egyptian myth is one of the unique of the ancient world, for it contains many basic characteristics of religious belief and practice: polytheism, monotheism, henotheism, abundant rituals and magical practices, divine kingship, a professional priesthood, elaborately illustrated religious texts, a funerary cult, magical resurrection, a complex vision of an afterlife, and judgment of the dead. The great attraction of Egyptian religion may be found in its richness and complexity.

But the paradox of ancient Egypt becomes clear once one begins to list Egyptian accomplishments: They formulated surgical methods (without magic, ritual, and superstition) that still impress surgeons today. Their use of mathematics, and the lever as a tool in constructing the mammoth and shockingly precise pyramids, their use of copper tools, their sophistication in architecture and design with fluted columns, portals, pillared halls, and painted pottery and tomb paintings in four colors—all two thousand years before Athens was built—is little short of amazing. Their scientific and artistic accomplishments were far in advance of their age. They seemed to possess a kind of dualistic mentality, or coconsciousness, where reason was called upon when needed for the practical things of life, but where magic and pagan beliefs took in spiritual matters. This points to a kind of coexistence between myth and magic, in addition to a basic pragmatism. But perhaps this is the clue to explain their paradoxical nature. Their cosmology, beliefs in an afterlife, and religious teachings seem to be most often expressed in tangible, physical terms. They indicated little brilliance when it came to speculative thinking or abstract ideas. They were not theorizers, but doers. Perhaps this is why their religion and beliefs changed so little in almost three thousand years. Perhaps this is why they could be a sophisticated, advanced civilization in terms of the practical world, and yet remain an animistically dominated religion. It may also explain how their religion came to be so complex, with so many available interpretations of each event or each god's role. During the early period of Egypt's religion, for example, there was great tolerance for alternative ideas. There was little rigid doctrine. A priest or scribe could accept various contradictory ideas on the same subject—a god or creation, for instance. This tolerance opened the way for change and diversity. Rather than cause major alterations in their beliefs, a new idea would simply be adopted into their scheme of things.

One of the major concerns of the Egyptians was the afterlife. Survival was vitally important—perhaps because of their attachment to the physical, real world. There is no proof of any of these theories. There was less concern about the origin of life, however, which again emphasizes their lack of interest in cosmological theories or metaphysics. Their views of the afterworld were tangible and grounded in the physical.

EGYPTIAN CREATION MYTHS

The Gods[1]

Tem, or Atmu, the oldest of the gods, and he is called the "divine god," the "self-created," the "maker of the gods," the "creator of men," "who stretched out the heavens," who illumineth the Tuat with his Eyes (the sun and moon). He existed when not was sky, not was earth, not were men, not were born the gods, not was death.

In what form he existed no one knows, but he created for himself, as a place wherein to dwell, the great mass of Celestial Waters to which the Egyptians gave the name of Nu. In these, for a time, he lived quite alone, and then, in a series of efforts of thought, he created the heavens and the celestial bodies in them, and the gods, and the earth, and men and women, animals, birds, and creeping things, in his own mind. These thoughts or ideas of creation were translated into words by Thoth, or the intelligence or mind of Temu, and when he uttered these words all creation came into being.

Nu is the name given to the vast mass of water which existed in primeval times, and was situated presumably in the sky; it formed the material part of the great god Tem, or Atmu, who was the creator of the universe and of gods and men. In this mass, which was believed to be of fathomless depth and of boundless extent, were the germs of all life, and of all kinds of life, and for this reason the god who was the personification of the water, i.e., Nu, was called the "Father of the Gods," and the "producer of the Great Company of the Gods." The watery mass of Nu was the prototype of the great World-Ocean which later ancient nations believed to

---

[1] In order to better understand the complicated pantheon of Egyptian gods and their myths, this interesting description has been included as a primer. Further, it simply and clearly relates some of the main themes of the Egyptian cosmic creation. From E. Wallis Budge, *The Book of the Dead, The Papyrus of Ani* (London: British Museum Pamphlet, 1920).

surround the whole world. Out from Nu came the river which flowed through the Tuat, or Other World, and divided its valley into two parts, making it to resemble Egypt. From Nu also came the waters which appeared in the two famous caverns in the First Cataract, and which, flowing from their mouths, formed the river Nile. The waters of Nu formed the dwelling place of Tem, and out of them came the sun, which was the result of one of Tem's earliest acts of creation. The early inhabitants of Egypt thought that the sun sailed over the waters of Nu in two magical boats, called Mantchet, or Matet, or Atet, and Semktet, or Sektet, respectively; in the former the sun set out in the morning on his journey, which he finished in the latter. A very ancient tradition in Egypt asserted that Nu was the head of a divine company, which consisted of four gods and four goddesses. These were: Nu, Hehu, Kekui, Kerth, Nut, Hehut, Kekuit, Kerhet.

The gods of these pairs were depicted in human form, with the heads and frogs, and the goddesses in the forms of women, with serpents' heads. Nu was the primeval water itself, Hehu personified its vast and endless extent, Kekui the darkness which brooded over the water, and Kerh its inert and motionless character. Very little is known about the three last-named gods and their female counterparts, for they belong to a system of cosmogony which was superseded by other systems in which the Sun-god Ra played the most prominent part. The goddess Nut, who was in the earliest times a Water-goddess, was depicted under the New Empire in the form of a woman, and also in the form of a cow.

Ptah the Creator

Ptah, the great, is the mind and tongue of the gods. . . .
It (the mind) is the one that bringeth forth every successful
   issue.
It is the tongue which repeats the thought of the mind:
It (the mind) was the fashioner of all gods . . .
At a time when every divine word
Came into existence by the thought of the mind,
And the command of the tongue.

Ra the Creator[1]

The Chapter of the divine god, the self-created being, who made the heavens and the earth, and the winds which give life, and the fire, and the gods, and men, and beasts, and cattle, and reptiles, and the fowl of the air and the fish of the sea; he is the king of men and of gods, he hath one period of life and with him periods of one hundred and twenty years each are but as years; his names are manifold and unknown, the gods even know them not.

Before the world and all that therein is came into being, only the great god Neb-er-tcher existed, for even the gods were not born. Now when the time had come for the god to create all things he said, "I brought (*i.e.*, fashioned) my mouth, and I uttered my own name as a word of power, and thus I evolved myself under the evolutions of the god Khepera, and I developed myself out of the primeval matter which had evolved multitudes of evolutions from the beginning of time. Nothing existed on this earth before me, I made all things. There was none other who worked with me at that time."

The god Khepera says, "I developed myself from the primeval matter which I made, I developed myself out of the primeval matter. My name is 'Osiris,' the germ of primeval matter. I am the great god Nu, who gave birth unto himself, and who made his name to become the company of the gods." Then the question, "What does this mean?" or "Who is this?" is asked. And this is the answer: "It is Ra, the creator of the names of his limbs, which came into being in the form of the gods who are in the following of Ra."

[1] This creation story is related in the *Papyrus of Nesi-Amsu*. Ra is first a human god (the Pharaoh), then a world god like Ptah in his giant form, and finally a cosmic deity. While the Egyptian priests were systematizing their theology of the sun cult, Ra, the sun, is exalted continuously. Ra is shown to be greater than his father Nu, and a legend created for the benefit of the worshippers of Isis clearly credits Ra with imparting her powers to her. Horus is also given powers by Ra, for he becomes possessor of the "eyes" of Ra (the sun and moon).

Birth of the Sun

When at the end of the twelfth hour the last door had
swung to, then there was great mourning among the souls who
dwell in Amenti and remain behind in darkness. But Isis and
Nephthys, each in the form of a uraeus, sit by the gates to
protect the young Sun god, even as they protected Horus the
son of Isis. Before them stretches Nu, the primeval water,
from which, as one myth tells us, all things came forth. From
this Ra too must rise, and to effect his rising the god of the
water uplifts him together with his Madet bark. Ra is in
the midst of the bark, and beside him stand Isis and Nephthys
as his guardians, while aft are Seb, Shu, the god Hek, who
knows the magic formulas, and two steersmen. Forward are
the three porters who have opened the gates of the day, and
who will open also the various doors of the upper heaven.
Nut, goddess of the day sky, reaches from the other side to
receive the Sun. She stands upon a figure which by touching
its head with its feet forms a circle and is designated the
"Osiris who encloses Duat," the whole arrangement signifying
that the day sky is here uplifted above the night sky, the
realm of Nut above that of Osiris.

Creation Myth of the
Sun Worshipers

At the begining the world was a waste of water called Nu,
and it was the abode of the Great Father. He was Nu, for
he was the deep, and he gave being unto the sun god who hath
said: "Lo! I am Khepera at dawn, Ra at high noon, and Tum
at eventide.[11] The god of brightness first appeared as a shining
egg which floated upon the water's breast, and the spirits of
the deep, who were the Fathers and the Mothers, were with
him there, as he was with Nu, for they were the companions
of Nu.

Now Ra was greater than Nu from whom he arose. He was
the divine father and strong ruler of gods, and those whom
he first created, according to his desire, were Shu, the wind
god, and his consort Tefnut, who had the head of a lioness

and was called "The Spitter" because she sent the rain. In aftertime these two deities shone as stars amidst the constellations of heaven, and they were called "The Twins."

Then came into being Seb, the earth god, and Nut, the goddess of the firmament, who became the parents of Osiris and his consort Isis and also of Set and his consort Nephthys.

Ra spake at the beginning of Creation, and bade the earth and the heavens to rise out of the waste of water. In the brightness of his majesty they appeared, and Shu, the uplifter, raised Nut upon high. She formed the vault, which is arched over Seb, the god of earth, who lies prostrate beneath her from where, at the eastern horizon, she is poised upon her toes to where, at the western horizon, bending down with outstretched arms, she rests upon her finger tips. In the darkness are beheld the stars which sparkle upon her body and over her great unwearied limbs.

When Ra, according to his desire, uttered the deep thoughts of his mind, that which he named had being. When he gazed into space, that which he desired to see appeared before him. He created all things that move in the waters and upon the dry land. Now, mankind were born from his eye, and Ra, the Creator, who was ruler of the gods, became the first king upon earth. He went about among men; he took form like unto theirs, and to him the centuries were as years.

Ra had many names that were not known unto gods or men, and he had one secret name which gave to him his divine power.[1] The goddess Isis, who dwelt in the world as a woman, grew weary of the ways of mankind; she sought rather to be amidst the mighty gods. She was an enchantress, and she desired greatly to have power equal with Ra in the heavens, and upon the earth. In her heart, therefore, she yearned to know the secret name of the ruling god, which was hidden in his bosom and was never revealed in speech.

Each day Ra walked forth, and the gods who were of his train followed him, and he sat upon his throne and uttered decrees. He had grown old, and as he spake moisture dripped from his mouth and fell upon the ground. Isis followed after him, and when she found his saliva she baked it with the earth on which it lay. In the form of a spear she shaped the substance, and it became a venomous serpent. She lifted it up; she cast it from her, and it lay on the path which Ra was

---

[1] The secret name is Ran.

wont to traverse when he went up and down his kingdom, surveying that which he had made. Now the sacred serpent which Isis created was invisible to gods and men.

Soon there came a day when Ra, the aged god, walked along the path followed by his companions. He came nigh to the serpent, which awaited him, and the serpent stung him. The burning venom entered his body, and Ra was stricken with great pain. A loud and mighty cry broke from his lips, and it was heard in highest heaven.

Then spake the gods who were with him, saying: "What hath befallen thee?" and "What thing is there?"

Ra answered not; he shook; all his body trembled and his teeth clattered, for the venom overflowed in his flesh as does the Nile when it floods the land of Egypt. But at length he possessed himself and subdued his heart and the fears of his heart. He spake, and his words were:

"Gather about me, ye who are my children, so that I may make known the grievous thing which hath befallen me even now. I am stricken with great pain by something I know not of . . . by something which I cannot behold. Of that I have knowledge in my heart, for I have not done myself an injury with mine own hand. Lo! I am without power to make known who hath stricken me thus. Never before hath such sorrow and pain been mine."

He spake further, saying: "I am a god and the son of a god; I am the Mighty One, son of the Mighty One. Nu, my father, conceived my secret name which giveth me power, and he concealed it in my heart so that no magician might ever know it, and, knowing it, be given power to work evil against me.

"As I went forth, even now, beholding the world which I have created, a malignant thing did bite me. It is not fire, yet it burns in my flesh; it is not water, yet cold is my body and my limbs tremble. Hear me now! My command is that all my children be brought nigh to me so that they may pronounce words of power which shall be felt upon earth and in the heavens."

All the children of Ra were brought unto him as was his desire. Isis, the enchantress, came in their midst, and all sorrowed greatly, save her alone. She spoke forth mighty words, for she could utter incantations to subdue pain and to give life unto that from which life had departed. Unto Ra spake Isis, saying: "What aileth thee, holy father? . . . Thou hast been bitten by a serpent, one of the creatures which thou didst create. I shall weave spells; I shall thwart thine enemy with magic. Lo! I shall overwhelm the serpent utterly in the brightness of thy glory."

He answered her, saying: "A malignant thing did bite me. It is not fire, yet it burns my flesh. It is not water, yet cold is my body, and my limbs tremble. Mine eyes also have grown dim. Drops of sweat fall from my face."

Isis spake unto the divine father and said: "Thou must, even now, reveal thy secret name unto me, for, verily, thou canst be delivered from thy pain and distress by the power of thy name."

Ra heard her in sorrow. Then he said: "I have created the heavens and the earth. Lo! I have even framed the earth, and the mountains are the work of my hands; I made the sea, and I cause the Nile to flood the land of Egypt. I am the Great Father of the gods and the goddesses. I gave life unto them. I created every living thing that moves upon the dry land and in the sea depths. When I open my eyes there is light: when I close them there is thick darkness. My secret name is known not unto the gods. I am Khepera at dawn, Ra at high noon, and Tum at eventide."

So spake the divine father; but mighty and magical as were his words they brought him no relief. The poison still burned in his flesh and his body trembled. He seemed ready to die.

Isis, the enchantress, heard him, but there was no sorrow in her heart. She desired, above all other things, to share the power of Ra, and she must needs have revealed unto her his sacred name which Nu conceived and uttered at the beginning. So she spake to Ra, saying:

"Divine father, thou has not yet spoken thy name of power. If thou shalt reveal it unto me I will have strength to give thee healing."

Hotter than fire burned the venom in the heart of Ra. Like raging flames it consumed his flesh, and he suffered fierce agony. Isis waited, and at length the Great Father spake in majesty and said:

"It is my will that Isis be given my secret name, and that it leave my heart and enter hers."

When he had spoken thus, Ra vanished from before the eyes of the gods. The sun boat was empty, and there was thick darkness. Isis waited, and when the secret name of the divine father was about to leave his heart and pass into her own, she spake unto Horus her son and said:

"Now, compel the ruling god, by a mighty spell, to yield up also his eyes, which are the sun and the moon."

Isis then received in her heart the secret name of Ra, and the mightly enchantress said:

"Depart, O venom, from Ra; come forth from his heart and from his flesh; flow out, shining from his mouth. . . . I have worked the spell. . . . Lo! I have overcome the serpent and caused the venom to be spilled upon the ground, because that the secret name of the divine father hath been given unto me. . . . Now let Ra live, for the venom hath perished."

So was the god made whole. The venom departed from his body and there was no longer pain in his heart or any sorrow.

As Ra grew old ruling over men, there were those among his subjects who spake disdainfully regarding him, saying: "Aged, indeed, is King Ra, for now his bones are silvern and his flesh is turned to gold, although his hair is still true lapis lazuli (dark)."

Unto Ra came knowledge of the evil words which were spoken against him, and there was anger in his heart, because that there were rebellious sayings on the lips of men and because they sought also to slay him. He spake unto his divine followers and said:

"Bring before me the god Shu and the goddess Tefnut, the god Seb and his consort Nut, and the fathers and mothers who were with me at the beginning when I was in Nu. Bring Nu before me also. Let them all come hither in secret, so that men may not behold them, and, fearing, take sudden flight. Let all the gods assemble in my great temple at Heliopolis."

The gods assembled as Ra desired, and they made obeisance before him. They then said: "Speak what thou desirest to say and we will hear."

He addressed the gods, saying: "O Nu, thou the eldest god, from whom I had my being, and ye ancestral gods, hear and know now, that rebellious words are spoken against me by mankind, whom I did create. Lo! they seek even to slay me. It is my desire that ye should instruct me what ye would do in this matter. Consider well among yourselves and guide me with wisdom. I have hesitated to punish mankind until I have heard from your lips what should now be done regarding them.

"For lo! I desire in my heart to destroy utterly that which I did create. All the world will become a waste of water through a great flood as it was at the beginning, and I alone shall be left remaining, with no one else beside me save Osiris and his son, Horus. I shall become a small serpent invisible to the gods.

To Osiris will be given power to reign over the dead, and Horus will be exalted on the throne which is set upon the island of fiery flames."

Then spake forth Nu, god of primeval waters, and he said: "Hear me now, O my son, thou who art mightier far than me, although I gave thee life. Steadfast is thy throne; great is the fear of thee among men. Let thine eye go forth against those who are rebels in the kingdom."

Ra said: "Now do men seek escape among the hills; they tremble because of the words they have uttered."

The gods spake together, saying: "Let thine eye go forth against those who are rebels in the kingdom and it shall destroy them utterly. When it cometh down from heaven as Hathor, no human eye can be raised against it."

Ra heard, and, as was his will, his eye went forth as Hathor against mankind among the mountains, and they were speedily slain. The goddess rejoiced in her work and drove over the land, so that for many nights she waded in blood.

Then Ra repented. His fierce anger passed away, and he sought to save the remnant of mankind. He sent messengers, who ran swifter than the storm wind, unto Elephantine, so that they might obtain speedily many plants of virtue. These they brought back, and they were well ground and steeped with barley in vessels filled with the blood of mankind. So was beer made and seven thousand jars were filled with it.

Day dawned and Hathor[2] went upstream slaughtering mankind. Ra surveyed the jars and said: "Now shall I give men protection. It is my will that Hathor may slay them no longer."

Then the god gave command that the jars should be carried to the place where the vengeful goddess rested for the night after that day of slaughter. The jars were emptied out as was his desire, and the land was covered with the flood.

When Hathor awoke her heart was made glad. She stooped down and she saw her beauteous face mirrored in the flood. Then began she to drink eagerly, and she was made drunken so that she went to and fro over the land, nor took any heed of mankind.

Ra spake unto her, saying:: "Beautiful goddess, return to me in peace."

Hathor returned, and the divine father said: "Henceforward

---

[2] The feline goddess Sekhet is also given as the slaughterer. In a temple inscription there is the chant: "Hathor overcometh the enemy of her sire by this her name of Sekhet."

shall comely handmaidens, thy priestesses, prepare for thee in jars, according to their number, draughts of sweetness, and these shall be given as offerings unto thee at the first festival of every New Year.[3]

So it came that from that day, when the Nile rose in red flood, covering the land of Egypt, offerings of beer were made unto Hathor. Men and women partook of the draughts of sweetness at the festival and were made drunken like the goddess.

Now when Hathor had returned to Ra he spake unto her with weariness, saying:

"A fiery pain torments me, nor can I tell whence it comes. I am still alive, but I am weary of heart and desire no longer to dwell among men. Lo! I have not destroyed them as I have power to do."

The gods who followed Ra said: "Be no longer weary. Power is thine according to thy desire."

Ra answered them, saying: "Weary indeed are my limbs and they fail me. I shall go forth no longer alone, nor shall I wait until I am stricken again with pain. Help shall be given unto me according to my desire!"

Then the ruler of the gods called unto Nu, from whom he had being, and Nu bade Shu, the atmosphere god, and Nut, goddess of the heavens, to give aid unto Ra in his distress.

Nut took the form of the Celestial Cow, and Shu lifted Ra upon her back. Then darkness came on. Men issued forth from their hiding places in great fear, and when they beheld Ra departing from them they sorrowed because of the rebellious words which had been spoken against his majesty. Indeed they cried unto Ra, beseeching him to slay those of his enemies who remained. But Ra was borne through the darkness, and men followed him until he appeared again and shed light upon the earth. Then did his faithful subjects arm themselves with weapons, and they sallied forth against the enemies of the sun god and slaughtered them in battle.

Ra beheld that which his followers among men had done, and he was well pleased. He spake unto them saying: "Now is your sin forgiven. Slaughter atones for slaugther. Such is sacrifice and the purport thereof."

When Ra had thus accepted in atonement for the sin of men

---

[3] This occurs on July 20, when the star Sirius appears as the morning star. The Nile is generally in full flood at this time.

the sacrifice of his enemies who desired to slay him, he spake unto the heavenly goddess Nut, saying:

"Henceforth my dwelling place must be in the heavens. No longer will I reign upon the earth."

So it happened, according to his divine will. The great god went on his way through the realms which are above, and these he divided and set in order. He spake creating words, and called into existence the field of Aalu, and there he caused to assemble a multitude of beings which are beheld in heaven, even the stars, and these were borne of Nut. In millions they came to praise and glorify Ra. Unto Shu, the god of atmosphere, whose consort is Nut, was given the keeping of the multitude of beings that shine in thick darkness. Shu raised his arms, uplifting over his head the Celestial Cow[4] and the millions and millions of stars.

Then Ra spake unto the earth god, who is called Seb, and said:

"Many fearsome reptiles dwell in thee. It is my will now that they may have dread of me as great as is my dread of them. Thou shalt discover why they are moved with enmity against me. When thou hast done that, thou shalt go unto Nu, my father, and bid him to have knowledge of all the reptiles in the deep and upon the dry land. Let it be made known unto each one that my rays shall fall upon them. By words of magic alone can they be overcome. I shall reveal the charms by which the children of men can thwart all reptiles, and Osiris, thy son, shall favor the magicians who protect mankind against them."

He spake again and called forth the god Thoth who came into being by his word.

"For thee, O Thoth," he said, "I shall make a resplendent abode in the great deep and the underworld which is Duat. Thou shalt record the sins of men, and the names of those who are mine enemies; in Duat thou shalt bind them. Thou shalt be temporary dweller in my place; thou art my deputy. Lo! I now give messengers unto thee."

So came into being by his power the ibis, the crane, and the dog ape,[5] the messengers of Thoth.

Ra spake again, saying: "Thy beauty shall be shed through the darkness; thou shalt join night with day."

---

[4] Hathor, the sky goddess, in one of her many forms is the cow.

[5] The chattering of apes at sunrise gave rise to the idea that they worshipped the rising sun, and thereby also became messengers of the old lunar deity, Thoth, who is here associated with the dawn.

So came into being the moon (Ah) of Thoth, and Ra said: "All living creatures shall glorify and praise thee as a wise god."

When all the land is black, the sun bark of Ra passes through the twelve hour-divisions of night in Duat. At eventide, when the god is Tum, he is old and very frail. Five-and-seventy invocations are chanted to give him power to overcome the demons of darkness who are his enemies. He then enters the western gate, through which dead men's souls pass to be judged before Osiris. In front of him goes the jackal god, Anubis, for he is "Opener of the Ways." Ra has a scepter in one hand: in the other he carries the Ankh, which is the symbol of life.

When the sun bark enters the river Urnes of the underworld, the companions of Ra are with him. Watchman is there, and Striker, the Steersman is at the helm, and in the bark are also those divinities who are given power, by uttering magical incantations, to overcome the demons of evil.

The gloomy darkness of the first hour-division is scattered by the brightness of Ra. Beside the bark gather the pale shades of the newly dead, but none of them can enter it without knowledge of the magical formula which it is given unto few to possess.

At the end of the first hour-division is a high and strong wall, and a gate is opened by incantations so that the bark of Ra may pass through. So from division to division, all through the perilous night, the sun god proceeds, and the number of demons that must be thwarted by magic and fierce fighting increases as he goes. Apep, the great Night serpent, ever seeks to overcome Ra and devour him.

The fifth hour-division is the domain of dreaded Sokar, the underworld god, with three human heads, a serpent's body, and mighty wings between which appears his hawk form. His abode is in a dark and secret place which is guarded by fierce sphinxes. Nigh to him is the Drowning Pool, watched over by five gods with bodies like to men and animals' heads. Strange and mysterious forms hover nigh, and in the pool are genii in torture, their heads aflame with everlasting fire.

In the seventh hour-division sits Osiris, divine judge of the dead. Fiery serpents, which are many-headed, obey his will. Feet have they to walk upon and hands, and some carry sharp knives with which to cut to pieces the souls of the wicked. Whom Osiris deems to be worthy, he favors; such shall live in the Nether World: whom he finds to be full of sin, he rejects; and these do the serpents fall upon, dragging them away, while they utter loud and piercing cries of grief and agony, to be tortured and devoured; lo! the wicked perish utterly. In this divison of peril the darksome Night serpent Apep attacks the sun bark, curling its great body around the compartment of Ra with ferocious intent to devour him. But the allies of the god contend against the serpent; they stab it with knives until it is overcome. Isis utters mighty incantations which cause the sun bark to sail onward unscathed nor stayed.

In the eighth division are serpents which spit forth fire to illumine the darkness, and in the tenth are fierce water reptiles and ravenous fishes. The god Horus burns great beacons in the eleventh hour-division; ruddy flames and flames of gold blaze aloft in beauty: the enemies of Ra are consumed in the fires of Horus.

The sun god is reborn in the twelfth hour-division. He enters the tail of the mighty serpent, which is named "Divine Life," and issues from its mouth in the form of Khepera, which is a beetle. Those who are with the god are reborn also. The last door of all is guarded by Isis, wife of Osiris, and Nephthys, wife of Set, in the form of serpents. They enter the sun bark with Ra.

Now Urnes, the river of Duat,[6] flows into the primeval ocean in which Nu has his abode. And as Ra was lifted out of the deep at the beginning, so he is lifted by Nu at dawn. He is then received by Nut, goddess of the heavens; he is born of Nut and grows in majesty, ascending to high noon.

The souls of the dead utter loud lamentations when the sun god departs out of the darkness of Duat.

Hymn to the Creation of the Cosmos and Man by Aten

Beauteous is thy resplendent appearing on the horizon of heaven,
O Aten, who livest and art the beginning of life!
When thou risest on the horizon of the east thou fillest every land with thy beauties;
Fair shining art thou, great and radiant, high above the earth,
Thy beams encompass the lands to the measure of all that thou has made;

6 The underworld.

Thou art the sun, thou bringest what is needful to them by
thy love;

Thou stretchest out thy beams to the earth.

When thou art above the earth, day follows thy steps;

When thou settest on the western horizon then is the earth in
darkness like unto one that is dead;

They (men) repose in their dwellings, their heads are covered,
none seeing his fellow,

They are robbed of all the things beneath their heads and
they know it not;

Every lion cometh forth out of his cave, all snakes bite;

Night darkens, earth becomes silent, their maker hath set on
his horizon.

Light is the earth when thou risest on the horizon and shinest
at Aten by day; darkness flees;

Thou sendest forth thy rays and the world is full of joy day by
day.

They (men) awake standing on their feet;

They purify their limbs, they take their garments

And uplift their hands in adoration, because thou illuminatest
the whole earth. They perform their labors.

All cattle rest in their pastures, the trees and the plants grow
green;

The birds fly out of their nests, their outspread wings praise
thee.

All flocks leap on their feet, birds and all fowl live; thou risest
for them.

Barks go up and down stream, thy road (the Nile) is opened
at thy rising;

The fish in the river rise to the surface toward thy face, and
thy rays penetrate the great waters;

They cause women to be fruitful and men to beget,

They quicken the child within the body of its mother.

Thou soothest it that it cry out,

Thou dost nourish it within the body of its mother,

Thou givest breath to give life to all its functions.

It cometh forth from the body of its mother . . . on the day of
its birth;

Thou openest its mouth that it may speak.

The chick is in its egg, cheeping within its shell,

Thou givest it breath therein that it may live;

Thou makest it complete (fully developed) that it may break
out of the egg;

It cometh forth from the egg to cheep, to be made complete;
It runneth on its feet when it cometh forth from the egg.
. . .
Thou createdst the earth according to thy will when thou wast
    alone:
Men, herds, all flocks,
All that is upon earth and goeth upon feet,
All that is on high and flieth with wings,
The lands of Syria, of Kush, and of Egypt;
Thou settest each in its right place;
Thou providest each with that which pertaineth to it.
Thou measurest to them the duration of their lives,
Their tongues are loosened that they speak, their forms are
    according to the complexions of their skins:
Ordaining them, thou hast ordained the inhabitants of the
    lands.
Thou makest the Nile in the Underworld (Duat), thou con-
    ductest it hither at thy pleasure,
That it may give life to men whom thou hast made for thyself,
    Lord of All!
Thou givest the Nile in heaven that it descendeth to them.
It causeth its waters to rise upon the rocks like the sea; it
    watereth their fields in their districts.
So are thy methods accomplished, O Lord of Eternity! thou
    who art thyself the celestial Nile;
Thou art the King of the inhabitants of the lands.
And of the cattle going upon their feet in every land, which
    go upon feet.
The Nile cometh out of the Underworld to Egypt.
Thy rays nourish every field, thou risest and they live for thee.
Thou makest the seasons of the year that they may bring into
    existence all that thou hast made:
The winter to refresh them, the heat to warm them.
Thou createdst the heaven which is outspread that thou might-
    est rise in it,
That thou mightest see all which thou didst create.
Thou art the Only One, when thou risest in thy form as the
    living Aten, splendid, radiant, fair-shining.
Thou createdst the forms of the beings who are in thee.
Thou art the Only One in respect of cities, fields, roads, water-
    ways of the Nile.
All behold thee in their midst, for thou art the Aten of day
    above the earth.
At thy rising all live: at thy setting they die by thee.

The Destruction of Mankind

Ra is the god who created himself, and was king over gods and men alike. Mankind took counsel against his majesty and spake: "Behold, his majesty the god Ra is grown old; his bones are become silver, his limbs gold, and his hair pure lapis lazuli." His majesty heard the words which men spake concerning him. His majesty spake to those who were in his train: "Call unto me mine eye (the goddess Hathor Sekhet), and the god Shu and the goddess Tefnut, the god Seb and the goddess Nut, and the fathers and the mothers who were with me when I was in Nu (the primeval waters), and also Nu (the god of the primeval waters). Let him bring his companions with him; let him bring them in all secrecy, that men may not see them and flee. Let him go with them to the great temple at Heliopolis, that they may give counsel, for I will go forth out of the primeval waters to the place at which I shall be: let these gods be brought to me."

Now when these gods came to the place at which Ra was, they cast themselves down to earth before his majesty, and he spake before Nu, the father of the oldest gods, he who created mankind, he who was king of the spirits that know. They spake before his majesty: "Speak unto us that we may hear thy words." And Ra spake unto Nu: "O thou eldest god by whom I first had my being, and ye ancestral gods! behold, mankind, who had their being from mine eye, hold counsel against me. Tell me what ye would do in face of this. Take ye counsel for me. I will not slay them until I have heard what ye say concerning it."

Then spake the majesty of the god Nu: "O my son Ra, thou the god who art greater than his creator (Nu himself), and than those who formed him! Thy throne standeth fast, great is the fear of thee. Turn thine eye against those who conspire against thee." The god Ra spake: "Behold, men flee into the hills; their heart is full of fear because of that which they said." Then spake the gods before his majesty, Ra the king: "Send forth thine eye; let it destroy for thee the people which imagined wicked plots against thee. There is no eye among mankind which can withstand thine eye when it descendeth in the form of the goddess Hathor."

Then went forth this goddess, and she slew mankind upon the hills. Then spake the majesty of this god: "Approach in peace, Hathor! Never will I be parted from thee." Then spake the goddess: "Mayst thou live for me! When I took possession of mankind, then was my heart rejoiced." Then spake the majesty of the god Ra: "I will take possession of mankind as their king, and destroy them." And it came to pass that for several nights Sekhet waded in the blood of men, beginning at Heracleopolis Magna.

Then spake Ra: "Call unto me swift messengers; let them run like a blast of wind." The messengers were forthwith brought. The majesty of this god spake: "Let them run to Elephantine; let them bring me many mandrakes." These mandrakes were brought to him. They were given to the god Sekti (the grinder), who dwells in Heliopolis, that he should grind these mandrakes. Behold, when the women slaves had crushed corn for beer, then these mandrakes were put in the jars in which was the beer and also human blood. Seven thousand beer jars of this were made.

When the majesty of Ra, King of Upper and Lower Egypt, came with the gods to see this beer, and day dawned, after this goddess had been slaughtering men as she went up stream, then spake the majesty of this god: "This is excellent. I shall protect mankind against her."

Ra spake: "Let these jars be carried and brought to the place at which men are being slaughtered." The majesty of Ra, King of Upper and Lower Egypt, commanded that this soporific drink should be poured forth during the fine night. The fields on all four sides were overflowed, as the majesty of this god had commanded.

And the goddess Sekhet came in the morning; she found the fields inundated, she was rejoiced thereat, she drank thereof, her heart was rejoiced, she went about drunken and took no more cognisance of men. Then spake the majesty of Ra to this goddess: "Approach in peace, thou charming goddess" (*amit*). From this the pleasant damsels in Amu have their origin.[1] And the majesty of Ra spake to this goddess: "Soporific drinks shall be prepared for thee at every New Year's feast, and verily their number (the number of the jars containing the drink) shall correspond to that of my hand-maidens." Therefore from that day soporific drinks are made

---

[1] This is because Ra had called Sekhet "amit," or "charming," and attractive women were installed as priestesses in the city of Amu in the western Delta, a city the Greeks called Apis.

by all men at the feast of Hathor, according to the number of the handmaidens.[2]

And the majesty of Ra spake to this goddess: "I suffer from a burning pain; whence is this pain?" The majesty of Ra spake: "Truly I am alive, but my heart is weary of being together with men; I have not destroyed them, they are not destroyed as befits my might." Then spake the gods who were of his following: "Let thy weariness alone; thy might is according to thy desire." But the majesty of this god spake unto the majesty of Nu (the god of the primeval waters); "For the first time my limbs ail; I will not wait until this weakness seizeth me a second time."

He reached it while it was still night. But when the earth grew light and it was morning, the men went forth with their bows and marched to battle against the enemies of the god Ra. Then spake the majesty of this god: "Your crime is forgiven you; the slaughter (which ye have executed for me) atoneth for the slaughter (which the rebels had purposed against me)." And this god spake unto the goddess Nut: "I have determined to cause myself to be uplifted into the sky, to join the blessed gods and to renounce rule of the world." His desire was fulfilled, and having reached the upper regions he inspected the territory which he had there chosen for his own, declared his purpose of gathering many men about him in it, and created for their future accommodation the various divisions of the heavenly world. His majesty—to whom Life! Prosperity! Health!—spake: "Let there be set a great field," and there appeared the Field of Rest. "I will gather plants in it," and there appeared the Field of *Aaru*; "Therein do I gather as its inhabitants things which hang from heaven, even the stars." Then Nut trembled exceedingly.[3]

And the majesty of the god Ra spake: "I excogitated millions of beings that they may extol me." And there appeared millions. And the majesty of Ra spake: "O my son Shu, do thou unite thyself with my daughter, Nut, and there watch for me over the millions of millions who are there, who there tarry in darkness."[4]

[2] The feasts of Hathor were festivals at which drinking and drunkenness were common. One inscription even mentions a festival known as the Intoxication Festival held in Hathor's honor.

[3] The vault of heaven shook so that the stars were dislodged and fell, as Ra commanded, into the land which he had also made.

[4] Ra appoints Shu to be a light unto men on earth, and he is installed by old Sun as the new.

Ra Creates the Sacred Animals

The majesty of the god Ra spake: "Let Thoth be called unto me." He was forthwith brought. The majesty of this god spake unto Thoth: "Let us go, leaving heaven and my dwelling, for I will make something shining and resplendent in Duat and in the Land of the Deep. There shalt thou register those who did wicked deeds as inhabitants, and there shalt thou imprison them, and the servants whom my heart hateth. But thou art in my place, the dweller in my place; thou shalt be called Thoth, the Resident (representative) of Ra. I give unto thee power to send forth thy messengers"[1] (*hab*)—thereupon the ibis (*habi*) of Thoth came into being. "I cause thee to uplift thine hand before the great Enneads of the gods: good is the deed (*khen*) which thou accomplishest—thereupon the sacred bird (*tekhni*) of Thoth came into being. "I cause thee to embrace (*anh*) the two heavens (the day and the night sky) with thy beauties"—thereupon the moon (*aah*) of Thoth came into being. "I cause thee to turn (*anon*) to the people of the North" —thereupon the cynocephalus (*anan*) of Thoth, who shall be [Ra's] representative, came into being. "Thou, Thoth, dost now possess my place in the sight of all who turn themselves toward thee; all creatures extol thee as a god."

Hymn to Aten

How many are the things which thou hast made:
Thou createst the land by thy will; thou alone,
With peoples, herds, and flocks,
Everything on the face of the earth that walketh on its feet,
Everything in the air that flieth with its wings,
In the hills from Syria to Kush, and the plain of Egypt,
Thou givest to every one his place, thou framest their lives,
To every one his belonging, reckoning his length of days.

[1] Throughout this text Ra pronounces the word which phonetically corresponds to the name of a sacred animal. Upon the sound of its secret name, the animal comes into being. The other sacred words spoken by Ra are part of the magical formula that, overall, initiates creation.

An Egyptian Gnostic Creation Myth

And the God laughed seven times. Ha-Ha-Ha-Ha-Ha-Ha-Ha. God laughed, and from these seven laughs seven Gods sprang up which embraced the whole universe; those were the first Gods.[1]

When he first laughed, light appeared and its splendor shone through the whole universe. The God of the cosmos and of the fire. Then: BESSEN BERITHEN BERIO, which are magic words.

He laughed for the second time and everything was water; the earth heard the sound and saw the light and was astonished and moved, and so the moisture was divided into three and the God of the abyss appeared. The name is ESCHAKLEO: you are the OE, you are the eternal BETHELLE!

When the God wanted to laugh for the third time, bitterness came up in his mind and in his heart and it was called Hermes, through whom the whole universe is made manifest. But the one, the other Hermes, through whom the universe is ordered, remains within. He was called: SEMESILAMP. The first part of the name has to do with Shemesh, the sun, but the rest of the word is not explained.

Then the God laughed for the fifth time and while he was laughing he became sad and Moira (fate) appeared, holding the scales in her hand, showing that in her was justice. So you see justice comes from a state between laughing and sadness. But Hermes fought with Moira and said, "I am the just one!" While they were quarreling, God said to them, "Out of both of you justice will appear, everything should be submitted to you."

When the God laughed for the sixth time, he was terribly pleased and Chronos appeared with his scepter, the sign of power, and God said to him that he should have the glory and the light, the scepter of the ruler, and that everything present and future, would be submitted to him.

Then he laughed for the seventh time, drawing breath, and *while he was laughing he cried, and thus the soul came into being.* And God said, "Thou shalt move everything, and every-

---

[1] This text has no exact date or origin. All that is known is that it comes from late antiquity, probably from Hellenized Egypt. The text begins with a list of angels and invocations to the godhead: "The first angel praises you in the language of birds, ARAI, ARAI. The sun praises you in the holy language LAILAM (Hebrew), with the same name." The 36-letter name means: "I go before you, I, the Sun, and it is through you that the sun boat comes up."

thing will be made happier through you. Hermes will lead you." When God said this, everything was set in motion and filled with breath.

When he saw the soul he bent down to the earth and whistled mightily and hearing this, the earth opened and gave birth to a being of herself. She gave birth to a being of her own, the Pythic dragon, who knew everything ahead through the sound of the Godhead. And God called him ILLILU ILLILU ILLILU ITHOR, the shining one, PHOCHOPHOBOCH. When he appeared, the earth swelled up and the pole stood still and wished to explode. And God saw the dragon and was afraid and through his fright there came out Phobos (terror), full of weapons and so on.

The Book of Knowing the Genesis of the Sun-God and of Overthrowing Apop[1]

The Master of Everything saith after his forming:
"I am he who was formed as Khepri.
When I had formed, then only the forms were formed.
All the forms were formed after my forming.
Numerous are the forms from that which proceeded from my mouth.
The heaven had not been formed,
The earth had not been formed,
The ground had not been created
For the reptiles in that place.
I raised myself among them in the abyss, out of its inertness.
When I did not find a place where I could stand,
I thought wisely in my heart,
I founded in my soul.
I made all forms, I alone.
I had not yet ejected as Shu,
I had not spat out as Tefenet,
None else had risen who had worked with me.
Then I founded in my own heart;

---

[1] This myth is from a single papyrus copy written during the reign of Alexander II, around 310 B.C. It is one of the fullest extant Egyptian texts dealing with the creation of the world. This rendition is taken from E. A. Wallis Budge's "The Hieratic Papyrus of Nesi-Amsu," in *Archaeologia*, lii, pp. 557ff (1890).

There were formed many forms,
The forms of the forms in the forms of the children,
And in the forms of their children.
What I ejected was Shu,
What I spat out was Tefenet.
My father, the abyss, sent them.
My eye followed them through ages of ages.
As they separated from me. After I was formed as the only god,
Three gods were separated from me since I was on this earth.
Shu and Tefenet rejoiced in the abyss in which they were.
They brought me my eye back following after them.
After I had united my members, I wept over them.
The origin of men was thus from my tears which came from my eye.
It became angry against me after it had come back,
When it found that I had made me another eye in its place
And I had replaced it by a resplendent eye;
I had advanced its place in my face afterward,
So that it ruled this whole land.
Now at its time were their plants (?)
I replaced what she had taken therefrom.
I came forth from the plants.
I created all reptiles and all that was in them.
Shu and Tefenet begat Qeb and Nut.
Oeb and Nut begat Osiris, Horus (the one before the eyeless),
Seth, Isis, and Nephthys from one womb,
One of them after the other;
Their children are many on this earth."

SELECTIONS FROM THE EGYPTIAN
BOOK OF THE DEAD[1]

Creation Themes from the Papyrus of Ani

God is One and only, and none other existeth and Him.—
God is the One, the One who hath made all things.—God is a
spirit, a hidden spirit, the spirit of spirits, the great spirit of
the Egyptians, the divine spirit.—God is from the beginning,
and He hath been from the beginning. He hath existed from of
old, and was when nothing else had being, He existed when
nothing else existed, and what existeth He created after He had
come into being. He is the Father of beginnings,—God is the
eternal One, He is eternal and infinite, and endureth for ever
and aye.—God is hidden and no man knoweth His form. No
man hath been able to seek out His likeness; He is hidden to
gods and men, and He is a mystery unto His creatures. No man
knoweth how to know Him.—His name remaineth hidden; His
name is a mystery unto His children. His names are innumerable, they are manifold, and none knoweth their number.—God
is truth, He liveth by Truth, He feedeth thereon. He is the King
of Truth, and He hath established the earth thereupon.—God
is life, and through Him only man liveth. He giveth life to
man. He breatheth the breath of life into his nostrils.—God
is father and mother, the father of fathers and the mother of
mothers. He begetteth, but was never begotten; He produceth,
but was never produced; He begat Himself and produced
Himself. He createth, but was never created. He is the maker

---

[1] The "Book of the Dead" is a term used to describe Egyptian funerary
literature. In it there are many formulas for use by the dead in the
afterworld. They also contain many basic ideas of the Egyptian religion.
The earliest-known collection of Egyptian funerary writing dates from
the XVIII dynasty, between 1580–1350 B.C. This collection also contains
texts compiled from earlier religious writings—the Coffin Texts (c. 2000
B.C.) and the Pyramid Texts (c. 3000–2600 B.C.). The two best-known
translations of these collections are those by Sir Peter Le Page Renouf
and Sir E. Wallis Budge. I have used the Budge translations wherever
possible.

of His own form, and the fashioner of His own body.—God Himself is existence, He endureth without increase or diminution, He multiplieth Himself millions of times, He is manifold in forms and in members.—God hath made the universe, and He hath created all that therein is. He is the Creator of what is in this world, and of what was, and of what is, and of what shall be. He is the creator of the heavens, and the earth, and of the deep, and of the water, and of the mountains. God hath stretched out the heavens and founded the earth.—What His heart (*i.e.*, mind) conceived straightway came to pass. When He hath spoken it cometh to pass and endureth forever. —God is the father of the Gods. He fashioned man and formeth the gods.—God is merciful unto those who reverence Him, and He heareth him that calleth upon Him. God knoweth him that acknowledgeth Him. He rewardeth him that serveth Him, and He protecteth him that followeth Him.[2]

This holy god, the lord of all the gods, Amen-Ra; the lord of the Throne of the Two Lands, the governor of Apt; the holy soul who came into being in the beginning; the great god who liveth upon Truth; the First God of primeval time, who produced the Ancient Gods, the being through whom every [other] god hath existence; the One One who hath made everything which hath come into existence since primeval time when the world was created; the being whose birth is hidden, whose evolutions are manifold, whose growth is incomprehensible; the holy form, beloved, terrible, and mighty in his risings; the lord of space the Power, Khepera who createth every evolution of his existence, except whom at the beginning none other existed; who at the dawn of primeval time was Atmu, the prince of light and splendor; who having made himself, made all men to live.

The god Tem existed by himself, and that it was he who, by a series of efforts of his mind, created the heavens and the earth, and gods and men, and every creature which has life. He was self-created and self-existent, and that he was One

---

[2] The above are extracts compiled by Dr. Heinrich Brugsch, the German philologist and Egyptologist, from many different texts. They are not all of the same date, but accurately reflect the ideas of monotheism and creation in ancient Egypt. In fact, all of the selections in this section have been chosen because they clearly show the Egyptians' ideas about God, cosmic powers, and their creations. The selections are from a number of different sources gathered by Dr. Brugsch, but not given by him. The dashes indicate separation between the different selections.

Only, and he was quite alone when he arrived at the decision to create the heavens and the earth, and gods and men. The gods proceeded from his body, and men from the words of his mouth.[3]

The first act of creation was the sending forth from Nu of the ball of the sun, the creation of light.[4] Temu evolved the thought in Nu, and when the thought was expressed in a word, or words, the sun appeared as the result. Every succeeding act of creation represented a thought of Temu and its expression in words, which probably took the form of commands. The God of the Sun was, under the second half of the period of the Ancient Empire, called Ra, but it is very probable that Ra was identified with Temu at an early date, and that to the creature was paid the worship due to the Creator.

The Book of Knowing How Ra Came into Being

The desire to create the heavens and the earth arose in his heart, or mind, and he assumed the form of the god Khepera, who from first to last was regarded as a form of Nu, or the Creator, *par excellence*. At this time nothing existed except the vast mass of Celestial Waters which the Egyptians called Nu, and in this existed the germs of all living things that subsequently took form in heaven and on earth, but they existed in a state of inertness and helplessness. When Khepera rose out of this watery mass, he found himself in an empty space, and he had nothing to stand upon. Khepera came into being by pronouncing his own name, and when he wanted a place whereon to stand, he first conceived the similitude of that standing place in his mind, and when he had given it a name, and uttered that name, the standing place at once came into being.[1] Khepera also possessed a *Ba* or Heart-soul, which

[3] Here we have a recurrent theme, not ony in Egyptian creation myth but in many cultures and lands—that of a single God who was self-created, self-existent, who created the universe. According to the Egyptian *Book of the Dead*, however, he possessed a dual soul, a shadow and a humanlike soul. These aspects of spirit lived in Nu, or Celestial waters.
[4] The body, and material, of the sun was worshiped as the source of all heat, light, and life by many of the ancient Egyptians.

[1] This process of thinking out the existence of things is expressed in Egyptian by words, which mean literally "laying the foundation in the heart," or, that is, in the mind.

assisted him in depicting in his mind the image of the world
which was to be. And he was also assisted in this work by
maat.[2]

Khepera next created the first triad of gods. He had union
with his shadow, and so begot offspring, who proceeded from
his body under the forms of Shu (air and dryness), and Tefnut
(water and moisture). Shu and Tefnut were next united, and
their offspring were Keb the Earth-god, and Nut, the Sky-god-
dess. Keb and Nut were united, and the offspring of their
embraces were Osiris, Horus, Set, Isis and Nephthys. Of these,
Osiris is "the essence of the primeval matter" of which Khepera
himself was formed. Thus, Osiris was of the same substance as
the Great God who created the world, and was a reincarnation
of his great-grandfather. Osiris was also the great Ancestor-
god, who when on earth was the great benefactor of the
Egyptians, and who, after his murder and resurrection, became
the savior of their souls.

The creation of man sprang, not from the earth, but directly
from the body of the god Khepera, or Neb-er-tcher. He joined
his members together, and then wept tears upon them, and men
and women came into being from the tears which fell from his
eyes. Men and women and all other living creatures which were
made by the god then reproduced their species, each creature
in its own way, and so the earth became filled with their
descendants.

Another Telling of the Origin of the Gods[1]

In the beginning there existed neither heaven nor earth, and
nothing existed except the boundless mass of primeval water
which was shrouded in darkness, and which contained within
itself the germs and beginnings, male and female, of everything which was to be in the future world. The divine primeval
spirit, which formed an essential part of the primeval matter,
felt within itself the desire to begin the work of Creation, and

[2] *Maat* can mean many things, including law, order, truth, but here
it refers to wisdom.

[1] Again, this is not an ancient text, but a compilation by Dr. Heinrich
Brugsch of selections from various different sources, showing the origin
of the gods. See also note 2, page 276.

its word woke to life the world, the form and shape of which it had already depicted within itself. The first act of creation began with the formation of an egg out of the primeval water, from which emerged Ra, the immediate cause of all life upon the earth. The almighty power of the divine spirit embodied itself in its most brilliant form in the rising sun. When the inert mass of primeval matter felt the desire of the primeval spirit to begin the work of creation, it began to move, and the creatures which were to constitute the future world were formed according to the divine intelligence *Maat*. Under the influence of Thoth, or that form of the divine intelligence which created the world by a word, eight elements, four male and four female, arose out of the primeval Nu, which possessed the properties of the male and female. These eight elements were called Nu and Nut, Heh and Hehet, Kek and Keket, and Nen and Nenet; collectively they were called "Khemenu," or the "Eight," and they were considered as primeval fathers and mothers. They appear in two forms: 1. As apes, four male and four female, who stand in adoration of the sun when he rises, and greet him with songs and hymns of praise. 2. As human beings, four having the heads of frogs, and four the heads of serpents. The birth of light from the waters, and of fire from the moist mass of primeval matter, and of Ra from Nu, formed the starting point of all else. The light of the sun gave birth to itself out of chaos, and the conception of the future world was depicted in Thoth, the divine intelligence; when Thoth gave the word, what he commanded at once took place by means of Ptah and Khnemu, the visible representatives who turned Thoth's command into deed. Khnemu made the egg of the sun, and Ptah gave to the god of light a finished body. The first company of the gods were Shu, Tefnut, Keb, Nut, Osiris, Isis, Set, Nephthys, Horus, and their governor Tem, or Atmu.

The Legend of Ra and Isis

The Chapter of the Divine God, who created himself, who made the heavens and the earth, and the breath of life, and fire, and the gods, and men, and beasts, and cattle, and reptiles, and feathered fowl, and the fish; who is the king of men and gods, the one Form, to whom periods of one hundred and twenty years are as single years, whose multitudinous names are unknowable, for even the gods know them not.

Behold, the goddess Isis lived in the form of a woman, who had the knowledge of words of power. Her heart turned away in disgust from the millions of men, and she chose for herself the millions of the gods, but she esteemed more highly the millions of the spirits. Was it not possible to become even as was Ra in heaven and upon earth, and to make herself mistress of the earth and a mighty goddess by means of the knowledge of the Name of the holy god? Thus did she meditate in her heart.

Behold, Ra entered heaven each day at the head of his mariners, establishing himself upon the double throne of the two horizons. Now the divine one had become old, he dribbled at the mouth, and he let his emissions go forth from him upon the earth, and his spittle fell upon the ground. This Isis kneaded with dust in her hand, and she fashioned it in the form of a sacred serpent with dartlike fangs, so that none might be able to escape alive from it, and she placed it on the path whereon the great god was about to travel, according to his desire, around about the Two Lands (*i.e.*, Egypt). Then the holy god rose up in the tabernacle of the gods in the Great House (the sky), Life, Strength, Health among those who were in his train, and as he journeyed on his way according to his custom daily, the holy serpent drove his fangs into him. The living fire began to depart from the god's body, and the reptile destroyed the dweller among the cedars. Then the might god opened his mouth, and the cry of His Majesty, Life, Strength, Health rang through the heavens. The Company of the gods said, "What it is?" and the gods of Ra said, "What is the matter?" Now the god found no words wherewith to answer concerning himself, for his jaws shut, his lips trembled, and the poison conquered all his members, just as Hapi (the Nile) conquereth all the land through which he floweth.

Then the great god made firm his heart, and he cried out to the gods who were in his following saying: "Come ye unto me, O ye who have sprung from my members, ye gods who have proceeded from me, for I wish to tell you what hath happened. I have been stung by some deadly thing, of which my heart hath no knowledge, and which I have neither seen with my eyes nor made with my hand. I have no knowledge whatsoever of that which hath done this thing to me. Never before have I felt pain like unto this, and no pain can be worse than this. I am a Prince, and the Son of a Prince, I am a divine emanation, I was produced by a god. I am a Great One, and the son of a Great One, and my father determined for me my name. My names are multitudinous, my forms are manifold, and my being existeth in every god. I am invoked as Thoth and Heru-Hekenu. My father and my mother uttered my name, and they hid it in my body when I was born, so that none of those who would use against me words of power might succeed in making their enchantments to have dominion over me. I was coming forth from my tabernacle to look upon that which I had made, and was making my way through the Two Lands (i.e., Egypt), which I made, when I was stung, but by what I know not. Can it be fire? Can it be water? My heart is full of burning fire, my limbs are shivering, and in my members are shooting pains. Let there come to me my children the gods, who possess words of power, whose mouths are skilled in uttering them, and whose powers reach to the very heavens."

Then his children came unto him, and every god was there uttering cries of lamentation. And Isis came with her words of power, and in her mouth was the breath of life. Now the words which she stringeth together destroy diseases, and they make to live those whose throats are stopped up (the dead) and she said, "What is this, O divine father? What is the matter? Hath a serpent shot his venom into thee? Hath anything which thou hast fashioned (dared) to lift up his head against thee? Verily, it shall be overcome by effective words of power, and I will drive it away before thy light." The holy god opened his mouth and said, "I was coming along the road, and was passing through my country of Egypt, for I wished to look upon what I had made, when lo! I was bitten by a serpent. Can it be fire? Can it be water? I am colder than water. I am hotter than fire. All my members sweat, my body quaketh, mine eyes faileth me, I cannot look at the heavens. Water exudeth from my face, as in the time of the Inundation."

Then Isis said unto Ra, "O my divine father, tell me thy name, for he who is able to pronounce his name shall live." And Ra said, "I am the maker of the heavens and the earth. I have knit together the mountains, and I have created everything which existeth upon them. I am the maker of the waters. I have made Mehturt to come into being. I made Ka-en-mut-f, and I have created the joys of love. I am the maker of heaven. I have made to be hidden the two gods of the horizon. I have placed the soul of the gods in them. I am the Being who openeth his eyes and the light cometh; I am the Being who shutteth his eyes and darkness cometh. I am he who commandeth, and the waters of the Nile flow forth. I am he whose name the gods know not. I am the maker of the hours and the creator of the days. I inaugurate festivals. I make the water-flood. I am the creator of the fire of life through which the products of the workshops come into being. I am Khepera in the morning, Ra at mid-day, and Temu in the evening." Nevertheless the poison was not turned aside from its course, and the pain of the great god was not relieved.

Then Isis said unto Ra: "Among the words which thou hast said unto me there is no mention of thy name. Declare thou to me thy name, and the poison shall leave thee, for he who declareth his name shall live." Meanwhile the poison burned like blazing fire and the heat, thereof was stronger than that of a fire that burneth brightly. Then the Majesty of Ra said: "I will permit Isis to search me, and my name shall come forth from my body and go into hers." Then the divine one hid himself from the gods, and the throne in the Boat of Millions of Years was empty. And when the time came for the heart of the god to come forth, Isis said unto her son Horus: "The great god bindeth himself by an oath to give his two Eyes" (*i.e.*, the sun and moon). Thus was the great god made to yield up his name. Then Isis, the great lady of words of power, said: "Flow poison, come out of Ra. Let the Eye of Horus come forth from the god and shine outside his mouth. I work, I make the poison to fall on the ground, for the venom is conquéred. Verily the name of the great god hath been taken away from him. Ra shall live, and the poison shall die; if the poison liveth, then Ra shall die. Similarly so-and-so if he hath been poisoned and these words be said over him shall live, and the poison shall die." These were the words which Isis spake, the great lady, the Queen of the gods, and she had knowledge of Ra's own name.

Here begin the praises and glorifyings of coming out from and of going into the glorious Khert-Neter, which is in the Beautiful Amentet, of coming forth by day in all the forms of existence which it may please the deceased to take, of playing at draughts, of sitting in the Seh Hall, and of appearing as a living soul:

The Osiris the scribe Ani saith after he hath arrived in his haven of rest—now it is good for a man to recite this work whilst he is upon earth, for then all the words of Tem come to pass—

I am the god Tem in rising. I am the Only One. I came into existence in Nu. I am Ra who rose in the beginning, the ruler of this creation.

Who is this?

It is Ra, when at the beginning he rose in the city of Hensu (Herakleopolis), crowned like a king for his coronation. The Pillars of the god Shu[1] were not as yet created, when he was upon the steps of him that dwelleth in Khemenu.

I am the Great God who created himself, even Nu, who made his names to become the Company of the Gods as gods.

Who is this?

It is Ra, the creator of the names of his limbs, which came into being in the form of the gods who are in the train of Ra.

I am he who cannot be replaced among the gods.

Who is this?

It is Temu, the dweller in his disk, but others say that it is Ra when he riseth in the eastern horizon of the sky.

I am Yesterday, I know. To-day.

Who is this?

Yesterday is Osiris, and Today is Ra, when he shall destroy the enemies of Neb-er-tcher (the lord to the uttermost limit), and when he shall establish as prince and ruler his son Horus.

Others, however, say that Today is Ra, on the day when we commemorate the festival of the meeting of the dead Osiris with his father Ra, and when the battle of the gods was fought, in which Osiris, the Lord of Amentet, was the leader.

What is this?

It is Amentet, that is to say, the creation of the souls of the gods when Osiris was leader in Set-Amentet.

Others, however, say that it is the Amentet which Ra hath given unto me; when any god cometh he must rise up and fight for it.

I know the god who dwelleth therein.

Who is this?

It is Osiris. Others, however, say that his name is Ra, and that the god who dwelleth in Amentet is the phallus of Ra, wherewith he had union with himself.

I am the Benu (Phoenix) bird which is in Anu (Heliopolis). I am the keeper of the volume of the book (the Register, or the Tablet of Destiny) of the things which have been made, and of the things which shall be made.

Who is this?

---

[1] Shu is the first born son of Ra by the goddess Hathor. He represented light and the atmosphere, and supported the sky (Nut) in the daytime. The "Pillars" mentioned are the four pillars which supported the sky, and were used as markers for the four cardinal points of the world.

It is Osiris.

Others, however, say that it is the dead body of Osiris, and yet others say that it is the excrement of Osiris. The things which have been made, and the things which shall be made refer to the dead body of Osiris. Others again say that the things which have been made are Eternity, and the things which shall be made are Everlastingness, and that Eternity is the Day, and Everlastingness the Night.

I am the god Memu in his coming forth; may his two plumes be set on my head for me.

Who is this?

Menu is Horus, the Advocate (or, Avenger) of his father (Osiris), and his coming forth means his birth. The two plumes on his head are Isis and Nephthys, when these goddesses go forth and set themselves thereon, and when they act as his protectors, and when they provide that which his head lacketh.

Others, however, say that the two plumes are the two exceedingly large uraei which are upon the head of their father Tem, and there are yet others who say that the two plumes which are upon the head of Menu are his two eyes.

The Osiris the scribe Ani, whose word is true, the registrar of all the offerings which are made to the gods, riseth up and cometh into his city.

What (or, where) is this city?

It is the horizon of his father Tem.

I have made an end of my shortcomings, and I have put away my faults.

What is this?

It is the cutting of the navel string[2] of the body of the Osiris the scribe Ani, whose word is true before all the gods, and all his faults are driven out.

What is this?

It is the purification of Osiris on the day of his birth.

I am purified in my great double nest which is in Hensu (Herakleopolis) on the day of the offerings of the followers of the Great God who dwelleth therein.

What is the "great double nest"?

The name of one nest is Millions of Years, and Great Green Sea is the name of the other, that is to say Lake of Natron and Lake of Salt.

Others, however, say the name of the one is Guide of Millions of Years, and that Great Green Lake is the name of the

[2] That is, the umbilical cord.

other. Yet others say that Begetter of Millions of Years is the name of one, and Great Green Lake is the name of the other. Yet others say that Begetter of Millions of Years is the name of one, and Great Green Lake is the name of the other. Now, as concerning the Great God who dwelleth therein, it is Ra himself.

I pass over the way, I know the head of the Island of Maati. What is this?

It is Ra-stau, that is to say, it is the gate to the South of Nerutef, and it is the Northern Gate of the Domain or, Tomb of the god.

Now, as concerning the Island of Maati, it is Abtu (Abydos).

Others, however, say that it is the way by which Father Tem travelleth when he goeth forth to Sekhet-Aaru, the place which produceth the food and sustenance of the gods who are in their shrines.

Now the Gate Tchesert is the Gate of the Pillars of Shu, that is to say, the Northern Gate of the Tuat.

Others, however, say that the Gate of Tchesert is the two leaves of the door through which the god Tem passeth when he goeth forth to the eastern horizon of the sky.

O ye gods who are in the presence of Osiris, grant to me your arms, for I am the god who shall come into being among you.

Who are these gods?

They are the drops of blood which came forth from the phallus of Ra when he went forth to perform his own mutilation. These drops of blood sprang into being under the forms of the gods Hu and Sa, who are in the bodyguard of Ra, and who accompany the god Tem daily and every day.

Chapter of Making the Transformation into the Benu (Phoenix) Bird

The Osiris, the scribe Ani, whose word is truth, saith: I flew up out of primeval matter. I came into being like the god Khepera. I germinated or, grew up like the plants. I am concealed or, hidden like the tortoise (or, turtle) in his shell. I am the seed of every god. I am Yesterday of the Four Quarters of the Earth, and the Seven Uraei, who came into being in the Eastern land. I am the Great One (Horus) who illumineth the Hememet spirits with the light of his body. I am that god in respect to Set. I am Thoth who stood between them (Horus and Set) as the judge on behalf of the Governor of Sekhem (Letopolis) and the Souls of Anu (Heliopolis). He was like a stream between them. I have come. I rise up on my throne. I am endowed with a Khu (Spirit-soul). I am mighty. I am endowed with godhood among the gods. I am Khensu, the lord of every kind of strength.

Egyptian Hymns to the Creator

Praise to Amen-Ra,
the Bull in An,[1] Chief of all gods,
the good god beloved,
giving life to all animated things,
to all fair cattle.
Hail to thee Amen-Ra, Lord of the thrones of the earth,
Chief in Thebes,
Husband of his mother in his field,
turning his feet toward the land of the South,
Lord of the heathen, Prince of Arabia,
the Ancient of heaven, the Oldest of the earth,
Lord of all existences, the Support of things, the Support of all
    things.
The One in his works,[2] single among the gods,
the beautiful Bull of the cycle of gods,
Chief of all the gods,
Lord of truth, Father of the gods,
Maker of men, Creator of beasts,
Lord of existences,[3] Creator of fruitful trees,
Maker of herbs, Feeder of cattle,
Good Being begotten of Ptah, beautiful youth beloved,
to whom the gods give honor,
Maker of things below and above, Enlightener of the earth,
sailing in heaven in tranquility,
King Ra true speaker,[4] Chief of the earth,
Most glorious one, Lord of terror (awe),

---

[1] The house of the obelisk, Heliopolis.
[2] An alternative translation is: "Alone in his forms."
[3] Another translation reads: "Of things which are."
[4] Also "King of Upper and Lower Egypt."

Chief creator of the whole earth.
Making the attributes of every god,
in whose goodness the gods rejoice,
to whom adoration is paid in the great house,[5]
crowned in the house of flame,[6]
whose fragrance the gods love,
when he comes from Arabia.
Prince of the dew, traversing foreign lands,
benignly approaching Arabia.
The gods attend his feet,
while they acknowledge his Majesty as their Lord.
Lord of terror most awful,
greatest of spirits,
bring offerings, make sacrifices,
salutation to thee, Maker of the gods,
Supporter of the heavens, Founder of the earth.
Awake in strength Min Amen,[7]
Lord of eternity, Maker everlasting,
Lord of adoration dwelling in Thebes,
strong with beautiful horns,
Lord of the crown high plumed,
of the fair turban wearing the white crown,
the coronet and the diadem are the ornaments of his face,
he is invested with *Ami-ha*,
the double crown is his head-gear, he wears the red crown,
benignly he receives the Atef-crown,
on whose south and on whose north is love,[8]
the Lord of life receives the scepter,
Lord *of the breastplate* armed with the whip.
Gracious ruler crowned with the white crown,
Lord of rays, Maker of light,
to whom the gods give praises,
who stretches forth his arms at his pleasure,
consuming his enemies with flame,
whose eye subdues the wicked,
sending forth its dart to the roof of the firmament,
sending its arrows against the devourer of Nu,

[5] The temple of Amen.
[6] That is, when he is led forth in solemn procession.
[7] Amen as creator.
[8] The two divisions of Egypt (upper and lower), which is symbolized
by the crown.

it causeth the serpent to spit forth what it hath eaten.
Hail to thee Ra Lord of truth,
whose shrine is hidden, Lord of the gods,
Khepera, the Creator, in his boat,
at whose command the gods were made,
Tum, Maker of men,
supporting their works, giving them life,
distinguishing the color of one from another,
listening to the poor who is in distress,
gentle of heart when one cries unto him.
Deliverer of the timid man from the violent,
judging the poor, the poor and the oppressed,
Lord of wisdom whose precepts are wise,
He cometh as the Nile to those who love him.
Lord of mercy most loving,
He maketh to live intelligent beings,
opener of every eye,
proceeding from the firmament.
He is made out of Nu,
causer of pleasure and light,
at whose goodness the gods rejoice,
their hearts revive when they see him.
O Ra adored in Thebes,
high-crowned in the house of the obelisk (Heliopolis),
King (Ani) Lord of the New-moon festival,
to whom the sixth and seventh days are sacred,
Sovereign of life health and strength, Lord of all the gods,
who are visible in the midst of heaven,
whose name is hidden from his creatures,
in his name which is Amen.[9]
Hail to thee who art in tranquility,
Lord of magnanimity strong in apparel,
Lord of the crown high plumed,
of the beautiful turban, of the tall white crown,
the gods love thy presence,
when the double crown is set upon thy head,
thy love pervades the earth,
thy beams *arise*, men are cheered by thy rising,
the beasts shrink from thy beams,
thy love is over the southern heaven.

[9] *Amen* means "secret" or "hidden."

Hymn to Amen-Ra

Thy heart is not unmindful of the northern heaven,
thy goodness . . . all hearts,
love subdues all hands,
thy creations are fair overcoming all the earth,
all hearts are softened at beholding thee.
The One maker of existences,
creator of . . . maker of beings,
from whose eyes mankind proceeded,
of whose mouth are the gods,
maker of grass for the cattle (oxen, goats, asses, pigs, sheep),
fruitful trees for men,
causing the fish to live in the river,
the birds to fill the air,
giving breath to those in the egg,
feeding the bird that flies,
giving food to the bird that perches,
to the creeping thing and the flying thing equally,
providing food for the rats in their holes,
feeding the flying *things* in every tree.
Hail to thee for all these things,
the One alone with many hands,
lying awake while all men lie asleep,
to seek out the good of his creatures,
Amen (the hidden) sustainer of all things,
Athom Horus of the horizon,
homage to thee in all their voices:
salutation to thee for thy mercy unto us,
protestations to thee who hast created us.
Hail to thee say all creatures,
salutation to thee from every land,
to the height of heaven, to the breadth of the earth,
to the depths of the sea,
the gods adore Thy Majesty,
the spirits thou hast created exalt thee,
rejoicing before the feet of their begetter,
they cry out welcome to thee,
father of the fathers of all the gods,
who raises the heavens who fixes the earth.
Maker of beings, Creator of existence,
Sovereign of life, health, and strength, Chief of the gods,

we worship thy spirit *who alone* hast made us,
we whom thou hast made (thank thee) that thou hast given us
    birth,
we give to thee praises on account of thy mercy to us.
Hail to thee Maker of all beings,
Lord of truth father of the gods,
Maker of men creator of beasts,
Lord of grains,
making food for the beast of the field,
Amen the beautiful Bull,
beloved in Thebes,
high crowned in the house of the obelisk (Heliopolis),
twice turbaned in An,
judge of combatants in the great hall,
Chief of the great cycle of the gods,
The One alone without peer,
Chief in Thebes,
King over his cycle of gods,
living in truth forever,
Lord of the horizon, Horus of the East,
he who hath created the soil with silver and gold,
the precious lapis lazuli at his pleasure,
spices and incense various for the peoples,
fresh odors for thy nostrils,
benignly come to the nations,
Amen-Ra Lord of the thrones of the earth,
Chief in Thebes,
the Sovereign *on his throne*.
King alone, *single* among the gods,
of many names, unknown is their number,
rising in the eastern horizon setting in the western horizon,
overthrowing his enemies,
dawning on (his) children daily and every day,
Thoth raises his eyes,
he delights himself with his blessings,
the gods rejoice in his goodness who exalts those *who are lowly*,
Lord of the boat and the barge,
they conduct thee through the firmament in peace.
Thy servants rejoice,
beholding the overthrow of the wicked,
his limbs pierced with the *sword*
fire consumes him,
his soul and body are annihilated.
Naka (the serpent) saves *his feet*,

the gods rejoice,
the servants of the Sun are in peace,
An is joyful,
the enemies of Athom are overthrown and Thebes is in peace,
    An is joyful,
the giver of life is pleased,
at the overthrow of the enemies of her Lord,
the gods of Kher-sa make salutations,
they of the Adytum prostrate themselves.
They behold the mighty one in his strength,
the image of the gods of truth the Lord of Thebes,
in thy name of Doer of justice,
Lord of sacrifices, the Bull of offerings,
in thy name of Amen the Bull of his mother,
maker of men,
causing all things which are to exist,
in thy name of Athom Khepera (the Creator),
the great Hawk making each body to rejoice,
benignly making each breast to rejoice,
type of creators high crowned,
the Diadem (Uati) is on his forehead,
the hearts of men seek him,
when he appears to mortals,
he rejoices the earth with his goings forth,
Hail to thee Amen-Ra Lord of the thrones of the world,
beloved of his city when he shines forth.

PART NINE

Near East

INTRODUCTION

Indian Cosmogony

THE INDIAN RELIGION is rivaled by none in its complexity and subtlety. Its philosophy, psychology, and spirituality developed over thousands of years, ever growing and expanding. Its myths are no less complex. Indian mythology spans perhaps the longest period in world history. It is further distinguished from other mythologies because it is still a part of the living Indian culture from which it sprang.

As will be seen in the selections in *Sun Songs*, there are several distinct traditions in India. The first involved the early Vedic[1] myths and beliefs, various forms of Hinduism, and finally several other religions such as Buddhism and Jainism occured in India. Many of the Vedic gods (Indra, Agni, Soma, Vayu, Yama, Varuna, and so forth) were absorbed into the Hindu pantheon, whose primary gods were Brahma, Vishnu, and Shiva. Many of these names consequently are found throughout Aryan myths.

In the Indian cosmogony, universal time is conceived as a never-ending cycle of alternating creation and destruction, not unlike some contemporary scientific cosmological theories. Each cycle is believed to equal one hundred years in Brahma's life. At the conclusion of this expanding universe the entire cosmos, including the supreme god Brahma, all other gods,

---

[1] The Vedas are the oldest scriptures of Hinduism, but are also revered by other Indian religions including Buddhism and Jainism. They comprise the oldest religious texts in the Indo-European language, and are the literature of the Aryans who invaded India from the north about 1500 B.C. Much of the Veda deals with fire sacrifice. The Vedic hymns were probably first compiled (although written much earlier) during a five-hundred-year period. The Vedas consist of four types of writings—the *Samhita, Brahmana, Aranyaka*, and *Upanishad*. The Samhitas are songs, of which there are four—*Rig, Sama, Yajur* and *Atharva*. These comprise the basic Veda. The Brahamanas are prose explanations of religious rituals, the Aranyaka give instructions in meditation, and the Upanishads are speculative, philosophical writings often on mystical themes.

wise men, demons, animals, mankind, and matter are to be dissolved in a Great Cataclysm the Hindus call *Mahapralya.* Then one hundred years of chaos occur, after which Brahma is born again and another cycle begins. Thus, creation is a continuum. At the beginning of each creation cycle there will be a flood that covers the universe. These cycles are broken down into divisions and subdivisions, each with judgment, morality, and virtue playing an integral and important causative role. The most important cycle is the Kalpa, which is one day in the life of Brahma, but equivalent to 4,320 million earth years.

The beginning of each cycle of creation is described by many myths. One of the most popular, included in *Sun Songs* on page 331 is the Vedic conception of a golden cosmic egg floating on the cosmic water. After a thousand years the egg bursts open and gives birth to the Lord of the Universe, who becomes the first, eternal man whose soul is in perfect unity with the Universal Spirit. This first man is called Purusha because he is the first to destroy all sin by fire. Purusha, however, experiences fear when he first casts his eyes on the empty waters of the cosmos—for he realizes he is completely alone. But he also immediately sees that there is nothing to fear—precisely because he is alone. However, Purusha feels no delight in being alone, so he divides himself in two—half female and half male. But now feeling disunited, Purusha joins himself to his male part and then makes the female part his wife. Together they take the forms of many creatures and thereby give birth to all sorts of animals. Thus, life was created.

In other versions of this creation myth the creator is Narayana, but the result is the same. Later myths tend to refer to Brahma as the creator. In these myths the Lord of the Universe broods over the cosmic egg as it lies on the watery abyss for a thousand years, until Brahma springs forth from a lotus, self-created but possessing the powers of the Lord of the Universe.

The creation story in the *Laws of Manu*[2] combines many of

---

[2] See the selection, the "Laws of Manu," and note 1 on page 323. Manu is a semilegendary Hindu lawgiver. Nothing is known about Manu, but the writings attributed to him date from somewhere between 200 B.C. and A.D. 200. The writings deal only tangentially with myths and basically provide rules for priests on the performance of ritual and the conduct of daily life. But their influence on Indian life over the ages has been tremendous.

these same elements but brings in a new idea: Manu is a sage and a human being who survives the Mahapralya, or destruction, and takes a leading role in the creation of the next period.

Persian Cosmogony

The ancient Persians are closely akin to the Aryan races of India. Their religion, which is similar in many ways to the Vedic teachings, was dominant in Persia until the Arab conquest in the seventh century. The Persian mythology involves a central struggle between the forces of light and darkness, between good and evil, which was a dominant theme among all Indo-European peoples. Throughout these myths, giants are killed by sky or storm gods. Or a heavenly being slays a dragon hidden in a cloud whose moisture waters the earth. In still other myths the fire of heaven is brought by a hero like the Greek Prometheus or by some spirit-animated animal such as a bird. All such myths involve a struggle against darkness.

The Persian legend of creation describes how Ahura Mazda, a god of light, lives eternally within his infinite illumination, while Angra Mainyu, a god of darkness, stays in an abyss of endless blackness. Between these two opposing principles is empty space—the air. Ahura Mazda first creates "Good Mind," then creates life (sky, water, earth, plants, animals, and mankind). The evil spirit, Angra Mainyu, rises from the abyss and attempts to destroy what has been created. But Ahura Mazda is too powerful and forces the evil spirit to retreat back into his gloomy darkness where he creates many fiends and other evil spirits to help him in his battle. The two deities, each seeing how powerful the other is, then forge an agreement whereby three thousand years pass until the will of Ahura Mazda will be done; for the next three thousand years the two gods' wills are to be merged, and in the last three thousand the evil spirit is to be overcome. Angra Mainyu agrees to this arrangement because he is ignorant and unobservant, so at the end of time the god of light will be supreme.

Most of the Persian myths are contained in their sacred book, the *Zend Avesta* (*Zend* = commentary, *Avesta* = law). While the major source for ancient Persian myths, the book itself is confused by many fragmentary entries written by many people, over many years. Zoroaster, the prophet and founder of the ancient Persian, or Zoroastrian religion, probably contributed to the *Gathos* (or "Songs") part of the *Zend Avesta* in his own hand. The Zoroasterian religion is ditheistic, with a righteous god, Ahura Mazda (also Ormazd, or Ormuzd), and evil god, Ahriman (also Aharman, or Angra Mainyu). The continual war between these two deities will end only when mankind asserts its collective willpower in favor of one or the other. Out of this ongoing battle the cosmogony and eschatology of the Zoroastrian religion are developed.[3]

---

[3] For more detailed information on the religion of Zoroaster, see R. C. Zaehner, *The Dawn and Twilight of Zoroastrianism*; M. N. Dhalla, *History of Zoroasterianism*, and Raymond Van Over, *Eastern Mysticism*, vol. 1 (New York: The New American Library, Inc., 1977).

INDIAN CREATION MYTHS

The Muria[1]

Creation of the Cosmos

When this world was first made, there was neither sun nor moon and the clouds and the earth were like husband and wife, they lay so close together. Men were very small and had to move between them. They ploughed with rats and to pick brinjals they had to reach up as though they were getting mangoes from a tree. As they walked to and fro, they used to knock their heads against the clouds.

Then Lingo and his brothers raised the clouds into the sky and there was room for men on earth, but there was no sun or moon and everything was dark. There was a tree called Huppe Piyer. When this tree blossomed it was day, when it dried up it was night. The twelve Lingo brothers and the thirteen Bhimul brothers thought and thought how they could bring more light to the world. "Where can we find something which will make light and darkness?" So thinking they came to the tree Huppe Piyer. "This is what we want," they said and began to cut it down. It was so big that the twelve Lingo brothers and the thirteen Bhimul brothers could cook their food and sleep in the space cut by their axes. When it was nearly cut through, it still did not fall for on the top of the tree sat the bird called Gara-surial-pite holding it up. Said Lingo his brother, "We must kill this bird," and Kosa Kana took his ax and killed it. Then the tree fell to the ground.

When the tree came down, it fell on the thirteen Bhimul brothers and they shouted with fear. Lingo picked it up with one hand and threw it aside. Now this tree stood in the kingdom of twelve Rajas, and when these heard the noise they sent

---

[1] The Muria is a tribe of the Bastar State in the Central Provinces of India, between the coastal cities of Bombay and Calcutta. See Verrier Elwin, *The Muria and Their Ghotul* (Bombay, India: Oxford University Press, 1947), for more information on the culture and society of the Muria.

their police to see if the tree was safe. The police reported that someone or other had cut it down and the Rajas sent their soldiers to arrest the culprits. Lingo said to the soldiers, "We have come to make two lanterns so that there may be light by day and light by night. We have done no evil." So said Lingo. But the soldiers took no heed of what he said and attacked the brothers with their spears and swords. Lingo took all the blows in his own body and saved his brothers. Then he himself took his sword and fought and killed the soldiers. With their blood the tree became red, for its roots drank it up. Then the brothers stripped off the bark and cut the wood into two great circles.

They made the lower circle into the sun and the upper circle into the moon. The sun was as big as the kingdoms of the twelve Rajas, but the moon was smaller. When they were ready, the brothers wondered how to put into them a living soul. Mahapurub had a son. "Only by killing Mahapurub's son and giving his blood to the sun and moon to drink will they become alive and be man and woman," so said Lingo. The brothers thought and thought how to match Mahapurub's son, but at last Lingo said, "I will catch him" and went to Porrobhum.

Mahapurub was working in his fields. His wife put the child in a swing and went for water. Lingo stole the child and brought him down to earth. There he sacrificed him and offered his blood to the sun and moon. The sun, who is a man, drank a lot of the blood and that is why he is always red. The moon, who is a woman, only drank a little and is always pale.

When Mahapurub's wife returned and could not find her son, she ran to tell her husband and they were full of sorrow. But next morning when the sun rose red into the sky, Mahapurub cried to his wife, "Look there's your baby in the sky; don't weep, for you will always be able to look at him."

Another Creation Tale

In the old days there was an earth. At the time when Lingo and his brothers were born Mahapurub turned the world topsy-turvy and it was eaten by the earthworm, so the Middle World became nought but water. There were two young children on the earth. God put life into their bodies by poking them in the back: the marks of his fingers still remain. They hid inside a gourd which grew up out of the water as a great creeper and reached the heavens.

Presently the worm excreted the earth and some of it fell on a siari leaf. That earth began to weep, "Who is there to serve me, for all mankind are drowned?" When Lingo heard that weeping he went to see what was the matter. Meanwhile, Mahapurub had plucked the gourd growing from the great creeper in the heavens and found inside the two small children. "Where can these children live?" So thinking he sent his crow to search for it. The crow flew and flew across the ocean until at last it saw Lingo and his brothers driving their harrow over the sea. Wherever the harrow went there was land, where it went crooked or missed a place there was water and a river, where the earth was piled up at the side there was a mountain. When the crow saw this it flew back and told Mahapurub that the earth was made again, and the two children were sent to live there.

Mahapurub told the boy and girl that they should marry each other but they refused saying, "We are brother and sister." So the smallpox goddess came and separated them and each got smallpox. Afterward when they met they did not know who they were, for their faces were covered with the marks of disease, and they got married. Now these two, man and woman, had no knowledge of sex. They lived together working in their fields, but the man never went to his wife. Presently Mahapurub sent Lingo to see how they were getting on. "They know nothing of love or copulation, they are living as brother and sister," so said Lingo. This made Mahapurub anxious about the peopling of the world. So he gave Lingo two pills filled with his love charms to give them.

When Lingo reached the house, he found the man had gone to hunt but the woman was bathing. He gave her the two pills and told her to eat one of them after the bath and to give the other to her husband when he returned. Having done this, Lingo went away. The woman ate one pill but was so pleased with it that she ate the second also, leaving nothing for her husband. Directly she swallowed the pills she was filled with excitement and passion and ran into the forest to seek her man.

At last when he returned from hunting, instead of giving him his food she took him into the house and pulled him down to the ground beside her. But for all her caresses there was no desire in him and he did nothing. He ate a heavy meal but she could not eat. All night she tried to rouse him, but without success. Then once again Lingo came to see how they were. He peeped through the door and saw the woman trying to rouse her husband. So he brought two more pills and this time gave them one each. Now at last the husband's desire was awakened and he went to his wife again and again, but since the woman had a greater number of pills she was much the more passionate. That is why the Muria say women remain more passionate than men unto this day.

So strong was their passion that the very next morning a child was born. After this, children were born throughout the world and men and women increased in number.

Creation of Fire

At the begining of the world, when the earth sank beneath the great waters, there were no men left but the seven Koroho-Lingo brothers. When the water went down again, they set out to find fire to warm themselves and cook their food. Presently they saw a Maharin whose name was Parajunge; she had a fire. They made their camp near her house and went to get fire from her. The girl gave the eldest brother some fire in a bundle of grass but it went out. Then the next brother went, and the next, but every time the fire went out. At last Lingo himself went. When she offered him fire in the grass, he hit her twice and picked up a burning log from her fire and took it to his camp.

The brothers went away, but the girl soon found that she was pregnant from the two blows which Lingo had struck. The boy grew up, and when he was old enough he went with the other boys and girls to dance in Lingo's ghotul. Parajunge, his mother, followed him. Now Lingo was leading the dance with a tuft of palm leaves in his turban. When the dancers got tired, they sat down to smoke and the boy said to his mother, "All these other children have fathers, but where is my father?" Parajunge said, "It is the one who is wearing leaves in his hair, go and catch him." The boy caught him by the leg and cried, "You are my father." When the brothers heard it they were very angry with Lingo and said, "We would have given you a kingdom, but he who makes a Maharin pregnant becomes a Mahara." Lingo said, "I never went to her, I only hit her and she became pregnant of her own accord." They disputed this for many days and at last Lingo said, "You may test me by oil and fire; make a great iron vessel and fill it with twelve pots of oil; put me in it and boil me on a hearth lit with twelve cartloads of wood; if I am unhurt, it will prove me innocent." The brothers carried out the test and Lingo was unharmed; he sat in the fire playing his eighteen instruments. The brothers then believed Lingo and gave him the kingdom. The name of the boy was Son Kuar and he was admitted into the ghotul as a Muria, but they would not accept his mother.

Kumis Creation Myth

(Eastern India)

God made the world and the trees and the creeping things first, and after that he made one man and one woman, forming their bodies of clay; but every night, when he had done his work, there came a great snake, which, while God was sleeping, devoured the two images. This happened twice or thrice, and God was at his wits' end, for he had to work all day and could not finish the pair in less than twelve hours; besides, if he did not sleep, "he would be no good," as the native narrator observed with some show of probability. So, as I have said, God was at his wits' end. But at last he got up early one morning and first made a dog and put life into it; and that night, when he had finished the images, he set the dog to watch them, and when the snake came, the dog barked and frightened it away. That is why to this day, when a man is dying, the dogs begin to howl; but the Kumis think that God sleeps heavily nowadays, or that the snake is bolder, for men die in spite of the howling of the dogs. If God did not sleep, there would be neither sickness nor death; it is during the hours of his slumber that the snake comes and carries us off.

Korkus Creation Myth

(Central Provinces)

Rawan, the demon king of Ceylon, observed that the Vindhyan and Satpura ranges were uninhabited, and he besought the great god Mahadeo to people them. So Mahadeo, by whom they mean Siva, sent a crow to find for him an anthill of red earth, and the bird discovered such an anthill among the mountains of Betul. Thereupon the god repaired to the spot, and taking a handful of the red earth he fashioned out of it two images, in the likeness of a man and a woman. But no

sooner had he done so than two fiery horses, sent by Indra, rose
from the earth and trampled the images to dust. For two days
the Creator persisted in his attempts, but as often as the images
mere made they were dashed in pieces by the horses. At last
the god made an image of a dog, and breathed into it the
breath of life, and the animal kept off the fiery steeds of Indra.
Thus the god was able to make the two images of man and
woman undisturbed, and bestowing life upon them, he called
them Mula and Mulai. These two became the ancestors of the
Korku tribe.

Creation Myths from the *Bhagbata*

In attempt at creation he tumbled upon Ignorance which he
cast away; and this became Night. Out of Night sprang forth
the Beings of Darkness. Brahma having created nothing else
at the time, the hungry beings of the void rushed toward
Brahma himself to devour him. Thus assailed, Brahma cried
out to his hungry sons: "Eat me not, I am your father." But
some of the hungry ones cried: "Eat him even if he is our
father." These became Yakshas; the others who cried: "Do not
let him be saved," became Rakshasas.

Becoming wiser, Brahma next created beings in whom the
Satwa quality predominated and they became celestials. From
his hip he created Asuras, from his feet the earth, from his
smile fairies, etc., etc.[1]

Prakriti (nature) is said to be the mainstay of the three
fundamental qualities, Satwa, Rajas and Tamas which were
originally in a passive state; but on their agitation by the resist-
less destiny of creatures, the Prime Person presiding over
Prakriti, and Kala (Time), the principle of Mahatawa, came

---

[1] This is a rare creation myth in which the god of creation makes a
mistake and has to begin again. In another place in the revered book,
Bhagbata, Brahma created four Munis, or sages, after his initial failure.
But these sages were not inclined toward the work of creation and
instead spent their existence meditating and worshiping Vasudeva, thus
defeating the very purpose for which Brahma created them. This second
failure filled Brahma with anger and out of his wrath sprang the mighty
storm god of the Vedas, Rudra, who carried on the work of creation.

into being. From this by a process too lengthy to be given in detail here, Tanmatras were produced. These, when combined with the Divine Power, generated the Golden Egg. The Lord of the Universe reposed for over thousand years on that egg devoid of any living creatures and lying on the surface of the ocean. While the Lord was so lying in self-communion, there issued from his navel a lotus with the shining brilliance of one thousand suns together. So large was the lotus that it could be the dwelling place of all the creatures. From this lotus sprang up Brahma, the self-created. Thereupon, being endowed with the powers of the Reverend One lying on the waters, Brahma created all beings and assigned to each of them name and form.[2]

Prajapati coming into existence from nonexistence wept, exclaiming, "for what purpose have I been born if (I have been born) from this which forms no support? The tears which fell into the water became the earth. That which he wiped away became the air. That which he wiped away upward became the sky.[3]

Maitri Upanishad

Creation of Mankind

In the beginning Pragapati, the lord of creatures, stood alone. He had no happiness, when alone. Meditating on himself, he created many creatures. He looked on them and saw they were, like a stone, without understanding, and standing like a life-less post. He had no happiness. He thought, I shall enter within, that they may awake. Making himself like air (vayu), he entered within. Being one, he could not do it. Then dividing himself fivefold, he is called Prana, Apana, Samana, Udana, Vyana. Now that air which rises upward, is Prana. That which moves downwards, is Apana. That by which these two are supposed to be held is, Vyana. That which carries the grosser

2 This is another version of the cosmic egg myth, which is so popular in many of the Indian myths of creation.
3 This is another rare myth in which the world is created by the tears of the great god Prajapati.

material of food to the Apana, and brings the subtler material to each limb, has the name Samana. That which brings up or carries down what has been drunk and eaten, is the Udana.[1]

Now the Upamsu-vessel (or prana) depends on the Antaryama-vessel (apana) and each upon the other; between these two the self-resplendent (Self) produced heat.[2] This heat is the purusha (person), and this purusha is Agni Vaisvanara. And thus it is said elsewhere: "Agni Vaisvanara is the fire within man by which the food that is eaten is cooked, (i.e., digested). Its noise is that which one hears, if one covers one's ears. When a man is on the point of departing this life, he does not hear that noise."

Now he,[3] having divided himself fivefold, is hidden in a secret place (buddhi), assuming the nature of mind, having the pranas as his body; resplendent, having true concepts, and free like ether.[4] Feeling even thus that he has not attained his object, he thinks from within the interior of the heart, "Let me enjoy objects." Therefore, having first broken open these five apertures of the senses, he enjoys the objects by means of the five reins. This means that these perceptive organs (ear, skin, eye, tongue, nose) are his reins; the active organs (tongue, hands, feet, anus, generative organs) are his horses; the body his chariot, the mind the charioteer, the whip being the temperament. Driven by that whip, this body goes around like

---

[1] These five kinds of wind are symbols for the functioning of life. The prana and apana, the up-breathing and down-breathing, keep the bodily warmth alive, as a bellows keeps up a fire. The food cooked in it is distributed by the samana, so that the coarse material becomes waste, as well as the middle flesh, and the subtle material of mind (manas). The udana brings up waste, while the vyana gives strength to the whole being.

[2] These two vessels were traditionally placed on either side of the stone on which the Soma (a sacrificial, sacred hallucinogen) is squeezed. Here it is compared to the prana and apana, between which the Self assumes heat and thereby thrives.

[3] The purusha, but originally the Pragapati, who had made himself like air and divided himself into five vital airs. The purusha in an individual is equivalent to the soul. On a universal scale it becomes a world soul, and can therefore be identified with Pragapati, the maker of all. Thus, the individual contains the godhead, or universal cause, within. The pure Self, which is also called atma, brahma, etc., after entering what he had himself created, no longer distinguishes himself from the created things (bhuta), and is called Bhutatma.

[4] Thus the atma, with his own unique qualities and those which he assumes, becomes a living being.

the wheel driven by the potter. This body is made intelligent, and he is the driver thereof.[5]

This is indeed the Self, who seeming to be filled with desires, and seeming to be overcome by bright or dark fruits of action, wanders about in every body (himself remaining free). Because he is not manifest, because he is infinitely small, because he is invisible, because he cannot be grasped, because he is attached to nothing, therefore he, seeming to be changing, an agent in that which is not prakriti, is in reality not an agent and unchanging. He is pure, firm, stable, undefiled, unmoved, free from desire, remaining a spectator, resting in himself. Having concealed himself in the cloak of the three qualities he appears as the enjoyer of rita (of his good works).

Svetasvatara Upanishad[1]

There is one Rudra only, they do not allow a second, who rules all the worlds by his powers. He stands behind all persons and after having created all worlds he, the protector, rolls it up at the end of time.[2]

That one god, having his eyes, his face, his arms, and his feet in every place, when producing heaven and earth, forges them together with his arms and his wings.

He, the creator and supporter of the gods, Rudra, the great seer, the lord of all, he who formerly gave birth to Hiranyagarbha,[3] may he endow us with good thoughts. . . .

This whole universe is filled by this person (purusha), to whom there is nothing superior, from whom there is nothing

---

[5] Compare this analogy of the body and chariot, horses and driver with Plato's almost identical image. For a summary, see Raymond Van Over, *Total Meditation* (New York: Macmillan Pub. Co., 1978), p. 32ff. Or see Plato's dialogue *Phaedrus*.

---

[1] This is the Third Adhyaya of the upanishad where the Highest Self represents the personified deity, or Rudra, involved in the full sway of his own creative power (or prakriti). In earlier Vedic writings, Rudra is a storm god.

[2] Rudra, after having created all things, draws together, and takes them all back into himself at the end of time.

[3] This is a Sanskrit word for "Golden Child," or, more literally, the "golden embryo" or "golden germ."

different, than whom there is nothing smaller or larger, who stands alone, fixed like a tree in the sky.

That which is beyond this world is without form and without suffering. They who know it, become immortal, but others suffer pain indeed.

That Bhagavat exists in the faces, the heads, the necks of all, he dwells in the cave of the heart of all beings, he is all-pervading, therefore he is the omnipresent Siva.

That person (purusha) is the great lord; he is the mover of existence, he possesses that purest power of reaching everything, he is light, he is undecaying.

Some wise men, deluded, speak of Nature, and others of Time as the cause of everything, but it is the greatness of God by which this Brahma-wheel is made to turn.

It is at the command of him who always covers this world, the knower, the time of time, who assumes qualities and all knowledge; it is at his command that this work (creation) unfolds itself, which is called earth, water, fire, air, and ether.

He who, after he has done that work and rested again, and after he has brought together one essence (the self) with the other (matter), with one, two, three, or eight, with time also and with the subtle qualities of the mind,

Who, after starting the works endowed with the three qualities can order all things, yet when, in the absence of all these, he has caused the destruction of the work, goes on, being in truth different from all he has produced.

He is the beginning, producing the causes which unite the soul with the body, and, being above the three kinds of time (past, present, future), he is seen as without parts, after we have first worshiped that adorable god, who has many forms, and who is the true source of all things, as dwelling in our own mind.

He is beyond all the forms of the tree (of the world), and of time. He is the other, from whom this world moves around, when one has known him who brings good and removes evil, the lord of bliss, as dwelling within the self, the immortal, the support of all.

Let us know that highest great lord of lords, the highest deity of deities, the master of masters, the highest above, as god, the lord of the world, the adorable.

There is no effect and no cause known of him, no one is

seen like unto him or better; his high power is revealed as manifold, as inherent, acting as force and knowledge.

There is no master of his in the world, no ruler of his, not even a sign of him. He is the cause, the lord of the lords of the organs, and there is of him neither parent nor lord.

That only god who spontaneously covered himself, like a spider, with threads drawn from the first cause (pradhana), grant us entrance into Brahman.

He is the one God, hidden in all beings, all-pervading, the self within all beings, watching over all works, dwelling in all beings, the witness, the perceiver, the only one, free from qualities.

He is the one ruler of many who seem to act, but really do not act; he makes the one seed manifold. The wise who perceive him within their self, to them belongs eternal happiness, not to others.

He is the eternal among eternals, the thinker among thinkers, who, though one, fulfills the desires of many. He who has known that cause which is to be apprehended by Sankhya (philosophy) and Yoga (religious discipline), he is freed from all fetters.

The sun does not shine there, nor the moon and the stars, nor these lightnings, and much less this fire. When he shines, everything shines after him; by his light all this is lightened.

He is the one bird[4] in the midst of the world; he is also like the fire of the sun that has set in the ocean. A man who knows him truly, passes over death; there is no other path to go.

He makes all, he knows all, the self-caused, the knower, the time of time (destroyer of time), who assumes qualities and knows everything, the master of nature and of man, the lord of the three qualities (guna), the cause of the bondage, the existence, and the liberation of the world.[5]

He who has become that, he is the immortal, remaining the lord, the knower, the ever-present guardian of this world, who rules this world forever, for no one else is able to rule it.

Seeking for freedom I go for refuge to that God who is the light of his own thoughts, he who first creates Brahman[6] and delivers the Vedas to him.

---

[4] This allusion frequently is used to refer to the Highest Self.

[5] He binds, sustains, and dissolves worldly existence.

[6] Brahman is used here in the sense of the Hiranyagarbha, or the golden germ that gives birth to everything. It can also mean "the living world as a whole."

Mundaka Upanishad

Brahma was the first of the Devas,[1] the maker of the universe, the preserver of the world. He told the knowledge of Brahman, the foundation of all knowledge, to his eldest son Atharva.

That which cannot be seen, nor seized, which has no family and no caste,[2] no eyes nor ears, no hands nor feet, the eternal, the omnipresent (all-pervading), infinitesimal, that which is imperishable, that it is which the wise regard as the source of all beings.

As the spider sends forth and draws in its thread, as plants grow on the earth, as from every man hairs spring forth on the head and the body, thus does everything arise here from the Indestructible.

The Brahman swells by means of brooding (penance); hence is produced matter (food); from matter breath, mind, the true, the worlds (seven), and from the works performed by men in the worlds, the immortal (the eternal effects, rewards, and punishments of works).

From him who perceives all and who knows all, whose brooding (penance) consists of knowledge, from Him (the highest Brahman) is born that Brahman,[3] form, and matter (food).

This is the truth. As from a blazing fire sparks, being like unto fire, fly forth a thousandfold, thus are various beings brought forth from the Imperishable, my friend, and return thither also.

That heavenly Person is without body, he is both without and within, not produced, without breath and without mind, pure, higher than the high Imperishable.[4]

[1] *Deva* means "shining one," and the devas are good spirits of Hindu mythology; also "a high god."

[2] This doesn't mean the social caste system, but rather belonging to no genus or species: "without origins and without qualities."

[3] The multiple uses of the word *Brahman* can be confusing. That is because in Sanskrit there are different meanings according to the gender of the noun. Brahman as an undifferentiated god-principle is neuter. When Brahman takes on attributes, and manifests in the physical world, his name is masculine. As masculine Brahman with attributes, he becomes the creator, or creative aspect of the neuter Supreme Spirit. It is important to keep the distinction in mind. In this instance, Brahman is used as the creator god who permeates the living world as a whole. In this guise, Brahman is also Hiranyagarbha, the golden child, or golden germ.

[4] The "high Imperishable" here is the creative Brahman, the "higher," the noncreative Brahman.

From him, when entering on creation, is born breath, mind, and all organs of sense, ether, air, light, water, and the earth, the support of all.

Fire (the sky) is his head, his eyes the sun and the moon, the quarters his ears, his speech the Vedas disclosed, the wind his breath, his heart the universe; from his feet came the earth; he is indeed the inner Self of all things.

From him comes Agni (fire),[5] the sun being the fuel; from the moon (Soma) comes rain (Parganya); from the earth herbs; and man gives seed unto the woman. Thus many beings are forgotten from the Person (purusha).

From him come the Rik, the Saman, the Yagush, the Diksha (initiatory rites), all sacrifices and offerings of animals, and the fees bestowed on priests, the year too, the sacrificer, and the worlds, in which the moon shines brightly and the sun.

From him the many Devas too are begotten, the Sadhyas (genii), men, cattle, birds, the up- and down-breathings, rice and corn for sacrifies, penance, faith, truth, abstinence, and law.

The seven senses (prana) also spring from him, the seven lights (acts of sensation), the seven kinds of fuel (objects by which the senses are lighted), the seven sacrifices (results of sensation), these seven of fuel (objects by which the senses are lighted), the seven sacrifices (results of sensation), these seven worlds (the places of the senses, the worlds determined by the senses) in which the senses move, which rest in the cave of the heart, and are placed there seven and seven.

Hence come the seas and all the mountains, from him flow the rivers of every kind; hence come all herbs and the juice through which the inner Self subsists with the elements.

The Person is all this, sacrifice, penance, Brahman, the highest immortal; he who knows this hidden in the cave of the heart, he, O friend, scatters the knot of ignorance here on earth.

Taittiriya Upanishad

He who knows the Brahman attains the highest (Brahman). On this the following verse is recorded:

He who knows Brahman, which is (i.e. cause, not effect), which is conscious, which is without end, as hidden in the

---

[5] There are five fires: those of heaven, rain, earth, man, and woman.

depth (of the heart), in the highest ether, he enjoys all blessings, at one with the omniscient Brahman.[1]

From that Self (Brahman) sprang ether (akasa, that through which we hear); from ether air (that through which we hear and feel); from air fire (that through which we hear, feel, and see); from fire water (that through which we hear, feel, see, and taste); from water earth (that through which we hear, feel, see, taste, and smell). From earth herbs, from herbs food, from food seed, from seed man. Man thus consists of the essence of food.

From food[2] are produced all creatures which dwell on earth. Then they live by food, and in the end they return to food. For food is the oldest of all beings, and therefore it is called panacea (sarvaushadha, i.e. consisting of all herbs, or quieting the heat of the body of all beings).

They who worship food as Brahman[3] obtain all food. For food is the oldest of all beings, and therefore it is called panacea. From food all creatures are produced; by food, when born, they grow. Because it is fed on, or because it feeds on beings, therefore it is called food (anna).

Different from this, which consists of the essence of food, is the other, the inner Self, which consists of breath. The former is filled by this. It also has the shape of man. Like the human shape of the former is the human shape of the latter. Prana (up-breathing) is its head. Vyana (back-breathing) is its right arm. Apana (down-breathing) is its left arm. Ether is its trunk. The earth the seat (the support).

Creation Myth from *Vishnu Purana*

Maitreya: Tell me, mighty sage, how, in the commencement of the present age, Brahma created all existent things.

Parasara: In what manner the divine Brahma, who is one with Narayana, created progeny, and is thence named the lord of progeny (Prajapati), the lord god, you shall hear.

---

[1] See note 3, page 310 for an explanation of the different names of Brahman. The same distinctions apply here where the masculine "Brahman" (of the manifested physical world) is the creative aspect of the neuter, undifferentiated godhead Brahman.

[2] *Anna* is sometimes used in the more general sense of matter.

[3] Worship consisting and in the knowledge that they are born of food, live by food, and end in food, all of which is Brahman.

At the close of the past Padma period, the divine Brahma, endowed with the quality of goodness, awoke from his night of sleep, and beheld the universe void. He, the supreme Narayana the incomprehensible, the sovereign of all creatures, invested with the form of Brahma, the god without beginning, the creator of all things; of whom, with respect to his name Narayana, the god who has the form of Brahma, the imperishable origin of the world, this verse is repeated: "The waters are called Nara, because they were the offspring of Nara (the supreme spirit); and, as, in them, his first (Ayana) progress in the character of Brahma took place, he is thence named Narayana (he whose place of moving was the waters)." He, the lord, concluding that within the waters lay the earth, and being desirous to raise it up, created another form for that purpose; and, as, in preceding ages (Kalpas), he has assumed the shape of a fish or a tortoise, so, in this, he took the figure of a boar. Having adopted a form composed of the sacrifices of the Vedas, for the preservation of the whole earth, the eternal, supreme, and universal soul, the great progenitor of created beings, eulogized by Sanaka and the other saints who dwell in the sphere of holy men (Janaloka); he, the supporter of spiritual and material being, plunged into the ocean. The goddess Earth, beholding him thus descending to the subterranean regions, bowed in devout adoration, and thus glorified the god:

Prithivi (Earth): Hail to thee, who art all creatures; to thee, the holder of the mace and shell: elevate me now from this place, as thou hast upraised me in days of old. From thee have I proceeded; of thee do I consist; as do the skies and all other existing things. Hail to thee, spirit of the supreme spirit; to thee, soul of soul; to thee, who art discrete and indiscrete matter; who art one with the elements and with time. Thou art the creator of all things, their preserver, and their destroyer, in the forms, O lord, of Brahma, Vishnu, and Rudra, at the seasons of creation, duration, and dissolution. When thou hast devoured all things, thou reposest on the ocean that sweeps over the world, meditated upon, O Govinda, by the wise. No one knoweth thy true nature; and the gods adore thee only in the forms it hath pleased thee to assume. They who are desirous of final liberation worship thee as the supreme Brahma; and who that adores not Vasudeva shall obtain emancipation? Whatever may be apprehended by the mind, whatever may be perceived by the senses, whatever may be discerned by the intellect, all is but a form of thee. I am of thee, upheld by thee; thou art my creator, and to thee I fly for refuge: hence, in this universe, Madhavi (the bride of Madhava or Vishnu) is my designation. Triumph to the essence of all wisdom, to the unchangeable, the imperishable: triumph to the eternal; to the indiscrete, to the essence of discrete things: to him who is both cause and effect; who is the universe; the sinless lord of sacrifice; triumph. Thou art sacrifice; thou art the oblation; thou art the mystic Omkara; thou art the sacrificial fires; thou art the Vedas, and their dependent sciences; thou art, Hari, the object of all worship. The sun, the stars, the planets, the whole world; all that is formless, or that has form; all that is visible, or invisible; all. Purushottama, that I have said, or left unsaid; all this, Supreme, thou art. Hail to thee, again and again! hail! all hail!

Parasara: The auspicious supporter of the world, being thus hymned by the earth, emitted a low murmuring sound, like the chanting of the Sama Veda; and the mighty boar, whose eyes were like the lotus, and whose body, vast as the Nila mountain, was of the dark color of the lotus leaves, uplifted upon his ample tusks the earth from the lowest regions. As he reared his head, the waters shed from his brow purified the great sages, Sanandana and others, residing in the sphere of the saints. Through the indentations made by his hoofs, the waters rushed into the lower worlds with a thundering noise. Before his breath the pious denizens of Janaloka were scattered; and the Munis sought for shelter among the bristles upon the scriptural body of the boar, trembling as he rose up, supporting the earth, and dripping with moisture. Then the great sages, Sanandana and the rest, residing continually in the shere of saints, were inspired with delight; and, bowing lowly, they praised the stern-eyed upholder of the earth.

The Yogins: Triumph, lord of lords supreme; Kesava, sovereign of the earth, the wielder of the mace, the shell, the discus, and the sword: cause of production, destruction, and existence. *Thou art*, O god: there is no other supreme condition but thou. Thou, lord, art the person of sacrifice: for thy feet are the Vedas, thy tusks are the stake to which the victim is bound; in thy teeth are the offerings; thy mouth is the altar; thy tongue is the fire; and the hairs of thy body are the sacrificial grass. Thine eyes, O omnipotent, are day and night; thy head is the seat of all, the place of Brahma; thy name is all the hymns of the Vedas; thy nostrils are all oblations: O thou, whose snout is the ladle of oblation; whose deep voice is the

chanting of the Sama Veda;[1] whose body is the hall of scarifice;
whose joints are the different ceremonies; and whose ears have
the properties of both voluntary and obligatory rites; do thou,
who are eternal, who art in size a mountain, be propitious. We
acknowledge thee, who hast traversed the world, O universal
form, to be the beginning, the continuance, and the destruction
of all things: thou art the supreme god. Have pity on us, O lord
of conscious and unconscious beings. The orb of the earth is
seen seated on the tip of thy tusks, as if thou hadst been sporting amidst a lake where the lotus floats, and hadst borne away
the leaves covered with soil. The space between heaven and
earth is occupied by thy body, O thou of unequaled glory,
resplendent with the power of pervading the universe, O lord,
for the benefit of all. Thou art the aim of all: there is none
other than thee, sovereign of the world: this is thy might, by
which all things, fixed or moveable, are pervaded. This form,
which is now beheld, is thy form, as one essentially with wisdom. Those who have practiced devotion conceive erroneously
of the nature of the world. The ignorant, who do not perceive
that this universe is of the nature of wisdom, and judge of it
as an object of perception only, are lost in the ocean of spiritual
ignorance. But they who knew true wisdom, and whose minds
are pure, behold this whole world as one with divine knowledge, as one with thee, O god. Be favorable, O universal spirit:
raise up this earth, for the habitation of created beings. In-
scrutable deity, whose eyes are like lotuses, give us felicity. O
lord, thou art endowed with the quality of goodness: raise up,
Govinda, this earth, for the general good. Grant us happiness,
O lotus-eyed. May this, thy activity in creation, be beneficial to
the earth. Salutation to thee. Grant us happiness, O lotus-eyed.

Parasara: The supreme being thus eulogized, upholding the
earth, raised it quickly, and placed it on the summit of the
ocean, where it floats like a mighty vessel, and from its ex-
pansive surface, does not sing beneath the waters. Then, having leveled the earth, the great eternal deity divided it into
portions, by mountains. He who never wills in vain created,
by his irresistible power, those mountains again upon the
earth, which had been consumed at the destruction of the

---

[1] There are four Vedas, of which the *Rig Veda* is the oldest. Together
they are called the Samhitas. The other Vedas are *Yajur Veda, Sama
Veda*, and *Atharva Veda*, which deal with rituals for sacrifice, chanting,
spells, and incantations.

world. Having then divided the earth into seven great portions
or continents, as it was before, he constructed, in like manner,
the four lower spheres, earth, sky, heaven, and the sphere of
the sages (Maharloka). Thus Heri, the four-faced god, invested
with the quality of activity, and taking the form of Brahma,
accomplished the creation. But he (Brahma) is only the instrumental cause of things to be created; the things that are capable
of being created arise from nature as a common material
cause. With exception of one instrumental cause alone, there is
no need of any other cause; for imperceptible substance becomes perceptible substance according to the powers with
which it is originally imbued.

Brihadaranyaka Upanishad[1]

The Creation of Ego and Mankind

In the beginning was Self (Atman) alone, in the shape of a
person.[2] He, looking around, saw nothing but his Self. He first
said, "This is I"; therefore he became "I" by name. Therefore
even now, if a man is asked, he first says, "This is I," and then
pronounces the other name which he may have. And because
before all this he (the Self) burned down all evils, therefore he
was a person (purusha). Verily he who knows this burns down
everyone who tries to be before him. He feared, and therefore
anyone who is lonely fears. He thought, "As there is nothing
but myself, why should I fear?" Then his fear passed away.
For what should he have feared? Verily fear arises from a
second only. But he felt no delight. Therefore a man who is
lonely feels no delight. He wished for a second. He was as large
as man and wife together. He then made this, his Self, to fall in
two, and thence arose husband (pat) and wife (patni). Therefore Yagnavalkya[3] said, "We two are thus, each of us, like half

[1] See the "Second Brahmana" of this Upanishad (p. 317), where
there are greater details supplied about the creation of the world
through the sacrifice of a horse. It is part of the familiar motif in
myths of a "first victim." For more information on this theme in
creation myths, see Marie-Louise Von Franz, Creation Myths (Zurich:
Spring Pub., 1972) pp. 96ff, and 118.

[2] Person here means "Purusha," or spiritual self in human form.
Max Muller, the translator of this selection, renders the self as "Atman,"
so in a sense Atman was in the shape of Purusha, or the human "self,"
or "person."

[3] In this text, Yagnavalkya is the sage who is being instructed.

a shell." Therefore the void which was there is filled by the wife. He embraced her and men were born. She thought, "How can he embrace me after having produced me from himself? I shall hide myself." She then became a cow, the other became a bull and embraced her, and hence cows were born. The one became a mare, and the other a stallion, the one a male ass, and the other a female ass. He embraced her, and hence one-hoofed animals were born. The one became a she-goat the other a he-goat; the one became a ewe, the other a ram. He embraced her and embracing each other through the whole of creation they produced all kinds of animals and beings.

Creation of Fire and Light

Second Brahmana[1]

In the beginning there was nothing to be perceived here whatsoever. By Death indeed all this was concealed—by hunger; for death is hunger. Death, the first being, thought: "Let me have a body." Then he moved about, worshiping. From him thus worshiping, water was produced. And he said: "Verily, there appeared to me, while I worshiped, water (ka)." This is why water is called arka.[2] Surely there is water (or pleasure) for him who thus knows the reason why water is called arka.

Verily, water is arka. And what was there as the froth of the water, that was hardened, and became the earth. On that earth he (Death) rested, and from him, thus resting and heated, Agni proceeded, full of light.

That being divided itself threefold, Aditya (the sun) as the third, and Vayu (the air) as the third. That spirit (prana), became threefold. The head was the Eastern quarter, and the

[1] The object of this whole Brahmana is to show the origin and true character of fire (arka). *Arka* here means fire as part of sacrifice, and in a wider sense the Brahmana also teaches the origin of Agni, the god of fire from the Vedas. Another, more roundabout description of arka as sacrificial fire is the interpretation that arka originally springs from water, out of which fire was first created indirectly. The reasoning is: from water springs the earth; on that earth he (Pragapati) rested from his task of creation, and from him, while resting, fire was first produced. That fire assumed three forms: fire, sun, and air, and in its full three fold form it is called prana, or spirit. As involuted as this may appear, it is a fair representation of the early Indian proclivity for ever more refined definitions of substances. Matter or form rarely stood unqualified before the intensely curious, inquiring Indian mentality.

[2] See the descriptions of water indirectly giving rise to fire in note 1.

arms this and that quarter. Then the tail was the Western
quarter, and the two legs this and that quarter (the N.W. and
S.W.) The sides were the Southern and Northern quarters,
the back heaven, the belly the sky, the dust the earth. Thus he
(Pragapati as arka) stands firm in the water, and he who knows
this stands firm wherever he goes.

He[3] desired, "Let a second body be born of me," and he
(Death or Hunger) embraced Speech in his mind. Then the
seed became the year. Before that time there was no year.
Speech bore him so long as a year, and after that time sent him
forth. Then when he was born, he (Death) opened his mouth,
as if to swallow him. He cried Bahn! and that became speech.

He thought, "If I kill him, I shall have but little food." He
therefore brought forth by that speech and by that body (the
year) all whatsoever exists, the Rik, the Yagus, the Saman, the
meters, the sacrifices, men, and animals.

And whatever he (Death) brought forth, that he resolved to
eat (ad). Verily because he eats everything, therefore is Aditi
(Death) called Aditi. He who thus knows why Aditi is called
Aditi, becomes an eater of everything, and everything becomes
his food.

He desired to sacrifice again with a greater sacrifice. He
toiled and performed penance. And while he toiled and performed penance, glorious power went out of him. Verily glorious power means the senses (prana). Then when the senses
had gone out, the body took to swelling, and mind was in the
body.

He desired that his body should be fit for sacrifice (medhya),
and that he should be embodied by it. Then he became a
horse (asva), because it swelled (asvat), and was fit for
sacrifice (medhya); and this is why the horse-sacrifice is called
Asva-medha.

Verily he who knows him thus, knows the Asva-medha.
Then, letting the horse free, he[4] thought, and at the end of a
year he offered it up for himself, while he gave up the other
animals to the deities. Therefore the sacrificers offered up the
purified horse belonging to Pragapati, as dedicated to all the
deities.

---

[3] "He" is the same as death, who, after becoming self-conscious, produced water, earth, fire, etc. He now wishes for a second body which
will be the year, or the annual sacrifice; the year being dependent on
the sun (Aditya).

[4] "He" considered himself the same as the horse, as he is identified
with all the animals. Thus he is involved in all sacrifices.

Hymn of Narayana[1]

Spirit of Spirits, who, though every part
Of space expanded, and of endless time,
Beyond the stretch of lab'ring thought sublime
Bad'st uproar into beauteous order start,
Before heaven was thou art:
Ere spheres beneath us roll'd, or spheres above,
Ere earth in firmamental ether hung,
Thou sat'st above; till, through thy mystic love,
Things unexisting to existence sprung,
And graceful descant sung.
What first impelled thee to exert thy might?
Goodness unlimited. What glorious light
Thy power directed? Wisdom without bound.
What proved it first? oh! guide my fancy right;
Oh! raise from cumbrous ground
My soul is rapture drowned,
That fearless it may soar on wings of fire;
For Thou, who only know'st. Thou only can'st inspire.
Wrapt in eternal solitary shade,
Th' impenetrable gloom of light intense,
Impervious, inaccessible, immense,
Ere spirits were infused or forms displayed,
Brahm his own mind surveyed.
As mortal eyes (thus finite we compare
With infinite) in smoothest mirrors gaze:
Swift, at his look, a shape supremely fair
Leap'd into being with a boundless blaze,
That fifty suns might daze.
Primeval Maya was the Goddess named,
Who to her sire, with love divine inflame;
A casket gave with rich ideas filled,
From which this gorgeous universe he framed;
For, when the Almighty will'd,
Unnumbered worlds to build,

---

[1] In some Hindu myths Narayana is considered "The Primal Lord,"
and is shown floating on a banyan leaf amidst the primal waters, suck-
ing his toe, the symbol of eternity. For more detailed information on
Narayana and myths of ancient India, see P. Thomas, *Epics, Myths,
and Legends of India*, (Bombay, India: DB. Taraporevala Sons & Co.,
n.d.).

From Unity, diversified he sprang,
While gay creation laughed and procreant Nature rang.
First an all-potent, all-pervading sound
Bade flow the waters, and the waters flow'd.
Exulting in their measureless abode,
Diffusive, multitudinous, profound,
Above, beneath, around;
Then o'er the vast expanse primordial wind
Breath'd gently, till a lucid bubble rose,
Which grew in perfect shape, an egg refined:
Created substance no such luster shows,
Earth no such beauty knows.
Above the warring waves it danc'd elate.
Till from its bursting shell with lovely state,
A form cerulean flutter'd o'er the deep,
Brightest of beings, greatest of the great:
Who, not as mortals steep,
Their eyes in dewy sleep,
But heavenly pensive on the lotus lay,
That blossom'd at his touch and shed a golden ray.
Hail, primal blossom! hail empyreal gem
Kamal or Padma, or whate'er high name
Delight thee, say, what four-formed Godhead came,
With graceful stole and beamy diadem,
Forth from thy verdant stem?
Full gifted Brahma! Rapt in solemn thought
He stood, and round his eyes fire-darting threw;
But whilst his view-less origin he sought
One plane he saw of living waters blue,
Their spring nor saw nor knew.
Then in his parent stalk again retired.
With restless pain for ages he inquired,
What were his powers, by whom and why conferr'd:
With doubts perplex'd, with keen impatience fired
He rose, and rising heard
Th' unknown, all-knowing word
"Brahma! no more in vain research persist:
My veil thou canst not love—go, bid all worlds exist."

A Shaivite Creation Myth[1]

"In the night of Brahma, when all beings and all worlds are resolved together in one equal and inseparable stillness, I beheld the great Narayana, soul of the universe, thousand-eyed, omniscient, Being and non-Being alike, reclining on the formless waters, supported by the thousand-headed serpent Infinite; and I, deluded by his glamor touched the Eternal Being with my hand and asked: 'Who art thou? Speak.' Then he of the lotus eyes looked upon me with drowsy glance, then rose and smiled and said: 'Welcome my child, thou shining grandsire.' But I took offense thereat and said: 'Dost thou O sinless god, like a teacher to a pupil call me child, who am the cause of creation and destruction, framer of the myriad worlds, the source and soul of all? Tell me why dost thou speak foolish words to me?' Then Vishnu answered: 'Knowest thou not that I am Narayana, creator, preserver, and destroyer of the worlds, the Eternal Male, the undying source and center of the universe? For thou wert born from my own imperishable body.'

"Now ensued an angry argument between us twain upon that formless sea. Then for the ending of our contention there appeared before us a glorious shining Lingam, a fiery pillar, like a hundred universe-consuming fires, without beginning, middle, or end, incomparable, indescribable. The divine Vishnu, bewildered by its thousand flames, said unto me, who was as much astonished as himself: "Let us forthwith seek to know this fire's source. I will descend, do thou ascend with all thy power.' Then he became a boar, like a mountain of blue collyrium, a thousand leagues in width, with white sharp-pointed tusks, long-snouted, loud-grunting, short of foot, victorious, strong, incomparable—and plunged below. For a thousand years he sped thus downward, but found no base at all of the Lingam. Meanwhile I became a swan, white, fiery-eyed, with

[1] While the Hindus were accepting of many gods into their pantheon, each sect tended to alter legends and myths to suit their own particular beliefs. This Shaivite myth places Shiva in the forefront of power and creation. And as each sect alters stories and texts to their needs, there is, not surprisingly, a Vaishnavite version of this same myth twisted to establish the supremacy of Vishnu. According to this second version, Brahma falsely claims to have reached the top of the Lingam while Vishnu admits he could not find its base. Shiva cuts off one of Brahma's heads and acknowledges Vishnu as the greatest of the Hindu Triad for having spoken the truth.

wings on every side, swift as thought and as the wind; and I
went upward for a thousand years seeking to find the pillar's
end, but found it not. Then I returned and met the great
Vishnu, weary and astonished, on his upward way.

"Then Shiva stood before us, and we whom his magic had
guiled bowed unto him, while there arose about us on every
hand the articulate sound of Aum clear and lasting."

Creation in the *Mahabharata*

Manu,[1] who was equal unto Brahma in glory, had practiced
austerities for 10,000 years. One day while he was meditating
on the Infinite, standing on one leg with uplifted hand by the
bank of a stream, a fish rose from the water and asked for
Manu's protection from the bigger fish that was chasing it.
Manu took the fish from the stream and placed it in an earthen
jar. The fish grew too big for the jar. Then Manu took it to a
pond. The fish grew too big for the pond and begged to be
taken to the Ganges. It was taken to the Ganges but it grew big
for the Ganges too, and had to be taken to the ocean. In the
ocean the fish smiled and revealed to Manu its identity as
Brahma. It also predicted the approaching end of the world by
a deluge, and asked Manu to build an ark and take in it "the
seven Rishis and all the different seeds enumerated by Brah-
mins of yore and preserve them carefully." Manu did as he
was told, and when the deluge began, he set sail in his ship and
fastened the cables of the ship to the horns of the fish.

"Along the ocean in that stately ship was borne the lord
   of men and through
Its dancing, tumbling billows, and its roaring waters;
   and the bark,
Tossed to and fro by violent winds, reeled on the surface
   of the deep.
Staggering and trembling like a drunken woman. Land
   was seen no more,

[1] In Indian legend, Manu is a divinely inspired law-giver. In some
places, as in this myth, he is entirely divine. In the *Mahabharata*, a
huge Sanskrit epic composed between 200 B.C. and A.D. 200, the sage
Markandeya relates how Manu is threatened, saved, and eventually
continues his work of creation.

Nor far horizon, nor the space between; for everywhere
   around
Spread the wild waste of waters, reeking atmosphere,
   and boundless sky.
Now when all the world was deluged, nought appeared
   above the waves
But Manu and the seven sages, and the fish that drew
   the bark.
Unwearied, thus for years on years, the fish propeled the
   ship across
The heaped-up waters, till at length it bore the vessel to
   the peak
Of Himavan."

Now the waters began to descend and Manu with them. In
due time he reached the plains and took up the work of creation for the next Kritayuga.

The Account of Creation by
Manu and the *Mahabharata*[1]

Vyasa said: In the commencement exists the Brahman without beginning or end, unborn, luminous, free from decay, im-
mutable, eternal, unfathomable by reasoning, not to be fully
known.

The sun divides days and nights, both human and divine, the
night being intended for the repose of created beings and the
day of exertion.

A month is a day and a night of the manes, but the division
is according to fortnights. The dark fortnight is their day for
active exertion, the bright fortnight their night for sleep.

A year is a day and night of the gods; the division is as follows: the half year during which the sun progresses to the
north will be the day, that during which it goes southward
the night.

---

[1] Equivalents of the *Laws of Manu* appear throughout the *Mahabharata* writings. Their duplication of the creation, and its subsequent
movement throughout the great ages of time, is frequent. I have compared and collated the two accounts of creation to make them more
palatable for the modern reader. I have also excluded the more tedious,
longer descriptions of the time span of millions of years for the various
ages as not germane to the creation myth.

But hear now the brief description of the duration of a night and day of Brahman and of the several ages of the world according to their order. They declare that the Krita age consists of four thousand years of the gods; the twilight preceding it consists of as many hundreds, and the twilight following it of the same number.

In the other three ages, with their twilights preceding and following, the thousands and hundreds are diminished by one in each. These support the eternal, everlasting worlds; this is known as the eternal Brahman to those who know Brahman.

In the Krita age Dharma is four-footed and entire, and so is Truth; nor does any gain accrue to men by unrighteousness.

In the other three ages, by reason of unjust gains, Dharma is deprived successively of one foot, and unrighteousness increases through theft, falsehood, and fraud.

Men are free from disease, accomplish all their aims, and live four hundred years in the Krita age, but in the Treta, and in each of the succeeding ages, their life is lessened by one quarter.

And the doctrines of the Veda decrease, as we hear, in each successive age, as well as the lives of men, their blessings, and the rewards which the Veda yields.[2]

One set of duties is prescribed for men in the Krita age, different ones in the Treta and in the Dvapara, and again another set in the Kali age, in proportion as those ages decrease in length.

In the Krita age the chief virtue is the performance of austerities, in the Treta divine knowledge is most excellent, in the Dvapara they declare sacrifices to be best, in the Kali liberality alone.

The wise know such a period of twelve thousand divine years to be understood by the term an age of the gods; that period being multiplied by one thousand is called a day of Brahman.

Know his night to be as long. At the beginning of that day the lord who is the Universe finally awakes, after having entered deep meditation and having slept during the period of destruction.

Those only who know that Brahman's day ends after the completion of one thousand ages of the gods and that his night

[2] This verse states simply that the age of men, their blessings, and the rewards of deeds, such as are promised in the Veda, diminish in each successive age.

last a thousand ages, are really men acquainted with the length of days and nights.

When imperishable Brahman awakes at the end of his night, he modifies himself and creates the element called the Great One and from that mind which is discrete.

Luminous Brahman is the seed from which single element this whole twofold creation, the immovable and the movable, has been produced.

Awaking at the beginning of his day, he creates the world by means of Ignorance—even first the element, called the Great One, next speedily mind which is discrete;

And conquering here resplendent mind which goes far, enters many paths, and has the nature of desire and doubt, creates the seven mind-born ones.

Mind, impelled by the desire to create, perform the work of creation by modifying itself; thence ether is produced; they declare that sound is the quality of the latter.

But from ether, modifying itself, springs the pure, powerful wind, the vehicle of all perfumes; touch is considered to be its quality.

Next from wind, modifying itself, proceeds the brilliant light which illuminates and is white; that is declared to possess the quality of color;

And from light, modifying itself, comes water which possesses taste; from water, smell and earth; such is declared to be the creation of them all.

Those Atmans of seven kinds, which possess various powers, were severally unable to create beings without fully uniting themselves.

These great Atmans, uniting and mutually combining with each other, entered the body; hence one speaks of Purusha.

In consequence of that entering, the body becomes endowed with a perceptible form, and consists of sixteen constituent parts.[3]

That the great elements enter together with the karma (merit and demerit).

Taking with him all the elements, that first creator of created beings enters it in order to perform austerities; him they call the lord of created beings.

---

[3] The sixteen constituent parts are apparently the five gross elements and the eleven organs of sensing.

He, indeed, creates the creatures, both the immovable and the movable; then that Brahma creates gods, sages, manes, and men,

The worlds, rivers, oceans, the quarters of the compass, mountains, trees, men, Kinnaras, Rakshas, birds, tame and wild beasts, and snakes, the imperishable and the perishable, both the immovable and the movable.

Whatever course of action they adopted in a former creation, even that alone they adopt in each succeeding creation.

They turn to noxiousness or harmlessness, gentleness or ferocity, virtue or sin, truth or falsehood, according to the disposition with which they were first created; hence that particular course of action pleases each.[4]

Laws of Manu

The great sages approached Manu, who was seated with a collected mind, and, having duly worshiped him, spoke as follows:[1]

For thou, O Lord, alone knowest the purport, the rites, and the knowledge of the soul, taught in this whole ordinance of the Self-existent, which is unknowable and unfathomable.[2]

He, whose power is measureless, being thus asked by the high-minded great sages, duly honored them, and answered, "Listen!"

This universe existed in the shape of Darkness, unperceived, destitute of distinctive marks, unattainable by reasoning, unknowable, wholly immersed, as it were, in deep sleep.

---

[4] The remainder of this narrative, twenty-six more verses, simply continues on in the same vein; finally the Lord assigns his creatures their names and conditions in life, in accordance with the words in the Vedas.

---

[1] In an alternative translation the next verse reads: "The origin of the whole multitude of created beings, of those born from the womb, of those born from eggs, of those produced from exudations and from germinating seeds, and their destruction."

[2] The ordinance of the Self-existent is "the Veda." Another rendering of this verse explains the unfathomability of the universe: "For thou, O Lord, alone knowest the nature and the object of the products employed in the creation of this universe, which is unthinkable on account of its greatness and unknowable." The "unknowable" quality of the universe is also explained in still another place by being "undefinable by words or authoritative statement."

Then the divine Self-existent, himself indiscernible, but making all the great elements and the rest discernible, appeared with irresistible creative power, dispelling the darkness.

He who can be perceived by the internal organ alone, who is subtle, indiscernible, and eternal, who contains all created beings and is inconceivable, shone forth of his own will.

He, desiring to produce beings of many kinds from his own body, first with a thought created the waters, and placed his seed in them.

That seed became a golden egg, in brilliancy equal to the sun; in that egg he himself was born as Brahman, the progenitor of the whole world.

The waters are called narah for the waters are, indeed, the offspring of Nara; as they were his first residence, he thence is named Narayana.

From that first cause, which is indiscernible, eternal, and both real and unreal, was produced that male (Purusha), who is famed in this world under the appellation of Brahman.

The divine one resided in that egg during a whole year, then he himself by his thought alone divided it into two halves;

And out of those two halves he formed heaven and earth, between them the middle sphere, the eight points of the horizon, and the eternal abode of the waters.

From himself (atmanah) he also drew forth the mind, which is both real and unreal, likewise from the mind egoism, which possesses the function of self-consciousness and is lordly;

Moreover, the great one, the soul, and all products affected by the three qualities, and, in their order, the five organs which perceive the objects of sensation.

But, joining minute particles even of those six, which possess measureless power, with particles of himself, he created all beings.

Because those six kinds of minute particles, which form the creator's frame, enter these creatures, therefore the wise call his frame sarira, (the body).

That the great elements enter, together with their functions and the mind, through its minute parts the framer of all beings, the imperishable one.

But from minute body-framing particles of these seven very powerful Purushas springs this world, the perishable from the imperishable.

Among them each succeeding element acquires the quality of the preceding one, and whatever place in the sequence each of them occupies, even so many qualities it is declared to possess.

But in the beginning he assigned their several names, actions, and conditions to all created beings, even according to the words of the Veda.

He, the Lord, also created the class of the gods, who are endowed with life, and whose nature is action; and the subtle class of the Sadhyas, and the eternal sacrifice.

But from fire, wind, and the sun he drew forth the threefold eternal Veda, called Rik, Yagus, and Saman, for the due performance of the sacrifice.

Time and the divisions of time, the lunar mansions and the planets, the rivers, the oceans, the mountains, plains, and uneven ground,

Austerity, speech, pleasure, desire, and anger, this whole creation he likewise produced, as he desired to call these beings into existence.

Moreover, in order to distinguish actions, he separated merit from demerit, and he caused the creatures to be affected by the pairs of opposites, such as pain and pleasure.

But with the minute perishable particles of the five elements which have been mentioned, this whole world is framed in due order.

But to whatever course of action the Lord at first appointed each kind of beings, that alone it has spontaneously adopted in each succeeding creation.

Whatever he assigned to each at the first creation, noxiousness or harmlessness, gentleness or ferocity, virtue or sin, truth or falsehood, that clung afterward spontaneously to it.

As at the change of the seasons each season of its own accord assumes its distinctive marks, even so corporeal beings resume in new births their appointed course of action.

But for the sake of the prosperity of the worlds, he caused the Brahmana, the Kshatriya, the Vaisya, and the Sudra to proceed from his mouth, his arms, his thighs, and his feet.

Dividing his own body, the Lord became half male and half female; with that female he produced Virag.

But know me, O most holy among the twice-born, to be the creator of this whole world, whom that male, Virag, himself produced, having performed austerities.

Then I, desiring to produce created beings, performed very difficult austerities, and thereby called into existence ten great sages, lords of created beings,

When he whose power is incomprehensible, had thus pro-

duced the universe and me, he disappeared in himself, re-
peatedly suppressing one period by means of the other.

When that divine one wakes, then this world stirs; when he
slumbers tranquilly, then the universe sinks to sleep.

But when he reposes in calm sleep, the corporeal beings
whose nature is action, desist from their actions and mind
becomes inert.

When they are absorbed all at once in that great soul, then
he who is the soul of all beings sweetly slumbers, free from all
care and occupation.

When this soul has entered darkness, it remains for a long
time united with the organs of sensation, but performs not its
functions: it then leaves the corporeal frame.

When, being clothed with minute particles only, it enters into
vegetable or animal seed, it then assumes, united with the
fine body, a new corporeal frame.

Thus he, the imperishable one, by alternately waking and
slumbering, incessantly revivifies and destroys this whole
movable and immovable creation.

Creation of the Cosmos in Manu

The Golden Egg[1]

The primeval God transformed himself into a golden egg
which was shining like the sun and in which he himself, Brahman, the father of all worlds, was born. He rested a whole year
in this egg and then he parted it into two parts through a mere
word. From the two shells he formed heaven and earth, in the
middle he put the air, and the eight directions of the world,
and the eternal dwelling of the water.

---

[1] I include two short examples of the golden embyro, or golden cosmic egg theme, which is so common to creation myths. I didn't include
egg creation texts—of which there are many—because they all express
the same basic idea. In the Rig Veda 10: 82, for example, a verse
says: "What germ primeval did the waters cherish. Wherein the gods
all saw themselves together, which is beyond the earth, beyond the
heaven, beyond the mighty gods' mysterious dwelling?" The golden
germ, or egg, is often identified with the whole universe, and sometimes as Hiranyagharbha, the spirit of the living world. It is also often
identified with the rising sun as in the selection here from the *Khan-
dogya Upanishad*. The idea of a golden egg giving birth to the universe
is one of the oldest creation themes, found in many cultures.

The Golden Embryo in the Khandogya Upanishad

In the beginning this was nonexistent. It became existent, it grew. It turned into an egg. The egg lay for the time of a year. The egg broke open. The two halves were one of silver, the other of gold. The silver one became this earth, the golden one the sky, the thick membrane (of the white) the mountains, the thin membrane (of the yoke) the mist with the clouds, the small veins the rivers, the fluid the sea.

Aitareya Upanishad

There are these worlds; shall I send forth guardians of the worlds? He then formed the Purusha, taking him forth from the water. He brooded on him[1] (that is, he exercised Tapas on him), and when that person had thus been brooded on, a mouth burst forth like an egg. From the mouth proceeded speech, from speech Agni, fire.

Creation Myths in the Vedic Hymns[1]

To the Unknown God

In the beginning there arose the Golden Child. As soon as born, he alone was the lord of all that is. He established the earth and this heaven: Who is the God to whom we shall offer sacrifice?

He who gives breath, he who gives strength, whose command all the bright gods revere, whose shadow is immortality, whose shadow is death: Who is the God to whom we shall offer sacrifice?

---

[1] That is, he used Tapas on him. The translator of this verse, Max Muller, writes that *Tapas* appears to have two meanings in English, that of warmth and that of thought, or meditation. By fire and meditation (brooding) a swelling occurs that finally bursts forth with new life. See the selection from the *Mundaka Upanishad,* page 310.

---

[1] For a larger collection of Vedic hymns, and selections from the Upanishads, see Raymond Van Over, *Eastern Mysticism,* vol. 1 (New York: Mentor Books, 1977).

He who through his might became the sole king of the breathing and twinkling world, who governs all this, man, and beast: Who is the God to whom we shall offer sacrifice?

He through whose might these snowy mountains are, and the sea, they say, with the distant river; he of whom these regions are indeed the two arms: Who is the God to whom we shall offer sacrifice?

He through whom the awful heaven and the earth were made fast, he through whom the ether was established, and the firmament; he who measured the air in the sky:: Who is the God to whom we shall offer sacrifice?

He to whom heaven and earth, standing firm by his will, look up, trembling in their mind; he over whom the risen sun shines forth: Who is the God to whom we shall offer sacrifice?

When the great waters went everywhere, holding the germ, and generating light, then there arose from them the breath of the gods: Who is the God to whom we shall offer sacrifice?

He who by his might looked even over the waters which held power and generated the sacrifice, he who alone is God above all gods: Who is the God to whom we shall offer sacrifice?

May he not hurt us, he who is the begetter of the earth, or he, the righteous, who begat the heaven; he who also begat the bright and mighty waters: Who is the God to whom we shall offer sacrifice?

Pragapati, no other than thou embraces all these created things. May that be ours which we desire when sacrificing to thee: may we be lords of wealth!

Rig Veda X. 129

There was neither existence nor nonexistence,
The Kingdom of air, nor the sky beyond.
What was there to contain, to cover, in—
Was it but vast, unfathomed depths of water?
There was no death there, nor Immortality:
No sun was there, dividing day from night.

1 Translations often vary widely, and because the *Rig Veda* X. 129, is so famous, and central, to early Hindu myth, I have included two versions. It is interesting to compare the two. Note especially the altered emphasis on key ideas, such as the germ being born in "heat" in one version, and in the other "desire" gave rise to a "primal germ of mind."

Then was there only *That*, resting within itself.
Apart from it, there was not anything.
At first within the darkness veiled in darkness,
Chaos unknowable, the All lay hid.
Till straitway from the formless void made manifest
By the great power of heat was born the germ.

A Second Rendition of *Rig Veda* X. 129

Then there was neither Aught nor Nought; nor air nor
    sky beyond.
What covered all? Where rested all? In watery gulf
    profound?
Nor death was then, nor deathlessness, nor change of
    night and day.
That one breathed calmly, self-sustained; nought else
    beyond it lay.
Gloom hid in gloom existed first—one sea, eluding view.
That One, a void in chaos wrapt, by inward fervor grew.
Within it first arose desire, the primal germ of mind,
Which nothing with existence links, as sages searching
    find.
The kindling ray that shot across the dark and drear abyss.
Was it beneath? or high aloft? What bard can answer this?
There fecundating powers were found, and mighty forces
    strove.
A self-supporting mass beneath, and energy above.
Who knows, whoever told, from whence this vast creation
    rose?
No gods had then been born. Who then can e'er the truth
    disclose?
Whence sprang this world, and whether framed by hand
    divine or no.
Its lord in heaven alone can tell, if even he can show.

Sama Veda

The Universal Soul took the shape of man. Beholding nothing but himself, he said first *This I am*. Hence the name of *I*
was produced. Therefore even now a man, when called, says

first "It is I," and tells afterward any other name that belongs to him. And because he, as the first of all of them, consumed by fire all the sin, therefore he is called Purusha.

He was afraid; therefore man, when alone, is afraid. He then looked around and said: "Since nothing but myself exists, of whom should I be afraid?" Hence his fear departed; for whom should he fear, since fear arises from another?

He did not feel delight. Therefore nobody when alone feels delight. He was desirous of a second. He was in the same state as husband and wife. He divided his self two-fold. Hence were husband and wife produced.[1] Therefore was this only a half of himself as a split pea is of the whole. This void is thus completed by woman. He approached her. Hence were men born.

[1] In some of these Indian creation myths you will find mention of the cooperation of a female principle, an idea that is reflected often in the pairing of other symbols of creation—earth and heaven, fire and water, sun and moon. But in the Indian (and Chinese) myths the blending of the male and female principles in nature is a more fully expressed idea than in other cultures. In fact, a complete system of yoga and meditation has derived from this impulse, the Indian concept of Sakti and Sakta, male and female elements in human nature. Monier Williams makes the point that "Brahma was made to possess a double nature, or, in other words, two characters—one quiescent, the other active." These same characteristics can be found in the Chinese Taoist concept of yin and yang, male and female principles made manifest from the neuter source of all—Ch'i.

PERSIAN CREATION MYTHS

Creation of Yima, the First Man

Zarathustra asked Ahura Mazda:

O Ahura Mazda, most beneficent Spirit, Maker of the material world, thou Holy One!

Who was the first mortal, before myself, Zarathustra, with whom thou, Ahura Mazda, didst converse, whom thou didst teach the law of Ahura, the law of Zarathustra?

Ahura Mazda answered:

The fair Yima, the great shepherd, O holy Zarathustra! he was the first mortal, before thee, Zarathustra, with whom I, Ahura Mazda, did converse, whom I taught the law of Ahura, the law of Zarathustra.

Unto him, O Zarathustra, I, Ahura Mazda, spake, saying: "Well, fair Yima, son of Vivanghat, be thou the preacher and the bearer of my law!"

And the fair Yima, O Zarathustra, replied unto me, saying: 'I was not born, I was not taught to be the preacher and the bearer of thy law."[1]

Then I, Ahura Mazda, said thus unto him, O Zarathustra:

"Since thou wantest not to be the preacher and the bearer of my law, then make thou my worlds thrive, make my worlds increase: undertake thou to nourish, to rule, and to watch over my world."

And the fair Yima replied unto me, O Zarathustra, saying:

"Yes! I will make thy worlds thrive, I will make thy worlds increase. Yes! I will nourish, and rule, and watch over thy world. There shall be, while I am king, neither cold wind nor hot wind, neither disease nor death."

---

[1] In the Vedas, Yama is the first man, as well as the first priest. Yima once had the same right as the Indian Yama to claim the title of the founder of a religion, but he lost it as Mazdaism developed with Zoroaster as its law-giver and chief priest. See Raymond Van Over, *Eastern Mysticism*, op. cit., the section on Zoroastrianism, for more details on this religion and its beliefs.

Then I, Ahura Mazda, brought two implements unto him: a golden ring and a poniard inlaid with gold. Behold, here Yima bears the royal sway!

Thus, under the sway of Yima, three hundred winters passed away, and the earth was replenished with flocks and herds, with men and dogs and birds and with red blazing fires, and there was no more room for flocks, herds, and men.

Then I warned the fair Yima, saying: "O fair Yima, son of Vivanghat, the earth has become full of flocks and herds, of men and dogs and birds and of red blazing fires, and there is no more room for flocks, herds, and men."

Then Yima stepped forward, toward the luminous space, southward to meet the sun,[2] and afterward he pressed the earth with the golden ring, and bored it with the poniard, speaking thus:

"O Spenta Armaiti,[3] kindly open asunder and stretch thyself afar, to bear flocks and herds and men."

And Yima made the earth grow larger by one-third than it was before, and there came flocks and herds and men, at his will and wish, as many as he wished.

Thus, under the sway of Yima, six hundred winters passed away, and the earth was replenished with flocks and herds, with men and dogs and birds and with red blazing fires, and there was no more room for flocks, herds, and men.

And I warned the fair Yima, saying: "O fair Yima, son of Vivanghat, the earth has become full of flocks and herds, of men and dogs and birds and of red blazing fires, and there is no more room for flocks, herds, and men."

Then Yima stepped forward, toward the luminous space, southward to meet the sun, and afterward he pressed the earth with the golden ring, and bored it with the poniard, speaking thus:

"O Spenta Armaiti, kindly open asunder and stretch thyself afar, to bear flocks and herds and men."

And Yima made the earth grow larger by two-thirds than it was before, and thence came flocks and herds and men, at his will and wish, as many as he wished.

---

[2] In Aryan mythology the sun is the symbol and source of royalty. In Persia, kings are the "brothers of the sun." By Yima's going between the heaven and the sun, and his enlarging the surface of the earth, he is also taking royal power for "three times three hundred years."

[3] The genius of the earth.

Thus, under the sway of Yima, nine hundred winters passed away, and the earth was replenished with flocks and herds, with men and dogs and birds and with red blazing fires, and there was no more room for flocks, herds, and men.

And I warned the fair Yima, saying: "O fair Yima, son of Vivanghat, the earth has become full of flocks and herds, of men and dogs and birds and of red blazing fires, and there is no more room for flocks, herds, and men."

Then Yima stepped forward, toward the luminous space, southward, to meet the sun, and afterwards he pressed the earth with the golden ring, and bored it with the poniard, speaking thus:

"O Spenta Armaniti, kindly open asunder and stretch thyself afar, to bear flocks and herds and men."

And Yima made the earth grow larger by three-thirds than it was before, and there came flocks and herds and men, at his will and wish, as many as he wished.

And Ahura Mazda said unto Yima: "O fair Yima, son of Vivanghat! Crush the earth with a stamp of thy heel, and then knead it with thy hands, as the potter does when kneading the potter's clay."

And Yima did as Ahura Mazda wished; he crushed the earth with a stamp of his heel, he kneaded it with his hands, as the potter does when kneading the potter's clay.

And Yima made a Vara,[4] long as a riding ground on every side of the square. There he brought the seeds of sheep and oxen, of men, of dogs, of birds, and of red blazing fires. He made a Vara, long as a riding ground on every side of the square, to be an abode for men; a Vara, long as a riding ground on every side of the square, to be a fold for flocks.

There he made waters flow in a bed a hathra long; there he settled birds, by the evergreen banks that bear never-failing food. There he established dwelling places, consisting of a house with a balcony, a courtyard, and a gallery.

There he brought the seeds of men and women, of the greatest, best, and finest kinds on this earth; there he brought the seeds of every kind of cattle, of the greatest, best, and finest kinds on this earth.

There he brought the seeds of every kind of tree, of the greatest, best, and finest kinds on this earth; there he brought the seeds of every kind of fruit, the fullest of food and sweetest

[4] Vara is the land where the departed live, and are therefore immortal.

of odor. All those seeds he brought, two of every kind, to be kept inexhaustible there, so long as those men shall stay in the Vara.

And there were no humpbacked, none bulged forward there; no impotent, no lunatic; no poverty, no lying; no meanness, no jealousy; no decayed tooth, no leprous to be confined, nor any of the brands wherewith Angra Mainyu stamps the bodies of mortals.

In the largest part of the place he made nine streets, six in the middle part, three in the smallest. To the streets of the largest part he brought a thousand seeds of men and women; to the streets of the middle part, six hundred; to the streets of the smallest part, three hundred. That Vara he sealed up with the golden ring, and he made a door, and a window self-shining within.

O Maker of the material world, thou Holy One! What lights are there to give light in the Vara which Yima made?

Ahura Mazda answered: "There are uncreated lights and created lights.[5] There the stars, the moon, and the sun are only once a year seen to rise and set, and a year seems only as a day.

"Every fortieth year, to every couple two are born, a male and a female. And thus it is for every sort of cattle. And the men in the Vara which Yima made live the happiest life."

Creation in the *Zend-Avesta*[1]

Ahura Mazda spake unto Spitama Zarathustra, saying:

I have made every land dear to its people, even though it had no charms whatever in it: had I not made every land dear to its people, even though it had no charms whatever in it, then the whole living world would have invaded the Airyana Vaego. The first of the good lands and countries which I, Ahura Mazda, created, was the Airyana Vaego, by the Vanguhi

---

[5] Heavenly lights and material lights. Another translation reads: "All created lights shine from above; created lights shine from below."

---

[1] This text is an enumeration of the sixteen perfect lands first created by Ahura Mazda, the Persian god of light. It also involves Ahura Mazda's continuing battle with the dark principle of Zoroastrian religion —Angra Mainyu, as Ahura Mazda resists the constant plagues created by Angra Mainyu. The *Zend-Avesta* is the holy book of the ancient Zoroastrians.

Daitya. Thereupon came Angra Mainyu, who is all death, and he counter-created the serpent in the river and Winter, a work of the Devas. There are ten winter months there, two summer months; and those are cold for the waters, cold for the earth, cold for the trees. Winters fall there, the worst of all plagues. The second of the good lands and countries which I, Ahura Mazda, created, was the plain which the Sughdhas inhabit. Thereupon came Angra Mainyu, who is all death, and he counter-created the locust, which brings death unto cattle and plants. The third of the good lands and countries which I, Ahura Mazda, created, was the strong, holy Mouru. Thereupon came Angra Mainyu, who is all death, and he counter-created plunder and sin. The fourth of the good lands and countries which I, Ahura Mazda, created, was the beautiful Bakhdhi with high-lifted banners. Thereupon came Angra Mainyu, who is all death, and he counter-created the ants and the anthills. The fifth of the good lands and countries which I, Ahura Mazda, created, was Nisaya, that lies between Mouru and Bakhdhi. Thereupon came Angra Mainyu, who is all death, and he counter-created the sin of unbelief. The sixth of the good lands and countries which I, Ahura Mazda, created, was the house-deserting Haroyu. Thereupon came Angra Mainyu, who is all death, and he counter-created tears and wailing. The seventh of the good lands and countries which I, Ahura Mazda, created, was Vaekereta, of the evil shadows. Thereupon came Angra Mainyu, who is all death, and he counter-created the Pairika Knathaiti, who clave unto Keresaspa. The eighth of the good lands and countries which I, Ahura Mazda, created, was Urva of the rich pastures. Thereupon came Angra Mainyu, who is all death, and he counter-created the sin of pride. The ninth of the good lands and countries which I, Ahura Mazda, created, was Khnenta which the Vehrkanas inhabit. Thereupon came Angra Mainyu, who is all death, and he counter-created a sin for which there is no atonement, the unnatural sin. The tenth of the good lands and countries which I, Ahura Mazda, created, was the beautiful Harahvaiti. Thereupon came Angra Mainyu, who is all death, and he counter-created a sin for which there is no atonement, the burying of the dead. The eleventh of the good lands and countries which I, Ahura Mazda, created, was the bright, glorious Haetumant. Thereupon came Angra Mainyu, who is all death, and he counter-created the evil work of witchcraft. And this is the sign by which it is known, this is that by which it is seen at once: wheresoever they may go and raise a cry of sorcery, there the worst works of witchcraft go forth. From there they come to kill and strike at heart, and they bring locusts as many as they want. The twelfth of the good lands and countries which I, Ahura Mazda, created, was Ragha of the three races. Thereupon came Angra Mainyu, who is all death, and he counter-created the sin of utter unbelief. The thirteenth of the good lands and countries which I, Ahura Mazda, created, was the strong, holy Kakhra. Thereupon came Angra Mainyu, who is all death, and he counter-created a sin for which there is no atonement, the cooking of corpses. The fourteenth of the good lands and countries which I, Ahura Mazda, created, was the four-cornered Varena, for which was born Thraetaona, who smote Azi Dahaka. Thereupon came Angra Mainyu, who is all death, and he counter-created abnormal issues in women and barbarian oppression. The fifteenth of the good lands and countries which I, Ahura Mazda, created, was the Seven Rivers. Thereupon came Angra Mainyu, who is all death, and he counter-created abnormal issues in women and excessive heat. The sixteenth of the good lands and countries which I, Ahura Mazda, created, was the land by the sources of the Rangha, where people live who have no chiefs. Thereupon came Angra Mainyu, who is all death, and he counter-created Winter, a work of the Devas. There are still other lands and countries, beautiful and deep, longing and asking for the good, and bright.

Opinions of the Spirit of Wisdom

The sage asked the spirit of wisdom thus: "How and in what manner has Ahura Mazda created these creatures and creation? And how and in what manner were the archangels and the spirit of wisdom formed and created by him? And how are the demons and fiends, and also the remaining corrupted ones of Aharman, the wicked,[1] miscreated? How do every good and evil happen which occur to mankind and also the remaining creatures? And is it possible to alter anything which is destined, or not?"

The spirit of wisdom answered thus: "The creator, Ahura Mazda, produced these creatures and creation, the archangels

[1] For a brief description of Zoroastrianism and the various names of the righteous god and the evil god, see the introduction to this section.

and the spirit of wisdom from that which is his own splendor, and with the blessing of unlimited time (Zurvan). For this reason, because unlimited time is undecaying and immortal, painless and hungerless, thirstless and undisturbed; and forever and everlasting no one is able to seize upon it, or to make it nonpredominant as regards his own affairs.

"And Aharman, the wicked, miscreated the demons and fiends, and also the remaining corrupted ones,[2] by his own unnatural intercourse. A treaty of nine thousand winters[3] in unlimited time was also made by him with Ahura Mazda; and, until it has been fully completed, no one is able to alter it and to act otherwise. And when the nine thousand years have become completed, Aharman is quite impotent; and Srosh, the righteous, will smite Aeshm, and Mitro and unlimited time and the spirit of justice, who deceives no one in anything, and destiny and divine providence will smite the creatures and creation of Aharman of every kind, and, in the end, even Azo, the demon. And every creature and creation of Ahura Mazda becomes again as undisturbed as those which were produced and created by him in the beginning.

"Every good and evil which happen to mankind, and also the other creatures, happen through the seven planets and the twelve constellations.[4] And those twelve constellations are such as in revelation are the twelve chieftains who are on the side of Ahura Mazda, and those seven planets are called the seven chieftains who are on the side of Aharman. Those seven planets pervert every creature and creation, and deliver them up to death and every evil. And, as it were, those twelve constellations and seven planets are organizing and managing the world.

Ahura Mazda is wishing good, and never approves nor contemplates evil. Aharman is wishing evil, and does not meditate

---

[2] Wizards.

[3] In the beginning, Ahura Mazda created the spiritual prototypes who remained undisturbed for the first three thousand years when Aharman (also Ahriman) appeared and agreed to a conflict for the remaining nine thousand years during the first three of which Ahura Mazda's will is undisputed. During the next three, Aharman is active and interferring, while in the last three Aharman's influence and power slowly diminishes until, in the end, it disappears entirely. The nine thousand years of this conflict between light and dark, between good and evil is supposed to extend from about 5400 B.C. to about 3600 A.D. Compare with Christian apocalyptic prophecy.

[4] The zodiacal signs.

nor approve anything good whatever. Ahura Mazda, when he wishes it, is able to alter as regards the creatures of Aharman; and Aharman, too, it is, who, when he wishes it, can do so as regards the creatures of Ahura Mazda, but he is only able to alter so that in the final effect there may be no injury of Ahura Mazda, because the final victory is Ahura Mazda's own."

The sage asked the spirit of wisdom thus: "Is it possible to go from region to region, or not? From what substance is the sky made? And how and in what manner is the mingling of the water in the earth?"

The spirit of wisdom answered thus: "Without the permission of the sacred beings, or the permission of the demons, it is then not possible for one to go from region to region. The sky is made from the substance of the bloodstone,[5] such as they also call diamond (almast). And the mingling of the water in the earth is just like the blood in the body of man."

The sage asked the spirit of wisdom thus: "Wherefore is it when the treasure of the spiritual existence is allotted so truly, and that of the worldly existence so falsely?"

The spirit of wisdom answered thus: "The treasure of the worldly existence was allotted as truly, in the original creation, as that of the spiritual existence. And the creator, Ahura Mazda, provided the happiness of every kind, that is in these creatures and creation, for the use of the sun[6] and moon and those twelve constellations which are called the twelve chieftains by revelation; and they, too, accepted it in order to allot it truly and deservedly.

"And, afterward, Aharman produced those seven planets, such as are called the seven chieftains of Aharman, for dissipating and carrying off that happiness from the creatures of Ahura Mazda, in opposition to the sun and moon and those twelve constellations. And as to every happiness which those constellations bestow on the creatures of Ahura Mazda, those planets take away as much of it as it is possible for them (the constellations) to give, and give it up to the power of the demons and fiends and the bad.

"And the treasure of the spiritual existence is so true on this account, because Ahura Mazda, the lord, with all the angels and archangels, is undisturbed, and they make the struggle with Aharman and the demons, and also the account of the souls of

---

[5] Or ruby, referring to the rosy tints of dawn and sunset.
[6] The angel of the sun is Mithra.

are equal is among the ever-stationary, and when the crime is more, his path is then to hell."
men, with justice. And the place of him whose good work is more is in heaven, the place of him whose good work and sin

Sikand-Gumanik Vigar

In the name of Ahura Mazda, the lord, the greatest and wise, the all-ruling, all-knowing, and almighty, who is a spirit even among spirits, and from his self-existence, single in unity, was the creation of the fruitful. He also created, by his own unrivaled power, the seven supreme archangels,[1] all the angels of the spiritual and worldly existences, and the seven worldly creations which are man, animals, fire, metal, earth, water, and plants.

And man was created by him, as a control of the creatures, for the advancement of his will. From him likewise came at various times, through his own compassion, mercifulness to his own creatures, religion, and a natural desire of the knowledge of purity and contamination. So, also, as to the intellect, understanding, wisdom, knowledge, consciousness, and guardian spirit—which are the appliances of the soil that are seeking information of these spiritual appliances, the five which are the sight, hearing, smell, taste, and touch, through the five worldly appliances, which are the eye, the ear, the nose, the mouth, and the rubbing surfaces of the whole body —he likewise created man with the accompaniment of these appliances, for the management of the creatures.

And as to that which is asked thus: "Why does not the creator Ahura Mazda keep Aharman back from evil-doing and evil-seeking, when he is the mighty maker? As I assert that no mighty maker is afterwards imperfect nor yet unresisting."

If I say that the creator Ahura Mazda is able to keep Aharman back from the evil which is his perpetual nature, it is possible to change that nature which is demoniacal into a divine one, and that which is divine into a demoniacal one; and it is possible to make the dark light, and the light dark.

Through the creator Ahura Mazda was the arrangement of these creatures and creation, methodically and sagaciously, and

---

[1] The seven archangels include Ahura Mazda himself.

for the sake of the continuance of the renovation of the universe. As the evil spirit was entangled in the sky, that fiend, with evil astuteness and with lying falsehood, encompassed and mingled with the light, together with the fiends of crimes of many kinds, who are those of a gloomy race, thinking thus: "I will make these creatures and creation of Ahura Mazda extinct, or I must make them for my own."

Those luminaries, the highest of those of the good being, became aware, by means of omniscience, of the blemishing operation and the lies and falsehoods of the fiend, and of this too, that is, of what extent was this power of his, by which this blemishing operation and work of ruin creep on, so that, henceforth, there exists no power whatsoever for its restoration, which is free from the complete daubing of restraint, pain, and entanglement that is inside the sky.

It is they[2] who are sagaciously mingled by him (the good being) with the substance of the luminaries, because that fiend encompassed and was entangled with his luminaries, therefore, all his powers and resources are for the purpose of not allowing the fiends of crimes of many kinds their own performance of what is desirable for them each separately; such as the fiendish venom of the noxious creatures which the four elements, pertaining to Ahura Mazda, keep enveloped.[3] For if this fiendish venom of the noxious creatures does not remain entangled with the four elements of the bodily formations pertaining to Ahura Mazda—which are water, fire, earth, and air—it is just as though they came to the sky and spiritual existence.

Moreover, if the births of the worldly existence are mostly manifest through the occurrence of death therein, even then it is seen that that death is not a complete dissolution of existence, but a necessity of going from place to place, from duty to duty. For, as the existence of all these creations is derived from the four elements, it is manifest to the sight that those worldly bodies of theirs are to be mingled again with the four elements. The spiritual parts, which are the rudimentary appliances of the life stimulating the body, are mingled with the soul—on account of unity of nature they are

2 This refers to the spiritual representatives of the luminaries, the angels.

3 Another translation reads: "Since the fiendish venom of the noxious creatures, that the four elements pertaining to Ahura Mazda—which are water, fire, earth, and air—have not entangled, is just as though they [the creatures] came to the sky and spiritual existence."

not dispersed—and the soul is accountable for its own deeds. Its treasurers, also, unto whom its good works and offenses are intrusted, advance there for a contest. When the treasurer of the good works is of greater strength, she preserves it, by her victory, from the hands of the accuser,[4] and settles it for the great throne and the mutual delightfulness of the luminaries; and it is assisted eternally in virtuous progress. And when the treasurer of its offenses is of greater strength, it is dragged, through her victory, away from the hands of the helper,[5] and is delivered up to the place of thirst and hunger and the agonizing abode of disease.[6] And, even there, those feeble good works, which were practiced by it in the worldly existence, are not useless to it; for, owing to this same reason, that hunger and thirst and punishment are inflicted on it proportionately to the sin, and not lawlessly, because there is a watcher[7] of the infliction of its punishment. And, ultimately, the compassionate creator, who is the forgiver of the creatures, does not leave any good creature captive in the hands of the enemy. But, one day, he saves even those who are sinful, and those of the righteous through atonement for sin, by the hands of the purifiers, and makes them proceed on the happy course which is eternal.

The conclusion is this, that the creator is the healer and perfect ruler, the maintainer and nourisher, portecting and preserving the creatures; not a producer of the disease, a causer of the pain, and an inflicter of the punishment of his own creatures. And it is more explicitly written below, with the arrangement of the two original evolutions, among the assertors of the nonexistence of a sacred being, and the contemplators of unity.

---

[4] The accuser is any person or thing of "the good creation" that has been injured by sin. The account is to be settled when the good works of the soul are rendered and seen to be sufficient to atone for the sin.

[5] The treasurer of good works.

[6] Hell.

[7] This means either the treasurer of good works or the good works themselves.

PART TEN

Far East

INTRODUCTION

As WITH THE other major mythologies, creation for the peoples of the Far East involved reducing chaos to order. Each of the major ancient religions in Japan, China, and Tibet express this need for structuring the world out of the primeval chaos.

Japan

In Shinto, the early religion of Japan, celestial deities emerge spontaneousy out of the primeval waters. The male and female creative deities, Izanagi and Izanami, become the begetters of the human race. But unlike those of many other mythological figures, their acts are often sexual. For example, in an attempt to lure the sulking Sun Goddess from her cave, one of the goddesses dancing before the cave entrance reminds the Sun Goddess of her responsibility to bring fertility to men and nature by pulling open her blouse, exposing her nipples, and then pushing down her skirt to reveal her pudenda. Also, until recent times the Shinto shrines contained many "fertility maidens," or temple prostitutes. The phallic elements in Shinto mythology are also very evident.[1] In fact, Japanese mythology, as can be seen in the selections that follow, is rich in sexual references and feats of magic. The first and most evident is in Izanagi's and Izanami's creation of an island by use of a Heavenly Jeweled Spear, an obvious phallic symbol. Further, these two deities are considered the World Parents, the Sky Father and Earth Mother. Their primary task is to create order out of chaos, to bring the cosmos under control. When they have finished their job, they dis-

---

[1] See, for example, Michael Czaja, *Gods of Myth and Stone, Phallicism in Japanese Folk Religion* (New York/Tokyo: Weatherhill, 1974).

appear or die and are replaced by other deities who also must give shape to what is formless.

The Japanese possessed a vivid animism in which the things of nature were endowed with great power or beauty. All of these objects or beings are called Kami, a deity or spirit. They are the functionaries of Japanese mythology. Often there is some degree of personification in Japanese mythology, but not as much as in Greek mythology. The Japanese do not seem to have been as concerned with systematizing their ideas in myths as other peoples—for example, the Babylonians and Greeks.

The mythologist Mircea Eliade has identified several successive stages in the cosmic myths of Japan.

1. A primordial state in which nothing is separate or differentiated, and identified as Chaos.
2. The existence of a germ or seed that will be the generator of a divine androgyny.
3. The first deities created brother and sister deities of heaven and earth.
4. The deities of heaven and earth marry and create form, that is, they separate heaven from earth.
5. After the separation, there is sexual union from which is established a spiritual principle and creation of the world.
6. The Earth Mother dies (is sacrificed) giving birth to the fire deity.
7. Earth and vegetative deities are born from the sacrifice of the fire deity, who is dismembered.
8. The Sky Father creates the sun, moon, and storm deities and disappears.[2]

This sequence is similar to creative cycles in other mythologies. There is the cycle of birth, the creation of separate being, fulfillment, and death. The stages of creation progress from the origin of the universe to the appearance of gods who shape the world and then sacrifice themselves. The Japanese creation myth ends, however, with the creation of the sun goddess, the moon god, and the storm god, each of whom must rule over his own sphere and thereby make the world livable. As Eric Neumann has observed regarding creation myths generally, "The world begins only with the coming of light which constellates the opposition between heaven

2 *Myths, Dreams and Mysteries* (New York: Harper & Row, 1960), pp. 182ff.

and earth as the basic symbol of all other opposites."[3] Thus, as in numerous other myths in *Sun Songs*, light battles darkness and illuminates the world of form through creation.

China

The Chinese have perhaps one of the largest bodies of literature in the world. There is nothing literary that they did not excel at except perhaps the epic tale. With such a literary tradition it is strange, therefore, that there is no clearly defined Chinese myth of the origin of the universe. There is an incomplete and unsatisfying description of an infinite creative power possessed by the deity Shang Ti. But the worship of Shang Ti was more closely associated with the spirite of air, earth, and ancestors rather than with any great act of cosmic creation. The Taoist sage Lao Tzu touched upon creation in one of the chapters of his book *Tao Teh Ching*. There are also pieces of cosmic musings in the Taoist philosophers Chaung Tzu and Huai-nan Tzu, selections from both of whom appear in *Sun Songs*.

One of the rare cosmic myths of ancient China involves the mythic figure of P'an Ku. According to a third-century A.D. text, Chaos was like a giant egg, from which P'an Ku emerged. During this period, Earth and Heaven did not yet exist. As the parts of the egg separated, the heavy parts formed the earth and the lighter, purer ones shaped the sky. P'an Ku labored on creation heavily until he died and the various parts of his body dispersed to become different natural elements. A version of this myth is included in *Sun Songs*.

P'an means the "shell of an egg" and *Ku* "to secure." Some translators have rendered his name to signify "aboriginal abyss," or, like the Babylonian Tiamat, to mean "the Deep." P'an Ku is often shown in pictures as a dwarf with two horns on his head. He holds a hammer and chisel with which he forms the world. Sometimes he is accompanied on his labors by four supernatural beings—a unicorn, phoenix, tortoise, and dragon. This version of P'an Ku and Chinese creation is Taoist in origin and not to be confused with a later Buddhist version

[3] *The Origins and History of Consciousness*. 2 vols. Trans. by R. F. C. Hull (New York: Harper Torchbooks, 1962), vol. 1, p. 106.

involving a Gold Colored Being and a divine Buddha that gives Pan Ku directions. The later version simply incorporates some Buddhist and Indian mythic elements and confuses them with the purely Chinese Taoist. But even within its Chinese heritage the legend of P'an Ku presents difficulty, for it is more personal in tone than the more impersonal Taoist cosmologies found in the *I Ching*, Lao Tzu, Chuang Tzu, or Huai Nan Tzu. Some scholars feel that the P'an Ku creation myth was a late creation by the Taoist recluse Magistrate Ko Hung (fourth century A.D.), who is the author of the Biographies of the Gods.

TAOISM AND THE I CHING

Taoism is peculiarly void of cosmic mythmaking. "Peculiar" because it is a religion full of metaphysical speculation and profound philosophical concepts. But mysteriously, these characteristics did not spill over into cosmic mythmaking. One of the principal Taoist books, the *I Ching*, or *Book of Changes*, seems devoid of a creation myth, beyond the creative elements of the Taoist concepts of yin and yang. The *I Ching*'s first two hexagrams, Ch'ien and K'un, represent the Taoist view of a universe in constant and perfect flux—movement and rest, penetrating and receptive—which are the basic ingredients for creation and continued existence. The connection between yang and yin, Ch'ien and K'un, is necessary to produce any single substantial thing. The yang originates a shadowy outline which the yin fills up with definite substance. So, actually, in nature, Heaven (Ch'ien) and Earth (K'un) operate together in the production of all material things and beings. I have included these first two hexagrams from the *I Ching* in *Sun Songs* even though the material is arcane and difficult to penetrate. It does offer a glimpse, no matter how fleeting and obscure, into one of the major philosophies and religions of ancient China.

Tibetan Myths

Bon Po (or Bonbo, Bea-ho) is a little-known pre-Buddhist cult. From the few references to Bon in early texts, it can only be surmised that it was a cult of divine kingship, with kings regarded as manifestations of the sky divinity. The cult had gods of the atmosphere, earth, and subterranean regions. It had oracular priests and practiced blood sacrifice. All of these characteristics have been absorbed into Tibetan Buddhism. All Bon material will have a decided Buddhist quality because everything known to us about this cult has been filtered through the Buddhist perspective— especially since literature began in Tibet as a result of Buddhist efforts. (The first Buddhist temples were built in Tibet in 649 A.D. Tibetan literature is also a development of Buddhist influence in the 7th century.) For example, the Bon idea of divine kingship took on a Buddhist form through the theory of reincarnating lamas. In fact, the old Bon rituals took on a decided Buddhist quality. Under Buddhist influence, the flesh offerings once prepared for bloodthirsty Bon deities became simple sacrificial cakes prepared so as to look gruesome.

In the upland regions between Tibet and Upper Burma there are a great number of primitive mongoloid peoples— the Garos, Abors, Kukis, Karens—who have not been as deeply influenced by Buddhist or Hindu beliefs. And in some of these tribal myths the old Bon beliefs can be seen, as with nature worship, and the personification of the sun, moon, and stars; with hills, streams, forests, and other realities of nature possessing their indwelling spirits. Amidst the fulsome worship of spirits, who are perceived as rulers of the universe and controllers of human destiny and all natural phenomenon, there are many fanciful legends. Thus, while the gods of the Garos are vague mythical entities, with no definite powers or attributes (for such powers are with the spirits), they are associated with wonderful cosmological legends. For example, Salgong, a Garos deity, marries Apongma, a divine princess who descends to earth and gives birth to the father of fire, Kengra Barsa, and all the heavenly bodies. A daughter of Apongma then marries Donjogma, and becomes the mother of mankind. From their offspring come the various kinds of people, including the Garos, and even the English (or Feringies). Another colorful legend from the Tawyans, a branch of the Chin family, relates how their once-powerful status was ruined by their insane efforts to capture the sun. They had struggled up a kind of Jacob's ladder, higher and higher toward the sun, until they grew tired and began arguing among themselves. One day, while half of them were continuing to climb upward, the half remaining below cut them down just as they were about to seize the sun.

According to another tribe, the Kuki, the face of the earth was originally covered with one vast sheet of water, which was inhabited by a huge worm, who became instrumental in creating the world. I have included this short myth in this collection because it is representative of the old nature-worship beliefs and pre-Buddhistic tribal myths.

JAPANESE CREATION MYTH

Nihongi (Chronicles of Japan)[1]

The Age of the Gods

Of old, Heaven and Earth were not yet separated, and the Yin (female and Yang (male) principles not yet divided. They formed a chaotic mass like an egg which was of obscurely defined limits and contained germs (life principle).

The purer and clearer part was thinly drawn out, ascended and formed Heaven, while the heavier and grosser element settled down and became Earth. The finer element easily became a united body, but the consolidation of the heavy and gross element was accomplished with difficulty. Heaven was therefore formed first, and Earth was established subsequently. Thereafter Divine Beings were produced between them.[2]

Hence, it is said that when the world began to be created, the soil of which lands were composed floated about in a

[1] The first two books of the *Nihongi*, or, the *Chronicles of Japan*, contain the myths which form the basis of the Shinto religion. Nihon is the name for Japan as pronounced by the Chinese, and further modified by European tongues. Nihon in Chinese means "sun-origin," that is, sunrise, and given to Japan because of its position east of the Asiatic continent. On old maps it is spelled Nippon, or Niphon. However, Yamato is the true old Japanese name of the country.

[2] The preceding opening sentences have been questioned by scholars as being only an essay of Chinese rationalism prefixed to the genuine Japanese traditions. A corresponding alternative translation reads: "Of old, the original essence was a chaotic mass. Heaven and Earth had not yet been separated, but were like an egg, of ill-defined limits and containing germs. Thereafter, the pure essence, ascending by degrees, became thinly spread out, and formed Heaven. The floating grosser essence sank heavily, and, settling down, became Earth. What we call countries were produced by the opening, splitting up, and dividing of the earth as it floated along. It might be compared to the floating of a fish which sports on the surface of the water. Now Heaven was produced first and Earth afterwards."

manner which might be compared to the floating of a fish
sporting on the surface of the water.

At this time a certain thing was produced between Heaven
and Earth. It was in form like a reed-shoot. Now this became
transformed into a God,[3] and was called Land-eternal-stand-
of-august-thing.

Next there was Land-of-right-soil-of-augustness, and next
Rich-form-plain-of-augustness—in all three deities.

These were pure males spontaneously developed by the
operation of the principle of Heaven (Yang).[4]

In one writing it is said: Before Heaven and Earth were
produced, there was something which might be compared to
a cloud floating over the sea. It had no place of attachment for
its root. In the midst of this a thing was generated which
resembled a reed-shoot when it is first produced in the mud.
This became straightway transformed into human (deity)
shape and was called Kuni no toko-tachi no Mikoto (Land-
eternal-of-august-thing).

Thereupon they thrust down the jewel-spear of Heaven,[5]
and groping about therewith found the ocean. The brine
which dripped from the point of the spear coagulated and
became an island which received the name of Ono-goro-jima
(Spontaneously-congeal-island).

The two Deities thereupon descended and dwelt in this
island. Accordingly they wished to become husband and wife
together, and to produce countries.

So they made Spontaneous-island, or Ahaji, the pillar of
the center of the land.

Two Kami, He-who-invites and She-who-invites, stood on
the floating bridge of Heaven and held counsel together, saying: "Is there not a country beneath?"

[3] The names of these gods are obscure and these translations should
be accepted with caution. The names can also be translated as Mid-
Sky-Master, High-Producer, and Divine-Producer.

[4] The principle of Heaven is the same thing as the Yo, or male
principle of Chinese philosophy. The words for male and female
throughout the original are Yo and In.

[5] The jewel-spear of Heaven was in the form of a wo-bashira, which
means literally a male-pillar. There is also a Chinese expression that
means jewel-stalk, which is an ornate word for the penis. Compare this
part of the myth with the huge lingam, or phallus, without top or bottom that Brahma and Vishnu circled in the section on Hindu myths.

Then the eight-great-islands country was produced by the coagulation of the foam of the saltwater.

It is also stated that they were produced by the coagulation of the foam of fresh water.

In one writing it is said: "The Gods of Heaven addressed He-who-invites and She-who-invites, saying: "There is the country Abundant-reed-plain. Do ye proceed and bring it into order?" They then gave them the jewel-spear of Heaven. Hereupon the two Gods stood on the floating bridge of Heaven, and plunging down the spear, sought for land. Then upon stirring the ocean with it, and bringing it up again, the brine which dripped from the spear-point coagulated and became an island, which was called Ono-goro-jima (Spontaneously-congeal-island). The two gods descended, dwelt in this island, and erected there an eight-fathom place.[6] They also set up the pillar of Heaven."

Then the male Deity asked the female Deity, saying: "Is there anything formed in thy body?"

She answered and said: "My body has a place completely formed, and called the source of femininity."

The male god said: "My body again has a place completely formed, and called the source of masculinity. I desire to unite my source of masculinity to thy source of femininity."

Having thus spoken, they prepared to go around the pillar of Heaven, and made a promise, saying: "Do thou, my younger sister, go around from the left, while I will go around from the right." Having done so, they went around separately and met, when the female Deity spoke first, "How pretty! a lovely youth!"

The male Deity then answered and said: "How pretty! a lovely maiden!"

Finally they became husband and wife. Their first child was the leech, whom they straightway placed in a reed boat and sent adrift.[7] Their next was the Island of Ahaji. This also was not included in the number of their children. Wherefore

---

[6] Eight-fathom is a poetical expression for great or large. There is no apparent mythic or sacred significance to the number eight. The central pillar of the house refers to a tradition in which the two gods made the jewel-spear the center of their palace. Early Japanese architecture incorporated this.

[7] The leech is the God Yebisu, and the reed boat recalls the Accadian myth of Sargon, with its ark of rushes; the Biblical story of Moses as an infant; the abandoned Indian Karna; Horus as a child floating in Argo; etc.

they returned up again to Heaven, and fully reported the circumstances. Then the Heavenly Gods divined this by the
greater divination. Upon which they instructed them, saying:
"It was by reason of the woman's having spoken first; ye had
best return thither again." Thereupon having divined a time,
they went down.

They next produced the sea, then the rivers, and then the
mountains. Then they produced the ancestor of the trees, and
next the ancestor of herbs.

After this He-who-invites and She-who-invites consulted
together, saying: "We have now produced the Great-eight-
island country, with the mountains, rivers, herbs, and trees.
Why should we not produce someone who shall be lord of
the universe?[8] They then together produced the Sun-Goddess,
who was called Great-noon-female-of-possessor.

The resplendent luster of this child shone throughout all the
six quarters.[9] Therefore the two Deities rejoiced, saying: "We
have had many children, but none of them have been equal
to this wondrous infant. She ought not to be kept long in this
land, but we ought of our own accord to send her at once to
Heaven, and entrust to her the affairs of Heaven."

At this time, Heaven and Earth were still not far separated.[10] and therefore they sent her up to Heaven by the
ladder of Heaven.

They next produced the Moon-god, or the Bow-of-darkness.
His radiance was next to that of the Sun in splendor. This
God was to be the consort of the Sun-Goddess, and to share
in her government. They therefore sent him also to Heaven.

Next they produced the leech-child, which even at the age
of three years could not stand upright. They therefore placed
it in the rock-camphor-wood boat of Heaven, and abandoned
it to the winds.

Their next child was Impetuous Male.

This God had a fierce temper and was given to cruel acts.
Moreover he made a practice of continually weeping and
wailing. So he brought many of the people of the land to an
untimely end. Again he caused green mountains to become

---

[8] In the original, this also means that which is under Heaven, and
often can stand for the word for Empire.

[9] That is, North, South, East, West, Above, and Below.

[10] Another translation reads: "In the beginning the Heaven, Rangi,
and the Earth, Papa, were the father and mother of all things. In
those days the Heaven lay upon the Earth, and all was darkness. They
had never been separated."

withered. Therefore the two Gods, his parents, addressed Impetuous Male, saying: "Thou art exceedingly wicked, and it is not meet that thou shouldst reign over the world. Certainly thou must depart far away to the Nether Land."[11] So they at length expelled him.

In one writing it is said: "After the sun and moon, the next child which was born was the leech-child. When this child had completed his third year, he was nevertheless still unable to stand upright. The reason why the leech-child was born was that in the beginning, when He-who-invites and She-who-invites went around the pillar, the female Deity was the first to utter an exclamation of pleasure, and the law of male and female was therefore broken. They next procreated Impetuous Male. This God was of a wicked nature, and was always fond of wailing and wrath. Many of the people of the land died, and the green mountains withered. Therefore his parents addressed him, saying: "Supposing that thou wert to rule this country, much destruction of life would surely ensue. Thou must govern the far-distant Nether Land." Their next child was the bird-rock-camphor-wood boat of Heaven. They forthwith took this boat and, placing the leech-child in it, abandoned it to the current. Their next child was Kagu tsuchi" (God of Fire).

Now She-who-invites was burned by Kag utsuchi, so that she died. When she was lying down to die, she gave birth to the Earth-Goddess (Hani-yama-hime) and the Water-Goddess (Midzu-ha-no-me). Upon this, Kagu tsuchi took to wife Hani-yama-hime, and they had a child. On the crown of this Deity's head were produced the silkworm and the mulberry tree, and in her navel the five kinds of grain.[12]

In one writing it is said: "The Sun-Goddess, aware from the beginning of the fierce and relentless purpose of Impetuous Male said (to herself) when he ascended: "The coming of my younger brother is not for a good object. He surely means to rob me of my Plain of Heaven." So she made manly warlike preparation, girding upon her a ten-span sword, a nine-span sword, and an eight-span sword. Moreover, on her back she slung a quiver, and on her forearm drew a dread loud-sounding elbow-pad. In her hand she took a bow and arrow, and going forth to meet him in person, stood on her defense. Then Impetuous Male declared to her, saying: "From

[11] Literally, the "root country," which means Hades.
[12] Hemp, millet, rice, corn, pulse.

the beginning I have had no evil intentions. All that I wished
was to see thee, my elder sister, face to face. It is only for a
brief space that I have come." Thereupon the Sun-Goddess,
standing opposite to Impetuous Male, swore an oath, saying:
"If thy heart is pure, and thou hast no purpose of relentless
robbery, the children born to thee will surely be males." When
she had finished speaking, she ate first the ten-span sword
which she had girded on, and produced a child. Moreover,
she ate the nine-span sword, and produced another child.
Moreover she ate the eight-span sword, and produced another
child—in all three female Deities. After this Impetuous Male
took the string of five hundred august jewels which hung upon
his neck, and having rinsed them in the Nuna (True) well of
Heaven, another name for which is the true-well of Isa, and
ate them. So he produced a child, in all five male Deities.
Therefore, as Impetuous Male had thus acquired proof of
his victory, the Sun-Goddess learned exactly that his intentions
were wholly free from guilt. The three female Deities which
the Sun-Goddess had produced were accordingly sent down
to the Land of Tsukushi. She therefore instructed them, saying: "Do you, three Deities, go down and dwell in the center
of the province, where you will assist the descendants of
Heaven,[13] and receive worship from them.' "

In one writing it is said: "The Sun-Goddess stood opposite
to Impetuous Male, separated from him by the Tranquil
River of Heaven,[14] and established a covenant with him,
saying, "If thou hast not a traitorous heart, the children which
thou wilt produce will surely be males, and if they are males,
I will consider them my children, and will cause them to
govern the Plain of Heaven." Hereupon the Sun-Goddess first
ate her ten-span sword, which became converted into a child,
the Goddess Oki-tsu-shima. Next she ate her nine-span sword,
which became converted into a child, the Goddess Tagi-tsu
hime. Again she ate her eight-span sword, which became
converted into a child, the Goddess Ta-giri hime. Upon this,
Impetuous Male took in his mouth the string of 500 jewels
which was entwined in the left knot of his hair, and placed
it on the palm of his left hand, whereupon it became converted into a male child. He then said: "Truly I have won."
In one writing it is said: "The august Sun-Goddess took an

13 That is, the Emperors.
14 The Milky Way.

enclosed rice field and made it her Imperial rice field. Now
Impetuous Male, in spring, filled up the channels and broke
down the divisions, and in autumn, when the grain was
formed, he forthwith stretched around them division ropes.[15]
Again when the Sun-Goddess was in her Weaving-Hall, he
flayed alive a piebald colt and flung it into the Hall. In all
these various matters his conduct was rude in the highest
degree. Nevertheless, the Sun-Goddess, out of her friendship
for him, was not indignant or resentful, but took everything
calmly and with forbearance.

When the time came for the Sun-Goddess to celebrate the
feast of first-fruits, Impetuous Male secretly voided excrement
under her august seat in the New Palace. The Sun-Goddess,
not knowing this, went straight there and took her seat.
Accordingly the Sun-Goddess drew herself up, and was sick-
ened. She therefore was enraged, and straightaway took up
her abode in the Rock-cave of Heaven, and fastened its Rock-
door.

Then all the Gods were grieved at this, and forthwith
caused Ama no nuka-do, the ancestor of the Be of mirror-
makers, to make a mirror, Futo-dama, the ancestor of the
Imibe, to make offerings, and Toyo-tama,[16] the ancestor of
the Be of jewel-makers, to make jewels. They also caused
Mountain God to procure eighty precious combs of the five-
hundred-branched true sakaki tree, and Moor God to produce
eighty precious combs of the five-hundred-branched suzuki
grass. When all these various objects were collected, Ama no
Koyane, the ancestor of the Nakatomi, recited a liturgy in
honor of the Deity. Then the Sun-Goddess opened the Rock-
door and came out. At this time, when the mirror was put
into the Rock-cave, it struck against the door and received a
slight flaw, which remains until this day. This is the great
Deity worshiped at Ise. After this, Impetuous Male was con-
victed, and fined in the articles required for the ceremony of
purification. Hereupon these were the things abhorrent of
luck of the tips of his fingers, and the things abhorrent of
calamity of the tips of his toes.[17] Again, of his spittle he made

---

[15] That is, ropes dividing the rice fields in token of ownership.

[16] These two are cloth and rich-jewel.

[17] This is an obscure sentence that has even confounded Shinto
scholars. One authority understands the things abhorrent of luck to be
things required for the purification service. These are vital concerns
for the Shinto religion, for Shinto is a religion steeped in ritual.

white soft offerings, and of his nose-mucus he made blue soft offerings, with which the purification service was performed. Finally he was banished according to the law of Divine banishment."

In one writing it is said: "After this the Sun-Goddess had three rice fields, which were called the Easy Rice field of Heaven, the Level Rice field of Heaven, and the Village-join Rice field of Heaven. All these were good rice fields, and never suffered even after continuous rain or drought. Now Impetuous Male had also three rice fields, which were called the Pile-field of Heaven, the River-border. Field of Heaven, and the Mouth-Sharp Field of Heaven. All these were barren places. In the rains, the soil was swept away, and in droughts it was parked up. Therefore, Impetuous Male was jealous and destroyed his elder sister's rice fields. In spring, he knocked away the pipes and troughs, filled up the channels, and broke down the divisions. He also sowed seed over again. In autumn, he set up combs,[18] and made horses lie down in the rice fields. Notwithstanding all these wicked doings, which went on incessantly, the Sun-Goddess was not indignant, but treated him always with calmness and forbearance, etc., etc.

When the Sun-Goddess came to shut herself up in the Rock-cave of Heaven, all the Gods sent the child of Kogoto Musubi, Ama no Koyane, and made him recite a liturgy. Hereupon Ama no Koyane rooted up a true Sakaki tree of the Heavenly Mount Kagu and hung upon its upper branches a mirror of eight hands, made by the ancestor of the mirror-makers; on the middle branches he hung curved jewels of Yasaka gem made by the ancestor of the jewel-makers.

Futo-dama was thereupon made to take these things in his hand, and, with lavish and earnest words of praise, to recite a liturgy.

When the Sun-Goddess heard this, she said: "Though of late many prayers have been addressed to me, of none has the language been so beautiful as this." So she opened a little the Rock-door and peeped out. Thereupon the God Ama no Tajikara-wo no Kami, who was waiting beside the Rock-door,

---

[18] Combs were stuck up in rice-fields with incantations written on them so if anyone wrongly claimed the fields he might be destroyed.

forthwith pulled it open, and the radiance of the Sun-Goddess
filled the universe.[19] Therefore all the Gods rejoiced greatly,
and imposed on Impetuous Male a fine of a thousand articles
of purification.

---

[19] Throughout the *Nihongi* the Sun-Goddess is an anthropomorphic
deity but little is mentioned about her solar functions. This confusion
between divine powers and natural functions is inherent in all mythologies. As John Muir points out (Vol. V, "Sanskrit Texts"): "The same
visible object was at different times regarded diversely as being either
a portion of the inanimate universe or an animated being and a cos-
mical power. Thus in the Vedic hymns, the sun, the sky, and the earth
are severally considered, sometimes as natural objects governed by
particular gods, and sometimes as themselves gods who generate and
control other beings." The complete title of John Muir's most notable
work, from which this quotation was taken, is *Original Sanskrit Texts
on the Origin and History of the People of India,* five volumes (1858–
70).

CHINESE CREATION MYTHS

Taoism

P'an Ku[1] and Chinese Creation

At first there was Chaos. From it pure light collected to itself and moved to create the sky. The darkness remaining moved and from itself formed the earth. From within this activity there arose two principles yang and yin, light and dark, sky and earth. From this movement of like to like a balancing of forces occurred and growth and increase brought forth the beginning and the ten thousand creations, all of which take the sky and earth (yang and yin) as their mode. Yang gives and yin receives, yang moves out and yin comes in, yang disperses and yin collects.

As yang and yin thus separated and become mixed, five elements gathered to form P'an Ku. Created in the shape of a man, P'an Ku immediately set about giving form to the remaining chaos. His task occupied him for 18,000 years, during which he formed the sun, moon, and stars, completed the heavens and earth. He increased in stature himself, each day being six feet taller than the day before, until, his labors ended, he died that his works might live. His head became the mountains, his breath the wind and clouds, his voice the thunder, his limbs the four quarters of the earth, his blood the rivers, his flesh the soil, his beard the constellations, his skin and hair the herbs and trees, his teeth, bones, and marrow the metals, rocks and precious stones, his sweat the rain, and the insects creeping over his body became human beings.

Creation in Chuang Tzu

At the begining of time there were two oceans—one in the south and one in the north—and there was land in the center. The Ruler of the southern ocean was Shu (Heedless), and the

---

[1] For further comment, see E.T.C. Werner, *Myths and Legends of China* (London: George Harrap & Co., 1922), pp. 76ff.

Ruler of the northern ocean was Hu (Hasty),[1] while the Ruler of the Center was Twun-tun (Chaos).

"Heedless" and "Hasty" were in the habit of paying regular visits to the land, and there they met and became acquainted. "Chaos" treated them kindly, and it was their desire to confer upon him some favor so as to give practical expression to their feelings of gratitude. They discussed the matter together, and decided what they should do.

Now Chaos was blind, his eyes being closed, and he was deaf, his ears being closed, and he could not breathe, having no nostrils, nor eat, because he was mouthless.

"Hasty" and "Heedless" met daily in the Central land, and each day they opened an orifice. One the seventh day their work was finished. But when he had ears and eyes opened, and could see and hear, and could breathe through his nostrils, and had a mouth with which to eat, old Chaos died.[2]

* * *

In the Grand Beginning of all things there was nothing in all the vacancy of space: there was nothing that could be named. It was in this state that there arose the first existence: the first existence, but still without bodily shape. From this, things could be produced, receiving what we call their several characters. That which had no bodily shape was divided, and then without intermission there was what we call the process of conferring. The two processes continued to operate, and things were produced. As they were completed, there appeared the distinguishing lines of each, which we call the bodily shape. That shape was the bodly preserving the spirit, and each had its peculiar manifestation which we call its nature.

Creation in Huai Nan Tzu

(1) There was "the beginning: (2) there was a beginning of an anteriority to this beginning: (3) there was a begining of an anteriority even before the beginning of this anteriority. (4) There was "the existence." (5) There was "the non-

---

[1] *Hu* has also been translated as "Sudden Energy," which is significant when considering creation of a universe. The "Heedless" is pure Taoist, however.

[2] This ingenious and amusing allegory is typical of Chuang Tzu's wit and irreverence. "It indicates," says one commentator, "how action (which, in Taoism, means the opposite of non-inaction) injures the first condition of things."

existence." (6) There was "not yet a beginning of non-existence." (7) There was "not yet a beginning of the not yet beginning of nonexistence."[1]

(1) The meaning of "There was the beginning" is that there was a complex energy which had not yet pullulated into germinal form, nor into any visible shape of root and seed and rudiment. Even then in this vast and impalpable void there was apparent the desire to spring into life; but, as yet, the genera of matter were not formed.

(2) At "the beginning of anteriority before the beginning" the fluid of heaven first descended and the fluid of earth first ascended. The male and female principles interosculated, prompting and striving among the elements of the cosmos. The forces wandered hither and thither, pursuing, competing, interpenetrating. Clothed with energy, they moved, sifted, separated, impregnated the various elements as they moved in the fluid ocean, each aura desiring to ally itself with another, even when, as yet, there was no appearance of any created form.

(3) At the stage "There must be a beginning of an anteriority even before the beginning of anteriority," Heaven contained the spirit of harmony, but had not, as yet, descended: earth cherished the vivifying fluid, but had not ascended, as yet. It was space, still, desolate, vapory, a drizzling humid state with a similitude of vacancy and form. The vitalizing fluid floated about, layer on layer.

(4) "There was the existence" speaks of the coming of creation and the immaterial fluids assuming definite forms," implying that the different elements had become stabilized. The immaterial nuclei and embryos, generic forms as roots, stems, tissues, twigs, and leaves of variegated hues appeared. Beautiful were the variegated colors. Butterflies and insects flew hither and thither: insects crawled about. We now reach the stage of movement and the breath of life on every hand. At this stage it was possible to feel, to grasp, to see and follow outward phenomena. They could be counted and distinguished both quantitatively and qualitatively.

---

[1] With few exceptions, like the story of P'an Ku, the Chinese creation myths are full of various philosophical abstractions. For the Chinese Buddhist, creation myths are very similar to the Indian myths. For the Taoist, the concepts of creation are laced with Taoistic abstraction and philosophy.

(5) "The nonexistence" period. It was so called because when it was gazed on no form was seen: when the ear listened, there was no sound: when the hand grasped, there was nothing tangible: when gazed at, it was illimitable. It was limitless space, profound and a vast void, a quiescent, subtle mass of immeasurable translucency.

(6) In "There was not yet a beginning of nonexistence," implies that this period wrapped up heaven and earth, shaping and forging the myriad things of creation: there was an all-penetrating impalpable complexity, profoundly vast and all-extending; nothing was outside its operations. The minutest hair and sharpest point were differentiated: nothing within was left undone. There was no wall around, and the foundation of nonexistence was being laid.

(7) In the period of "There was not yet a beginning of the not yet beginning of nonexistence," Heaven and Earth were not divided: the four seasons were not yet separated: the myriad things were not yet come to birth. Vast-like, even and quiet, still-like, clear and limpid, forms were not visible.

One says, "I can appreciate nonexistence, but the nonexistence of nonexistence is too profound for me to apprehend! How may one come to this apprehension?" These fluxes are most mysterious, beyond the ken of the mind. None can trace the workings of these mysterious operations and penetrate into ultimate depths.

Now Heaven has endowed me with a body and given me work in life. It has made it pleasant for me during old age and has prepared for my dissolution in death. The agencies that are good for life are those which are good for death. People assume that a boat hidden in a cave, or an island in a lake are safe and firm. Nevertheless, a man of mighty strength may carry them away at midnight and escape, without the sleeper's knowing anything about it.

If the world is hidden in the world, then there is no possibility of concealing it. In other words the Tao is coextensive with the universe and it is safe from change and decay.

The emergence of the human form in creation is pleasurable. If man undergoes a myriad transformations without end, dying and coming to renewed life, this is a source of joy that cannot be expressed. Decay and resurrection are triumphant sources of joy.

From the Book of Lao Tzu

EMBODYING THE TAO

The Tao that can be trodden is not the enduring and unchanging Tao. The name that can be named is not the enduring and unchanging name.

Conceived of as having no name it is the Originator of heaven and earth; conceived of as having a name, it is the Mother of all things.

Always without desire we must be found,
If its deep mystery we would sound;
But if desire always within us be,
Its outer fringe is all that we shall see.

Under these two aspects, it is really the same; but as development takes place, it receives the different names. Together we call them Mystery. Where the Mystery is the deepest is the gate of all that is subtle and wonderful.

NOURISHMENT OF THE PERSON

All in the world know the beauty of the beautiful, and in doing this they have the idea of what ugliness is; they all know the skill of the skillful, and in doing this they have the idea of what the want of skill is.

So it is that existence and nonexistence give birth the one to the idea of the other; that difficulty and ease produce the one the idea of the other; that length and shortness fashion out the one the figure of the other; that the ideas of height and lowness arise from the contrast of the one with the other; that the musical notes and tones become harmonious through the relation of one with another; and that being before and behind give the idea of one following another.

Therefore the sage manages affairs without doing anything, and conveys his instructions without the use of speech.

KEEPING PEOPLE AT REST

All things spring up, and there is not one which declines to show itself; they grow, and there is no claim made for their ownership; they go through their processes, and there is no expectation of a reward for the results. The work is accomplished, and there is no resting in it (as an achievement).

The work is done, but how no one can see;
'Tis this that makes the power not cease to be.

THE FOUNTAIN LESS

The Tao is like the emptiness of a vessel; and in our employment of it we must be on our guard against all fullness. How deep and unfathomable it is, as if it were the Honored Ancestor of all things!

We should blunt our sharp points, and unravel the complications of things; we should attemper our brightness, and bring ourselves into agreement with the obscurity of others. How pure and still the Tao is, as if it would ever so continue!

I do not know whose son it is. It might appear to have been before God.

THE USE OF EMPTINESS

Heaven and earth do not act from the impulse of any wish to be benevolent; they deal with all things as the dogs of grass are dealt with. The sages do not act from any wish to be benevolent; they deal with the people as the dogs of grass are dealt with.

May not the space between heaven and earth be compared to a bellows?

'Tis emptied, yet it loses not its power;
'Tis moved again, and sends forth air the more.
Much speech to swift exhaustion lead we see;
Your inner being guard, and keep it free.

THE COMPLETION OF MATERIAL FORMS

The valley spirit does not, aye the same;
The female mystery thus do we name.[1]
Its gate, from which at first they issued forth,
Is called the root which grew heaven and earth.
Long and unbroken does its power remain,
Used gently, and without the touch of pain.

[1] The "Female Mystery" is the same symbol as in "Embodying the Tao," and is the "Mother of All Things." Lao Tzu is thought to present life here as a process of evolving (instead of "creation") from a primal force or vital breath, which ultimately divides into two and appears only in the forms of things. The "valley spirit" stands for the active or vital force of the Tao, the *teh*, as seen in the title of Lao Tzu's book, *Tao Teh Ching*.

SHEATHING THE LIGHT

Heaven is long-enduring and earth continues long. The reason why heaven and earth are able to endure and continue thus long is because they do not live of, or for, themselves. This is how they are able to continue and endure. . . .

The Tao, considered as unchanging, has no name.

Though in its primordial simplicity[2] it may be small, the whole world dares not deal with one embodying it as a minister. If a feudal prince or the king could guard and hold it, all would spontaneously submit themselves to him.

Heaven and Earth under its guidance unite together and send down the sweet dew, which, without the directions of men, reaches equally everywhere as of its own accord.

As soon as it proceeds to action, it has a name. When it once has that name, men can know to rest in it. When they know to rest in it, they can be free from all risk of failure and error.

The relation of the Tao to all the world is like that of the great rivers and seas to the streams from the valleys. . . .

All-pervading is the Great Tao! It may be found on the left hand and on the right.

All things depend on it for their production, which it gives to them, not one refusing obedience to it. When its work is accomplished, it does not claim the name of having done it. It clothes all things as with a garment, and makes no assumption of being their lord—it may be named in the smallest things. All things return to their root and disappear, and do not know that it is it which presides over their doing so—it may be named in the greatest things.[3]

There was something undefined and complete, coming into existence before Heaven and Earth. How still it was and formless, standing alone, and undergoing no change, reach-

---

[2] The "primordial simplicity" is the Tao in its simplest conception, alone, and by itself. It is that Tao that comes forth into operation and manifests as the *teh*.

[3] This paragraph describes the effect of the Tao in the vegetable world.

ing everywhere and in no danger of being exhausted! It may be regarded as the Mother of all things.[4]

I do not know its name, and I give it the designation of the Tao (the Way or Course). Making an effort further to give it a name, I call it The Great.

Great, it passes on in constant flow. Passing on, it becomes remote. Having become remote, it returns. Therefore the Tao is great; Heaven is great; Earth is great; and the king (sage) is also great. In the universe there are four that are great, and the king (sage) is one of them.

Man takes his law from the Earth; the Earth takes its law from Heaven; Heaven takes its law from the Tao. The law of the Tao is its being what it is.

Selections from the I Ching

Ch'ien is the symbol of heaven, and hence is styled father. K'un is the symbol of earth, and hence is styled mother. Chen shows the first application of k'un to ch'ien, resulting in getting the first of its male or undivided lines, and hence we call it the oldest son. Sun shows a first application of ch'ien to 'un, resulting in getting the first of its female or divided lines, and hence we call it the oldest daughter.[2]

God comes forth in Chen to his producing work; He brings His processes into full and equal action in Sun; they are manifested to one another in Li; the greatest service is done for Him in K'un; He rejoices in Tui; He struggles in

---

[4] In these paragraphs, Lao Tzu again calls the Tao the "Mother of All Things," thereby almost giving it human character. But he does not follow that line of thought and instead returns to the Tao as the "Uncaused Cause." In the Tao, there cannot be a personalized god, an anthropomorphized being or creature. The Tao does not act from any personal will, the Tao is simply a spontaneity, evolving from itself.

---

[1] For more information, see the *I Ching*, edited by Raymond Van Over (New York: Mentor Books, 1971), pp. 384ff. I have included these selections from the *I Ching* because it is one of the five great Chinese classics, and captures the essence of Taoist cosmology, even though fleetingly.

[2] Ch'ien is symbolic of Heaven, and is called Father. K'un is Earth, and is called Mother. *Chen* is the first male and is called the eldest son, etc.

Ch'ien; He is comforted and enters into rest in K'an; and he completes the work of the year in Ken.

The Master said: "The trigrams[3] Ch'ien and K'un may be regarded as the gate of the *I*." Ch'ien represents what is of the yang nature (bright and active); K'un what is of the yin nature (shaded and inactive). These two unite according to their qualities, and there comes the embodiment of the result by the strong and weak lines. In this way, we have the phenomena of heaven and earth visibly exhibited, and can comprehend the operation of the spiritual intelligence.

CH'IEN HEXAGRAM (COMMENTARY)

Vast is the great and originating power indicated by Ch'ien! All things owe to it their beginning—it contains all the meaning belonging to the name heaven.

The clouds move and the rain is distributed; the various things appear in their developed forms.

The method of Ch'ien is to change and transform, so that everything obtains its correct nature as appointed by the mind of Heaven; and thereafter the conditions of great harmony are preserved in union. The result is "what is advantageous, and correct and firm."

K'UN HEXAGRAM (COMMENTARY)

Complete is the great and originating capacity indicated by K'un! All things owe to it their birth—it receives obediently the influences of Heaven.

K'un, in its largeness, supports and contains all things. Its excellent capacity matches the unlimited power of Ch'ien. Its comprehension is wide, and its brightness great. The various things obtain by it their full development.

---

[3] The first two hexagrams, Ch'ien and K'un, are composed of six lines each. In turn, each line possesses either yang or yin characteristics. The hexagrams, or six lines, are further broken down into two trigrams of three lines each. The trigrams also contain specific symbolic significance, and each line still has yin and yang characteristics.

BON PO AND
TIBETAN CREATION MYTHS

Creating the Family of Man

There are on the earth three great families, and we are all
of the great Tibetan family. This is what I have heard the
Lamas say, who have studied the things of antiquity. At the
beginning there was on the earth only a single man; he had
neither house nor tent, for at that time the winter was not
cold, and the summer was not hot; the wind did not blow so
violently, and there fell neither snow nor rain; the tea grew
of itself on the mountains, and the flocks had nothing to fear
from beasts of prey. This man had three children, who lived
a long time with him, nourishing themselves on milk and
fruits. After having attained to a great age, this man died.
The three children deliberated what they should do with the
body of their father, and they could not agree about it; one
wished to put him in a coffin, the other wanted to burn him,
the third thought it would be best to expose the body on the
summit of a mountain. They resolved then to divide it into
three parts. The eldest had the body and arms; he was the
ancestor of the great Chinese family, and that is why his
descendants have become celebrated in arts and industry, and
are remarkable for their tricks and stratagems. The second
son had the breast; he was the father of the Tibetan family,
and they are full of heart and courage, and do not fear death.
From the third, who had inferior parts of the body, are
descended the Tartars, who are simple and timid, without
head or heart, and who know nothing but how to keep themselves firm in their saddles.

The Birth of Gesar

One day Gesar's mother was sitting in her house and she
heard a voice saying:

"Mother, see if it is time for me to be born. It would be
best for all beings if I take birth from your head, but first
you must study the auspices.

"Have the animals you brought with you from the naga realm freshly given birth?

"Is the ground covered with a layer of new-fallen blue, yellow, red, and green snow?

"In addition, is there a rain of white rice whiter than the snow on Amne Machen?

"Have flowers blossomed that are the color of the Jobo's golden skin?

"Pray go and see for the happiness of many depend upon these signs!"

Gesar's mother was very amazed on hearing these words, but she hastened outside and was even more amazed on finding that these things had come to pass exactly as the voice had said. When she realized that she was really to have a child born of her, she ran back inside the small house where she lived.

From the center of the crown of her head opened a red and white vein from which issued a translucent white egg the color of Khotanese jade which seemed to be marked with three spots which resembled three eyes. She wrapped the egg in an orange-colored cloth and meant to put it in the pouch of her dress, but before she could do so the egg broke of itself.

Thus was born Gesar in the form of a male child with amber colored skin and a circle of down between his eyes. In the center of the downy circle was one long straight, thick hair like a bristle.

Holding Gesar in her arms she questioned him saying:

"Who are you and where do you come from? Why were you born and how is it you came from my head?"

Gesar replied:

"Many lifetimes I have studied and practiced the Buddha's deep doctrines.

"Many lifetimes I have lived as a Yogi in forests and on snow-clad peaks.

"By the virtue of these austerities I was reborn in Og Min as the son of Demchog Korlo and Dorje Pogmo, and I was named Tubpa Kawa.

"Presently, through evil oaths taken in previous existences, many demon-like beings have taken birth in this land of Tibet, intent on the purpose of destroying the Buddhist religion and its followers.

"Avalokitesvara, upon seeing these things happening, requested of Guru Padmasambhava that he send a protector to defend and preserve the Religion and at the same time convert and subdue those demon-like people who are so difficult to rescue.

"For this reason was I born, and my name is Gesar."

An Exposition Creation Myth from Tibet[1]

Formerly by the magical power of the gods, the *gSas* and the *dBal*,[2]
An egg formed of the five precious gems
Burst open by its own innate force
From the celestial womb of the empty sky.
The shell became protecting armor.
The tegument defending weapons,
The white became a strength-potion for heroes,
The inner tegument became a citadel for them to dwell in,
That obscure citadel the "Sky-Fort of the Waters of Wrath,"
It stole the sun's light, so bright was it.
From the very inner part of the egg
There came a man of magical powers.
He had the head of a lion and the ears of a lynx,
A fierce face and an elephant's nose,
A crocodile's mouth and a tiger's fangs,
Feet like swords and feathers like sabers,
And between his horns which were those of the King of Birds
He had a head-ornament a wish-granting gem.
No name was given him, so he had no name,
But the "Primeval Priest of Perfect Power" (*Ye-gshen-dbang-rdzogs*) conjured him with magical force,
Giving him the name Great Hero *War-ma Nyi-nya.*
He is the foremost of all the powerful ones,
Protecting the doctrines of *Bon* and of *gShen,*

[1] This exposition myth was intoned by the invoking priest (Bon) of ancient Tibet. It was meant to invoke the powers of the great beings of the Bon and Buddhist religions. Even these ancient rituals contain the recurring egg myth. Here it is the origin of the physical universe, of early man, of gods and demons alike.

[2] Early Tibetans believed mankind to be continually beset by demons and evil spirits. On the other side were beings of health and happiness, of which gSas and dBal were two of the most beneficent and powerful.

Overcoming the hordes of foes and opponents.
Acting as friend of goodness and virtue.[3]

A Kuki Creation Myth

The face of the earth was originally covered with one vast
sheet of water inhabited by a huge worm. One day the creator,
passing over this worm, dropped a small piece of clay, saying,
"Of this I mean to make a land and people it."

"Nonsense," said the worm. "Look here, I can swallow it."
But the lump passing out of his body grew and grew until it
became the world we now see. Then man spring out of the
ground by the will of the three gods, Lambra the Creator,
without whose consent nothing can be done, Golarai, god of
death, and the beneficent Dudukal, who operates through his
wife Fapite.[4]

---

[3] This myth continues with a list of how the egg let loose all manner
of things upon the world, and then lists various guardian divinities. Some
of what the egg let burst upon the world follows: "The egg burst open
and its out shell became the real of sprites and parasites, its inner
tegument became the eighty-one evil portents and the three hundred
sixty injuries. The white of the egg spilled on the ground and became
the four hundred and four kinds of disease. The center of the egg
became the three hundred and sixty classes of evil spirits. . . ."

[4] From C. A. Soppitt, *Kuki-Lushai Tribes* (1887).

PART ELEVEN

Oceania and South Sea Island Peoples

INTRODUCTION

OCEANIA IS A great area of islands and ocean in the southern hemisphere, including Polynesia, Melanesia, Indonesia, Micronesia, Australia, New Zealand, New Guinea, and the surrounding smaller islands. There are, of course, many races and cultures scattered over this vast expanse of water. Oceanic and South Sea Island myths are often adventuresome and romantic. The myths of the Micronesians, for example, involve wonderful tales where mankind survives enormous adversity. Logically enough, the myths of island peoples often deal with war and sailing, or with powers of nature like the wind and the sea. The different ethnic groups on these isolated land masses are almost as numerous as the islands. Some, such as the recently discovered New Guinea pygmies, are far down the scale of cultural development, while others, like the Polynesians, have highly sophisticated beliefs and customs. Their myths reflect this variation.

The Maoris of New Zealand and the Malaysians developed relatively complete creation myths, examples of which have been included here. But myths dealing with the origin of the world are scant in Australia and most of the other South Sea Islands. With many of the island cultures, the earth and sky seem to have been accepted as always existing, for little account is given of their creation. Occasionally myths of origin have grown up around certain special rivers, mountains, and other important places or objects, but this happens only rarely. Often a general statement describes creation, as in one saying found in Australia: "All things were made in the beginning by a deity or supernatural being."

Although the island people seem to have limited their speculations about the beginning of the world, they have developed many myths on the creation of mankind. In fact, there are enough to divide these myths into three groups: (1) man has an independent origin where he is made completely whole; (2) man is created an incomplete being who is then finished; (3) man is made or created by some deity and is thus dependent upon that god.

The Micronesian islands also lack detailed myths about creation, and those myths that are found seem to have strong relationships to Indonesian and Polynesian myths. Myths characteristic of the Indonesian tribes also lack any clear cosmogonic tales. The Papuan mythology is characterized by the prominence of ghost tales, by a general simplicity, and again by an absence of cosmogonic myths. The Melanesians, however, have a more developed vision of the universe and therefore have some cosmogonic myths, mixed in with their fondness for cannibalistic tales.

CREATION MYTHS IN ISLAND CULTURES

Maori Creation Myths of New Zealand

The Sons of Heaven and Earth

In the beginning, the Heaven, Rangi, and the Earth, Papa, were the father and mother of all things. "In these days the Heaven lay upon the Earth, and all was darkness. They had never been separated." Heaven and Earth had children, who grew up and lived in this thick night, and they were unhappy because they could not see. Between the bodies of their parents they were imprisoned, and there was no light. The names of the children were Tumatuenga, Tane Mahuta, Tutenganahau, and some others. So they all consulted as to what should be done with their parents, Rangi (the heavens) and Papa (the earth). "Shall we slay them, or shall we separate them?" "Go to," said Tumatuenga (the god of war), "let us slay them."

"No," cried Tane Mahuta (the forest god), "let us rather separate them. Let one go upward, and become a stranger to us; let the other remain below, and be a parent to us."

Only Tawhiri Matea (the wind) had pity on his own father and mother. Then the fruit gods, and the war god, and the sea god (for all the children of Papa and Rangi were gods) tried to rend their parents asunder. Last rose the forest god, cruel Tutenganahau. He severed the sinews which united Heaven and Earth, Rangi and Papa. Then he pushed hard with his head and feet. Heaven and Earth were divided. It is Tane who separated night from day. Then wailed Heaven and exclaimed Earth, "Wherefore this murder? Why this great sin? Why destroy us? Why separate us?"[1] But Tane pushed and pushed: Rangi was driven far away into the air. They became visible, who had hitherto been concealed between the hollows of their parents' breasts. Only the storm god differed

---

[1] This myth is still alive in Maori cultures. When a little boy behaves rudely to his parents, he is sometimes warned that he is "as bad as cruel Tutenganahau."

from his brethren: he arose and followed his father, Rangi, and abode with him in the open spaces of the sky.[2]

The Creation of Man

A certain god, variously named Tu, Tiki, and Tane, took red riverside clay, kneaded it with his own blood into a likeness or image of himself, with eyes, legs, arms, and all complete, in fact, an exact copy of the deity; and having perfected the model, he animated it by breathing into its mouth and nostrils, whereupon the clay effigy at once came to life and sneezed. So like himself was the man whom the Maori Creator Tiki fashioned that he called him Tiki-ahua, that is, Tiki's likeness.

An Australian Creation Myth

Pund-jel, the Creator, cut three large sheets of bark with his big knife. On one of these he placed some clay and worked it up with his knife into a proper consistence. He then laid a portion of the clay on one of the other pieces of bark and shaped it into a human form; first he made the feet, then the legs, then the trunk, the arms, and the head. Thus he made a clay man on each of the two pieces of bark; and being well pleased with his handiwork, he danced around them for joy. Next he took stringy bark from the eucalyptus tree, made hair of it, and stuck it on the heads of his clay men. Then he looked at them again, was pleased with his work, and again danced around them for joy. He then lay down on them, blew his breath hard into their mouths, their noses, and their navels; and presently they stirred, spoke, and rose up as full-grown men.

A Tahitian Creation Myth

In Tahiti was that the first human pair was made by Taaroa, the chief god. After he had formed the world he created man

---

[2] A number of similar myths occur in Samoa. There is one, Andrew Lang tells us, in which a serpent severs Heaven and Earth.

out of red earth, which was also the food of mankind until bread-fruit was produced. Further, some say that one day Taaroa called for the man by name, and when he came he made him fall asleep. As he slept, the Creator took out one of his bones (ivi) and made of it a woman, whom he gave to the man to be his wife, and the pair became the progenitors of mankind.

A Samoan Creation Myth

The God Tangaloa lived in the far spaces. He created all things. He was alone, there was no heaven, no earth. He was alone and wandered about in space. There was no sea, and no earth, but where he stood there was a rock: Tangaloa-faa-tutupu-nuu. All things are created from this rock but all things were not yet created. Heaven was not yet created, but the rock grew there where the God stood.

Then Tangaloa said to the rock: Split yourself open. Out came Papa-tao-to and Papa-soso-lo, then Papa-lau-a-au, then Papa-ano-ano, then Papa-ele, then Papa-tu and then Papa-amu-amu and their children.

And Tangaloa stood there and looked to the West and spoke to the rock: and he hit the rock with his right hand and it split again and out came the parents of all the nations of the earth, and the sea came also. And the sea covered Papa-soso-lo, and Papa-tao-to said to Papa-soso-lo: Blessed are you, that you own the sea.

Then Tangaloa turned to the right side and water came out. And again Tangaloa spoke to the rock and heaven was created. He spoke again to the rock and Tui-tee-langi came forth. And then Ilu came forth, which means immensity and Mamao, meaning space, came at the same time in female form. And then came Niu-ao. Tangaloa then spoke again to the rock and Luao, a boy, came out. Tangaloa spoke again to the rock and Lua-vai, a girl, came forth. Tangaloa put both of them on the island of Saa-tua-langi.

And again Tangaloa spoke and Oa-vali, a boy, was born and then Ngao-ngao-le-tei, a girl. Then man came forth, and then came the spirit (Anga-nga), then the heart (loto), then the will (fingalo), and finally thought (masalo).

A Creation Myth from New Hebrides

Taakeuta began, "Sir, I remember the voices of my fathers. Hearken to the words of Karongoa. . . ."

Naareau the Elder was the First of All. Not a man, not a beast, not a fish, not a thing was before him. He slept not, for there was no sleep; he ate not, for there was no hunger. He was in the void. There was only Naareau sitting in the Void. Long he sat, and there was only he.

Then Naareau said in his heart, "I will make a woman." Behold! a woman grew out of the Void: Nei Teakea. He said again, "I will make a man." Behold! a man grew out of his thought: Na Atibu, the Rock. And Na Atibu lay with Nei Teakea. Behold! their child—even Naareau the Younger.

And Naareau the Elder said to Naareau the Younger, "All knowledge is whole in thee. I will make a thing for thee to work upon." So he made that thing in the Void. It was called the Darkness and the Cleaving Together; the sky and the earth and the sea were within it; but the sky and the earth clove together, and darkness was between them, for as yet there was no separation.

And when his work was done, Naareau the Elder said. "Enough! It is ready. I go, never to return." So he went, never to return, and no man knows where he abides now.

But Naareau the Younger walked on the overside of the sky that lay on the land. The sky was rock, and in some places it was rooted in the land, but in other places there were hollows between. A thought came into Naareau's heart; he said, "I will enter beneath it." He searched for a cleft wherein he might creep, but there was no cleft. He said again, "How, then, shall I enter? I will go with a spell." That was the First Spell. He knelt on the sky and began to tap it with his fingers, saying:

Tap . . . tap, on heaven and its dwelling places.
It is stone. What becomes of it? It echoes!
It is rock. What becomes of it? It echoes!
Open Sir Stone! Open, Sir Rock!
It is open-o-o-o!

And at the third striking, the sky opened under his fingers. He said, "It is ready," and he looked down into the hollow place. It was black dark, and his ears heard the noise of breathing and snoring in the darkness. So he stood up and rubbed his fingertips together. Behold! the First Creature came out of them—even the Bat that he called Tiku-tiku-toumouma. And he said to the Bat, "Thou canst see in the darkness. Go before me and find what thou findest."

The Bat said, "I see people lying in this place." Naareau answered, "What are they like?" and the Bat said, "They move not; they say no word; they are all asleep." Naareau answered again, "It is the Company of Fools and Deaf Mutes. They are a Breed of Slaves. Tell me their names." Then the Bat settled on the forehead of each one as he lay in the darkness and called his name to Naareau: "This man is Uka the Blower. Here lies Naabawe the Sweeper. Behold! Karitoro the Roller-up. Now Kotekateka the Sitter. Kotei the Stander now—a great Multitude."

And when they were all named, Naareau said, "Enough. I will go in." So he crawled through the cleft and walked on the underside of the sky; and the Bat was his guide in the darkness. He stood among the Fools and Deaf Mutes and shouted, "Sirs, what are you doing?" None answered; only his voice came back out of the hollowness, "Sirs, what are you doing?" He said in his heart, "They are not yet in their right minds, but wait."

He went to a place in their midst; he shouted to them: "Move!" and they moved. He said again, "Move!" They set their hands against the underside of the sky. He said again, "Move!" They sat up; the sky was lifted a little. He said again, "Move! Stand!" They stood. He said again, "Higher!" But they answered, "How shall we lift it higher?" He made a beam of wood, saying, "Lift it on this." They did so. He said again, "Higher! Higher!" But they answered, "We can no more, we can no more, for the sky has roots in the land." So Naareau lifted up his voice and shouted, "Where are the Eel and the Turtle, the Octopus and the Great Ray?" The Fools and Deaf Mutes answered, "Alas! they are hidden away from the work." [Even then there were such people!] So he said, "Rest" and they rested; and he said to that one among them named Naabawe, "Go, call Riiki, the conger eel."

When Naabawe came to Riiki, he was coiled asleep with his wife, the short-tailed eel. Naabawe called him: he answered not, but lifted his head and bit him. Naabawe went back to Naareau, crying, "Alas! the conger eel bit me." So Naareau made a stick, with a slip-noose, saying, "We shall take him with this, if there is a bait to lure him." Then he called the

Octopus from his hiding place: and the Octopus had ten
arms. He struck off two arms and hung them on the stick as
bait: therefore the octopus has only eight arms to this day.
They took the lure to Riiki, and as they offered it to him,
Naareau sang:

> Rikki of old, Riiki of old!
> Come hither, Riiki, thou mighty one;
> Leave thy wife, the short-tailed eel,
> For thou shalt uproot the sky, thou shalt press
>   down the depths.
> Heave thyself up, Riiki, mighty and long,
> Kingpost of the roof, prop up the sky and have done.
> Have done, for the judgment is judged.

When Riiki heard the spell, he lifted up his head and the
sleep went out of him. See him now! He puts forth his snout.
He seizes the bait. Alas; they tighten the noose: he is fast
caught, they haul him! he is dragged away from his wife the
short-tailed eel, and Naareau is roaring and dancing. Yet pity
him not, for the sky is ready to be lifted. The day of sunder-
ing has come.

Riiki said to Naareau, "What shall I do?" Naareau answered,
"Lift up the sky on thy snout; press down the earth under
thy tail." But when Riiki began to lift, the sky and the land
groaned, and he said, "Perhaps they do not wish to be sundered." So Naareau lifted up his voice and sang:

> Hark, hark how it groans, the Cleaving Together of old!
> Speed between, Great Ray, slice it apart.
> Hump thy back, Turtle, burst it apart.
> Fling out thy arms, Octopus, tear it apart.
> West, East, cut them away!
> North, South, cut them away!
> Lift, Riiki, lift, kingpost of the roof, prop of the sky.
> It roars, it rumbles! Not yet, not yet is the Cleaving
>   Together sundered.

When the Great Ray and the Turtle and the Octopus heard
the words of Naareau, they began to tear at the roots of the
sky that clung to the land. The Company of Fools and Deaf
Mutes stood in the midst. They laughed; they shouted, "It
moves! See how it moves!" And all that while Naareau was
singing and Riiki pushing. He pushed up with his snout, he

pushed down with his tail; the roots of the sky were torn from
the earth; they snapped! The Cleaving Together was split
asunder. Enough! Riiki straightened out his body; the sky
stood high, the land sank, the Company of Fools and Deaf
Mutes was left swimming in the sea.

But Naareau looked up at the sky and saw that there were
no sides to it. He said, "Only I, Naareau, can pull down the
sides of the sky." And he sang:

> Behold I am seen in the West, it is West!
> There is never a ghost, nor a land, nor a man;
> There is only the Breed of the First Mother, and the
>   First Father and the First Begetting;
> There is only the First Naming of Names and the First
>   Lying Together in the Void;
> There is only the laying together of Na Atibu and Nei
>   Teakea,
> And we are flung down in the waters of the western sea.
> It is West!

So also he sang in the east, and the north, and the south.
He ran, he leaped, he flew, he was seen and gone again like
the lightnings in the sides of heaven; and where he stayed,
there he pulled down the side of the sky so that it was shaped
like a bowl.

When that was done, he looked at the Company of Fools
and Deaf Mutes, and saw that they were swimming in the
sea. He said in his heart, "There shall be the First Land." He
called to them, "Reach down, reach down-o-o! Clutch with
your hands. Haul up the bedrock. Heave."

MALAY CREATION MYTHS

Malay Creation of the World

From the Supreme Being first emanated light toward chaos; this light, diffusing itself, became the vast ocean. From the bosom of the waters thick vapor and foam ascended. The earth and sea were then formed, each of seven tiers. The earth rested on the surface of the water from east to west. God, in order to render steadfast the foundations of the world, which vibrated tremulously with the motion of the watery expanse, girded it around with an adamantine chain, the stupendous mountains of Caucasus, the wondrous regions of genii and aerial spirits. Beyond these limits is spread out a vast plain, the sand and earth of which are of gold and musk, the stones rubies and emeralds, the vegetation of odoriferous flowers.

From the range of Caucasus, all the mountains of the earth have their origin as pillars to support and strengthen the terrestrial framework.

Creation Myth from a Malay Charmbook[1]

In the days when Haze bore Darkness, and Darkness Haze, when the Lord of the Outer Silence Himself was yet in the womb of Creation, before the existence of the names of Earth and Heaven, of God and Muhammad, of the Empyrean and Crystalline spheres, or of Space and Void, the Creator of the entire Universe pre-existed by Himself, and He was the Eldest Magician. He created the Earth of the width of a tray and the Heavens of the width of an umbrella, which are the universe of the Magician. Now from before the beginning of time

386

existed that Magician—that is, God—and He made Himself manifest with the brightness of the moon and the sun, which is the token of the True Magician.

God created the pillar of the Ka'bah,[2] which is the Navel of the Earth, whose growth is comparable to a Tree, . . . whose branches are four in number, and are called, the first, "Sajeratul Mentahar," and the second "Taubi," and the third, "Khaldi," and the fourth "Nasrun Alam," which extend unto the north, south, east, and west, where they are called the Four Corners of the World.

Creation of Man from
a Malay Charmbook[3]

God Almighty spake unto Gabriel, saying,
"Be not disobedient, O Gabriel,
But go and get me the Heart of the Earth."

[1] The *Malay Charmbook* is a manuscript found by Walter W. Skeat during his travels and anthropological research in Malay. The Malay people depended heavily on charms and rituals, for they possessed a religion full of spirits and demons that had to be dealt with—and this was accomplished primarily by charms. See note 3, p. 387.

The mention of Muhammad, Mecca, Adam and Eve, in Malay folklore might seem surprising at first, but they were a sea-going people, situated in a sea channel between the East and West. The mention of Adam and Eve, for example, derives from Arab influence. They picked up many other traditions and beliefs and incorporated them into their own fluid, animistic religion. In his book on *Malay Magic* W. W. Skeat points out that Malay folklore is of a very mixed character, and has been modified over centuries by the Arabian and Indian cultures. In fact, linguistic analysis shows many Sanskrit and Arabic roots to Malay language.

[2] This is the famous mosque at Mecca which contains the black stone and in Malay means literally "a cube."

[3] The Malay Charmbook belonging to a Selangor magician named Abdul Razzak of Klang could not be bought or borrowed, so these two myths were copied by W. W. Skeat and reported in his book *Malay Magic* (see bibliography). The second *Charmbook* myth appears to be Malay modification of Arabic beliefs in which man is created from the four elements of earth, air, water and fire. The magician who reported this account of creation added that when Azrael stretched forth his hand to take the Heart of the Earth, the Earth-spirit caught hold of his middle finger, which yielded to the strain, and thus became longer than the rest, and received its Malay name of the "devil's finger," or *jari hantu.*

But he could not get the Heart of the Earth.
"I will not give it," said the Earth.
Then went the Prophet Israfel to get it,
But he could not get the Heart of the Earth.
Then went Michael to get it,
But he could not get the Heart of the Earth.
Then went Azrael to get it,
And at last he got the Heart of the Earth.
When he got the Heart of the Earth
The empyrean and crystalline spheres shook,
And the whole Universe shook.
When he got the Heart of the Earth he made from it the
    Image of Adam.
But the Heart of the Earth was then too hard;
He mixed Water with it, and it became too soft,
So he mixed Fire with it, and at last struck out the image
    of Adam.
Then he raised up the image of Adam,
And craved Life for it from Almighty God,
And God Almighty gave it Life.
Then sneezed God Almighty, and the image of Adam
    broke in pieces,
And he (Azrael) returned to remake the image of Adam.
Then God Almighty commanded to take steel of
    Khorassan,
And drive it down his back, so that it became the thirty-
    three bones,
The harder steel at the top, the softer below it.
The harder steel shot up skyward,
And the softer steel penetrated earthward.
Thus the image of Adam had life, and dwelt in
    Paradise.
There Adam beheld two peacocks of no ordinary beauty,
And the Angel Gabriel appeared.
"Verily, O Angel Gabriel, I am solitary,
Easier is it to live in pairs, I crave a wife."
God Almighty spake, saying, "Command Adam
To pray at dawn a prayer of two genuflexions."
Then Adam prayed, and our Lady Eve descended,
And was captured by the Prophet Adam;
But before he had finished his prayer she was taken back,
Therefore Adam prayed the prayer of two genuflexions
    as desired,

And at the last obtained our Lady Eve.
When they were married, Eve bore twins every time,
Until she had borne forty-four children,
And the children, too, were wedded, handsome with
handsome, and plain with plain.

Another Malay Myth of the Creation of The First Man

The Creator determined to make man, and for that purpose He took some clay from the earth and fashioned it into the figure of a man. Then He took the Spirit of Life to endue this body with vitality, and placed the spirit on the head of the figure. But the spirit was strong, and the body, being only clay, could not hold it, and was reft in pieces and scattered into the air. Those fragments of the first great Failure are the spirits of earth and sea and air.

The Creator then formed another clay figure, but into this one He wrought some iron, so that when it received the vital spark it withstood the strain and became Man. That man was Adam, and the iron that is in the constitution of his descendants has stood them in good stead. When they lose it they become of little more account than their prototype the first failure.

Polynesian Creation Myth

(Natives of Bowditch Island)

The first man was produced out of a stone. After a time he bethought him of making a woman. So he gathered earth and molded the figure of a woman out of it, and having done so he took a rib out of his left side and thrust it into the earthen figure, which thereupon started up a live woman. He called her Ivi (Eevee) or "rib" and took her to wife, and the whole human race sprang from this pair.

Karens Creation Myth

(Burma)[1]

The Karens of Burma say that God "created man, and of what did he form him? He created man at first from the earth, and finished the work of creation. He created woman, and of what did he form her? He took a rib from the man and created the woman."

Bila-an Creation Myth

(Mindanao Island, Philippines)

In the beginning there was a certain being named Melu, of a size so huge that no known thing can give any idea of it; he was white in color, and had golden teeth, and he sat upon the clouds, occupying all the space above. Being of a very cleanly habit, he was constantly rubbing himself in order to preserve the whiteness of his skin unsullied. The scurf which he thus removed from his person he laid on one side, till it gathered in such a heap as to fidget him. To be rid of it he constructed the earth out of it, and being pleased with his work he resolved to make two beings like himself, only much smaller in size. He fashioned them accordingly in his own likeness out of the leavings of the scurf whereof he had molded the earth, and these two were the first human beings.

But while the Creator was still at work on them, and had finished one of them all but the nose, and the other all but the nose and one other part, Tau Dalom Tana came up to him and demanded to be allowed to make the noses. After a heated argument with the Creator, he got his way and made the noses, but in applying them to the faces of our first parents he unfortunately placed them upside down. So warm had been the discussion between the Creator and his assistant

---

[1] Burma is not technically within Oceania. But I have included it in this part because it approximates the northern most islands of Oceania—Sumatra, Borneo, and Formosa. Further, the northern island cultures, like the rest of these island peoples cultures, did influence each other in their beliefs. See the introduction to this part.

in regard to the noses, that the Creator quite forgot to finish the other part of the second figure, and went away to his place above the clouds, leaving the first man or the first woman imperfect; and Tau Dalom Tana also went away to his place below the earth. After that a heavy rain fell, and the two first of humankind nearly perished, for the rain ran off the tops of their heads into their upturned nostrils. The Creator perceived their plight and coming down from the clouds to the rescue he took off their noses and replaced them right end up.

Dyaks of Sakarran Creation Myth

(British Borneo)

The Sea Dyaks think that a certain god named Salampandai is the maker of men. He hammers them into shape out of clay, thus forming the bodies of children who are to be born into the world. There is an insect which makes a curious clinking noise at night, and when the Dyaks hear it, they say that it is the clink of Salampandai's hammer at his work.

The story goes that he was commanded by the gods to make a man, and he made one of stone; but the figure could not speak and was therefore rejected. So he set to work again, and made a man of iron; but neither could he speak, so the gods would have none of him. The third time Salampandai made a man of clay, and he had the power of speech. Therefore the gods were pleased and said, "The man you have made will do well. Let him be the ancestor of the human race, and you must make others like him."

So Salampandai set about fashioning human beings, and he is still fashioning them at his anvil, working away with his tools in unseen regions. There he hammers out the clay babies, and when one of them is finished he brings it to the gods, who ask the infant, "What would you like to handle and use?" If the child answers, "A sword," the gods pronounce it a male; but if the child replies, "Cotton and a spinning wheel," they pronounce it a female. Thus they are born boys or girls, according to their own wishes.

Nias Creation Myth

(Sumatra)

The supreme god, Luo Zaho, bathed at a celestial spring which reflected his figure in its clear water as in a mirror, and how, on seeing his image in the water, he took a handful of earth as large as an egg, and fashioned out of it a figure like one of those figures of ancestors which the people of Nias construct. Having made it, he put it in the scales and weighed it; he weighed also the wind, and having weighed it, he put it on the lips of the figure which he had made; so the figure spoke like a man or like a child, and God gave him the name of Sihai. But though Sihai was like God in form, he had no offspring; and the world was dark, for as yet there was neither sun nor moon. So God meditated, and sent Sihai down to earth to live there in a house made of tree-fern. But while as yet he had neither wife nor child, he one day died at noon. However, out of his mouth grew two trees, and the trees budded and blossomed, and the wind shook the blossoms from the trees, and blossoms fell to the ground and from them arose diseases. And from Sihai's throat grew a tree, from which gold is derived; and from his heart grew another tree, from which men are descended. Moreover, out of his right eye came the sun, and out of his left eye came the moon.

A Creation Myth of
the Banks Islands

(Melanesia)

In Mota the hero Qat molded men of clay, the red clay from the marshy riverside at Vanua Lava. At first he made men and pigs just alike, but his brothers remonstrated with him, so he beat down the pigs to go on all fours and made man walk upright. Qat fashioned the first woman out of supple twigs, and when she smiled he knew she was a living woman. The natives of Malekula, one of the New Hebrides, give the name of Bokor to the great being who kneaded the first man and woman out of clay.

A Creation Myth of
the Kei Islands

(Indonesia)

The inhabitants of Noo-hoo-roa say that their ancestors were fashioned out of clay by the supreme god, Dooadlera, who breathed life into the clay figures. According to the Bare'e-speaking Toradjas of Central Celebes there were at first no human beings on the earth. Then i Lai, the god of the upper world, and i Ndara, the goddess of the under world, resolved to make men. They committed the task to i Kombengi, who made two models, one of a man and the other of a woman, out of stone or, according to others, out of wood. When he had done his work, he set up his models by the side of the road which leads from the upper to the under world, so that all spirits passing by might see and criticize his workmanship. In the evening the gods talked it over, and agreed that the calves of the legs of the two figures were not round enough. So Kombengi went to work again, and constructed another pair of models which he again submitted to the divine criticism. This time the gods observed that the figures were too pot-bellied, so Kombengi produced a third pair of models, which the gods approved of, after the maker had made a slight change in the anatomy of the figures, transferring a portion of the male to the female figure. It now only remained to make the figures live. So the god Lai returned to his celestial mansion to fetch eternal breath for the man and woman; but in the meantime the Creator himself, whether from thoughtlessness or haste, had allowed the common wind to blow on the figures, and they drew their breath and life from it. That is why the breath returns to the wind when a man dies.

SELECTED BIBLIOGRAPHY

Aiken, Charles F. *The Sacred Books and Early Literature of the East. Vol. X.* New York: Parke, Austin, and Lipscomb, Inc., 1917.

Anesaki, Masaharu. *Japanese Mythology. The Mythology of All Races*, Vol. VIII, Part 2. New York: Cooper Square Publishers, Inc., 1964.

Anuruddha, R. P. *An Introduction into Lamaism, The Mystical Buddhism of Tibet.* India: Vishveshvaranand Vedic Research Institute, 1959.

Aston, W. G. *Nihongi, Chronicles of Japan.* London: George Allen & Unwin Ltd. 1896.

Auerbach, Leo. *The Babylonian Talmud.* New York: Philosophical Library, 1944.

Avalon, Arthur. *The Serpent Power.* Madras: Ganesh and Co., 1913.

Banks, Rev. J., trans. *The Works of Hesiod, Callimachus and Theognis.* London: H. G. Bohn, 1856.

Barondes, R. De Rohan. *China, Lore Legend and Lyrics.* New York: Philosophical Library, Inc., 1960.

Batchelor, J. *The Ainu and their Folk-lore.* London: 1911.

Bellamy, H. S. *Moons, Myths and Man, A Reinterpretation.* London: Faber & Faber Limited, 1936.

Bellows, Henry Adam, trans. *The Poetic Edda.* New York: The American-Scandinavian Foundation, 1923.

The Bible. King James Version.

Blacker, Carmen, and Loewe, Michael. *Ancient Cosmologies.* London: George Allen & Unwin Ltd., 1975.

Bleek, W. H., and Lloyd, L. C. *Specimens of Bushman Folklore.* London: 1911.

Brown, G. *Melanesians and Polynesians.* London. 1910.

Brugsch, Dr. Heinrich. *Religion and Mythologie.* Leipzig. 1885-1888.

Budge, E. A. Wallis. *The Book of the Dead, The Papyrus of Ani.* London: British Museum Pamphlet, 1920.

Budge, E. A. Wallis. *Egyptian Magic*. London: Kegan Paul, Trench, Trubner & Co., Ltd., 1901.

Buhler, Georg. *The Sacred Books of the East*, vol. XXV. Edited by Max Muller. Oxford: Clarendon Press, 1886.

Bulfinch, Thomas. *The Age of Fable or The Beauties of Mythology*. New York: Heritage Press, 1942.

Childe, V. Gordon. *New Light on the Most Ancient East*. New York: D. Appleton-Century Company, 1934.

Clark, R. T. Rundle. *Myth and Man, Myth and Symbol in Ancient Egypt*. London: Thames and Hudson, 1959.

Colum, Padraic. *Orpheus: Myths of the World*. New York: Macmillan and Co., 1930.

Cox, M. *Introduction to Folklore*. London: 1897.

Crooke, W. *Popular Religion and Folklore of Northern India*. Philadelphia: The Westminster Press, 1896.

Crowther, S., and Taylor, J. C. *The Gospel on the Banks of the Niger*. London: 1859.

Cushing, Frank Hamilton. *Outlines of Zuni Creation Myths*. Thirteenth Annual Report of the U.S. Bureau of American Ethnology. Washington: Smithsonian Institute, 1891-1892.

Dahnhardt, Oskar. *Natursagen*, vol. I. Berlin: B. G. Trubner, 1907.

Danks, B. *Melanesians and Polynesians*. London: 1910.

Darmesteter, James. *The Sacred Books of the East*, vol. IV. Edited by Max Muller. London: Clarendon Press, 1880.

Dawson, J. *Australian Aborigines*. Melbourne: 1881.

de Bary, Wm. Theodore, et. al. *Sources of Chinese Tradition*. New York: Columbia University Press, 1960.

de Herrera, A. *General History of the Vast Continent and Islands of America*. Trans. by J. Stevens. London: 1725-26.

de Santillana, Giorgio, and von Dechend, Hertha. *Hamlet's Mill. An Essay on Myth & The Frame of Time*. Boston: Gambit, Inc., 1969.

Dixon, Roland B. *Maidu Myths*. Part II in *Bulletin of the American Museum of Natural History*, Vol. XVII. 1902-1907.

Dixon, Roland B. *Oceanic Mythology*. Boston: 1916.

Elwin, V. *The Muria and Their Ghotul*. Calcutta: Geoffrey Cumberlege, Oxford University Press, 1947.

Etter, Carl. *Ainu Folklore: Traditions and Culture of the Vanishing Aborigines of Japan*. Chicago: Wilcox and Follett, 1949.

Forrester-Brown, James S. *The Two Creation Stories in Genesis*. Berkeley: Shambhala Publications, Inc., 1974.

Frazer, Sir James George. *The Golden Bough*. London: Macmillan, 1911.

———. *Folk-Lore in the Old Testament*. London: Macmillan and Co., Ltd., 1923.

———. *The New Golden Bough*. Edited by Theodor H. Gaster. New York: Criterion Books, Inc., 1959.

———. *Adonis Attis Osiris* (Studies in the History of Oriental Religion). New York: University Books, 1961.

Gait, E. A. "Human Sacrifice (Indian)" in James Hastings, *Encyclopaedia of Religion and Ethics*. New York: Charles Scribner's Sons, 1928.

Gaster, T. H. *Thespis*. New York: W. W. Norton & Co., 1950.

———. *The Oldest Stories in the World*. Boston: Beacon Press, 1952.

———. *The Dead Sea Scriptures*, New York: Doubleday & Co., 1976.

Gesar. "The Story of Gesar," Vol. I No. I. California: Dharma Pub., 1973.

Gill, William Wyatt. *Myths and Songs from the South Pacific*. London: Henry S. King & Company, 1876.

Goodrich, Norma Lorre. *Ancient Myths*. New York: The New American Library, 1960.

Gordon, E. N. *Indian Folk Tales*. London. 1908.

Grant, Robert M., ed. *Gnosticism, An Anthology*. London: Collins, 1961.

Grinnell, George Bird. *Blackfoot Lodge Tales*. New York: Charles Scribner's Sons, 1916.

Hackin, J. *Asiatic Mythology*. New York: Thomas Y. Crowell Company, 1963.

Hale, H. *Huron Folk-Lore, Journal of American Folk Lore*, vol. I. New York: G. E. Stechert & Co., 1888.

Halliday, William Reginald. *The Ancient World, Lectures on the History of Roman Religion*. London: Hodder and Stoughton Ltd., 1922.

Hamilton, Edith. *Mythology*. Boston: Little, Brown and Company, 1940.

Hamilton, Edith, and Cairns, Huntingtin. *The Collected Dialogues of Plato*. New York: Bollingen Foundation (Pantheon Books), 1961.

Hardwick, Charles. *Christ and Other Masters*. Cambridge: Macmillan and Co., 1858.

Harper, Robert F. *Assyrian and Babylonian Literature.* New York: D. Appleton and Company, 1904.

Hawkes, Jacquetta. *Man and the Sun.* London: The Cresset Press, 1962.

Herzberg, Max J. *Classical Myths.* New York: Allyn and Bacon, 1948.

Hewitt, J. F. *History and Chronology of the Myth-Making Age.* London: James Parker and Co., 1901.

Hewitt, J. N. B. *Iroquoian Cosmogony.* Vol. XXI of the Annual Reports of the Bureau of American Ethnology. Washington: Smithsonian Institute, 1903.

Hocart, A. M. *The Life-Giving Myth.* New York: Grove Press, n.d.

Holmberg, Uno. *Finno-Ugric, Siberian Mythology. The Mythology of All Races,* vol. IV. Boston: Archaeological Institute of America, 1917.

Horne, Charles F., ed. *The Sacred Books and Early Literature of The East.* vol. II. New York: Parke, Austin and Lipscomb, 1917.

Huc, M. *Recollections of a Journey Through Tartary, Tibet and China.* London: 1852.

Jastrow, Morris, Jr. *Aspects of Religious Belief and Practice in Babylonia and Assyria.* New York: G. P. Putnam's Sons, 1911.

——. *The Religion of Babylonia and Assyria.* Boston: Ginn & Company, 1898.

Jewkes, W. T. *Man the Myth-Maker.* New York: Harcourt Brace Jovanovich, Inc., 1973.

Johnson, Obed Simon. *A Study of Chinese Alchemy.* Shanghai: 1928.

Judson, K. B. *Myths and Legends of Alaska.* Chicago: A. C. McClurg & Co., 1911.

——. *Myths and Legends of California and the Old Southwest.* Chicago: A. C. McClurg & Co., 1912.

——. *Old Crow Stories.* Boston: Little, Brown & Co., 1917.

Kirby, W. F., trans. *Kalevala, The Land of the Heroes.* London: Dent & Sons, 1907.

Kitagawa, Joseph M. *Religions of the East.* Philadelphia: The Westminster Press, 1960.

Kitagawa, Joseph M. and Long, Charles H. *Myths and Symbols, Studies in Honor of Mircea Eliade.* Chicago: The University of Chicago Press, 1969.

Klah, Hasteen, *The Navajo Creation Myth.* As recorded by Mary C. Wheelwright. New Mexico: The Wheelwright Museum of the American Indian, 1942.

Kramer, Samuel Noah. *Mythologies of the Ancient World.* New York: Doubleday & Company, Inc., 1961.

Lang, Andrew. *Custom and Myth.* London: Longmans, Green, and Co., 1910.

Langdon, S. *The Babylonian Epic of Creation.* London: Oxford University Press, 1923.

———. *Semitic Mythology. The Mythology of All Races,* vol. V. Boston: Marshall Jones Company, 1931.

Legge, Francis. *Forerunners and Rivals of Christianity. From 330 B.C. to 330 A.D.* New York: University Books, Inc., 1964.

Legge, James. *The Sacred Books of the East.* Edited by Max Muller. vols. XXXIX & XL. London: Oxford University Press, 1891.

Long, Charles H. *Alpha, The Myths of Creation.* New York: George Braziller, 1963.

Macdonald, J. *Religion and Myth.* New York: Negro Universities Press, 1969 (Reprint of 1893 ed.)

Mackenzie, Donald A. *Egyptian Myth and Legend.* London: Gresham Publishing Company, n.d.

———. *Indian Myth and Legend.* London: Gresham Publishing Company, n.d.

———. *Myths of Babylonia and Assyria.* London: Gresham Publishing Company, n.d.

———. *Myths of China and Japan.* London: Gresham Publishing Company, n.d.

———. *Myths of Crete and Pre-Hellenic Europe.* London: Gresham Publishing Company, n.d.

Maclagan, David. *Creation Myths.* London: Thames and Hudson, 1977.

Malinowski, Bronislaw. *Magic, Science and Religion.* New York: Macmillan Company, 1925.

Maspero, Gaston C. *Les Momies Royales De Deir al Bahari.* Paris. n.d.

Mead, G. R. S. *Fragments of a Faith Forgotten.* New York: University Books, Inc., 1960.

Middleton, John, ed. *Gods and Rituals.* New York: The Natural History Press, 1967.

Morgan, Evan. *Tao The Great Luminant.* Taipei: Ch'eng-Wen Publishing Company, 1966.

Morin, F. Alfred. *The Serpent and the Satellite*. New York: Philosophical Library, 1953.

Muller, Max. *Comparative Mythology, An Essay*. London: George Routledge & Sons, Ltd., n.d.

————, ed. *Sacred Books of the East*, vols. XV, XXV, IV, XXIV. Oxford: Clarendon Press, 1879-1886.

Murray, Alexander S. *Manual of Mythology*. New York: Tudor Publishing Company, 1935.

Murray, Henry A. *Myth and Mythmaking*. Boston: Beacon Press, 1960.

Nivedita, The Sister, and Coomaraswamy, Ananda K. *Myths of the Hindus & Buddhists*. London: George C. Harrap & Company, 1916.

Obermann, Julian. *Ugaritic Mythology*. New Haven: Yale University Press, 1948.

O'Connor, Capt. W. F. *Folk Tales from Tibet*. London: Hurst and Blackett, Ltd., 1906.

Pinchin, Edith F. *The Bridge of the Gods in Gaelic Mythology*. London: The Theosophical Publishing House, 1934.

Playfair, Archibald. *The Garos*. London: D. Nutt, 1909.

Porteous, A. *Forest Folklore, Mythology and Romance*. Detroit: Singing Tree Press, 1968 (Reprint of 1928 ed.)

Pritchard, J. B., ed. *Ancient Near Eastern Texts Relating to the Old Testament*. Princeton: Princeton University Press, 1950.

Rasmussen, Knud. *The Eagle's Gift*. Trans. by Isabel Hutchinson. New York: Doubleday & Co., 1932.

Recinos, Adrian. *Popol-Vuh, The Sacred Book of the Ancient Quiché Maya*. Trans. by D. Goetz and S. G. Morley. Norman, Oklahoma: University of Oklahoma Press, 1950.

Rohde, Erwin. *Psyche, The Cult of Souls and Belief in Immortality Among the Greeks*, vols. I & II. London: Kegan Paul, Trench, Trubner & Co., Ltd., 1925.

Robinson, Herbert Spencer, and Wilson, Knox. *Myths and Legends of All Nations*. New York: Doubleday & Company, 1950.

Roth, W. E. *Ethnol. Studies Among the N.W.-Central Queensland Aborigines*. Brisbane-London: 1897.

Rydberg, Viktor. *Teutonic Mythology*. London: Swan Sonnenschein & Co., 1891.

Sale, George. *The Koran*. New York: A. L. Burt Co., n.d.

Sandars, N. K. *Poems of Heaven and Hell from Ancient Mesopotamia*. London: Penguin Books Ltd., 1971.

Simpson, William Kelly, ed. *The Literature of Ancient Egypt.*
      Trans. by R. O. Faulkner, E. F. Wente, Jr., and W. K.
      Simpson. New Haven: Yale University Press, 1972.

Skeat, W. W. *Malay Magic, An Introduction to the Folklore
      and Popular Religion of the Malay Peninsula.* New York:
      Macmillan and Co., 1900.

Slote, Bernice. *Myth and Symbol, Critical Approaches and
      Applications.* Lincoln, Nebraska: University of Nebraska
      Press, 1963.

Snellgrove, David, and Richardson, H. *A Cultural History of
      Tibet.* New York: Frederick Praeger Pub., 1968.

Spence, Lewis. *Myths and Legends of Babylonia and Assyria.*
      London: George G. Harrap & Company Ltd., 1916.

Thomas, P. *Epics, Myths and Legends of India.* India: D. B.
      Taraporevala Sons & Co., n.d.

Thurston, E. *Castes and Tribes of Southern India.* Madras,
      India. 1909.

Tiele, Dr. C. P. *History of the Egyptian Religion.* Boston:
      Houghton, Mifflin and Company, 1882.

Tirard, H. M. *The Book of the Dead.* London: Society for
      Promoting Christian Knowledge, 1910.

Trevelyan, Marie. *Folk-lore and Folk-stories of Wales.* Lon-
      don. 1909.

Turner, G. *Samoa.* London. 1884.

Van Over, Raymond. *I Ching.* New York: The New Ameri-
      can Library, 1971.

————. *Chinese Mystics.* New York: Harper & Row, 1973.

Villas Boas, Claudio and Orlando. *Xingu, The Indians, Their
      Myths.* New York: Farrar, Straus and Giroux, 1970.

Von Franz, Marie-Louise. *Creation Myths.* Zurich: Spring
      Pub., 1972.

Werner, E. T. C. *A Dictionary of Chinese Mythology.* New
      York: The Julian Press, Inc., 1961.

————. *Myths & Legends of China.* London: George G.
      Harrap & Co. Ltd., 1923.

West, E. W. *The Sacred Books of the East.* vol. XXIV. Edited
      by Max Muller. Oxford: Clarendon Press, 1885.

Westropp, Hodder M. *Primitive Symbolism.* London: George
      Redway, 1885.

Wheeler, Post. *The Sacred Scriptures of the Japanese.* London:
      George Allen & Unwin, Ltd., 1952.

Wherry, Joseph H. *Indian Masks & Myths of the West.* New
      York: Bonanza Books, 1969.

Wiedemann, A. *Religion of the Ancient Egyptians*. London: H. Grevel & Co., 1897.

Wilde, Lady. *Ancient Legends, Myths, Charms and Superstitions of Ireland*. London. 1887.

Wilson, E., ed. *Sacred Books of the East*. New York: Colonial Press, 1900.

Wilson, E. *The World's Great Classics: Egyptian Literature*. New York: The Colonial Press, 1901.

Woodson, C. G. *African Myths*. Washington D. C.: The Associated Pub. Co., Inc., n.d.

Zaehner, R. C. *The Teachings of the Magi*. London: Sheldon Press, 1956.

Zimmer, Heinrich. *The Art of Indian Asia*. Edited by Joseph Campbell. New York: The Bollingen Series XXXIX, Pantheon Books, 1955.